ECONOMIC GROWTH
IN FRANCE AND BRITAIN
1851–1950

ECONOMIC GROWTH IN FRANCE AND BRITAIN 1851–1950

CHARLES P. KINDLEBERGER

HARVARD UNIVERSITY PRESS
CAMBRIDGE, MASSACHUSETTS

© Copyright 1964 by the
President and Fellows of Harvard College

All rights reserved

Second Printing, 1967

Publication of this volume has been aided
by a grant from the Ford Foundation.

Distributed in Great Britain by Oxford University Press, London

Library of Congress Catalog Card Number: 64–13424

Printed in the United States of America

TO K. S. M.

ACKNOWLEDGMENTS

In the course of research extending over four years and three cities, it is manifestly impossible properly to thank all who have helped. It is perhaps a mistake to list anyone, when such a list must be partial and since the honor is a doubtful one, but I must express my gratitude to:

— the students of a graduate course on the French economy at the Fletcher School of Law and Diplomacy in 1958–59 who turned in extra copies of their term papers for me to keep;

— Ralph W. Tucker and Felicity Hall Skidmore, research assistants in 1958–59 and 1959–60, respectively, and Beatrice A. Rogers who miraculously edits while she types;

— the faculty seminar on contemporary France at the Harvard Center for International Affairs in 1959–60, and especially to its regular members, Robert R. Bowie, chairman, Jean-Baptiste Duroselle, Stanley Hoffmann, Jesse Pitts, Jo W. Saxe, Nicholas Wahl, and Laurence Wylie;

— to Nuffield College, Oxford, and to the Ministry of Finance, Paris, which housed me in 1960–61, through the respective kind invitations of Warden Norman Chester and the Director of Economic Studies, Jean Serisé;

— the undergraduate seminar on the British economy in the nineteenth century in the Michaelmas term, 1960, at Oxford University, led by R. M. Hartwell and John F. Wright;

— Philip W. S. Andrews, Humphrey Cole, S. Herbert Frankel, H. J. Habakkuk, who answered specific inquiries in Oxford; Maurice Byé, Michel Crozier, David S. Landes, Jan Marczewski, Jean Mayer, Jean Weiller, in Paris;

— seminars which have listened to and criticized parts of this research at the University of Birmingham, Nuffield College, the Economic History Club of Oxford, the Ecole de Droit of the University of Paris, the Economic Club of Stockholm, the Graduate Students Club of Yale;

— individuals who have read and criticized parts of the first draft of the manuscript, especially Kenneth Berrill, Norman Birnbaum, Just Faaland, R. M. Hartwell, William Letwin, William N. Parker, Stein Rokkan, Jo W. Saxe, Paul Streeten;

— the Oxford University Institute of Statistics for permission to reprint material from its *Bulletin,* "Obsolescence and Technical Change" (August 1961), and the *Economic History Review* for permission to use sections of "Foreign Trade and Economic Growth: Lessons from Britain and France, 1850–1913" (December 1961);

— the staffs of Dewey Library, Massachusetts Institute of Technology, of Widener Library, Harvard University, of Nuffield Library, Oxford University, of the Ministry of Finance Library atop the Louvre on the Rue de Rivoli side, of the library of the Institut de Science Politique, of the OEEC, and of the Bibliothèque Nationale;

— the Ford Foundation, which provided research assistance through the Massachusetts Institute of Technology department research fund and a Ford Faculty Research Fellowship for the year 1960–61.

I have tried to resist the temptation to strew my prose with French phrases. Apology is offered for the pedantic mass of footnotes; in a work by an amateur historian, however, it is important to make clear to the professional whence various notions sprang. Sources are referred to in footnotes by abbreviated designations; full titles are set out in the bibliography.

One final explanation: I had to stop taking account of recent contributions to the literature at some point, and this I did in 1960 or 1961. The book is seriously deficient, therefore, in that it does not reflect the contribution of three important works which appeared in 1962: H. J. Habakkuk's subtly reasoned *American and British Technology in the Nineteenth Century, The Search for Labour-Saving Inventions,* Phyllis Deane and W. A. Cole, *British Economic Growth, 1688–1959,* and B. R. Mitchell (with the collaboration of Phyllis Deane), *Abstract of British Historical Statistics,* all of them published at Cambridge by Cambridge University Press in 1962. One table has been taken from the third at the last minute. But the entire argument is poorer throughout for not having been sharpened against and informed by these works.

It is customary at this juncture for a married male writer to thank his wife, and I am pleased to comply. However, this book is dedicated, in affectionate gratitude, to my mother-in-law.

C. P. K.

Massachusetts Institute of Technology
September 1963

CONTENTS

ECONOMIC GROWTH
IN FRANCE AND BRITAIN
1851–1950

"Il est très utile de se poser des questions, *mais très* dangereux d'y répondre."—Charles Seignobos

"Ici, le dix-neuvième siècle, ce n'est pas bien dangereux. Mais quand vous toucherez aux guerres de religion, soyez très prudent." -A lycée professor

[Quotations from Marc Bloch, *Apologie pour l'histoire ou métier d'historien*, 4th ed. (Paris, Colin, 1961), pp. xvi, 10.]

INTRODUCTION

This study attempts to thread its way between deductive and inductive treatments of economic growth by submitting some partial models of growth and decline to empirical testing. The result is neither analysis nor history. It may nonetheless have value for students of economics as a reminder of the dangerous ease of theorizing without facts or of interpreting facts with too limited theories.

This is not a search for such single-valued explanations of economic growth and decline as "England achieved economic growth only because of its coal, or its middle class, or the mercantile accumulation of capital." Nor would I be brash enough to tackle the necessary task of assigning weights to different ingredients of growth and distinguishing among sufficient, necessary, and contributing causes. Instead I present the models, implicit or overt, which have been used to explain the course of growth in Britain and France in the last one hundred years and attempt to indicate whether the models are relevant and the factors involved significant.

In this volume significance has been rated qualitatively. Time and again as I have worked through the literature, I have been reminded of the familiar story of the blind men and the elephant, the former, each at a separate quarter, variously describing the beast as a rope (trunk), wall (side), tree (leg), and cloth (ear). With vision restored, it may be possible to see the elephant as the sum of these parts, and more; but it would be very difficult to assign quantitative weights to the separate elements. Statistical methods are not used here, beyond the presentation of simple tables. The major technique is the straightforward examination of sources on economic history, and the purpose is to see how effectively the economic models conform to and inform historical fact.

The sources are secondary. I am not an economic historian, nor do I have the temerity to aspire to be one. The badge of an economic historian is won by working with primary sources, not in making syntheses of already synthetic materials. But criticism of economic history, even negative criticism, may not be altogether useless. And it is a thoroughly accepted principle of literature and art, which may extend to history by analogy, that critics need not know how to write, act, paint, or sing.

Little explanation is required for a cross-cultural comparison of France and Britain. Comparison frequently runs between France and Germany, as in the classic study of J. H. Clapham or in William Parker's more recent investigations in iron and steel and entrepreneurship. The Anglo-French comparison as a rule comes from the French side; the British tend to measure their performance against that of the United States or Germany. The French, however, have long adopted Britain as the standard of performance.[1] An American has the freedom to choose as he will. If the comparison has more value for one country than another, it cannot be helped.

The emphasis in my study is on France. Though not intentional, this proved inescapable. Most of the chapters start by addressing a proposition about French economic growth, and, after analyzing it for a number of pages, have too little room left thoroughly to pursue the British parallel, if any, by way of control. Four chapters or so deal evenly with France and Britain, and one on technology gives top billing to the British experience. But the result is not balanced.

The time period selected is easily defended. One hundred years is a good round number. For the beginning year one can support the choice of 1851, the date of the Great Exhibition in Britain, which is variously referred to as the zenith of industrial leadership[2] or the beginning of Britain's consciousness of the need for scientific education. Rostow, in *The Stages of Economic Growth*, gives 1851 as the culmination of the British "drive to maturity." But 1846 with the repeal of the Corn Laws, 1847 with its Factory Act, 1849 with the repeal of the Navigation Acts, the discovery of gold in California (1849) or in Australia (1851), the beginning of the golden age of British agriculture in 1853 — any would serve as well. And in France one has a choice between the Revolution of 1848, the election of Louis Napoleon as president in the same year, or the coup d'état of December 1851. But there is no need to be precise, for my interest begins in mid-century. At the other end, primary attention stops for some purposes at 1914, for most at 1939, the end of the interwar period; and I am particularly unconcerned with current rates

---

[1] See, e.g., de Tapiès, *La France et l'Angleterre* (1845); Demoulins, *Anglo-Saxon Superiority* (1899); and Passe, *Économies comparées* (1957). The French inferiority complex vis-à-vis Britain on economic matters carries through right up to 1950. See, e.g., the letter by one F. Herbet in 1858, quoted by Cameron (*France and the Development of Europe*, 1961, p. 327): "It remains for us to prove that businessmen are not more rare among us than soldiers, writers and thinkers, and that it is not only in England that one finds distinguished engineers, clever organizers, intelligent capitalists."

[2] See Marshall, *Industry and Trade* (1920), p. 87n: "In 1851 [there was the] Great Exhibition at which the whole world learned suddenly how great were the numbers of those things which could be bought in London better or cheaper than elsewhere; and of those which could not be bought at all elsewhere."

of growth. In a few cases, however, it is useful to extend the study to the period immediately following World War II. I want to take cognizance, for example, of the rapid French growth in the 1950s, instead of ending on the despairing note of the late 1930s.

The theme of this work is essentially negative and paradoxical. Big theories of economic growth fail to account for the complex facts of life, and little theories frequently contradict one another. Paradox abounds, especially of course in any subject which touches upon the French. If France suffered from lack of coal, did Britain suffer from too much? Does the head start help — nothing succeeds like success? Or is early success fatal — three generations from shirtsleeves to shirtsleeves ("clogs to clogs" in translation from American idiom to English), and the bigger they come, the harder they fall? The resolution of many of these apparent conflicts turns on disparities in implicit assumptions, including particularly the time span chosen. Did British capital export, extending overseas markets in cotton textiles, galvanized iron, and rails, help or hurt? In the short run, it clearly helped; over a longer period, it may have hurt if it prevented an adaptation of industry to production of commodities with greater long-run growth prospects. One historian says "helped"; another (or sometimes the same one) says "hurt." And the critic's task is not to grade the papers and award the medals, but to understand the basis for the differences.

Still, it is hoped that the value of this exercise is not all negative. The amateur economic historian may have turned up a few leads that the literature has neglected: the existence in complex market structures of external diseconomies which block technical change; regional capital formation in Lorraine and Haute Savoie in a France whose primary capital market was engaged in the diversion of funds abroad; the role of agriculture in the Great Depression in France; the speed with which the British entrepreneur abandoned business for Parliament. The main "positive" theme, however, is the differences between British and French economic aging, rather than growth. I had anticipated that a secular decline in capacity for growth could be detected in the two countries, arising from the increasing inability of a country, once it achieved economic success, to adapt to new situations. This proves true for Britain, but not for France, despite the widespread discussion of economic senility in both countries.[3] In Britain it is fascinating to see how many changes in the direction of reduced capacity for growth con-

---

[3] All through the period the literature is full of titles emphasizing decline: e.g., Lédru-Rollin, *De la décadence de l'Angleterre* (1850); Mourre, *Décadence économique de la France* (1900); Brooks, *Our Present Discontents* (1933); Pommera, *Grandeur ou déclin de la France* (1940); Hutchison, *Decline and Fall of British Capitalism* (1950); Richmond, *The English Disease* (1959).

verge in the last quarter of the nineteenth century: the loss of technological leadership; the failure of agriculture to adjust to new demand and supply functions; an abrupt decline in the birth rate; the shift of foreign trade from Europe to the dominions and the empire; the rise of foreign lending to the empire at the expense of borrowers in Europe and at home. One might have reached much the same conclusion about France at various times — at the turn of the century when there was a wave of discussion of French economic decadence, later in the 1930s, or even immediately after the Second World War. But here there was no convergence of symptoms of economic decline — rather, we find a contrapuntal play between vigorous technical capacity and drive, on the one hand, and conservative and restraining practices, on the other. By 1960 it appeared that expansion had again taken over, that what the French call the Malthusian practices of monopoly, restriction, and immobility had again been defeated. Whether the defeat will be lasting, however, is an unanswerable question.

There is no need to describe the organization of this book. The next chapter contains a brief analytical account of the growth of the two economies since 1850. The limits and drawbacks of the statistical evidence, which is not relied upon, are discussed in the appendix. Beginning with Chapter 2, there is paraded a series of separate causes of the speed or slowness of French and British growth. The last chapter briefly draws the threads together in conclusion. This catalogue of subjects makes clear the partial-equilibrium nature of the method. I have analyzed single-valued explanations and have found them inadequate. Although this critical, negative task may be of some value, I recognize that it cannot take the place of the job which needs to be done: the provision of an adequate explanation of the course of economic growth of France and Britain since 1850, indicating the quality and quantity of the various causal factors in the two settings and how they differ. My last chapter attempts no such summation. But in the course of attacking the partial-equilibrium explanations, I may have uncovered some of the materials needed for a general theory of growth.

CHAPTER 1

AN OUTLINE OF FRENCH
AND BRITISH ECONOMIC
GROWTH SINCE 1851

The story of economic growth in France and Britain emerges in the analytical chapters that follow. But a brief sketch may be helpful as background. The outline given is not statistical: the appendix at the back of the book gives the best-known series for British and French national income, overall and per capita, along with discussion of the gaps and the weaknesses of existing series. Let us begin here with French growth.

THE PERIODS OF FRENCH ECONOMIC GROWTH

The early 1840s in France were a period of rapid expansion, especially in textiles.[1] But the crisis which led to the Revolution of 1848 decisively interrupted the upward movement. This revolution has been intensively studied by French economic historians, particularly Labrousse.[2] Their conclusion, as I interpret it, is that it was in large part brought on by the accident of harvest — first by the worst in fifty years in 1846 and then by the best in 1847, sending prices sky high to impoverish the urban dweller and then plunging them to the depths to ruin the farmer (who had not benefited from the high prices because of a lack of marketable supplies).[3] The scissors movement on agricultural incomes marked a deep divide in the demographic history of France.[4] But the depth of the economic crisis in 1849 provides the low point of the two decades.

[1] Marczewski, "Aspects of the Growth of France" (1961), p. 380, gives five industries whose rate of growth exceeds the general growth of industrial product and whose share in this product exceeds 2 percent, from 1825/34 to 1835/44. Four of these are textiles with a total weight of 19 percent. Iron and steel have a weight of 2.2 percent. My appendix gives certain objections why long-term averages of this sort may not be helpful for short-run analysis.
[2] See Labrousse, *Aspects de la crise* (1956).
[3] But Cameron (*France and the Development of Europe,* 1961), insists that the "crisis of 1848 was first and foremost a financial and banking crisis" (p. 125).
[4] Pouthas, *La Population française* (1956), p. 29.

The basis of the boom in the early fifties was, first, railroads and, second, public works. Both were overdue. State railway projects had been halted in 1847 and the canal program in the following year. Although both had been resumed, there was little force behind them because of the state of government credit. The coup d'état of Napoleon III on December 2, 1851, produced the first reversal in the situation. The establishment of the Crédit Mobilier by the Pereire brothers in 1852 did more to provide new means of finance. The demand for iron rails far exceeded the supply, and in 1853 and 1855 tariffs were lowered. The extension of the French railway network, with private bonds guaranteed by the government, and the building of the Paris boulevards and the ports of Marseilles, Rouen, and Le Havre, drew labor from the farms to the cities. The transformation of local into national markets by the railroads killed off a number of weaker industries, but it opened up opportunities for the expansion of many others. France grew rapidly.

How long this period of rapid growth may be said to have continued is a troublesome question. We are not interested in cycles but in trends. There was one cyclical crisis in 1858, another in 1865, another in 1868. The early 1870s are thoroughly confused by the Franco-Prussian War of 1870, the Treaty of Frankfort in 1871, and the payment of the indemnity which followed. But there was clearly a boom from 1879 to 1882, followed by a crisis and a long period of stagnation. Did the growth period beginning in 1851 last only to 1857, to 1859, to 1868 (when the Crédit Mobilier fell), to 1873?[5] Or, with the brief interruption for 1858 and 1859, is it better to regard 1852–1857 as a period of very fast growth and 1860–1882 as growth interrupted by war?[6] Again, one might view 1860–1875 as a time of considerable stability, preceded and followed by spurts of growth from 1851–1859 and 1879–1882, followed in turn by stagnation.[7]

In the absence of dependable statistics, the choice of dates depends largely on the implicit weights used by the observer. There can be no doubt that there was a boom from 1851 to 1857 and stagnation from 1882 to 1895. Railroads, coal, iron and steel (largely iron), textiles,

---

[5] Cameron regards 1857 as the apogee of the Second Empire (p. 157), and the year of the "revolution" in banking technique (p. 171). The deflation (p. 157) of 1857–58 inaugurated a forty-year deflationary trend (p. 190). But later (p. 485) he indicates that the long depression began in 1882. Perroux, "Croissance de l'économie française" (1955), p. 48, chooses 1859. For a picture of 1867, the year of the Paris exhibition, as the peak of the Second Empire, see Zola, L'Argent (1891), the opening of chap. viii. Clough, "Retardative Factors" (1946), p. 99, chooses 1873 as the end year.

[6] Cameron, "Profit, croissance et stagnation" (1957), p. 410.

[7] Lévy, Histoire économique de la France (1951–52), p. 185.

agriculture, building, and public works, all expanded in the early period and all stagnated in the later. But in the interval they behaved disparately. Agriculture did well up to 1875, although it is difficult to demonstrate this in the absence of adequate data.[8] Iron and steel declined relatively in rate of growth from 1856, food fabrication, tobacco, and railway passengers in 1867, wool in 1868; cotton, after the interruption created by the American Civil War, in the mid-1870s. The picture in construction is obscure owing to the lack of national indexes, but rapid rates of building occurred in Paris in the 1860s and early 1880s, following the increased urban populations of the 1850s and 1870s.[9] But Marseilles and Dijon did not enjoy a boom during the 1850s or 1860s, though they did in the period up to 1882.[10] Whether the earlier expansion was limited to Paris is unclear; if the Halbswachs figure given by Girard, which reached 550, is on the base of the average of 1880, 1885, and 1889 as 100, the peak was very high indeed.

For our purposes it is sufficient to note that economic growth was substantial under the Second Empire, especially in the 1850s; that the first half of the 1870s showed little growth; that a brief boom took place from about 1879 to 1882. During the latter period, agriculture was already suffering from the phylloxera that hit the vineyards in 1875 and from the growth of wheat imports that became serious in 1879.

That there was stagnation from 1882 to about 1896 is generally agreed upon. The few indications of national income for 1882 and 1892 show little movement in money terms.[11] Prices declined — agricultural prices steadily up to 1890, industrial prices mainly in the slump following that year. Agricultural production fell in the bad harvest of 1893 to the lowest level since the disastrous 1879. The only, and inadequate,

[8] The best annual index is heavily overweighted with grain and altogether omits meat and fresh vegetables which were rising in this period. See Sirol, Le Rôle de l'agriculture (1942), app. 2. But cattle numbers are difficult to measure in France, even in the twentieth century, given the large number of illiterate small farmers, some using cattle for draft purposes.

[9] See Halbswachs, La Population à Paris (1928), p. 209, for an index of construction and additions to structures in Paris from 1862 to 1889. Girard, Travaux publics (1951), p. 165, quotes Halbswachs' figures for 1852–1858, which show much higher index numbers for the period to 1857, but I have been unable to find the original source to see whether these use the same base. The largest increases in urbanization in the second half of the nineteenth century occurred in the five-year periods ending in 1856 and 1881.

[10] See Rambert, Marseille (1934), p. 415; and Laurent, "Les Archives d'octroi" (1956), esp. diagram 2, p. 201.

[11] See Perroux, "Croissance de l'économie française," p. 53, who gives money income in 1882 and 1892 as 26 billion francs. Perroux's dates for turning points are naturally for the years he investigates, which are typically based on Census of Production material. They are therefore statistical rather than historical turning points.

industrial production index shows a decline from 45 in 1883 to 37 in 1886, a rise to 49 in 1892, and that level held to 1895.[12] Real income may have expanded to some extent, as in Britain, especially for the limited numbers of salaried personnel. But expansion was minimal; the economy was stagnant.

After 1896 a vigorous upturn took place, which lasted until the world war. Industrial production rose briskly; at the turn of the century, the rate of its expansion exceeded Britain's.[13] Even agriculture improved.[14] There is a difference of opinion about which industries led the growth — but growth there was, and vigorous it was.

The familiar post–World War I story can be briefly summarized: expansion with inflation, but vigorous expansion nonetheless, to 1929; thereafter deflation, stagnation, and inflation without expansion to World War II; a slow climb to recovery after 1945, becoming rapid after 1953 despite monetary disorder. After 1957 there was some cyclical setback, but with basically vigorous growth underneath. The development of the 1920s depended particularly on the reconstruction of the destroyed northeast, as well as governmental activity in the provision of canals and the improvement of railway equipment. Coal mines were electrified and steel plants modernized. Agriculture and private building were left behind.

The disastrous 1930s were the result of overvaluation, an attempt at deflation, and the Popular Front experiment with the forty-hour week. Prices declined until 1935 and rose up to 1939, but production recovered only under the Reynaud administration, which took over in November 1938 after Munich. The early postwar recovery was the result of massive investment, based to a large extent on foreign aid. But the expansion ultimately revealed itself to have a basis in strong technological change.[15]

SINGLE-VALUED EXPLANATIONS OF THE ALLEGED SLOWNESS OF FRENCH GROWTH

The last century has thus produced four and possibly five periods of rapid growth and two periods of stagnation and decline, apart from three wars and their immediate aftermaths. The expansions are 1851–

---

[12] Kuczynski, *Weltproduktion und Welthandel* (1935), pp. 20–21. This index is based exclusively on coal and iron and steel, and uses 1913 as a base. The Dessirier index ("Production industrielle et agricole," 1928, p. 104) gives slightly more coverage, since it includes textiles, but has figures for only three separate years prior to 1898.

[13] Paretti and Bloch, "Industrial Production in Western Europe" (1956), p. 195.

[14] See Institut de Conjuncture, *Production agricole* (1944), cited by Walter, "Développement économique de la France" (1957), pp. 53ff.

[15] I have discussed this in "Postwar Resurgence" (1963).

1868, 1896–1913, 1919–1929, and 1946 more or less to date. The probable expansion period is 1879–1882, probable because it was so brief. (There can be no doubt that French economic activity increased during these years, but the period is so short that it should perhaps not be counted as a growth period.) The stagnant periods are 1882–1895 and 1930–1939. With wars added, this leaves only the years from 1868 to 1870 and from 1872 to 1875, which can either be added to the war period or be regarded with the rather small war of 1870 as another short stagnant phase.

I have evaded and continue to evade the question of whether this expansion should be measured overall or per capita. The French record is much better on the second basis than on the first, given its relatively slow rate of population growth. But the overall rates in the expansion periods were substantial. This record of alternate spurts and pauses will be examined in detail below. Note now, however, that it casts doubt on any single-valued explanation of an overall slowness in French economic growth. To say that the French economy has not grown because it lacks cheap coking coal, because of the family firm, because of its slow population increase, and so on, would appear to suppose a rate which is continuously slow. It might be possible to construct a theory in which a lack of appropriate coal in appropriate abundance produces a slow average rate of growth, composed of alternate rapid and dead stretches, but the prima-facie case is against it. On the other hand, some of the explanation for French difficulties, such as class war or the drag of agricultural inefficiency, satisfactorily fit the rhythm of the French experience. We cannot use the fact of sporadic periods of rapid growth to exclude, without examination, single-valued explanations for slow overall performance, but at least the burden of proof is on their supporters to explain how these occasions of rapid expansion fit.

The commentators may also confuse the level of French output with its rate of change. There can be no doubt that income per capita in France was well below that of Britain in 1851, as it was in 1950 when the question was submitted to careful measurement.[16] Britain had been growing faster than France from 1760 to 1850, possibly earlier, and its lead was extensive. The two economies could thus grow at the same

[16] Gilbert and Kravis (*An International Comparison of National Products,* 1954) give British gross national product per capita as 17 percent higher than the French when based on United States weights, 25 percent higher based on European weights, or 21 percent higher using the geometric average of the two bases of weighting (p. 22). These calculations are from aggregations of real outputs priced in dollars, rather than national incomes in local currency, converted at the dollar exchange rate. On the latter basis, because of the overvaluation of the French franc in 1950, British superiority comes out at only 7 percent (p. 23).

rate, with the difference in level widening absolutely. It seems more likely that, on balance, France grew slightly faster on a per capita basis from 1851 to 1950 and that the difference between levels of output per capita narrowed to some extent in percentage terms, though they widened in absolute terms.

THE PROFILE OF BRITISH EXPANSION

The British economic performance over these years can be much more clearly perceived than the French, though it is not altogether without its puzzles. The 1850s were a period of rapid growth in Great Britain. Agriculture enjoyed a golden age, despite the repeal of the Corn Laws in 1846 that was precipitated by the famine in Ireland and the short crops of the "hungry forties." Building grew, despite the collapse in railway construction following the "railway mania" of 1844–1846 and the peak of construction in 1848. A notable contributing factor in the boom was exports, stimulated by the Crimean War, by the gold strikes in California and Australia, and, especially, by the wave of railway lending from London to the Continent, much of it spent on British equipment and technical assistance. Pressure from exports on iron and steel led to major technological advances, such as Bessemer's invention of 1856,[17] though they took many years to come to fruition. Exports of cotton textiles expanded rapidly without the same technological effects.

The crisis of 1857 provided an interruption, but the 1860s saw the expansion resumed. New industries boomed. Progress in cotton was interrupted by the American civil war, but wool, coal, shipbuilding, and building took up the slack. Exports of railway equipment continued to rise. The crash of the Overend, Gurney Company in 1866 gave brief pause to financial markets, but this proved merely the prelude to the boom of 1867–1873. New joint stock companies were formed under the limited-liability legislation of 1856. The cotton industry emerging from the cotton famine was reorganized and transformed. The shipbuilding boom of the 1860s was followed by one in the early 1870s. Exports of coal grew apace from the established center at Newcastle and the newly expanded Welsh industry, which exploded under the pressure of industrial and transport demand in Europe and in fact all over the world.

We may regard the period as one of unified growth from 1850 to 1873 or 1875 — for many of the investment projects floated before the crash in 1873 were constructed in the years that followed. This was a

[17] Habakkuk, "Free Trade and Commercial Expansion" (1940), p. 802.

remarkable period of expansion. Hoffmann's charts show that the rate of growth declined during most of the period, though it remained over 3 percent per annum until 1870, and that it was exceeded before in 1780 and in the early 1820s.[18] But these earlier periods are inflated by the small base from which they start and contain some statistical exaggeration.[19]

In the early seventies begin the Great Depression and possibly the Climacteric. Both provide puzzling issues. The Great Depression was a period of profitless prosperity, with substantial growth in the real income of the British masses; it is sometimes regarded as a real depression from 1873 to 1885 or 1886, followed by a boom, and another depression from the Baring crash to 1896.[20] The depression in agriculture, mainly or even exclusively in grain,[21] began in 1879 and lasted throughout the period.

The explanation for the Great Depression is sometimes given in terms of the overexpansion of industrial capacity, especially in coal and textiles in the boom of 1866–1873, which produced real output but cut off profits; or of a pause in the flow of inventions between the original wave — in steel, railroads, cotton textiles, and iron ships with screw propellers — linked to the 1850s and 1860s and the internal-combustion engine and electrical appliances of the 1890s;[22] or of the switch of investment from overseas to home construction, with the consequent improvement in the terms of trade;[23] or of the decline in demand resulting from the fall in railway investment, the capital-saving character of the innovations in the application of iron and steam to shipbuilding, and the fact of fewer wars.[24] But many industries, and especially building, remained high during the early period of the depression, fell off after, say, 1877, and stayed off during the recovery of the 1880s.[25] And agriculture remained cyclically depressed until 1894, with a long-term trend downward until imports were cut off by World War I.

The Climacteric and the Great Depression are related, but there is a dispute over exactly how. To Phelps-Brown and Handfield Jones, the Climacteric was a break in the rate of productivity increase and it occurred in the 1890s, at the end of the Great Depression.[26] Coppock

[18] See Hoffmann, *British Industry* (1955), diagram P, p. 319.
[19] See the appendix to this book.
[20] Beales, "The 'Great Depression' " (1934), p. 65.
[21] Fletcher, "The Great Depression of English Agriculture" (1961), *passim.*
[22] Musson, "The Great Depression in Britain" (1959), pp. 207–208.
[23] Rostow, *British Economy of the Nineteenth Century* (1948), p. 88.
[24] Coppock, "The Causes of the Great Depression" (1961), pp. 222–223.
[25] Cairncross, *Home and Foreign Investment* (1953), p. 168; Weber, "Residential Construction" (1955), p. 112.
[26] Phelps-Brown and Handfield Jones, "The Climacteric of the 1890s" (1952).

believes, on the other hand, that productivity had begun to flag in the 1870s, with the decline in the rate of growth of exports and with the improvement in the terms of trade.[27] The growth in real income of the working class during the Great Depression was a result of cheaper imports, not of increased productivity.

Growth was resumed after 1896. It started out with home investment, especially in urban transport and the like, spreading to exports and foreign lending. Profits were high, but productivity failed to increase. Real incomes of workers were held back by the 33 percent rise in import prices. Contrasted with the Great Depression of profitless prosperity, this was a period of profit inflation. Real output rose, with the lion's share of the increase going to profits. The 1920s are generally understood as a period of deflation and distressed areas. The indexes show little rise during the period, dragged down as they are by coal, steel, textiles, and shipbuilding. But building did not do badly,[28] and the new industries of automobiles, chemicals, and electricity came into their own. Sayers insists that productivity rose as much as 50 percent per man-hour between 1914 and 1931, from the application to British industry of innovations from Germany and the United States.[29] Real national income rose from 82 in 1921 to 105 in 1929, or 28 percent in eight years.[30]

After devaluation and the Ottawa Agreement, Britain emerged from depression faster than the rest of the world. A building boom in the early 1930s was followed by an armament boom late in the decade. The rate of growth was perhaps not tremendously high, at 26 percent a decade, but it was impressive against the background of world contraction. After another interruption for war, the British recovery was by no means rapid. Substantial investment from time to time led to balance-of-payments deficits, which, despite aid from the Commonwealth and the United States, caused investment and expansion to be cut back.

THE GROWTH OF FRANCE AND BRITAIN COMPARED

Britain's economic growth started out and ended up at higher levels of production and real income, overall and per capita, than France's.

[27] Coppock, "The Climacteric" (1956).
[28] Youngson (*British Economy*, 1960) dates the recovery in building from 1924 and calls it "almost uninterrupted" and, of housing, "continuous" (p. 49).
[29] Sayers, "Technical Progress" (1950).
[30] Svennilson, *Growth and Stagnation in the European Economy* (1954), table A.1, p. 233.

But the century shows an interesting parallelism and divergence in rates of growth. In the 1850s and early 1860s, both countries shared a rapid rate of expansion. In the 1850s, both were about the same in terms of rate of growth in industry, but the concomitant faster growth of productivity in agriculture resulted in a faster overall rate in Britain. Both industry and agriculture grew faster in Britain in the 1860s, when France, troubled by social and political struggles, failed to share in the boom of 1867–1873, even in the years before the outbreak of the war of 1870.

The economic experience of the two countries differed in the 1870s. Britain started out strong and ended up in depression; in France, it was the contrary. Positions were reversed again in the 1880s. The crash of the Union Générale bank in 1882 ushered in a period of stagnation in France, while Britain emerged from the early part of the decade into a respectable though brief expansion after 1885.

From the 1890s on, the two countries again marched in unison: depressed until 1896, prosperous to 1913. French growth, as we have seen, was more thoroughgoing than British growth. But there were other differences. Both countries loaned abroad on a large scale, but French lending reached its high point in 1906–1910, at close to 4.5 percent of national income; while British lending, doubling after 1906, hit 8.5 percent of national income and more than £200 million of foreign lending in 1913. French economic expansion also led to domestic investment and increases in industrial productivity. In Britain capacity

Table 1. The Course of Economic Growth in France and Britain, 1851–1950

Period	France	Britain
1851–1873	Very rapid to 1856 Moderate to 1867 Interruption, 1870–71	Very rapid to 1866 Recession to 1867 Boom to 1873
1873–1896	Sideways to 1877 Boom to 1882 Depression to 1896	Depression to 1885 Recovery to 1890 Depression to 1896
1896–1913	Rapid growth	Moderate growth
1919–1930	Boom	Stagnation
1930–1939	Stagnation	Moderate growth
1945–1950	Gathering force	Slow growth

expanded, especially up to 1907 and in steel and cotton textiles, not to mention coal, but productivity moved sideways.

After the war, there was more disparate behavior. The 1920s go to France, the 1930s to Britain. Again, after World War II the French economy started off more slowly, but achieved by the mid-1950s a faster rate of growth, and one which rested less on capital expansion than on increases in productivity deriving from innovations. The course of growth (but not the levels) over the century is summarized in Table 1.

This, then, is the framework. In the following chapters I shall have occasion to fill it out for both countries. Enough has been set out, however, to make it clear that the two nations have not responded passively to identical external forces, as the victims of world "trend periods." External influences there have been, as well as the intervention of random contingencies — natural, social, political. But there is enough difference in the characteristic behavior of the two economies to warrant an analytical examination of the various ingredients and processes of economic growth.

CHAPTER 2

RESOURCES

Economic development is a function of factor endowments, including land, labor, and capital, of the values of the society, especially its views on work and income, and of the state of the industrial arts. The level of development depends on the quantity of factors, social values, and technology; the rate of development depends on changes in endowments, values, and technology.

In this first analytical chapter I deal with resources, sometimes called land or "the original and indestructible bounty of nature." And I examine two widely held views: one, that French economic development has been held back by lack of coal (particularly in the rate of development when the steam engine and the conversion of iron manufacturing from wood to coal called for abundant supplies of this natural resource); the other, that while its resources favored Britain as the birthplace of the Industrial Revolution, subsequent technological change left its resources, especially of iron ore, less than optimally suited for continued rapid economic development and the maintenance of its industrial leadership.

THE MODELS

First I must translate these rather vague generalizations into terms that make economic sense. No country can hope to have large supplies of all resources. Trade enables it to exchange those it has in abundance for those it lacks. It would be absurd to suggest that Britain suffered from a lack of cotton. Why then did France suffer from a lack of coal? The point must be that coal is a bulky, heavy product of importance in many uses and that, even after importing, its price remains high. It can thus be seen that it is impossible to discuss coal without transport. One must go further and add that products which embody much coal, like iron and steel, are themselves heavy and cannot be imported without substantial cost, and that coal, iron, and steel are needed for economic development, without abundant and cheap substitutes.

The commonplace view is imprecise about whether the high price of coal in France has held down the level of economic development or the rate.[1] The questions are separable. The level may be affected without the rate, and, given sharply increasing costs in the short run which fall in the long run, the rate can be temporarily restrained — or the length of periods of expansion — without otherwise affecting the level. Resources are closely linked to technology, as the British theorem suggests. A change in technology can eliminate the restrictive effect of the high price of a commodity, or it can increase the demand for missing resources or resources located far from centers of population and development. In this way the handicap or benefit from an existing configuration of natural resources will alter through time, as technical change proceeds. But to blame the resources, where these help less after the change than before, is perhaps misleading.

In the same way, capital formation can be a substitute for resources. This is particularly true of investments which cheapen transport and make possible, say, the inexpensive import of land-intensive products from overseas. But it also applies to other investments. If depletion eliminates the hematite iron-ore deposits of Cumberland, the steel industry can be sustained either by investment abroad in nonphosphoric ores for importation or by constructing new capacity using the Thomas process at the site of phosphoric deposits. This will interrupt growth and, to this extent, reduce the level of growth ultimately achieved. But it will prevent a lack of resources from forestalling it.

Finally, we may note that after a given level of development has been achieved, a high price for resource products can be a stimulus to technological research and development, thus to growth, and that a low price can be a handicap. Under the static model, a high price handicaps. Under a dynamic model, with technical change, it helps. Chaptal in 1828 ascribed England's lead over France to the latter's cheap labor and dear fuel.[2] This applies different models to the differ-

---

[1] I speak of a high price, rather than a scarcity, since economics has no scarcities (or everything is scarce), except when shortages are created by the attempt to maintain a price below the equilibrium level. At the equilibrium level, demand equals supply and there is no scarcity. The price is "high," moreover, compared to some other country. It can be high in money terms, given an equilibrium exchange rate. Export prices will be low and import prices high, especially for commodities with substantial transport costs. But it can also be judged as "high" relative to the price of some other commodity or factor, e.g., the coal/wine ratio compared in France and Britain makes coal high-priced in France and wine high-priced in Britain. But there is no sense in which the price of a unique good is high in a single country (unless it is above the equilibrium price and there is a surplus). It is important also to observe that low wages (in terms of another country) do not inevitably lead to low labor costs, because of the possibility of differences in labor productivity. By analogy, low fuel prices need not make for low fuel costs if there are differences in fuel efficiency.

[2] Cited by Clapham, *Development of France and Germany* (1936), p. 233. Cameron, "Profit, croissance et stagnation" (1957), p. 441, gives the date as 1819.

ent factors.[3] Dear labor would presumably have stimulated development by encouraging investment in labor-saving devices, but dear fuel did not induce investment in transport to cheapen delivery or technological research into fuel economy. Below we shall see whether labor was really cheap. But here we may note that British writers have complained that their iron and steel industry failed to practice fuel economy in contrast to the Continent and to the United States, where the industry, faced with relatively expensive coal, "made fuel out of brains."[4]

FRENCH COAL

The thesis that France suffered in its industrial development as compared with Britain because of the high price of coal has an ancient origin,[5] a long list of distinguished adherents,[6] and thrives currently.[7] There are those who dissent.[8] Many ignore the issue.[9] But it is not

[3] The separate models are explicitly set out by Habakkuk, "Basic Conditions of Economic Progress" (1955), p. 156, in arguing against the view that French entrepreneurs acted in a noneconomic manner. He states that it still has to be demonstrated that the French adoption of coke instead of charcoal in iron production was slower than was warranted by its natural resources; and that it was not at all clear, given low efficiency wages, that it would have paid entrepreneurs to adopt new methods.

[4] Burnham and Hoskins, *Iron and Steel in Britain* (1943), p. 49; Burn, "American Engineering Competition" (1931), p. 301. For a French example, see Cameron, *France and the Development of Europe* (1961), pp. 100ff, which discusses the improvements in locomotives introduced by Schneider in the interest of fuel economy.

[5] In addition to Napoleon's minister, Chaptal, the scarcity of coal is cited by Raudot in 1849 and Cobden a few years later. (Cited by Cameron, "Profit, croissance et stagnation," p. 442; and in the semiofficial Ministère du Commerce, *Rapport générale* [1919], I, 33ff.) The thesis has been strongly advanced by the Comité des Forges, the national steel cartel, to excuse its alleged deficiencies in performance. See Comité des Forges, *La Sidérurgie française* (1920), p. 23.

[6] In addition to Habakkuk, among them may be cited Gerschenkron, "Social Attitudes" (1953), p. 11; Bettelheim, *Bilan de l'économie française* (1947), pp. 143–147; Walter, "Développement économique de la France" (1957), p. 40.

[7] For the fullest statement, see Chardonnet, *L'Économie française* (1958), vol. I, chap. i. An official French publication on energy after World War II states that the coal problem was more acute in France than in any other country (Institut de Conjoncture, *Bilan de l'énergie en France,* n.d. (post-1945), but the entire document seems to be a brief for rights in the Ruhr.

[8] For a dissent in 1835, see Tocqueville's conversation with the French consul at Liverpool, M. Laine (*Journeys to England,* 1958, p. 113):
"Q. Birmingham is placed over iron- and coal-mines; Manchester in a coal-mining district and two steps from the sea; Liverpool in the middle of all sorts of wealth. Nearby is Wales with the richest of iron-mines, so that iron, coming by sea, reaches Liverpool, Manchester and Birmingham almost without cost for transport. These are immense natural advantages. Do you not think that the unbeliev-

enough to count noses. The basic question is the cost of coal, after imports, and this turns on location, transport, and tariff policy.

To take tariffs first: a steeply rising supply price for domestic coal production does not necessarily hold back economic growth during periods of boom, if the supply price of imported coal is relatively constant. And there was very little reason for France to complain of the high price of coal, since a tariff was maintained on the commodity.

Tariffs on coal and iron were levied in 1819, 1821, and 1822, in order to reserve the coal market for the domestic producer.[10] These tariffs were levied in the interest of the landowner, who wanted a high price for charcoal. The progress in converting from charcoal to coke in smelting iron was accordingly slow.[11] But the boom of the 1830s brought about a change. Tariffs were reduced; there was a widespread public interest in and search for coal.[12] A large expansion in coal production in the Pas de Calais occurred. Tariffs then went back up, this time in the interest of the coal producers.[13] And they fell off and went

---

able prosperity of those districts and of England in general should be attributed to that?

"A. In my view, intellectual qualities, and in general practical knowledge and acquired advantages, play a much greater part still."

Mourre in 1899 (*Décadence économique de la France*, p. 421) dismisses coal from a long list of alleged causes of British superiority, in plumping for habits of work and order. The statistician Dessirier (*Conjoncture économique*, December 1943, quoted by Bettelheim, p. 146) argues that Britain is no more favored than France in raw materials; see also Dunham, *The Industrial Revolution in France* (1951), *passim*; Pitts, *Bourgeois Family and French Retardation* (1957), pp. 35ff. Gravier (*Décentralization*, 1954, p. 164) suggests that the examples of the Netherlands and Switzerland prove that economic development does not depend on the presence of coal. The Allais demonstration that natural resources are relatively unimportant to France (*L'Europe unie*, 1960, pp. 24–28) because, if resource products were free, French national income would be increased by only 33 percent is unacceptable. In arriving at this result from the statistic that French resource products account for 25 percent of national income, Allais uses the labor theory of value and constant costs. Given the possibility of increasing returns in other industries, and the likelihood of decreasing returns in resources, the percentage of resources allocated to resource-product output is not a measure of its general importance.

[9] It is especially noteworthy that the subject is not discussed in Sée, *Histoire économique de la France* (1942), II; in Lévy, *Histoire économique de la France* (1951–52); or in Jeanneney, *Forces et faiblesses* (1956).

[10] Gille, *Formation de la grande entreprise* (1959), p. 46.

[11] Dunham calls it "amazingly" slow (p. 134).

[13] See Amé, *Les Tarifs de douanes* (1876), I, 199. Lévy asserts that tariff reductions occurred in the booms of the middle 30s, 40s and 50s (p. 96). Presumably these tariffs were raised again in the slack periods. This was so in 1852 (see Dunham, *The Anglo-French Treaty*, 1930, p. 20). The changes in the tariff cannot be readily summarized because the schedules discriminated against England, and imports by sea, and in favor of imports from Prussia (the Ruhr) and Belgium. Within the category of imports by sea, imports on the channel (Sables d'Olonne to Dunkirk) paid a higher tariff than those to western or southern ports. On the public interest, see Gille, *Formation de la grande entreprise*, pp. 62ff.

[13] Gendarme, *La Région du Nord* (1954), p. 49.

up again. The railroad boom of the 1850s brought about a substantial reduction; so did the treaty with England, which also included a provision binding Britain to forswear export taxes on coal sold to France.[14] But the coal interests of the Nord were persistent. The duty rose again under the Méline tariff of 1892 and once more with the revision of 1910. Imports were substantial but so was protection. In the circumstances, it is hard to see how the French could continue to complain about the high price of coal.

Moreover, the price of coal to the consumer was declining in this period as the cost of transport fell. Sée lists the overall decline in the cost of transport with the advent of railroads as from 45 to 6 centimes a ton-kilometer between 1840 and 1870. Specific data for coal prices in particular localities can be adduced. The price of coal in Paris fell from 37 francs a ton in 1835 to 25 francs in 1851. There may have been some cyclical decline in this price, but Dunham attributes it to improved transport.[15] A substantial reduction in transport charges to 20 francs a ton took place after the introduction of the railroad from Charleroi to Rouen and reduced the cost of coal to 0.04 francs per kilogram of cotton spun, an inconsequential figure which suggested that the price of coal had no effect on the price of cotton textiles thereafter.[16] In the Dauphiné, consumption of coal was substantial already in 1847, but expanded rapidly in the 1850s and especially in the 1860s in Isère; it rose sharply from very low figures in Drôme after 1859; the Hautes Alpes slept undisturbed throughout the period.[17] The troubles of a badly located but originally highly progressive steel plant in the Nivernais were first caused by high coal prices, including the cost of large stocks since the Loire was navigable only for three months a year, but later, after a merger with an anthracite mine, the difficulties stemmed from exhaustion of the iron-ore supply and the falling price of coal.[18]

More undoubtedly could have been done, and sooner, to construct the social overhead capital of the country in transport, and so to have made good whatever shortage of resources existed. In the middle of the century, the delay was due to many possible reasons — the geographical spread of industry, drawn to supplies of workers who resisted movement off the farm, the "pettiness of Parliament" or the "rigidity of

[14] Levi, History of British Commerce (1880), p. 431.
[15] Sée, Histoire économique de la France, p. viii. Bouvier, Le Crédit Lyonnais (1961), notes that the Paris-Lyon-Marseilles railroad charged 10 centimes for Loire coal, reduced to 8 in 1863, rates which were regarded as "usurious" (p. 101). Dunham, The Industrial Revolution in France, p. 100; Renouard, Le Transport de la marchandise (1960), notes that the price of coal fell from 50 francs per ton in Paris in 1847 to 39 in 1875, while rising from 10.5 to 15.9 at the pithead (p. 43).
[16] Fohlen, L'Industrie textile (1956), p. 141.
[17] Léon, Naissance de l'industrie en Dauphiné (1954), II, 482, chart.
[18] Thuillier, Georges Dufaud (1959), pp. 33, 50, 76, 103.

Ponts et Chausées," quarrels between bankers or between bankers and the government, or the lack of coal itself.[19] For whatever reason, France arrived at the middle of the nineteenth century with only 3,000 kilometers of railroads, compared with 6,635 miles in Britain. Habakkuk voices the opinion that France fell ten years behind Germany in railroad building and that these ten years may have been critical in accelerating German development.[20]

Attempts were made after this to repair the gaps in the system, particularly those which would have helped to move coal cheaply. The Freyinet Plan of 1879 called for the Canal de l'Est to connect the Nord and Lorraine. This was declared a local utility in votes of July 26, 1881, and July 3, 1882; but action on it was blocked by the steel industry of the Nord which felt threatened. A similar project to shorten the length of the canal from the Seine to l'Escaut by 100 kilometers and reduce the 42 locks to 19 was not undertaken, despite the law of December 23, 1903.[21] The failure to construct a canal from Lille to Dunkirk, which would have made that city "another Antwerp," is part of the same discrimination against imports, especially British coal. The canals of the north were left more or less untouched after 1825, despite continuous building in Germany, the Netherlands, and Belgium.[22] The double-track electrified line from Valenciennes to Thionville, built after World War II, took the place of the Canal de l'Est and gave Lorraine an alternative to Saar, Upper Loire, and Ruhr coal. In the 1880s, however, when French Lorraine coal was in limited production, the connection would have been useful. It might have had to be combined with more imports, since the costs of Nord coal were sharply increasing, and its diversion from Paris to Lorraine would have raised prices.

What, then, was the situation? Cheaper coal could have been obtained by lower tariffs and by greater investment in transport. But there is very little evidence that the price of coal or physical limitations in its supply were a bottleneck after 1850. Coal output expanded rapidly

[19] Habakkuk, "Basic Conditions of Economic Progress," p. 157; Cameron, *France and the Development of Europe*, p. 207.

[20] Habakkuk, "Basic Conditions of Economic Progress," p. 165.

[21] Gendarme, *La Région du Nord*, pp. 120–122.

[22] Nistri and Prêcheur, *La Région du Nord et Nord-Est* (1959), pp. 15, 142. The Canal de l'Est by itself would have joined Lorraine to Dunkirk, but a direct canal from Dunkirk to Lille would have greatly improved transport. It is interesting to observe that Dunkirk is coming into its own as a petroleum port. See an article in *Le Monde* for November 30/December 1, 1958, on the thoughts of an electric brain on oil pipelines and refineries. The machine favored Dunkirk and Alsace because of the Common Market and was opposed to any further development of the remote Atlantic ports. The canals were hurt, of course, by the advent of the railroads and, some said, by discriminatory railway rates. See below, Chapter 9.

in the Nord after the discovery of the fields in 1847.[23] The process was accelerated from 1900 to 1913, with no discoveries but continuous improvement in equipment and mechanization.[24] Outside France, in German Lorraine, the Saar, and the Ruhr, near French borders, production expanded. The isolated French fields increased production very little; but the Nord and the Pas de Calais kept up with the Saar, with German Lorraine, and almost with the Ruhr.[25] Between 1880 and 1910 imports grew little faster than consumption, as Table 2 shows.

Table 2. French Coal Consumption and Imports

(millions of tons)

Year	Apparent consumption[a]	Imports
1880	28.7	9.9
1890	36.1	11.0
1900	48.1	15.4
1910	55.9	19.2

[a] Production plus imports less exports, adjusted for changes in mine stocks.
Source. INSEE, *Annuaire statistique, 1956*, p. 4.

On what terms was coal obtainable from the Ruhr, the Saar, or German Lorraine? That from the Ruhr was the best in coking quality. The prices at which it was sold are subject to some dispute. In 1919 the French Ministry of Commerce claimed that the German coal cartel discriminated against foreign buyers; but a separate portion of its report, dealing with the cartels rather than fuel, called the German organization moderate and useful.[26] Burn claims that firms in French Lorraine had an advantage over the German competitors, since they could buy coke, not coal, at lower prices than those obtaining in Germany.[27] It is of course possible that the Rheinische-Westphälische Kohlen Syndikat dumped coke and "reverse dumped" coal, but an attempt to ascertain the truth of these allegations some years ago failed to reach a clear-cut conclusion.[28]

[23] See Gendarme, *La Région du Nord*, p. 278, chart.
[24] See Parker, "Coal and Steel Output" (1957), pp. 217, 219, charts.
[25] Gignoux, *L'Industrie française* (1952), pp. 107–108.
[26] Ministère du Commerce, *Rapport générale*, I, 34; III, 226.
[27] Burn, *Economic History of Steelmaking* (1949), p. 159.
[28] See my *The Terms of Trade* (1956), p. 87, n. 31.

Cameron, who is interested in demonstrating the importance of France's capital contribution to European economic development, adduces a number of cases of French investment in Belgian and German coal mines. Here is another means of overcoming any possible handicap in raw materials, but of course the French could go further and invest not in German coal but in German steel.[29] The fact, however, is that French investments in German steel were relatively unimportant, covered more than half of Belgian coal, which was not useful for metallurgical purposes, and were relatively small in German coal.[30] The largest French producer in Lorraine also had the largest interests in the Ruhr, acquired to free himself from dependence on the Kartell — and still he had to buy almost half a million tons of Ruhr coke on the open market.[31] But while the Lorraine steelmakers had to import coal or coke, the producers in the Ruhr were obliged to seek iron ore abroad. "Though the cost of transporting their coke was heavy, the steelmakers in the Saar, and still more those in Lorraine and Luxembourg, had lower total transport costs in assembling materials than Westphalian makers using minette." [32]

There are questions of timing here. The French have always complained of lack of coal, from the Napoleonic period until after World War I. But some students think it counted more at some periods than

[29] Cameron asserts (*France and the Development of Europe*, p. 388) that France was ahead of Germany in iron and steel in the 1850s, but behind by 1870. This was owing in part, he states, to the opportunities for production and profit across the Rhine. But the only evidence cited is a loan by de Seillère to Krupp in 1865 (p. 397) and investment in Phoenix in the Ruhr, which turned out to be "one of those pompous Paris speculative enterprises" (p. 395) and collapsed.

[30] In 1852 the French owned 22 out of 40 Sociétés Anonymes in Belgian coal mining, plus several mines outright (*ibid.*, p. 348). Cameron offers a tentative estimate of 5 percent of German coal in French ownership (p. 300). He claims that all French investments in Germany were decisive for German development (p. 403). Both statements seem excessive.

[31] See the authorized history of de Wendel (Sédillot, *La Maison de Wendel*, 1958, p. 250), which discusses concessions or participations acquired in 1900, 1904, 1908.

[32] Burn, *Economic History of Steelmaking*, pp. 154–161, esp. 159. The French Ministry of Commerce (*Rapport générale*, pp. 33ff) claims that the French price of coal is 20 percent higher than the German and 40 percent higher than the British; the French coke price 54 percent higher than the British (34 francs per ton against 22) and 62 percent higher than the German (34 against 21). A series comparing the United Kingdom coke price at Middleborough with the French average is given by Burnham and Hoskins for the period 1870–1913, with seven separate years in all: the gap starts out at 60 percent and narrows to 10 percent (*Iron and Steel in Britain*, p. 127). But it is evidently misguided to compare the price of one ingredient. Ore costs were much lower in Lorraine than in the Ruhr or in Britain, and the cost of ore varies much more widely than the cost of coke. Basic pig iron was produced in Lorraine as cheaply as anywhere in the world (*ibid.*, p. 103). One should of course consider the cost of transporting the finished steel to the market, and here Lorraine is at a disadvantage compared with many other areas in France, as well as in Britain and Germany.

at others. Walter, for example, says that it counted for little after World War I; and d'Hérouville is prepared to admit that the lack of coal in France is not important now, but that it was a hundred or so years ago.[33] Nonetheless, it is hard to make a case that the French economic rate of growth, apart from the level, was handicapped at any time after 1836. From 1836 to 1848, "production of French coal grew greatly and ever more rapidly." [34] After 1847 there was the Pas de Calais expansion, which lasted to 1875. Production increased 534 percent on a base which was substantial, and capital expanded from 30 million francs to 200 million over the period, evoking a designation as "le 'rush' des capitaux pour l'exploitation du basin du Pas-de-Calais." [35] During the period up to 1896 there was, first, general stagnation and, second, lack of iron ore until the development of the Thomas process and the expansion of French Lorraine minette iron. But when these two obstacles had been overcome, steel output grew as fast in France as it did anywhere.[36]

One argument made against coal scarcity as a handicap to steel production is worth examination here. Pitts alleges that the slow development of French iron and steel, which we have had occasion just now to question, was not because of a lack of coal but because of the reluctance of family firms to maximize profits. Their interest, in this view, was to perpetuate the life of the family and, in the case of exhaustible natural resources, to make them last as long as possible. He cites the case of the rich iron mine at Briey. Iron ore had been mined at Briey in French Lorraine since the Middle Ages. The de Wendel interests obtained the concession in 1885, when the Thomas process made the high phosphorous-content ores workable. A shaft was sunk in 1891, and production began in 1894. But by 1901 output had reached less than 500,000 tons. At this time the Thomas patents that had been held by the de Wendel interests lapsed. Other firms took up steelmaking. Under the pressure of demand, iron ore production expanded. By 1913 Briey was producing 15 million tons of iron ore out of a total for French Lorraine of 19.6 million.[37]

Cameron wonders why Briey was so slow to develop; Pitts does not.

[33] Walter, "Développement de la France," p. 45. But note that Bettelheim claims (*Bilan de l'économie française*, p. 143) that the return of German Lorraine in 1919 made the high price of coal even more "poignant." D'Hérouville, "Niveau de la production manufacturière de la France" (1955), p. 213.
[34] Dunham, *Industrial Revolution in France*, p. 102.
[35] Gendarme, *La Région du Nord*, pp. 42, 43, 120ff.
[36] See Svennilson, *Growth and Stagnation* (1954), pp. 122–123. The rate of expansion of steel production by the new processes from as early as 1880 to 1913 was "extremely rapid" and "ranged from 8 per cent in France to about 10 per cent in Germany and Belgium-Luxembourg."
[37] Pitts, *Bourgeois Family and French Retardation*, pp. 55–56.

He rejects the explanation of the Comité des Forges, that there were technical difficulties, and accepts that of H. Grandet, that the de Wendels had enough ore in Hayange and Joeuf to take care of their needs and had no interest in producing iron ore for its own sake, no matter how profitable.[38] The character of the family firm made supply inelastic. This may be so (we shall examine the French family firm in a later chapter). But other testimony supports the technical explanation. The Briey ore beds lay below the water table and dipped in such a way that natural drainage could not be used. "The attempts to open mines were mismanaged, and for ten years there were no positive results." In 1896, however, the need for larger ore production became imperative; by 1899 a new process for handling the water was installed, and thereafter development was very rapid.[39]

We shall return to Lorraine iron ore later, once in connection with finance and again on the subject of war. Here it is worth mentioning that the Germans drew the new border in the Treaty of Frankfort with a view to depriving France of steel capacity and iron reserves — 80 percent of local capacity in each was lost.[40] But it was quickly made up. For France as a whole, in 1873 pig-iron production matched earlier all-time highs. For Meurthe-et-Moselle, in 1878 production reached the previous high for the two separate departments. Some labor and one firm moved across the border into France. Numerous new companies were formed. And geologists, operating with samples from greater depths, learned of the extent of the fields of Joeuf and Briey. Within a short time after 1880, France added 57,000 hectares of new reserves to replace the 43,000 lost in the Treaty of Frankfort.[41]

If the exploitation of Briey cannot be regarded as having been impeded by noneconomic factors, what about the de Wendel mine in German Lorraine, Petit Rosselle, which was nationalized in 1945? At the time of the nationalization, the de Wendels asserted that they had not operated it at full capacity because they had hoped to enjoy "the

[38] Cameron, "Profit, croissance et stagnation," p. 431; Pitts, "Bourgeois Family." See also Ehrmann, *Organized Business in France* (1957), p. 481. Ehrmann holds that it was not lack of coal which held back French development, but the mentality of producers and businessmen who use property as a promise of enjoyment and consumption rather than for growth.

[39] Pounds and Parker, *Coal and Steel* (1957), pp. 198–199. See also McKay, "Pre-war Development of Briey," (1936); Lévy (*Histoire économique de la France,* p. 236) and the biased Comité des Forges (*La Sidérurgie française,* pp. 70–71) which regard Briey as an example of speedy development.

[40] In 1869 the two departments of Meurthe and Moselle together produced 30.4 percent of French pig iron and 15.9 percent of steel and wrought iron. In 1872 the single department of Meurthe-et-Moselle produced 18.4 percent of French pig iron and .8 percent of French finished iron and steel. Comité des Forges, *La Sidérurgie française,* p. 174.

[41] See Sédillot, *La Maison de Wendel,* p. 241.

brightest jewel in the de Wendel crown" for a thousand years.[42] This claim is evidently partisan, since it objected to compensation for nationalization on the capitalized value of current output. We are in no position to evaluate the merits of this dispute over Petit Rosselle. But it may be relevant to note that its coal had to be mixed with German and Dutch coals in the nineteenth century for coking; that it grew fairly rapidly in the years before World War I; that it could not have been expected to grow in the depressed 1930s;[43] and that the Moselle is the region of France where one can least apply the theory that the French individual is uninterested in expanded income.[44]

A final mention of coal may be made in connection with the chemical industry. Here France is alleged to have suffered because of the deficiency of its coal, in both quality and uniformity, and its expense.[45] In addition, the industry had been handicapped by early reliance on and location near the southern coal fields, which played out fairly early.[46] This is only one part of an evidently complex story, to which we shall return. But it is of interest here to note the different interpretation of Maurice Lévy, who blames the poor showing of the chemical industry and the scarcity of coking by-products on the supply of capital. The capital shortage, in his view, is responsible for the fact that even when cokeries and gas plants consume 11 million tons of coking coal, they recover only 250,000 tons of coal tar.[47] With proper equipment, the yield should be twice that amount.

[42] This view of the de Wendels was kindly communicated to me by David Landes.

[43] Sédillot, *La Maison de Wendel*, p. 279. Nistri and Prêcheur, *La Région du Nord et Nord-Est*, p. 112, note that the de Wendels obtained the Petit Rosselle concession in 1850, produced a million tons of coal from it in 1900, more than 2 million tons in 1913, and 2.6 million tons in 1938. By 1954, under nationalization, production was up to 5 million tons. But this rise in production is no greater than that for all Lorraine coal, which expanded from 6.7 million tons in 1938 to 13 million tons in 1954. For the latter figures see Rideau, *Houillères et sidérurgie de Moselle* (1956), p. 21. Father Rideau gives the 1900 figure for Moselle as 630,000, but it is not clear whether this includes the Petit Rosselle, which was then on the German side of the border.

[44] Nistri and Prêcheur, p. 52: "Moselle is characterized by the energy of its labor, avid for income." This avidity may not, however, extend to the bourgeois classes.

[45] See Löffl, *Die Chemische Industrie Frankreichs* (1917), pp. 53ff; Baud, *Les Industries chimiques régionales* (1922), pp. 78ff; Grandmougin, *L'Essor des industries chimiques* (1919), chap. iii; and, for a recent treatment, Chardonnet, *Les Grandes puissances* (1960–61), I, 164. Paul Hohenburg, whose study of the French chemical industry I rely upon, notes that Löffl calls coal the "blood" of industry, whereas Baud speaks of it as the "bread." Cf. Clapham, *Development of France and Germany*, p. 403, who asserts that by 1894–1914 all proverbs about bread had gone out of use.

[46] Löffl, p. 57.

[47] Lévy, *Histoire économique de la France*, p. 228. Grandmougin notes, moreover,

The scarcity-of-coal argument as such is therefore not very convincing. But there are more subtle variations. Cameron points out how ironic it is that all French natural resources are located on its borders, rather than in the center of the country.[48] Or the objection is made that the resources are located far from the ports, where they might be appropriately combined with imported materials of other sorts, using inexpensive sea transport.[49] Again, Clapham bewails the lack of a bulk export product which would give France a cheap back-haul rate of the same sort that Britain was able to obtain in the tramp steamers returning for more coal cargoes.[50] Finally, and still more subtle, there is the suggestion that the lack of abundant coal hurt France by not providing it with a dense transport network which, by bearing a large part of the fixed charges of the system, would have enabled other commodities to be carried cheaply.[51]

These views amount to little more than that France lacked cheap and effective transport. Here is where lack of natural resources may have worked against it. But there is not a great deal that can be said on this score. The rivers of the north are effective highways and readily linked by canals to each other and to the great rivers, the Meuse, the Moselle, and the Rhône. The failure to achieve the canalization of the Meuse and the Moselle, except within France, doubtless lies at the door of international politics.[52] As we have seen, however, France had opportunities to build other canals. The Rhône and the Loire are difficult rivers, full for a short space of time during the year and dry the rest, difficult to link to the Seine and to each other.[53] A complaint can be lodged against nature for not having been more topographically generous. The Garonne connects the area of wine and naval stores, not with the rest of France but with the sea.[54] Nor is the

---

that Switzerland had a flourishing dyestuff industry without domestic coal supplies (p. 206).

[48] "Profit, croissance et stagnation," p. 433.

[49] Dunham, *Industrial Revolution in France*, p. 498. Dunham also blames the scattered character of French coal deposits in the upper Loire Valley, the Nord, the Massif, and Blanzy (p. 92), but this of course could save transport and be an advantage, unless there is a gain from large-scale coal transport.

[50] Clapham, *Development of France and Germany*, p. 244.

[51] Parker, "Comment" (1961), p. 189. Parker's view is that coal enabled Germany to acquire advantages of agglomeration which were missing in France.

[52] Nistri and Prêcheur, *La Région du Nord et Nord-Est*, stress the need for canalization of the Meuse and the Moselle to connect Lorraine to its natural market in Germany: "The center of France was too far" (p. 142). The same theme runs through the Sédillot account of de Wendel. The European Coal and Steel Community, after some hesitation, is now pushing the project. But the international difficulties remain substantial.

[53] See Dunham, *Industrial Revolution in France*, p. 48. See also Marshall, *Industry and Trade*, p. 108.

[54] See Girard, *Travaux publics* (1951), p. 30, on the two Frances of the pre-

other great port on the straight Atlantic coast, Nantes, equally remote
with Bordeaux from the economic centers of Paris and Lyon, much
more advantageously placed. It attracts little industry besides petroleum, naval training, and shipbuilding. But France barely developed
the industrial harbors it had. Marseilles and Rouen came in for attention, especially under Napoleon III, but not Dunkirk, as mentioned, or
Dieppe. These matters should properly be reserved for the later discussion of government and capital. A rearrangement of the landscape
would have been beneficial, but full advantage was not taken of what
existed.

Finally, there is one more highly intellectual point about French
resources. Dunham finds that France is a country of many little regions
of a similar sort, each largely self-sufficient.[55] This presumably inhibited
economic growth by limiting the gains from specialization when the
canals and railroads were built. More diversified resources would have
meant greater gains from trade, a higher level of real income, and
faster growth on the basis of the original input of higher savings and
investment. The suggestion is interesting. But the self-sufficiency of the
separate regions is not relevant, for any region is necessarily self-sufficient before trade arises. The question is merely one of whether the
regions are identical. It is true that wheat was grown in every department of France and on almost every farm. "In only ten of the eighty-
seven departments, including that of the Seine, did grain crops occupy
less than half the tillable land in 1882, and only in Corsica did they
fall below 40 per cent." [56] But the French farmer's resistance to specialization in wheat hardly makes the case for similarity among the regions of France. France has always been divided into three or more
different parts, at least since the days of Caesar.[57]

---

railway era, one of the mouth of the Loire, one of Burgundy. In the age of sail,
boats from Bordeaux or Nantes often had to wait days off Brittany for a fair wind
to run down the channel to Le Havre. Steam changed this, but shortly thereafter
the railroads ruined the business of *cabotage*.

[55] See his article, "The Industrial Revolution in France" (1951) and his review of
Morazé, "La France bourgeoise" (1946), p. 199.

[56] Golob, *Méline Tariff* (1944), p. 81. The structure of Alsace and Lorraine is
similar to the rest of France in this, and in all else but textiles and iron. See
Laufenburger, "Structure territoriale" (1939) pp. 2–5.

[57] The north and the east are evidently much more developed industrially than
the west and the south. For agricultural regions, see Fauchon, *Agriculture
française,* who divides France into six agricultural regions (p. 20); Augé-Laribé,
Politique agricole de la France (1950), who has seven (p. 19); Klatzmann,
"Grandes régions agricoles" (1957), who has twenty-four but admits that for
some purposes the Ministry of Agriculture's division into nine regions is satisfactory.
For private purposes I find it pleasant to contemplate Root's division of France
(*The Food of France,* 1958) into three regions which cook, respectively, with butter, olive oil, and goose grease; or those, not quite identical, which drink cider,
wine, and beer.

Moreover, as Dunham states elsewhere, as others assert, and as we shall have occasion to see, the French failed to take full advantage of the opportunities for specialization.[58] There was specialization, a great deal. Every grain except wheat is specialized by locality.[59] The wines of the Midi drove local vintages off the market by the hundreds with the coming of the railroad, and the same was true for textiles, forges, and so on.[60] The zone from which Paris drew provisions expanded from 50 kilometers in 1830 to 250 in 1855.[61] From 1865 on, France formed a single market in which there was a single price for each product. The average journey per ton rose from 62 kilometers in 1847 to 145 in 1854 and 197 in 1863 — the last figure was still unchanged in 1936.[62] It seems unreasonable to think that geography failed France completely, especially in the light of what further improvement in transport could have done to create opportunities for specialization.

We may conclude this discussion of French resources by a glance at agriculture. Here it is widely recognized that while France's natural resources are superior to Britain's, British agriculture has been far more effective.[63] No one blames the performance of French agriculture on lack of basic resources. Dozens of other reasons are given; the farmers could blame the government, industry, the banking system, large landowners — anybody but themselves. In industry, on the other

[58] Dunham, *Industrial Revolution in France*, p. 249. Gille, *Formation de la grande entreprise*, p. 33, quotes Schneider as having said in the 1830s that Britain's superiority was due to the greater specialization of firms, and he states that this was confirmed in a number of submissions to the inquiry of 1834. Specialization by firms is possible, of course, even when specialization by regions is not. And in increasing-returns industries, specialization by firms leads to specialization by regions, even between regions with identical resources.

[59] Augé-Laribé, *Politique agricole de la France*, p. 22.

[60] The "railroad sealed the triumph" and ushered in the golden age of Langue-doc. See Carrère and Dugrand, *La Région méditerranéene* (1960), p. 64. See, e.g., the studies of Fohlen, *L'Industrie textile*, esp. pp. 169ff; and *Une Affaire de famille* (1955), p. 92ff, on the need to specialize after the improvement of transport by railroads. Landes has a table of the decline in charcoal pig iron which he attributes, like Dunham, to the reduction in the tariff in the Anglo-French Treaty of 1860 ("Comment," pp. 262, 248). See also Dunham, *Anglo-French Treaty*, p. 141, who states that the treaty completed the conversion of the industry from wood to coal. Cf. Armengaud, "La Fin des forges catalanes" (1953), pp. 62–66. Production, with charcoal, hit a peak in 1853. The maîtres des forges blamed the Treaty of 1860, but the writer asserts that the damage was done by the railroad. The 55 furnaces of 1853 were already only 30 by 1860. The same point is made by Léon, *Naissance de l'industrie en Dauphiné*, pp. 823–824, where transport from the Loire basin ruined the industry, whose furnaces closed down one by one, while a local maître de forge, speaking in the name of the Comité des Forges, blamed the ruin on the treaties.

[61] Renouard, *Le Transport de la marchandise*, p. 44.

[62] *Ibid.*, p. 42.

[63] For an early view (1855), see de Lavergne, *The Rural Economy of England* (1855), chap. i; for a late one, Passe, *Économies comparées* (1957), p. 35.

hand, it was more difficult to find scapegoats. Hence, we find all the attention paid to the price of coal, which was seen almost exclusively as a "natural" phenomenon, sometimes assisted by foreign personalities — the German coal cartel or the "hated British coal monopoly." [64] — but seldom to the coal tariff imposed on behalf of the landowners and then the coal mines, or to the failure of the government to construct the needed transport. Coal may have had importance in the beginning, but each time after 1836 that the demand existed, coal was forthcoming.[65]

BRITISH RESOURCES

The simple view on the importance of coal to France has its corollary in reference to Britain — and is no more convincing. Britain was an unimportant country until the development of steam power, which made coal significant; after reaching the apogee of its economic leadership and influence between 1850 and 1870, it declined relative to Germany and the United States in the last quarter of the century, partly because of a lack of technical capacity, but also because of the shift from coal as a source of energy to electricity and oil.[66] This view neglects the other British natural advantages, the role of depletion, especially in iron, and the relative unimportance in an economy with capital and technical capacity of such natural resources as oilwells or hydroelectric-power sites.

There is little need to expatiate on the topographical advantages of Britain: its insular position, near a large land mass, accessible to supplies and markets but distinct from it, with all the encouragement that insularity gave to maritime intercourse and the relief from the necessity for large defensive forces. In contrast with the Biscay coast

[64] Brogan, *France under the Republic* (1940), p. 579.

[65] It is interesting to note the arithmetic, even if one does not believe the numbers, of the Ministry of Commerce's special study, which denigrates the importance of raw-material costs in the machinery industry. The machinery industry suffered from the tariff of 1910 which neglected mechanical construction and gave too much protection to primary products. But the difference in costs of primary materials was 25 percent, and the value of primary products in machinery ran between 30 and 50 percent. If one takes out the value added in steel, the 30 to 50 percent reduces to 20 to 30, and 25 percent of that is but 5 to 7.5 percent. (Ministère du Commerce, *Rapport générale*, I, 455.) As an indication of the difficulty of making these comparisons, note that Marcel Rist ("Le Traité de 1860," 1956, p. 925) states that just before the treaty of 1860, coal cost 8 francs (per quintal?) in the United Kingdom, and 30 francs in France, with the transport amounting to only 100 per cent; while Labrousse (*L'Évolution économique de la France*, 1954, II, 79) states that coal was more expensive in France than in Britain, but by no more than 8 percent.

[66] See Crouzet, *L'Économie du commonwealth* (1950), pp. 10ff.

of France, the islands have many harbors, on all coasts.[67] The islands are so small that no point on them is more than 110 miles from the sea. And the land is relatively flat, permitting easy construction of canals and railroads to provide good internal, as well as external, communication.

Climate has been important as well. Located where the warm Gulf Stream disperses, the islands enjoy mild temperature and much rainfall. The extreme southwest is subtropical. But the mildness and the rainfall combine to produce grass in luxuriant abundance, which had early advantages for sheepraising and therefore for wool and woolens. It provided west of the Pennines a moist atmosphere in which cotton thread was slow to break. The rainfall encouraged pink cheeks, pink roses, the Mackintosh industry (an early innovation in rubber), and oaks (an early advantage for ship construction).

Mineral resources were not lacking, even apart from coal. There were tin and copper, lead and iron, and the iron, coal, and limestone were frequently found together and in close proximity to the sea. Halévy calls these "an essential condition if not a sufficient cause" for the extraordinary development of British industry in the eighteenth century.[68] British satisfaction with its resource endowment proved less enduring than French envy of it. Already at the beginning of the nineteenth century, concern was being expressed at the pace at which coal fields were being worked. In 1865 W. Stanley Jevons published *The Coal Question*, predicting a rapid rise in costs because of diminishing returns. For some time depletion at the older fields was offset by the opening up of new ones — South Wales dominating the period of the 1870s and the East Midlands the period after World War I. But after the East Midlands, no new fields remained to be developed. The rate of technological progress in the mines, which had been rapid from 1850 to 1880, slowed down.[69]

There is considerable dispute in the literature over how to divide responsibility for the decline in coal productivity among natural conditions, industrial management, and the recalcitrance of labor. Even natural conditions have their man-made aspects: the mines of Birmingham would have lasted longer if the mineowners had been better able to agree on such questions as sharing the burden of pumping ground

---

[67] Burn notes, however, that the existence of many small harbors, which was originally an advantage, gradually became a handicap when the need was for large and deep-water harbors, capable of handling very large ore boats. See "Recent Trends in Steel" (1947). The same problem of expanding tanker size gave rise to the need to construct Milford Haven. But Britain had sites where such ports could be readily established.

[68] *History of the English People* (1937), I, 83.

[69] Beacham, "The Coal Industry" (1958), p. 114; Taylor, "Productivity and Innovation in British Coal" (1961), p. 49.

water, and if the industry had been organized on the basis of longer leases, thereby encouraging conservation practices.[70] But there can be little doubt that more mechanization was possible, despite the thinness and twist of the seams.[71] Capital was taken out of the industry and not invested in it.[72] Investment projects with short payouts were neglected.[73] Labor relations have a long history of bitterness, ca' canny, and obstruction of mechanization.[74] Foreign customers felt themselves robbed by extortionate prices charged in the period immediately after World War I up to 1921. Some of the British reaction to the resource industry is even noneconomic — the reluctance if not the refusal to undertake open-cast mining, whether of coal or of iron ore, and the early interest of miners in leisure rather than in income. Therefore, although I have no intention of rendering a verdict on how much weight should be accorded in the industry's decline to the separate factors or to the competition from oil,[75] it would be hard to make a case which relied heavily on depletion as mainly responsible for the difficulties.

The question of depletion is posed more insistently in iron ore. The wrought-iron age lasted to the peak of the boom in 1873, despite the invention of the Bessemer steel process in 1856 and of the Siemens-Martin open hearth in 1866. During the wrought-iron period the main center of production was the West Midlands, in South Staffordshire and South Lancashire, with a center in Birmingham, and in the West Riding of Yorkshire from Leeds to Sheffield. Toward the end of the 1860s there was a substantial rise in new producing areas: Scotland along the Clyde, South Wales, and the northeast coast on the Tyne.

[70] See Allen, *Birmingham and the Black Country* (1929), p. 386: "There can be no doubt that the Black Country's coal was brought to a premature end largely by faults in its organization." Local supplies of iron ore were also depleted after 1865 (pp. 194, 235) apparently without contributory negligence.

[71] An American mission to the United Kingdom during the war viewed the British coal fields as somewhat inferior to the American, but not by so much as has been widely held. The chairman took the view that they were comparable to the Appalachian fields, which accounted for 70 percent of United States production at that time.

[72] See Taylor ("Productivity," p. 64, n. 4), who quotes a witness before a Royal Commission on Coal Supplies of 1904: "I think the best plan in managing a colliery is to hand to your shareholders the money that is made."

[73] See Appendix 4 of the Reid Commission Report (1926).

[74] See Baldwin, *Beyond Nationalization* (1955). Most of the discussion of labor problems starts with World War I and the betrayal of the miners in 1921 by the government's refusal to nationalize the industry in accordance with the recommendations of the Sankey Commission. For a view of earlier worker attitudes, see McCormick and Williams, "The Miner and the Eight-Hour Day" (1959).

[75] The British comparative disadvantage after the widespread adoption of oil was serious as against the United States, but no worse than that of any other European country, and much better than most. Owing to its participations in the oil industry in Persia, Iraq, the United States, and Venezuela, Britain got its oil cheaper, net after profits, than the industrial countries of Europe, disregarding, as is appropriate, the small local production of Germany and the Netherlands.

With the coming of steel, however, it was necessary to limit the use of iron ore to hematite ores, free of phosphorus, until the introduction of the Gilchrist-Thomas process in 1878, which permitted the use of phosphoric ores to make basic Bessemer steel. But the industry was already expanding along different lines, in acid open-hearth steel. There was some increase in the 1880s in basic Bessemer steel using Durham coal and Cleveland ores. But the movement to the East Midland phosphoric ores of Northhamptonshire and Lincolnshire did not take place until the 1930s, when Stewart and Lloyds erected a plant at Corby and the United Steel Company expanded its Appleby-Frodingham works in 1938.

Again, there is controversy over whether the difficulties of the British iron and steel industry came from depletion of iron ore, as Marshall claimed,[76] or from a failure of management. It is difficult for the nonexpert to weigh the arguments on both sides. The East Midlands were relatively far from existing coal and from cheap scrap, such as would be generated by the steel-using industries of Birmingham or Sheffield. The ore was lower-grade than the Lorraine minette ores — averaging less than 27 percent as against the French figure of over 30 percent.[77] The Midlands lacked access to supply-oriented markets like those available to the shipbuilding of the Clyde and the Tyne, where local steelmaking relied on foreign ore. But other mills, like those of South Wales and the northwest coast, were also far from domestic markets. After its hematite ores had been exhausted and its export markets for rails lost, the latter had no advantages except deep water, but United Steel kept on investing at Workington, where "the company was very conscious of its responsibility as an important employer of labor in one of the depressed areas about which public opinion was very concerned."[78] There were other factors, such as the specification of acid steel by many users, until continental Bessemer steel had been bought for rerolling in tinplate on a substantial scale. And the Thomas process came along at a poor time, when the industry was still licking its wounds after the overexpansion in wrought iron and acid Bessemer and the loss of the United States rail market in the 1870s.

On balance, however, it seems evident that the industry was slow to

[76] Quoted by Burn, "British Steelmaking and Foreign Competition" (1940), p. 222.

[77] Nancy and Longwy, 33–40 percent; Briey, 36–40 percent; German Lorraine, 30 percent. See McKay, "Pre-war Development of Briey," p. 175.

[78] Andrews and Brunner, *Capital Development in Steel* (1951), p. 208. The most famous case is of course that of Richard Thomas, who was prevented by political pressure from establishing a tinplate mill in Lincolnshire in the East Midlands and was virtually required to build in the depressed area of Ebbw Vale. See Minchenton, *British Tinplate Industry* (1957), p. 194.

readapt, both in the 1880s and 1890s, when basic Bessemer steel failed to grow, as did acid open-hearth and even basic open-hearth. Burnham and Hoskins call the neglect "amazing." Burn states that the static pattern of production is a feature of great interest because underlying cost factors have changed greatly, and the response to these changes has been negligible.[79] A long list of critics has attacked the steel industry, as well as the coal, for a pricing policy, especially after the depression, which supported the high-cost producer at the expense of the low and seriously inhibited reallocation.[80] Andrews and Brunner defend the industry. They point out that expansion of Stewart and Lloyds in Corby, Northhamptonshire, has been handicapped by lack of housing; and they justify on various grounds the separate action of United Steel, formed in 1918, in expanding at the low-profit centers of Templeborough and Cumberland, while failing to invest in the East Midlands until 1938, despite the steady profits of the unit located there all during the difficult 1920s and 1930s.[81] Sinclair insists that good progress was made in the open-hearth section of the industry in the late nineteenth century, both technically and in terms of overall profit, and that it is a mistake to focus attention solely on the slow rate of advance in Bessemer.[82]

Under the pressure of circumstances, in the armament program of 1937–1939, and in the postwar period before, during, and after nationalization, the industry has moved in the direction in which the critics said it should have gone fifty years earlier. The critics have not been content and think it should have moved still faster.[83] And a further historical stage has been reached in depletion — the beginning of the exhaustion of the Spanish ores on which the South Wales industry depends,[84] although this source can be replaced by Algiers, Mauretania, and possibly Liberia.

[79] See Burnham and Hoskins, *Iron and Steel in Britain*, p. 120; Burn, "Steel" (1958), p. 276.

[80] In coal, see Beacham, "The Coal Industry," p. 137, and Jewkes, "Is British Industry Inefficient?" (1946), p. 13. These attacks are directed particularly against the Coal Mines Act of 1930. For steel, see Burn, "Steel," p. 297; and "Recent Trends" (1947), p. 101.

[81] Andrews and Brunner, *Capital Development in Steel*, p. 98. For information on the profitability of different works, especially the quotations from company reports, see pp. 128–130, p. 154, and the table, pp. 204–205.

[82] Sinclair, "The Growth of British Steel" (1959).

[83] See Burn, "Steel," p. 290, who claims that the investment plans after World War II do not involve enough radical change in location, given the high cost of foreign ores.

[84] See Flinn's two articles on the search for foreign ore by British entrepreneurs, the one in Spain a success, the other in Sweden a failure: "British Steel and Spanish Ore" (1955) and "Scandinavian Ore" (1954). The latter notes that the Spanish mines were beginning to become exhausted before 1913; the former, that

We shall not have an answer to the question of the importance of
resources to the relative decline of the British steel industry until we
examine other aspects of the industry — in particular, entrepreneurship
and technology.[85] But there is at least a possibility of oversimplification
in the view that depletion and changes in technology, which left resources inappropriate for a modern industry, slowed down the rate of
growth in British iron and steel. As depletion proceeded in hematite
ore, technology made possible the expansion of production in the East
Midlands; but the industry failed to adjust to maximum advantage. Its
response was to defend the existing structure rather than to adapt to
changes in underlying costs.

It may be appropriate here to refer back to the handicap imposed by
the headstart in making cheap fuel. American and continental economies in fuel have been mentioned at the start of this chapter. Allen
points out that the cheapness and high quality of British coal in the
past produced wasteful methods of utilization that are difficult to abandon now (1939). Andrews and Brunner note a technical problem of
coking fines at Frodingham, which did not reach a full solution for
thirty years, and that United Steel's decision to establish a central research department was taken only in 1930–31.[86] Technology is a substitute for resources; and resources, unfortunately for economic development, constitute a substitute for technological efficiency and progress.

DEVELOPMENT AND RESOURCES

In his *Strategy of Economic Development* Albert O. Hirschman suggests that, rather than resources leading to development, development
leads to the discovery and use of resources. That this is true above a
certain level is abundantly borne out by the recent history of France:
the discovery of oil in Algeria, natural gas in Lacq, even oil near
Bayonne. But it is also supported by the earlier record: the rapid development of coal in the Nord and Pas de Calais after 1847; the less
rapid, but more far-reaching expansion in iron ore after 1896; and the

---

dependence on rich hematite ores was reduced in the twentieth century by the
turn to the Thomas process. While British entrepreneurs did not succeed in producing the hematite Swedish ores effectively, Swedish producers after 1891 expanded
production and export of both hematite and phosphoric ores.

[85] In the view of the leading authority, Burn, the chief obstacles to the emergence
of new high-capacity plant in Britain have been "imperfections of competition"
and the structure of the British capital market, which limited the access of the
steel companies to long-term sources. See Burn, *Economic History of Steelmaking*
(1940), p. 262.

[86] Allen, *British Industries* (1939), pp. 56–57; Andrews and Brunner, *Capital Development in Steel*, pp. 135, 200.

development of Lorraine coal, under German sovereignty in the 1890s but for the French in the 1920s and 1950s.

Certainly resources count. At an early stage, when techniques are rudimentary and factors of production respond sluggishly to economic challenge, the richest countries will be those with the greatest resources, of a type appropriate to the stage of technology. Later, more resources are always better than less resources, except in the case where resources substitute for economic response.[87] But the case that scarcity of coal deposits was the villain in the drama of retarded French economic development is difficult to support. If one discusses the rate of growth, rather than the level, one is obliged to explain away the rapid bursts of energy, which brought coal in their wake, in 1851–1868, 1896–1913, and 1919–1929. If one worries about the level of growth, it is necessary to explain why coal was kept out by tariffs and why France did not substitute other elements of growth for coal — more transport facilities and more technical ingenuity. To insist that a static model applies in coal — a high price hurts — whereas a dynamic model is relevant to labor — a high price helps and a low price hurts — calls for a defense of the discrimination. But the main point is that any time France grew, coal came along too.

The British use of resource deficiencies to rationalize a slower rate of growth than that of the United States or Germany is somewhat more satisfactory in timing. Britain was ahead until 1870. After that, depletion and a change in taste against wrought iron left Britain with a smaller gain from trade (reduced comparative advantage), which slowed down growth. But the argument, as I have shown, is thin. Other explanations abound for the slow productivity rise in coal, for the failure to keep abreast of technology. British industry failed to adapt to the resources made valuable by technical change.

In both cases we shall have to reserve a final verdict until other elements of the analysis have been completed. But for the moment, and until it is reversed by further evidence, we may say that inadequate resources neither prevented economic growth in France after 1850 nor were responsible for any loss of leadership in Britain after 1875.

[87] This is a big subject which has occupied profound minds. Ciriacy-Wantrup in *Resource Conservation* (1952), p. 252, notes that an abundance of exhaustible resources can make for specialization, rather than diversification, and, with depletion, lead to retarded and abortive growth, dead end, stagnation, and the death of species. He cites as authorities: Dobzhansky, *Genetics and the Origin of Species* (1941); Toynbee, *A Study of History* (1935); and Kroeber, *A Configuration of Culture Growth* (1944).

CHAPTER 3

CAPITAL

The Harrod-Domar model of economic growth, as is well known, is one in which growth proceeds through capital formation at what Rostow calls compound interest. From higher levels of income come more savings, which result in more investment, which in turn produces still more income, savings, investment, and so on. This model was originally developed from concern about dynamic stability, rather than growth. Harrod emphasized that because today's investment in an instantaneous model results in an increment of capacity, tomorrow's effective demand has to be larger to produce full employment. Domar, on the other hand, observed that today's investment, by enlarging capacity, or potential supply, permits real income to expand.

Many observers have sought to apply the Harrod-Domar model to economic history and to explain the course of income in terms of capital investment.[1] This is not entirely satisfactory as historical explanation. We want to know, for example, whether capital formation fell short of what it might have been because of a lack of effective demand along the lines, say, of Hansen's model of secular stagnation — a Harrodian model. This question has been examined particularly in relation to France. Or savings may have been insufficient — the Domar version — which has been suggested for application to Britain. Realized savings may be the same in both countries and, with an equal capital/output ratio, rates of growth may have been identical. But the historian must not stop here. In the Harrod-Hansen stagnation version of the model, with inadequate demand for abundant savings, there will be low interest rates and unemployed or underemployed resources. In the Domar variant, on the other hand, with an inadequate supply of savings relative to the demand for investment, there will be full employment and relatively high rates of interest.

Nor is it sufficient to deal with the overall demand for capital and supply of savings. If the former is weak, it is necessary to ascertain why. And on the supply side, there is the possibility, discussed at length in both France and Britain, that though overall savings are sufficient, as measured by some test, they are being wasted or frittered

[1] See, e.g., Maddison, "Growth in Western Europe" (1959).

away in inefficient uses — for example, by being loaned abroad when they are "needed" at home.

The Harrod-Domar model links new investment to increments in income by means of a capital/output ratio. Additional capital is assumed to produce more income in perpetuity because, implicitly or explicitly, there is excess capacity of other factors in the system — typically, unutilized or underutilized land and labor. When this condition exists, the investment to obtain the largest increment in income is the project or sector where there is the lowest capital/output ratio (or highest ratio of output yield to capital invested).

Where the capital/output ratio is the appropriate criterion for choice among investments, a strong bias arises against foreign loans. The capital/output ratio is typically somewhere between 2 or 3 to 1, which would mean an increment in income on domestic investment of 33 to 40 percent, compared with the 5 to 10 percent which can be earned on foreign loans. The difference between the two yields is the income earned by the previously under- or unused land and labor. The investor may get as much or more abroad as at home. But with foreign loans the country fails to obtain an external economy — employment for its previously unused or poorly used factors.

When, however, domestic factors are effectively allocated and fully employed, increments of capital cannot be taken up into use without reallocation of land and labor in other industries. The investment criterion is now not the ratio of output to capital, but the marginal productivity of capital. A fully employed economy grows faster by investing abroad at a 6 percent return than at home at 4 percent because in this way it obtains the highest increase in income, and therefore in savings, and therefore in income again.

Nor is this all. For one thing, there may be economies of scale in the export industries, stimulated by the export of capital. Or there may be external economies abroad resulting from foreign investment in, say, railroads, and these lead to cheaper imports for the lending country, enlarged gains from trade, and hence more growth in the next time period. The output term in the capital/output ratio should include the private return *and* the sum of all external economies, positive or negative, at home and abroad.

According to this analysis, we should not judge foreign investment without examining the relevant investment criteria in Britain and France, and in particular the questions of the full and efficient employment of factors other than capital.[2] Considering the efficiency of

[2] For a discussion of the investment criteria in relation to foreign lending, see Johnson, *International Trade and Economic Growth* (1958), pp. 1–5; Jasay, "Home and Overseas Investment" (1960); Streeten, *Economic Integration* (1961), chap.

British and the inefficiency of French agriculture, there is a presump-
tive case that British foreign lending was warranted by the absence
of evidence of external economies in domestic investment (the investment criterion being the marginal efficiency of capital rather than the
capital/output ratio), and not warranted in the French case.

The existence of external economies in foreign investment is a
matter which can be dismissed from a comparative study, though it
belongs in any systematic account of British economic history,[3] because
those economies gained by Britain are available to France as well. It
is true that the French have been less willing than the British to take
advantage of the resulting opportunities — to adjust domestic production, for example, to the supplies of cheap wheat made available from
overseas by ocean shipping and the railroads of Argentina, Australia,
Russia, and the United States. This is a question of transformation,
rather than an essential element in capital lending. British lending
could have benefited France in this way, as French lending benefited
Britain.[4]

The models are easily adduced. Starting from a given position,
change occurs in the system and variables respond to it. But in the
world of history there is the identification problem, made worse by the
interaction of the variables. Did limited lending at home slow down
growth, or did a slow rate of growth check domestic investment and
therefore spill savings over into foreign loans? Does the fact that institutions favoring foreign investment exist alongside unsuccessful would-
be borrowers mean that the domestic investor is slighted? It is easy
to argue the contrary by pointing to the borrowers and banks that
failed and to the existence of successful borrowers and successful banks
and bankers that supported them, asserting that anyone really worthy
of credit receives it. Potentially successful frustrated borrowers leave
no trace. The most we can do, as before, is to summarize the evidence
and come to a reasonable conclusion.

---

iv. In another essay, Streeten touches upon another external economy from foreign
lending — the impact of increased exports on technological change (p. 123). This
is mentioned below in Chapter 12. Parenthetically, it may be remarked that
Keynes's view that foreign lending was inferior to domestic, because in the case
of bankruptcy the domestic economy lost real assets in the former but not in the
latter, is invalid. To the extent that the investment is uneconomic, the loss is the
same in both cases. And that part of the investment which retains value can be
used or sold, again equally well, in either situation.
   [3] See, e.g., the treatments by Cairncross, Colin Clark, Lewis, Brinley Thomas,
and Rostow, although they are not all systematic.
   [4] See below, Chapter 12.

FRANCE — THE OVERALL SUPPLY OF CAPITAL

There is general agreement that the overall supply of savings in France was sufficient between 1851 and, say, 1930 and that the difficulty in investment lay in the mechanism for directing its allocation. Before 1851 there may have been too little saving: Dunham amasses a series of conflicting opinions, but concludes that most French writers believe there was not enough capital for the "expansion and transformation of French industry." [5] Gille, on the other hand, believes that the overall mass of savings was sufficient, but that before it could be used effectively it was necessary to evolve the industrial bank.[6] After 1930 there is the possibility that inflation reduced the propensity to save,[7] but again it may merely have changed its form. The typical French bourgeois, artisan, and peasant were all thrifty or stingy types, prone to miserliness on one showing, prudent for the future on another. There was a strong affinity for saving over which control could be exercised: the family firm, land, or the strong box.[8] But the Frenchman was also attracted to the *rente* and caught up in waves of speculation,[9] despite

[5] Dunham, *Industrial Revolution in France* (1951), p. 213. On pages 326 and 359 he notes that the French literature of the period is full of references to the abundant supply of capital in Britain, but he himself states that it is impossible to say whether capital was scarce or not (p. 240). Capital accumulated slowly because industrialization proceeded slowly — or possibly vice versa.

[6] See Gille, *Formation de la grande entreprise* (1959), p. 8; and, by the same author, *Banque et crédit* (1959), *passim*, but esp. pp. 184 and 375.

[7] See Bettelheim, *Bilan de l'économie française* (1947), p. 126.

[8] Clapham, *Development of France and Germany* (1936), p. 132. Clapham blames this attitude on three bankruptcies of the nation in the eighteenth century. Fouillée, *Esquisse psychologique* (1903), p. 507, states that the French spirit of saving contrasts with the British spirit of spending. In Britain the individual counts on his energy to continue to earn for the sake of spending. He also leaves to his children the task of handling their affairs. The Frenchman dreams of the future, not only for himself but for his family. "From this it follows that the spirit of personality is more developed in England, and the spirit of solidarity more developed in France." Note Baum, who claims that France is a country of *rentes* and not of profits (*French Economy and the State*, 1958, p. 354); and Sée, who expresses roughly the same sentiments while warning against excessive generalization in characterizing the psychology of a people (*Histoire économique de la France*, 1942, p. 247).

[9] The love of the *rente*, which was regarded as an investment suitable for a family man, is sometimes said to be ingrained in the French and sometimes said to be stimulated (Dunham, *Industrial Revolution in France*, pp. 68, 225). The link between bonds and the family implicit in referring to the *rente* as an investment suitable for the head of a family recurs in the Ministère du Commerce, *Rapport générale* (1919), I, xi, and in Sée, *Historie économique de la France*, p. 272. Lévy notes that the *rente* spread to the provinces in the first half of the nineteenth century, as the state freed itself from reliance on the *hautes banques* in selling its securities (*Histoire économique de la France*, 1951–52, p. 47). The provinces owned none of the debt in 1815, 10 percent in 1830, 30 percent in 1840. Girard claims that the Revolution of 1848 democratized the *rente* and the state guarantees

having his fingers burned on frequent occasions.

> After 1851 the problem was not to find savings, but to avoid speculation.[10]

> In the last four or five years (1856) the mass of savings has been taking a different direction [from agriculture]. Billions of francs a year are now going into loans of the state or cities, or to enlarge the funds sterilized by speculation on the exchanges [which reduces the harvest and raises agricultural prices].[11]

> For ten years (1866) we have been lending abroad in frenzied fashion at rates of 8 to 11 percent, making it hard for agriculture and industry to acquire capital.[12]

From the beginning of our period, then, most observers agree that the problem has not been overall savings, but their allocation. The blame, moreover, has been placed on capital exports. The issue was raised long before Mourre or the debate between Lysis and Testis, as the quotation from Halévy makes clear.[13]

Whereas widespread opinion believes that French capital exports slowed down French economic expansion, few go so far as Cairncross, who asserts that French industry was "starved for capital." [14] Some are cautious and qualified, like White. Sée is disposed to see little harm in the lending from 1880 to 1896 — in this period of depression it positively helped — but he believes it was a handicap afterwards,

---

of 1852 the railroad bond (*Travaux publics*, 1951, p. 100). Bouvier (*Le Crédit Lyonnais*, 1961, pp. 203–204) believes that the Thiers loan of 1871 helped to educate the French public in *rentes*.

The love of speculation which is widely mentioned in the literature (see Bouvier, I, 188, and Dunham, pp. 71, 223) would seem to contrast with the fear of companies and the need for safety found in the *rente*. So it does. But the speculation was frequently in bonds, especially foreign bonds, which combined the form of safety with the risks of speculation (and high yield). For a literary discussion of the Bourse's excesses of speculation, see Zola's *L'Argent* (1891), esp. pp. 166ff.

[10] Girard, *Travaux publics*, p. 86.

[11] Gille, *Banque et crédit*, p. 375, quoting a contemporary text. Gille wonders whether the analysis does not apply earlier.

[12] Daniel Halévy in 1866, quoted by Duveau, *La Vie ouvrière* (1946), p. 122.

[13] Cameron ("The Crédit Mobilier and the Development of Europe," 1953, p. 461) says the question was raised by Mourre, and not in the period 1850 to 1870. But he changed his mind (see end of note). The reference is to *La Décadence économique de la France*. I find little trace in Mourre, however, of a tendency to blame capital exports. Cf. p. 257: "The form of government, the régime of inheritance [of land], the intervention of the state, protectionism, our pedantic instruction, the climate, the disdain of the higher classes for the lucrative professions, all these closely connected causes contribute to the decline of France."

Landes gives citations for the debate in "Comment" (1954), p. 260, n. 9. In *France and the Development of Europe* (1961), Cameron finds concern over capital exports in 1836 (p. 123) and especially in 1855 (p. 152)

[14] *Home and Foreign Investment* (1953), p. 225.

especially to agriculture.[15] Lévy found evidence of capital shortage, especially in the chemical industry and in urban transport, and blames it on the foreign lending. On the other hand, Goldenberg, a disciple of Hansen, thinks that the stationary population in the presence of so much saving made the capital exports necessary.[16]

FORMERS OF CAPITAL

The state. The demand for capital may be said to have come from the state, from large-scale industry, small industry, agriculture, commerce, the mortgage market, and foreign borrowers. We can discuss supply in terms of the relations of various suppliers of capital, direct and indirect, to these demanders. Let us start with government. Note that the emphasis in this chapter is on the supply of savings, and later I devote separate chapters to government, entrepreneurship, population, and agriculture and their influence on the demand.

The state was both a supplier of savings for capital formation and a demander. In the latter capacity, it undertook public works; in the former, it furnished its credit to railroads, industry, agriculture, housing — to construct capital in their respective spheres. The distinction is not worth drawing sharply. For our purposes, it does not matter whether the state is forming capital directly or indirectly.

The state drew on the savings of France for capital formation in the period we are considering: first, under the Second Empire, for public works, to guarantee railroad bonds, to assist urban construction and agricultural improvement, and to assist industry to re-equip in the face of British competition after the reduction of duties; second, in the Thiers loan, raised to pay the Prussian indemnity; third, for the Freycinet Plan of 1879, to extend the railroad, canal, and road network; fourth, for wars; fifth, for the reconstruction of shattered territory after World War I; and sixth, after World War II, for the reconstruction and modernization of the infrastructure, nationalized industry and private industry. The state was not an active seeker of savings 1896–1913 or in the 1930s.

The early struggles of the state with its creditors form an important part of the economic history of France. The delay in building the railroad system, for which a variety of reasons have been adduced, is

[15] White, *French International Accounts* (1933), esp. chaps. xii, xiii. Cameron observes (*France and the Development of Europe*, p. 487) that restraint on French capital exports in the 1880s deepened the depression. It is not clear, however, whether he is referring to market caution or to some unspecified policy restraint. Sée, *Histoire économique de la France*, p. 360.

[16] Lévy, *Histoire économique de la France*, p. 228; Goldenberg, "Savings and a Stationary Population" (1946), p. 42.

generally attributed to the disagreement between the government and
the bankers over how it should be financed.[17] The program finally got
under way after two important innovations — the guarantee of railroad
bonds and the establishment of the Crédit Mobilier as an industrial
bank, both in 1852. After the completion of the original Le Grand
design[18] — a star with lines radiating out from the center at Paris —
the government of Louis Napoleon proposed the extension of the
system, on terms to which the banks again objected. The crisis of 1857
and the conventions of 1858 between the bankers and the state were
the consequence.[19] And the Freycinet Plan twenty years later, when
the Third Republic thought to meet the recession of the late 1870s
with a governmental program of extending canals, roads, and railroads,
was again objected to by the bankers, changed in financing, and reduced in scope by the conventions of 1883.[20]

State financing after 1871 was carried through on terms satisfactory
to the banks, which indeed made large profits out of the Morgan
loan of 1870 and the Thiers loan of 1871. Bouvier attaches great importance to the effect of these profits, which followed the losses of
the Crédit Lyonnais in gas companies in Spain, a chemical company
near Lyon, and the local Lyon railroad network, in turning this large
bank from industrial loans to financial manipulation — *grosses affaires*
— in issues for large industry, in *rentes*, or in foreign loans.[21] The usual
view is that the Crédit Lyonnais changed from an industrial bank to a

[17] See Renouard, *Le Transport de la marchandise* (1960), introduction, for a
concise account. The Le Grand plan was conceived in 1832, rejected by the Chamber in 1838, and replaced by the Law of 1842. The original plan called for state
finance; the Law of 1842 provided that the state would look after the infrastructure, leaving the superstructure to the companies. Construction was interrupted in
1847 and 1848 by the crisis, resumed in 1849, but especially after the coup d'état,
the restoration of government credit, and the state guarantee of bonds. For a detailed bibliography of sources, see Landes, "Comment," p. 247, esp. notes 5, 6, 7,
and 8 on p. 260. Landes' interpretation differs slightly from the one here. He
blames the hesitant and suspicious capital market which made the promoters turn
to the merchant banks. But the merchant banks and the promoters were often
closely linked, and both were unwilling that the government substitute for their
efforts. A contemporary discussion of the war between Ponts et Chaussées and
industry observes that this could not have occurred in England. See de Tapiès, *La
France et l'Angleterre* (1845), p. 595.

[18] Le Grand was the head of Ponts et Chaussées. The real author of the plan was
Michel Chevalier (Cameron, *France and the Development of Europe*, p. 134).

[19] Girard, *Travaux publics*, pp. 163ff.

[20] Lévy, *Histoire économique de la France*, p. 189. Brunschwig (*Impérialisme
colonial français*, 1960) says that the Freycinet Plan, once the pride of France,
turned into its humiliation, since the Germans executed it, after French capital was
diverted into capital exports (p. 146). It is not clear to what he is referring, since
German investment occurred largely in iron, Belgian in tramways, and no foreign
investment in canals, railroads, or roads.

[21] Bouvier, *Le Crédit Lyonnais, passim*, esp. chap. vi, "Entreprises vs. Affaires."

deposit bank only after the crash of the Union Générale in 1882.[22]
This is insufficiently subtle. The Crédit Lyonnais either had discovered
that industrial credit ran large risks or had made a mess of the affairs
it was involved in,[23] but in any case it found large-scale security issues
very profitable. Three years after its founding in 1863, the Crédit
Lyonnais started to lend abroad. In 1871 Henri Germain, the leading
founder of the Crédit Lyonnais and its long-time head, had become
less interested in *entreprises* and more interested in *affaires*. The year
1882 confirmed the bank in conclusions already held.[24]

After World War I, the state resorted to inflationary financing for its
capital formation, at least until 1926. This was excused by the prospect
of reparation from Germany to pay for the reconstruction of the destroyed territory. After the restoration of confidence in the franc under
the Poincaré government, state calls on the capital market declined.
After World War II, state needs for capital were met by foreign aid,
inflation, and some taxation. But this period is of limited interest for
this discussion, since there was a shortage of capital rather than a
plethora.

Under the Second Empire state credit was employed not only for
railroad construction but also for urban works, agriculture, and industry. The urban works involved many cities and ports, although the rebuilding of Paris, largely under the prefecture of Baron Haussmann, is
the best known. The work preceded Haussmann's transfer to Paris from
Bordeaux in 1853 and even the coup d'état of December 1851.[25] But
both events lent force. The development of Paris has been attributed
to the glory — the inspiration of all Caesars — to furnish work for the
rootless workers of 1848, and to open roads to lend troops maneuver-
ability in suppressing revolution.[26] But the growth of Paris was a function of the railroad system, which consisted in separate lines running

[22] See, e.g., Cameron, *France and the Development of Europe*, p. 196; de Feuilhade, *Une Grande banque de dépôts* (1959), p. 26; and Bigo, *Les Banques
françaises* (1947), p. 172. Bigo says that the Crédit Lyonnais restricted its loans
to industry "a little." This is an understatement.

[23] The Crédit Mobilier had had many imitators in Britain up to the crash of
the most distinguished of them, Overend, Gurney & Company, in 1866. (Newbold,
"Beginnings of the World Crisis, 1873–1896," 1932, p. 428. Cameron, p. 163,
takes a contrary view.) The Crédit Mobilier itself was brought down in 1868 by
the hostility of the Bank of France, which refused to rediscount its paper, and the
merchant banks. (For an account partisan to the Pereires, see Cameron, pp. 191ff.)
Georges Lefèvre, *Politique intérieure du Second Empire* (ca. 1953) p. 56, states
that the history of the Second Empire can be written in terms of the conflicts of
rival financiers. See also below, pp. 109ff, esp. n. 125.

[24] Bouvier, *Le Crédit Lyonnais*, chap. xi and p. 384.

[25] See Girard, *Travaux publics*, p. 121, who states that the plans had long
been laid.

[26] Lefèvre, *Politique intérieure du Second Empire*, p. 68.

out from the city. Halbswachs has shown that the construction was a
response to, not the cause of, the movement to the city of masses of
workers, although there was much interaction. And the decline in Paris
building only partly stemmed from the waning of Louis Napoleon's
interest and from the financial difficulties into which Haussmann and
the city fell. After having grown in population from a million in 1851
to 1,825,000 in 1866, Paris slowed down and, with it, the rate of construction.[27]

Agriculture and commerce. In 1845 de Tapiès could say that agricultural credit was good in France, much better than in Britain.[28] In 1856
the observer quoted by Gille noted that the flow of credit into agriculture had stopped. Louis Napoleon tried to revive it. A law had been
enacted in 1854 enabling the government to lend money to people for
draining land. When this produced few results because of its administration by the state and the need to protect the rights of mortgage
lenders, the matter was turned over to the Crédit Foncier in 1868.[29]
In 1860 the Crédit Agricole was established as a special subsidiary of
the Crédit Foncier to occupy itself with rural loans. Some state works
of drainage had been successful.[30] But by 1870 the Crédit Agricole
had made drainage loans of only 1.1 million, out of an authorized
100 million; rural mortgage loans formed only a small part of the
Foncier's total loans on construction.[31] By 1873 the Crédit Agricole
was buying Egyptian bonds. In all, it lent 168 million francs to the
Egyptian government between 1873 and 1876.[32]

One reason for this dismal record may have been the original lending
technique, which called for the Crédit Agricole to issue its bonds to a
borrower who sold them in the open market. When interest rates were
tight, as in 1873, the discount rate would go as high as 15 percent.[33]
Another may have been the farmer's fear of debt[34] and his unwillingness to borrow, except for buying land. Farm indebtedness was heavy
in the middle of the nineteenth century, peasants borrowing largely

[27] Halbswachs, *La Population à Paris* (1928), p. 14. All the great works projected
by Napoleon III had been constructed, and the Caisse des Travaux de Paris was
liquidated by the end of 1869. Unfortunately, Halbswachs' index of building has
a break in it between 1868 and 1873. The 1867 figure is the high for the 1860s;
1868 is only slightly lower.

[28] *La France et l'Angleterre,* pp. 591–592.

[29] Jousseau, *Traité du Crédit Foncier* (1884), p. lix.

[30] Lévy, *Histoire économique de la France,* p. 140, notes that Napoleon III
established model farms.

[31] Jousseau, *Traité du Crédit Foncier,* p. xli; Robert-Coutelle, *Le Crédit Foncier*
(ca. 1876), p. 58. Of 480 million mortgage loans in 1865–69, 400 million, or 83
percent, were for Paris and the rest for rural property and provincial towns.

[32] Jousseau, *ibid.,* p. lxv.

[33] *Ibid.,* p. lxxi.

[34] Baum, *French Economy and the State,* p. 292. This refers to a later period.

for the purpose of buying land, mostly from notaries and frequently at usurious rates.[35] Side by side with this indebtedness were the savings of peasants that were drained off by the banking system and invested in *rentes* and foreign bonds. If agriculture was handicapped for lack of capital,[36] the remedy seemed to lie in organization. Ultimately, the French peasant discovered agricultural credit cooperatives and embraced this device despite his alleged mistrust of his fellow man and lack of the "spirit of association." [37] But for most of the years up to 1929, any shortage of capital in agriculture was attributable to ineffective machinery, given the annual flow of a large volume of savings from the rural sector.[38]

The banks did not altogether neglect agriculture. Local banks in the Nivernais, with great care and maintaining high rates of liquidity, assisted in the equipment of large estates.[39] In Seine-et-Marne close to Paris, large farms may even have been overcapitalized, since they were bought up by wealthy owners with access to borrowed funds.[40] Labasse discusses at length the availability of capital to certain types of agriculturists who are highly commercial — the *emboucheurs* who fatten cattle in feeder lots, the vineyards in the Burgundy area, and the cheese finishers. But not the fruitgrowers of Brieux near Lyon who finance themselves and put back the surplus into land — and not the cheese-makers.[41] Carrère and Dugrand give an instructive account of how the large Paris and Lyon banks loaned for the replanting of the Midi vineyards in the 1890s, after the area had been blighted by phylloxera and the local banks had failed. The small holders had been ruined along with the banks, and the bottom land bought up by industrialists like Rothschild, who were followed by the introduction of large vine-

[35] The usurious practices of the notaries lending to peasants are discussed by Gille, *Banque et crédit*, p. 136; Bigo, *Les Banques françaises*, pp. 40–49; Valarché, *L'Économie rurale* (1960), p. 86; and others. Bigo notes (p. 49) that usury was no longer effective after 1880 because of the decline in interest rates. After 1880, however, the price of land declined and made the burden of existing debt crushing.

[36] See Augé-Laribé, *Politique agricole* (1950), p. 152.

[37] Wilson, *French Banking Structure* (1957), p. 225.

[38] See, e.g., Labasse, *Capitaux et région* (1955), on how the deposit banks regarded credit as traveling a one-way street from the countryside to Lyon and Paris; or Bouvier, *Le Crédit Lyonnais*, chap. v, on "drainage," or the task of gathering savings from the countryside. For examples of rural portfolios of foreign bonds, see Labasse, p. 27; Bigo, *Les Banques françaises*, p. 244; Carrère and Dugrand, *La Région méditerranéenne* (1960), p. 80.

[39] Thuillier, "Une Histoire bancaire régionale (1955), pp. 511–512.

[40] Bernard, *Économie de la Seine-et-Marne* (1953), p. 98; Hunter (*Peasantry in France*, 1948) remarks on the industrial families who own large farms in the Soissonais and the Aisne country (p. 70).

[41] *Capitaux et région*, esp. pp. 58, 241–268. Labasse points out that the *emboucheur* has always had credit. Some fruitgrowers are industrialists who run farms of 100 hectares like a corporation.

yards, planted to grapes of low quality, and were assisted by the big banks.[42]

The system of agricultural credit grew slowly after World War I, largely with government help. Prior to that time, agriculture was a source of saving rather than an outlet for investment, except perhaps for the large estates near Paris and a few industrial farms, including vineyards. Lack of credit was not the only problem faced by French agriculture, nor the most serious, but the sector can hardly be regarded as unified in its relations to the capital market.

Commerce was always able to get credit. Occasionally it may have been reluctantly given, and for limited periods. But, provided that there were two names on paper, banks were prepared to lend; and, with three, the Bank of France was anxious to discount. Labasse notes that the grain and wine merchants enjoyed a preferred position among creditors, but only if they offered the appropriate paper. After them in standing came leather and groceries. Without commercial paper, discounts might be limited to very short periods, up to ten days.[43] The Crédit Lyonnais opened its first branch near the abattoir in Paris, hoping for commissionaire business, and then three bank branches in the abattoir in Lyon.[44] But the Crédit Lyonnais, as one bank, was interested in no local outlets, either commercial or industrial.[45] It tolerated commercial accounts for the sake of the savings that they provided.

Commerce with the right paper benefited from the competition between the Bank of France and the deposit banks. The latter insisted on two-name paper, so that it could add its own and have the requisite three names for discount. It is not clear that the big banks actually did discount; but the Bank of France actively sought this business from the smaller banks, ultimately abandoning its three-signature requirement.[46] A group in the Chamber of Deputies attached significance to the opening of branches by the Bank of France in many small communities to bring banking service to the provinces. Pose regards this policy, which was forced on the Bank of France at each renewal of its charter, but especially that of 1897, as born of ignorance on the part of Parliament.[47] But even before this period, the Bank of France

[42] Carrère and Dugrand, *La Région méditerranéenne*, p. 80.

[43] Labasse, *Capitaux et région*, pp. 35, 65. Bouvier (*Le Crédit Lyonnais*, p. 339) states that the Crédit Lyonnais refused commercial credits above 30 or 40 days if the paper was not bankable.

[44] Bouvier, p. 298; Labasse, p. 276.

[45] Bouvier, pp. 306–307.

[46] Dauphin-Meunier, *La Banque de France* (1936), p. 130. Dauphin-Meunier is a strong critic of the Bank of France and an admirer of Governor Georges Pallain, who pushed the opening of branches after 1897.

[47] Pose, *La Monnaie* (1942), I, 256, 286.

and the deposit banks were ostensibly cooperating, covertly competing, for this limited type of accommodation.[48]

A feature of French economic growth is that after the innovation of the department store, in the 1850s, that institution apparently did not grow or spread as rapidly as department stores, multiple shops, and chain stores in the United States, Britain, and Germany. Did lack of capital have anything to do with the alleged slow expansion of modern retailing? It seems unlikely. Pasdermadjian makes the point that department stores in France catered to the middle classes, as contrasted with Central Europe, where the large store addressed itself above all to the masses.[49] In discussing capital, moreover, his argument runs the other way: the large stores did not take advantage of small shops, as some claim, because of their readier access to organized capital markets; on the contrary, in France as elsewhere, from 1880 to 1914 they grew at a rapid rate, plowing back their own profits.[50] After World War II, the Paris department stores were limited in their attempts at expansion by the high cost of bank loans in a capital-scarce environment, and perhaps by their unwillingness, in the case of family firms, to dilute their capital. There is no evidence of capital shortage before that time.

Housing. We shall have occasion below in Chapter 13 to discuss French construction directly, and the subject arises naturally in Chapter 4 on population. Here a brief word is appropriate on the question of whether housing finance was a handicap. The evidence seems to indicate that private funds did little to promote mortgage financing, except in the speculative burst from 1877 to 1882, but that government filled the void. In the 1850s it founded the Crédit Foncier, which was said in 1882 to own 2 billion of the 21 billion francs of mortgage credits in France.[51] In the period prior to World War I, the government supported low-cost housing by making mortgages on specified types of rental housing eligible for special finance by the Caisse de Dépôts and by trusts.[52] In the 1920s the government financed a large proportion of housing through its war compensation.

The bursting of the bubble in the private mortgage financing of the 1877–1881 period may have had some effect in slowing down building in the long phase of stagnation after 1882.[53] But government finance

[48] Bouvier, *Le Crédit Lyonnais*, p. 322.

[49] *Le Grand magasin* (1949), p. 15.

[50] *Ibid.*, pp. 17–32, esp. p. 12. Baldy (*Les Banques d'affaires* (1922), p. 186) notes that the Société Générale, a deposit bank, loaned to the large stores, and lists Au Printemps, Galéries Lafayettes, and Galéries du Havre. The time referred to is 1900–1913.

[51] Jousseau, *Traité du Crédit Foncier*, p. xxiv.

[52] D'Avout, *Le Crédit immobilier en France* (1914).

[53] In 1879 Soubéyron, a former subdirector of the Crédit Foncier, formed a Banque Hypothécaire de France for building loans, with the support of the

was available, and not under strain. The likelihood is that until the prosperity of the period after 1896 drew workers off the farm into the city, the demand for more house building was so low that no limitations existed on the financial side.

Industry. Our real concern is the supply of capital to industry. Here it is useful to make a distinction between large and small firms, though the line is a delicate one to draw. Large firms had access to capital through the state, merchant banks, industrial banks, and flotation of stocks and bonds. It is not clear that they have always had all the capital they needed, even after the establishment of the Crédit Mobilier in 1852. Merchant banks were connected with the railroads and the iron and coal companies. Gille's description of the banking system prior to 1848 deals at length with the connections — such as those among Talabot, the Paris-Lyon-Marseilles railroad, Grand' Combe de la Loire (a steel company), and the Rothschild bank.[54] Thuillier mentions that in the crisis of 1848 the Fourchambault iron and steel company obtained from the Bank of France a loan which was guaranteed both by de Wendel and Schneider. This was a firm which normally relied on its own small merchant bank in Paris.[55] But the system was inadequate until the Crédit Mobilier; and even then, Gille states, the combinations of merchant bankers and industrialists were only temporary, so individualistic were the bankers.[56] And it is clear that, even with the Crédit Mobilier, the state guarantee of railroad bonds was needed in 1852, and the Bank of France elected to discount railroad bonds in 1857.[57]

The need for capital for industry was understood by Louis Napoleon, at whose insistence the Société Générale included in its title the rest of its name "pour favoriser le commerce et l'industrie en France." [58] But, like the Crédit Lyonnais, it was largely interested in *affaires* rather than *entreprises*, maintaining relations with local business at its

Banque de Paris et des Pays-Bas (Collas, *La Banque de Paris et des Pays-Bas* (1908), p. 21. The Banque Hypothécaire de France was mortally hurt in the crash of 1882 and was merged with the Crédit Foncier. Collas said that the Crédit Foncier gained by suppressing a dangerous competitor for the future. Soubéyron was attacked earlier for having been the head of a syndicate selling Egyptian bonds and, at the same time, an official of the Crédit Agricole, later absorbed by the Crédit Foncier, which bought the bonds (150 million out of a total of 177 million francs) when the syndicate had difficulty in selling them. See Robert-Coutelle, *Le Crédit Foncier*, pp. 119–121.

[54] Gille, *Formation de la grande entreprise*, pp. 96ff.

[55] Thuillier, *Georges Dufaud* (1959), pp. 39, 72, 81.

[56] Gille, *Banque et crédit en France*, p. 52.

[57] Dauphin-Meunier, *La Banque de France*, p. 100. This policy was sharply attacked by Victor Hugo. It is upheld in an uncritical defense of the Bank of France by Gabriel Ramon, *Histoire de la Banque de France* (1929), pp. 248–250.

[58] Bigo, *Les Banques françaises*, p. 179.

many branches primarily for the sake of attracting deposits and building customers for its security distribution system.

Bouvier has set out in detail the evolution of the attitude of the Crédit Lyonnais, its original interest in industrial loans and its early mistakes, including particularly la Fuchsine, the chemical company established to exploit the early French analine-dye patent, where the cause of failure may have been the domination of the company by the bank, anxious to get rich quick. To insiders in the bank Henri Germain, the president, made no secret of his preference for big affairs over business loans.[59] To the outside world he insisted that industrial loans were unsafe and that a great deposit bank had to restrict itself, like the British banks or the Bank of France, to the purest of self-liquidating commercial transactions.[60] It is far from clear whether French bankers, in talking of the security of their loans while they were speculating in foreign bonds, were being cynical or practicing self-delusion.[61]

[59] Bouvier, Le Crédit Lyonnais, passim. The three early failures are discussed in Chapter 5 below. The failure of the financiers and engineers to agree on policy justifies not only banking unwillingness to lend to industry, but the reluctance of family firms to admit foreign capital and to borrow from banks. There were three grades of information—one for the true insiders, one for directors, one for stockholders. The public at large got virtually none (p. 164).

[60] The bank was conscious of the possibility of investing in industrial concerns. Pose, who approves its attitude, quotes Henri Germain at a stockholders' meeting as saying: "People have wanted us to look into industrial loans. There are certainly excellent ones, but industrial enterprises, even the best conceived and even the most wisely administered, carry risks which we consider incompatible with the indispensable security with which the funds of deposit banks should be employed. We have taken a long time, but the Crédit Lyonnais can find no better example for the employment of its funds than the Bank of France" (La Monnaie, p. 212). Lévy, Histoire économique de la France, p. 228, calls the French banks uninterested in the French economy and quotes Henri Germain in 1908 as saying to stockholders: "You have illusions, but that is excusable since the government also has illusions. It, like you, is convinced that we have not completed its task and it wished to create, two years ago, an establishment with a capital of six million. Do you know how much it has advanced to business? Nothing, and I extend my compliments to it." Note also the ironic footnote of Georges Charpenay referring to the president of a large credit establishment (Germain?) who in April 1903 reproached a stockholder who wanted him to invest in domestic industry, saying: "There are many advantages and more security in lending abroad since the credit of a state represents the best guarantee." Charpenay, Les Banques régionalistes (1939), p. 28.

[61] The point has been widely commented on. See White, French International Accounts, pp. 276ff, who quotes Keynes on the "limit of . . . imprudence reached in France. . . . No investments have ever been made so foolish and so disastrous." (From "Foreign Investments and National Advantages," London Nation, August 9, 1924.) Bigo contrasts the unwillingness to lend to industry and (quoting Germain as above) the big loans abroad "on the best of intentions" (Les Banques françaises, p. 172). But he apparently sees no incongruity between the position of Germain, as quoted, and the statement on the following page (213) that the Société Générale ran into difficulty over the failure of some Peruvian bonds, which led to a change of management, and required it to take a long time to build

The deposit banks issued securities for large-scale business, took flyers in insurance and municipal bonds, and distributed bonds, largely foreign, to their networks of customers. Starting out as industrial banks, they turned away from industry. Credits were not absolutely forbidden: agencies were instructed to tell industrialists that the bank liked guaranteed credits. Others should be liquidated because industry tends to regard them as part of its capital — but with measure, not precipitously. Loans to regular clients were called when an opportunity presented itself to plunge in a Spanish loan at 9.5 percent (1878). The head of the Lyon office raised the question of whether it would not be "wise to sacrifice certain *grosses affaires* which disturb the regularity of our banking operations." The head office, in the person of Germain, writing in the margin of the Lyon memorandum, decreed that it was not. The Crédit Lyonnais was not interested in "aid" to business.[62]

If the deposit banks were unwilling to lend to industry, there were still the industrial banks. The Crédit Mobilier, established in 1852, was a pioneering innovation which is frequently given substantial credit for the expansion of the French economy under the Second Empire.[63] It is possibly significant that the doldrums followed soon after its demise in 1868, and it is frequently claimed that the next generation of industrial banks, especially the Banque de Paris et des Pays-Bas ("Parisbas") and the Union Parisienne, played a major role in the expansion from 1896 to 1914.[64] But the claim is difficult to verify. The Crédit Mobilier quickly turned from loans to industry to securities promotion abroad — setting the pattern for the Crédit Lyonnais which we have already examined; and the industrial banks, so-called, were similarly much more concerned with foreign security flotations than with domestic industry.

It is difficult to be precise about the industrial banks, since they have not opened up their archives to scholars and there is no detailed study

---

back. It is a fact that the Crédit Lyonnais was skillful and plowed back its extraordinary profits from "big affairs" into reserves, while distributing only ordinary profits from ordinary operations (Bouvier, *Le Crédit Lyonnais*, pp. 163, 231ff). Pose attributes the crashes of the Union Générale, the Comptoir d'Escompte, and Baring Brothers to bad management, while accepting the principle of deposit banks making commissions on selling securities to their customers. He also defends the much greater width of the underwriting margins in France than in England (pp. 338ff).

[62] Bouvier, *Le Crédit Lyonnais*, pp. 50–55, 339.

[63] Gerschenkron, "Economic Backwardness" (1952), pp. 9ff; Hoselitz, "Entrepreneurship and Capital Formation" (1956), pp. 306ff.

[64] Cameron, *France and the Development of Europe*, p. 203, reaches a sweeping conclusion: "The major synthesis of these experiments in the Crédit Mobilier and the ultimate refinements represented by the Crédit Lyonnais on the one hand and the Banque de Paris et des Pays-Bas on the other, markedly hastened the process of development and the growing industries which they were created to serve."

of them comparable to that on the early days of the Crédit Lyonnais. But it is also hard to interpret the general studies in support of the view that the industrial banks contributed significantly to the expansion of industry. The brilliant start of the Banque de Paris et des Pays-Bas, mentioned by Pose,[65] was based largely on speculation in *rentes*, issues for the Chemin de Fer de la Turquie and a mortgage bank in Spain in 1872, and a killing from selling off its portfolio in the bubble of 1879.[66] The success of the Parisbas was in surviving the depression when all other *banques d'affaires* founded between 1878 and 1882 had disappeared, and it alone "was ready" in 1900.[67] Details of industrial lending after 1900 are hard to find. Sée states that the Parisbas launched a good many industrial enterprises after 1895, and Wilson says that this class of banks had many successes to its credit and that without them industrial development would have been much slower.[68] Cameron mentions that the Parisbas was "active" in the electrical industry after 1897.[69] Robert Aron in a pamphlet on the Parisbas names two private loans — one of them foreign — and refers to "railroad and government bonds." [70] But the most detailed studies by Collas and Baldy, still not very complete, make clear that the industrial banks, like the Crédit Lyonnais, were mainly interested in underwriting foreign bonds. Collas mentions only one domestic participation by name[71] and states further: "As for the distinction between foreign and domestic affairs, it is difficult to give a figure but one can state with certainty that, without being committed especially to foreign loans the Bank [Parisbas] devoted its attention above all to them (loans to states, cities, mortgage banks and railroads in particular)." [72]

Baldy, who views the Parisbas as the "perfect type of *banque d'affaires*," [73] gives more details on domestic operations[74] but indicates

[65] *La Monnaie*, p. 239.

[66] Collas, *La Banque de Paris*, pp. 13, 19.

[67] Baldy, *Les Banques d'affaires*, pp. 12, 19.

[68] Sée, *Histoire économique de la France*, p. 265; Wilson, "The French Banques d'Affaires" (1954), p. 198. In his *French Banking Structure* (p. 118) Wilson says that the industrial banks' resources were inadequate to meet the needs of industry.

[69] *France and the Development of Europe*, p. 197.

[70] *Une Grande banque d'affaires* (1959), p. 20. The companies were the Compagnie Parisienne de Distribution d'Electricité (p. 23) and La Société Norvégienne de l'Azote (p. 15).

[71] Collas, *La Banque de Paris*, p. 152. The company was the Société des Ateliers et Chantiers de la Loire.

[72] *Ibid.*, p. 163.

[73] Baldy, *Les Banques d'affaires*, p. 139.

[74] *Ibid.*, esp. pp. 151–153 and pp. 39, 42. The bank's interest in electricity was mainly in 1906–1908 and again in 1910–1914 and in the Paris area. There were participations and security issues for the metal industry with seven companies specifically named, but also participations in domestic financial operations — the Société Générale, with which the Parisbas worked closely, private banks, and insurance companies.

that the bank "played in foreign loans an entirely primordial role."[75] As for other banks, the activity of the Union Parisienne was much more important abroad, the Crédit Français had only very limited activity in France, the Société Centrale des Banques de Province gave French affairs a second place, and so on.[76] Baldy defends the *banques d'affaires*, which he says filled their role toward industry. He also claims that large industry developing from 1900 to 1914 used its own resources above all, with such calls as it made upon the market being easily filled. Medium industry needed only limited bank credit, and small industry got such support as it required from local banks.[77] In short, the *banques d'affaires* failed to help domestic industry to any great extent because they were not needed.

There is still less evidence by which to judge the role of the merchant banks in the industrial development after the Second Empire. It is clear that they contributed importantly to the sale of foreign securities, but whether they issued any significant volume of securities for domestic industry or made advances to it is doubtful. Pose asserts that they played an important role in large-scale industry up to 1870 but that this role diminished after the Third Republic.[78] Bigo, in possible contradiction but in any event enigmatically, says that these banks are "less rich than people say, but more powerful than anyone believes."[79]

There is more information, and more controversy, on the role played by the regional banks. Part of the controversy arises from the fact that the Banque Charpenay, a private regional bank in Grenoble, with a distinguished record of having financed early industry in the Dauphiné, was allowed to fail in 1931, without the help it felt it should have received from the Bank of France. In a book written as an old man, the founder's son accuses the Bank of France, and in particular its local manager, of having deliberately changed its procedures for rediscounting in order to permit him to fail, in behalf of the large banks.[80] Charpenay and Buffet believe that regional banks were a powerful factor in the growth of the Dauphiné and Lorraine regions

[75] *Ibid.*, p. 154.

[76] *Ibid.*, pp. 38–39, 162, 178, 181. Some domestic operations are mentioned on p. 161. I omit from the text the Crédit Mobilier Française, successor to the Crédit Mobilier, which gave first place to the domestic metallurgical industry (p. 180), though it had foreign operations (p. 172); and the offsetting Banque Française, which had some domestic operations (p. 174) but whose activity abroad, like that of other banks, was very important (p. 175).

[77] *Ibid.*, pp. 201, 204–205, 209.

[78] *La Monnaie*, p. 241.

[79] *Les Banques françaises*, p. 124.

[80] Charpenay, *Les Banques régionalistes*, esp. pp. 98–99, 113. Dauphin-Meunier, who is a strong critic of the Bank of France, supports M. Charpenay, *La Banque de France* (p. 166), referring to methods of the Bank of France which were debatable, if not menacing, but referring in a footnote to the personal ambitions of the Grenoble administrator of the Bank. Morazé (*La France bourgeoise*, 1952)

which were, it is clear, among the leaders of France in the period before World War I.[81] Their claim is supported by a number of writers — Dauphin-Meunier, Bigo, Baldy, Labasse. It is dismissed by Pose and Aron.[82] The Ministry of Commerce report on industry in 1919 comes out strongly on the side of Charpenay and Buffet; but Buffet was a member of the study group, and some of the language was taken almost verbatim from his collected speeches.[83]

It seems clear, however, that in Lorraine, the Dauphiné, and to a lesser extent the Nord, the regional banks, supported by the Bank of France, contributed significantly to the provision of credit for local industry, both by direct advances and by marketing securities. The Lorraine banks are said to have placed 250 million francs of obligations for their customers[84] and in particular to have helped, along with the plowback of profits and German investments, to finance the rapid growth of the steel industry. The Charpenay bank alone placed 73 out of 402 million francs of securities issued by hydroelectric, electric-chemical, and electric steel plants in the Dauphiné and Haute Savoie area in the period from 1890 to 1930. This includes part of the war period, when governmental finance assisted. Advances in forty-four years were above three quarters of a billion francs in eight industries and more than fifty firms.[85] Between 1908 and 1914 the Banque Charpenay placed 28,420,000 francs in hydroelectric securities alone, organizing syndicates of the small private banks in the area.[86] The capital was enlarged in 1907, 1909, 1912, and 1913, indicating considerable activity before the war.[87] Another and perhaps the most prominent

---

observed that the Bank of France cut down on regional discounts in 1930, thereby contributing to the centralization of the economy (p. 194).

[81] Buffet, *Régionalisme financier* (1917). Buffet was a former inspector of finance and president of the Société Nancienne du Crédit Industriel et des Dépôts. His book refers to this bank and also to the Banque Renauld.

[82] Bigo, *Les Banques françaises*, pp. 147–148. Baldy, *Les Banques d'affaires*, pp. 179–180 (he states that the Société Centrale des Banques de Province gave "important support" to middle-sized industry). Labasse, *Capitaux et région*, p. 196. Bouvier (*Crédit Lyonnais*, p. 303) calls the Banque Charpenay an excellent example of a regional bank; but, given his time focus, his references to it deal largely with its founding. Pose dismisses the claims of the regional banks rather by indirection. He mentions that they formed a syndicate in 1904 to lend abroad (*La Monnaie*, II, 484–486) which did not prove very effective. The provincial banks did make loans during the war, especially for hydroelectricity and metals, but many collapsed after overexpansion in 1919. Aron states his view in a letter responding to a request for information on the Banque de Paris et des Pays-Bas.

[83] Ministère du Commerce, *Rapport générale*, esp. vol. I, the letter of the minister, pp. x and xi, and vol. III, pp. 372ff.

[84] *Ibid.*, p. 374.

[85] Charpenay, *Les Banques régionalistes*, pp. 28, 34.

[86] Ministère du Commerce, *Rapport générale*, III, 376.

[87] Charpenay, p. 28. Rediscounts at the Bank of France appear at 11 million in 1902 and reach 58 million francs in 1913 (p. 35).

regional bank, the Crédit du Nord, enlarged its capital in 1900, 1910, 1912, and 1913, reaching 125 million in the last period, of which one quarter paid in.[88] This was much larger than Charpenay at 2.5 million of capital, all paid in.

It can be argued that Grenoble was a curious locality, different from France as a whole. Labasse gives interesting sketches of the differences in the character of business and therefore in banking activity in Lyon (speculative, commercial rather than industrial), Roanne (serious small firms, interested in solid stocks, land, or gold), St. Étienne (does business at the café), and so on.[89] Grenoble he describes in particular: it is always changing equipment, which is not fully amortized, and hence is always in need of money. Banks must be careful of becoming frozen there. Building plays a large role. One bank found 55 percent of its debts in the building–public works sector. There are family enterprises, to be sure, but their financial conceptions are those of the artisan. People are particularly enterprising but difficult to deal with: they wriggle out of engagements. The city has an "imperious need for money." Like Annecy, which attracted a "rush des investissements" after World War II, Grenoble is a poor town in which to sell securities.[90] Bouvier notes that the Société Générale had trouble at Grenoble: it maladroitly let it be seen that its only interest in the area was to drain funds off, which aroused the characteristic Dauphinois mistrust of banks.[91] In November 1872, the Crédit Lyonnais briefly decided against establishing a branch in Grenoble, with its poor prospects for "drainage" and dangerous temptation for local engagements.[92]

No such allegations have been made about Meurthe-et-Moselle. There were German, Belgian, Luxemburg, and Saar investments there, in addition to those of the regional banks. There was local capital. And the big national banks started to get interested only after other interests had made a start, "late" in the eyes of some.[93]

We should note that both the Banque Charpenay and the Société Nancienne de Crédit et de Dépôts discounted their paper with the Bank of France.[94] At the beginning of the twentieth century, the Bank

[88] See the centenary brochure of the bank, put out in 1948, which, however, gives no details of interest on its lending activities.

[89] Labasse, *Capitaux et région*, pp. 277ff.

[90] *Ibid.*, pp. 280–281, 338, 455.

[91] Bouvier, *Le Crédit Lyonnais*, p. 312.

[92] *Ibid.*, p. 305.

[93] See Nistri and Prêcheur, *La Région du Nord et Nord-Est* (1959), p. 133. See also Labasse, *Capitaux et région*, for the fact that Paris investment prefers urban groups already endowed with economic potential and trained people (p. 496). As soon as a new success is achieved, as in electricity or at Annecy after World War II, Paris rushes in (p. 498).

[94] Charpenay notes that over the years the Bank of France had earned 50 million francs on the rediscounts of his bank and illogically compares this sum with the 51

started to discount industrial credits. The regional banks "and more particularly those in Lorraine, benefited from this system which contributed to the development of that part of France." [95] This paper contributed to the inflationary finance of French industry during the 1920s, when private capital was going abroad, until Governor Moreau brought the use of credit paper to a halt in 1926.[96] With the return flow of capital, to which its cessation contributed, this was hardly needed. After the war, the deposit banks had recognized the existence of a gap in their provision of credit to industry and had established separate affiliates for making one- to six-year loans to industry.[97] Prior to that time, the Bank had not changed its rules requiring three signatures and three-month paper. It merely indicated a willingness to renew such three-month paper when it matured and to let banks provide the second signature, as well as the third, for paper which did not arise in commercial transactions.[98] In 1931 the separate official Caisse des Dépôts et Consignations entered the field to make industrial loans of one to five years. After World War II, this organization was allowed to rediscount its obligations at the Bank of France.[99]

Another possible source of capital for industry above and beyond the Bank of France is the government. "The textile industry was characterized in the first half of the century by protectionism; in the second,

---

million francs owing to the bank when his institution's doors were closed (*Les Banques régionalistes*, p. 83), observing further that it was ultimately repaid in full. Buffet states that the Bank of France has not withheld its indispensable help, making itself the powerful instrument of industrial expansion in defiance of all criticism. The Nancy branch of the Bank of France occupied the first rank in the class by profits and seventh in the volume of operations. In addition, Longwy reached eighth largest in volume (*Régionalisme financier*, p. 24).

[95] Caboue, "Medium-Term Lending" (1954), p. 129.

[96] Moreau, *Souvenirs* (1954), p. 12. Dauphin-Meunier states that the Bank substituted an intensive drive of direct lending in commercial operations to use a part of its swollen reserves, claiming it was done without the knowledge of the top directorate, which was absorbed in monetary matters and regarded it as secondary. He quotes Moreau, however, on the matter of lending for three months subject to two renewals, and adds on his own authority that such loans would then be taken over by a bank for three months before coming back to the Bank of France for nine months (*La Banque de France*, pp. 163–164). Total amounts discounted rose from 45 billion francs in 1927 to 53 billion in 1928 and 104 billion in 1929. The monthly average discounts outstanding show a decline from 4.6 billion in 1926 to 2.3 billion in 1927, 2.6 billion in 1928; they rose to 7.0 billion in 1929 before declining to 6.0 billion in 1930.

[97] Caboue, "Medium-Term Lending," p. 131; Pose, *La Monnaie*, II, 548.

[98] Caboue, p. 131. Dauphin-Meunier, *La Banque de France*, p. 130, describes the change in the attitude of the Bank after Georges Pallain became governor in December 1897, calling it a return to its early traditions of credit. He notes that the Bank discounted some hotel warrants — a form of security which Labasse deprecates: "A hotel is a good risk after the second failure" (*Capitaux et région*, p. 286).

[99] Caboue, *ibid.*, pp. 135ff.

it was re-equipped with government credits." [100] The reference is presumably to the 40 million franc loan made available by the state after the enactment by decree of the Anglo-French Treaty of 1860. Lhomme disputes this view and notes that many industrialists refused a portion of the money.[101] But it was all used[102] and all repaid, except for one coal firm in Bordeaux that failed.[103] Still, it is difficult to regard this as sufficient to re-equip the industry when it had to be shared among so many industries. One is forced to agree that the government provided little direct aid.[104]

The other source of funds for industry which I have neglected so far is foreign borrowing. Lyon was frequently financed by Geneva and Alsace by Bâle. The Belgian-entangled interest in street railways has been mentioned. The Belgians are also said to have provided Paris with its Métro, and German capital played a role in the expansion of Lorraine iron and steel production, on the French as well as on the German side of the border.[105] But the backwash movements of capital are not so substantial that one can take seriously the charge that French industry had to rely on foreign capital.

In Chapter 6, I shall address the demand for savings emanating from industry, in particular the view that the French entrepreneur was unwilling to borrow or to sell securities for fear of bank interference and dilution of authority. Here it is enough to note the existence of the view that industry had all the capital it wanted from the banks and the capital market.[106] Unfortunately, industrial studies are lacking. The most information exists for the textile industry, which typically abhorred security issues and bank loans and expanded through plowed-back profits[107] — or what the French call "autofinancing." How gen-

---

[100] Morazé, *La France bourgeoise*, p. 144.

[101] Lhomme, *La Grande bourgeoisie* (1960), p. 180.

[102] Sée, *Histoire économique de la France*, p. 281, gives the amount as 38,410,000 francs — "too small to have a big effect."

[103] Lévy, *Histoire économique de la France*, p. 106.

[104] Lambert Dansette, *Quelques familles du patronat textile* (1954), p. 413.

[105] Lévy, p. 255. Buffet, *Régionalisme financier*, pp. 18–19: "No one denies that German and Belgian firms have contributed capital. In certain cases this intervention was the counterpart of a participation in German coal by a French metal firm." Brooks estimates the total of German holdings in French Lorraine as 7.4 percent of the value of all iron and steel plants (*The Iron Industries of Lorraine*, 1920, p. 30).

[106] Baldy, *Les Banques d'affaires*.

[107] See Gille, *Banque et crédit en France*, pp. 183–184, who states that textiles escaped the banks almost entirely and then adds, at least for fixed capital. Fohlen has described textile finance in general under the Second Empire (*L'Industrie textile*, 1956, pp. 95–124) and a case study for the entire nineteenth century in *Une Affaire de famille* (1955). He observes that while textile firms tried to eschew contact with banks, they did not always succeed in so doing, and that their contact with banks for working capital, collection, and discount grew after 1848–1850 (*L'Industrie textile*, p. 116). Dansette in *Quelques familles du patronat textile*,

erally this attitude extended has not been examined. There is information for the automobile industry later[108] and large-scale industry prior to 1848.[109] There is also, as we shall see, much generalization — but few facts.

THE FRENCH CAPITAL POSITION SUMMARIZED

How far have we come? It might be possible to say that French economic growth coincided with loans to industry — by the Crédit Mobilier under the Second Empire, by the regional banks supported by the Bank of France after 1896, by the subsidiaries of the deposit banks and the Bank of France in the 1920s, and by government agencies after 1945. Moreover, the economy stopped when the Crédit Mobilier was destroyed, when the government was either preoccupied with reparations or not allowed to invest in the social infrastructure under the Third Republic, and when the deposit banks found it more profitable to make money out of large commissions for selling securities than to earn interest on loans or industrial advances. The case is attractive. But the rebuttal is not without force: the government attempted to lend to agriculture, but it was not ready and would not borrow. When the basic railroad lines were built, progress was made; thereafter the difficulty was that secondary lines had no earning power, as the Crédit Lyonnais learned in its district and the Pereire brothers in the Massif Central. Interest rates fell to low levels in the 1870s, without evoking new and remunerative propositions. It was only when the new industries came along — electricity, chemicals, steel — that domestic loans were possible. And finance was found for them.

Re-rebuttal: existing credit institutions failed to provide adequate finance. A change was required in the personnel of the Bank of France as a consequence of the charter renewal and the vigor of small regional

---

scatters references to financing throughout his long thesis, but suggests that the role of banks is really not very well understood (p. 416), despite articles by Gille and Fohlen. At one stage he suggests that the capital requirements after 1860 went beyond the capacity of narrow family finance (p. 391) with 250,000 francs needed for an average mill of 16,000 spindles and 2 million for working capital. Various millowners received advances *en commandite;* security investment was virtually unknown (p. 628). In fact, the owners of the industry invested outside, in banks, insurance companies, chemicals (especially Kuhlmann), some mortgages, and some chateaux (pp. 630–631).

[108] Bauchet, "La Structure d'une branche d'industrie" (1952), p. 394: "Financial policy consisted in making only limited appeals to outside credit and limited investment. One is able to blame the individualist spirit of the French firms or the repugnance of banks in consenting to long-term loans. Louis Renault succeeded in escaping completely from dependence on banks at the price of an impoverishment of the capital of his enterprise. André Citroën was driven to bankruptcy for having led a risky policy without dependence on banks."

[109] See Gille, *Banque et crédit en France.*

institutions. Second rebuttal: the industrial banks of Paris were a much more important part of the finance of the upsurge than the dramatically appealing parochial banks; so were the merchant banks. The existing mechanism worked. When it did not, the deposit banks altered their structure to help, in 1919.

It is too early, perhaps, to judge the debate now; we need to delve more deeply into the demand for capital. The argument upholding the importance of the supply meanwhile seems persuasive. But observe this: foreign lending can hardly be blamed. The timing is wrong. Foreign lending built up rapidly in the 1850s, and especially after 1856; and growth, we decided, continued for another ten years, if at a somewhat reduced tempo. Foreign lending flourished concurrently with the boom of 1879–1881; and again from 1896 to 1913; and from 1919 to 1926, if not for the years of most rapid expansion from 1927 to 1930. Foreign investments amounted to 2 billion francs in 1850, rose to 14 billion by 1870. Two billion were used to help pay off the indemnity, drawing down the portfolio. The rest of the indemnity was paid off and the portfolio reconstituted, even built up. Cameron estimates that it amounted to 22 billion nominal, and 16 billion at market prices in 1880.[110] By 1896 it was 26 billion; by 1914, 50 billion.[111]

High rates of foreign lending coincided, then, with high rates of growth. The role of exports in that growth will be examined later, and foreign lending is of course an important determinant of exports. It is possible that foreign lending stimulated demand and the full utilization of French capacity from a Harrodian point of view,[112] even though it did not add to productive capacity and assist growth in line with the Domar version of the growth model.

Moreover, rates of interest strongly militate against the view that French industry was starved of capital by capital exports. Interest rates declined very rapidly in the early 1870s, after the crisis: this is what produced the large profits in *rentes* that helped to divert the deposit banks from industry. And they remained low, on the average. The rate on bonds went to 5.5 percent in the early 1880s during the crisis, declined to 3.3 percent in 1897 under the pressure of English and Belgian low-yield securities, and rose to 4.75 percent in 1912–1914.[113]

[110] Cameron, "L'Exportation des capitaux français, 1850–1880" (1955), p. 347, observes that government, industry, and foreign borrowers each absorbed one third of French net savings from 1850 to 1880. In another article he puts the fraction going abroad at one third to one half ("The Crédit Mobilier," p. 461).

[111] See White, *French International Accounts*, appendix, table 48, p. 316.

[112] Cameron, for example, claims that default on international bonds, international tension, and fear of war, in conjunction with world depression, restrained French investments in the 1880s and, feeding back, tended to prolong the depression in France (*France and the Economic Development of Europe*, pp. 70–71, 467).

[113] White, p. 112, and discussion, pp. 105ff.

Thus the notion that domestic and foreign investment were alternatives is oversimplified. The export of capital from France was wasted from the long-run point of view, and if use could have been made of it at home, it would have been desirable to do so. But the evidence is weak that if, for example, foreign lending had been forbidden, domestic investment would have responded to lower rates of interest or to more urgent searches for outlets by bankers. The supply of savings was inelastic, the demand inelastic, and the only way that the market could be cleared was by foreign lending. Foreign investment is better than no investment. But these conclusions remain tentative.

THE ADEQUACY OF BRITISH SAVINGS

I must deal with Britain more briefly and limit myself to four theses: (1) that in the later Victorian period, the British propensity to save declined, thereby slowing down growth; (2) that around 1875 foreign lending diverted capital needed by British industry and thereby slowed down growth; (3) that British industry was handicapped, particularly after World War I, by a lack of intermediate-term finance, owing to the rigidity of its institutions; and (4) that the main difficulty experienced from the side of finance was the occasional speculative excesses which weighed industry down under a burden of excess capacity and heavy fixed charges. These theses, which evidently have their counterparts in the French economic history of the last hundred years, are interrelated.

The possibility that the British supply of savings fell off after some uncertain date (1875? 1900? 1918? or even as late as 1930?) is largely related to the social structure. Up to the late Victorian or Edwardian era, there was abundant capital as the middle class expanded from its early group of merchants, shipowners, and bankers, plus the younger offspring of the gentry in the army and the church, to include manufacturers, doctors, lawyers, civil servants, and so on. This middle class had money and was willing to risk it to make more. Banks were called upon to provide working capital, but the Industrial Revolution could be carried through mainly by partnerships and sleeping partners because they were so many.[114] Incorporation was required in the middle of the nineteenth century, not to ease the task of raising capital, but to redistribute the profits from northern industrialists to London capitalists, who felt that they were receiving an inadequate share.[115]

[114] Jeffrys, *Trends in Business Organization* (1938), pp. 9, 441. For discussion emphasizing the role of the banks, see Pressnell, *Country Banking during the Industrial Revolution* (1956); Ashton, *Industrial Revolution* (1947), pp. 102ff; John. *Industrial Development of South Wales* (1950), Chap. ii, esp. pp. 47ff.

[115] Saville, "Sleeping Partnership" (1956), dissents from Jeffrys' interpretation

Between 1850 and 1913, however, the middle class began to consume capital, slowing down the rate of capital accumulation. Extravagance and debt can assist capital formation. High consumption in the late eighteenth and early nineteenth centuries on the part of the landed gentry had made them anxious to invest in industry, encouraging railroads, coal royalties, marriage with people of wealth.[116] Extravagance had fallen out of favor by the middle of the nineteenth century. But at some later stage it spread again more widely. A contributing factor may have been the Great Depression, with its redistribution of income from the saving to the consuming classes. But there seems to have been an upward shift in the consumption function of the upper classes, as well as a movement along it. Veblen comments on the conspicuous consumption of Britain and the cost of gentility per unit.[117] Fifty years before Galbraith, Masterman excoriates private ostentation and extravagance, accompanied by public penury.[118] Families which had built firms sold them off and changed from production to consumption.[119] Business lost its fortune-making capacity, which fact piled up savings; innovation became the prerogative of existing, not new, firms, run by employees, not self-made men, and paying their profits in · dividends.[120]

It can be argued, however, that some social group always arrives and ceases to save, or even dissaves on balance. What counts is the number of new arrivals and their accumulation. On this criterion, the slowdown of net personal saving may have occurred later, after World War I, after income tax had cut down the amounts of the fortunes that could be created and after social security, the rise of the Labour Party, and the acceptance of the doctrine of fair shares had reduced the urge

---

and believes that limited liability was demanded by the Christian Socialists to facilitate the growth of industry and enterprise. But he agrees that capital was abundant.

[116] Spring, "The English Landed Estate" (1951). In a sense it is appropriate for agriculture, which provided capital for industry, to have some of it returned. See Chapter 11 below.

[117] Veblen, *Imperial Germany* (1915), pp. 136–138. See also H. G. Wells, *Tono-Bungay* (1909): "We became part of what is nowadays an important element in the confusion of our world, that multitude of economically ascendant people who are learning how to spend money . . . They discover suddenly indulgences their moral code never foresaw and had no provision for, elaborations, ornaments, possessions beyond their wildest dreams. With an immense astonished zest they begin *shopping* . . . They plunge into it as one plunges into a career; as a class, they talk, think and dream possessions." (London, Collins, 1953, p. 222).

[118] *The Condition of England* (1909), chap. ii, esp. pp. 22, 24.

[119] Erickson, *British Industrialists* (1959), p. 52.

[120] *Ibid.*, p. 187. The true corporation had an advantage over the family firm, in which cutting the dividend in a period of reduced profits was equivalent to letting down one's kind (Florence, *The Logic of Industry*, 1953, p. 304).

to upward mobility.[121] Inequality of incomes, which is conducive to personal saving, began to change after World War I, but it went much further in the 1930s and the early postwar period.[122]

After World War II the decline in personal savings was offset by higher rates of corporate and governmental capital formation. Maddison puts the total of investment at 15.3 percent of income in 1948–1957, as compared with 10.5 percent for 1924–1938 and 12.5 percent for 1870–1913.[123]

THE DIVERSION OF INVESTMENT ABROAD

Assuming for the moment that savings were sufficient, at least until 1913, did London institutions divert them to foreign use at the expense of domestic industry?

As noted at the outset of this chapter, a precise statement of the effect of foreign lending on growth requires an examination of investment criteria and the external economies available in domestic and external capital formation — a task which I do not propose to undertake here. I repeat only that there is a presumption that the appropriate criterion in Britain was the marginal efficiency of capital rather than the capital/output ratio, given the efficient allocation of British resources and the absence of unused land or underemployed labor. But the Macmillan Report criticized London: "In some respects the City is more highly organized to provide capital to foreign investors than to British industry." [124] Burn gives the structure of the capital market

[121] Frost, "The Macmillan Gap" (1954), p. 197, observes that, while the freedom from capital-gains tax in Britain increases the incentive to build private companies for subsequent sale, the income tax more than offsets by reducing the capacity. Hancock and Gowing, *British War Economy* (1949), pp. 50–51, record a War Office memorandum of 1932 which provides the earliest mention of fair shares.

[122] See Cartter, *Redistribution in Britain* (1955), pp. 74–75, who gives an inequality index for post-tax net private income with social benefits which falls from .41 in 1880 to .38 in 1913; .30 in 1928; .23 in 1938; and .16 in 1948–1949. The index represents the percentage of total income which would have to be redistributed from higher- to lower-income groups to achieve perfect equality. See also Hicks, *British Public Finances* (1954), p. 94, who asserts that the Victorians kept the income tax low because they relied on personal savings and that the main source of savings, with the income tax, has become corporate savings. The notion of intention in the first part of this statement hardly seems reasonable, however.

[123] See Maddison, "Growth in Western Europe," p. 74; for figures by decades and single years, see the article's appendix. Gross investment is said to have gone from 13 percent in the 1870s and 1880s and 12.6 percent in the 1890s to 14.6 percent in 1900 and 16.6 percent in 1913, 12 percent in 1929, and 10.2 percent in 1938.

[124] Committee on Finance and Industry, *Macmillan Report* (1931), para. 397, p. 171.

as one of the two chief obstacles (before World War I) to the emergence of new high-capacity plants in the British steel industry.[125]

The difficulty stemmed partly from the government's action in making empire securities qualify for trustee investments along with British government securities. In part it arose from the experience acquired by the city in lending abroad. Capital flows in channels, and these had been dug between London and the far reaches of the empire, but not between London and the industrial north. A limited number of firms in a limited number of industries could get access to the London new-issues market — railroads, shipping, steel, cotton (after 1868), along with banks and insurance companies.[126] And some attention was devoted to refinancing existing private companies. For the most part, however, the flow of savings was aimed abroad and not to domestic industries. Nor did the banks help with fixed capital. The Overend-Gurney failure in 1866 halted any tendency for the movement away from commercial credit toward industrial banking along Crédit Mobilier or German D-bank lines, except just before 1913.[127]

There is, however, evidence to suggest that British industry got all the capital it could use. Burnham and Hoskins find no lack of capital in the steel industry;[128] Cairncross weighs the evidence carefully, including external economies, and concludes that foreign investment did pay.[129] Jeffrys notes the availability of the provincial stock markets, of the rise of debentures from 1860 to 1890, and of preference shares.[130] The number of investors, outside of the railroads and unincorporated enterprises, increased from 230,000 in 1860 to 500,000 in the first decade of the twentieth century.[131] If there was a strong demand for bonds

---

[125] Burn, *Economic History of Steelmaking* (1940), pp. 250–254, 262.

[126] Lavington, *The English Capital Market* (1921), p. 277.

[127] Jeffrys, *Trends in Business Organization*, p. 143.

[128] *Iron and Steel in Britain* (1943), p. 259. They are aware of and discuss the financial difficulties — the accumulation of private rather than public capital, lack of contact with the money market, and lack of bank support (p. 263), but assert that the difficulty lay not in lack of capital after 1880 but in its investment in the wrong directions. See also Erickson, *British Industrialists*, p. 165, on the fact that successful steel firms had resources before they built and that promoters, who borrowed first, failed either to get the funds — Burn, *Economic History of Steel-making*, p. 252: "The general investor does not favor schemes of this kind" — or to make steel. Jeffrys discusses the difficulty in effecting the transition from iron and steel companies owned by rich capitalists who had made or inherited money from private furnaces or mines (*Trends in Business Organization*, p. 219) to widespread marketing of shares by professional promoters in the 1880s (p. 306). The promoters of the 1860s and 1870s are called "embryo promoters," but by 1877 Chadwick had formed fifty to sixty companies in the steel industry of £40 million capital, with the smallest at £100,000.

[129] Cairncross, *Home and Foreign Investment*, chap. ix, "Did Foreign Investment Pay?"

[130] *Trends in Business Organization*, pp. 222, 249ff, 340, 371.

[131] *Ibid.*, p. 435.

from trustees (owing to primogeniture) and from oldfashioned investors, by 1900 50 percent of the savings in the United Kingdom came from business people rather than from landlords and salaried classes, thereby creating a market for more risk-taking investment.[132] And in those industries where there was a large need for capital — electricity, chemicals, motor cars, bicycles — companies either started large, particularly in electricity, or quickly became so.[133]

The London stock market played an important role in selling the securities of private companies. This provided no capital for industry, in the first instance, and gave the entrepreneurial family a chance to consume its capital, or to buy foreign bonds, if it did not take public shares in exchange for its original holding. But it was a necessary step in the expansion of the company to the size required by the increasing capital-intensive technology of the period. Once the shares had been placed, it was possible to raise more capital, whether through debentures, preference shares, or more equity.[134] It is true that small companies found borrowing through the London market expensive in view of the minimum commissions, and it is evident that industry would have liked better and cheaper facilities.[135] But this is a different question from whether new firms were handicapped or existing firms were restricted in trying to grow. The evidence is unpersuasive. Even the Macmillan gap seems relatively unimportant in the period before 1914, as the Macmillan Committee thought, because of the availability of sources of capital for innovating firms other than the London capital market and the joint stock banks.[136]

This conclusion is reinforced by timing. Foreign loans were an alternative to domestic investment.[137] When new construction went off in the 1880s, foreign investment picked up. The process had a positive feedback which led to exaggeration and trouble, particularly in Argentina, and new construction recovered before foreign investment had run its course. The same is true of the setback in domestic investment after 1902 — and the inverse in the period of recovery of domestic investment in 1895. It is true also that total investment moved in a

---

[132] *Ibid.*, pp. 263, 284.
[133] *Ibid.*, p. 132.
[134] See Hall, "The English Capital Market" (1957) and "A Reply" (1958).
[135] Cairncross, "The English Capital Market" (1958), p. 145.
[136] For a contrary view, see Marshall, *Industry and Trade* (1920), pp. 346–348. Henri Germain, who patterned his activities after the joint stock banks, when it came to refusing long-term lending to industry could not understand how they made ends meet without security operations. He asked his London branch to explain whether they had undisclosed sources of income (Bouvier, *Le Crédit Lyonnais*, pp. 779–780).
[137] See Cairncross, *Home and Foreign Investment*, esp. figure 14, p. 188. See also Rostow, *British Economy* (1948), chap. iii.

wide swing,[138] from £180 million in 1874 to £107 million in 1879, £190 million in 1890 and £125 million in 1894, before starting the only briefly interrupted (in 1909–1910) climb to £360 million in 1913.[139] But this was not because of stability in the structurally deficient domestic investment, since Cairncross's figures show wide swings here too.[140] They can hardly have been so wide as in foreign investment, which readily declined to zero or to negative quantities. Some capital widening and gross replacement went on at home; abroad, domestic sources of investment provide this base, and foreign borrowing, as a supplement, would change over a wider range.

A useful article by Raymond Frost summarizes the evidence on the Macmillan gap — that difficulty faced by companies too small to float long-dated capital in amounts of more than £200,000.[141] He observes that the Macmillan Report had stated that the gap did not exist before World War I; suggests that the problem exists for firms without freehold property, since mortgages can be obtained for amounts as low as £15,000; reduces the figure to £150,000; but argues that the gap has not been closed since World War II, despite the steps taken by government and banking in the early 1930s and again after World War II. Summarizing the structure of British industry, Burn holds that the institutional difficulties in finance have been reduced in the period after World War II by governmental bodies, private placements from insurance companies, bank advances, and investment allowances in taxation, but that high taxation discriminates against the little firm and still leaves an investment "gap." [142]

These views are not uncontested. Carter and Williams play down difficulties of access to capital. Lower taxes on industrial profits and easier terms for risk capital would help, along with twelve other things, but adequate finance is not found among the twenty-four characteristics of "good firms." [143] Bank lending is the main source of outside support for long-term capital investment, despite its alleged restriction to short-term finance.[144] Family firms may be reluctant to borrow because

---

[138] Saville, "Comment on Rostow" (1954), p. 77.

[139] Cairncross, *Home and Foreign Investment*, p. 203.

[140] Saville states that the London capital market was firmly oriented abroad and created a structural deficiency, citing Jeffrys and Burn. But as we have tried to show, the Burn discussion is unconvincing, and Jeffrys gives a rather different conclusion, especially his statement that the isolation of industry (with its other sources of finance) from London is not a true weakness but rather a compliment to German organization (*Trends in Business Organization*, p. 371).

[141] "The Macmillan Gap" (1954).

[142] Burn, "Retrospect" (1958), pp. 455–457.

[143] Carter and Williams, *Innovation* (1958), p. 142; *Technical Progress* (1957), pp. 183–184.

[144] *Technical Progress*, p. 143.

of an unwillingness to lose control; managers of corporations may not borrow for fear of the necessity for corporate reorganization if they seek outside funds rather than using profits, should investment plans misfire.[145] Barna's research into current conditions also finds that, while there are obstacles to investment — largely lack of managerial ability — finance is not one.[146] Lord Brand has stated categorically: "Since then the Macmillan Gap has been closed." [147]

Some part of the obstacle to financing domestic growth in Britain has arisen from the periodic bursts of investment in given lines that have left industry burdened with excess capacity and heavy fixed charges. The railroad mania of the 1840s and the investment splurges of 1869–1873 and 1919–1921 provide illustrations. The first was perhaps the least important. While railroad capital investment was very high in Britain, with heavy charges for parliamentary expenses and land damages, the railways had little difficulty in raising capital.[148] Then came the period of merger and absorption. In 1863 the Great Western Railway amalgamated with both the West Midland and the South Wales, after a struggle and on the basis of new loans. In the panic of 1867 the company passed its dividend. This experience colored investment attitudes for twenty years.[149] But the Great Depression was not severe on the railroad. Dividends were high, since costs fell faster than fares and rates.[150] Stockholders were happy and new shares or debentures (at falling interest rates) were issued successfully practically every year. Major railroad investment was postponed until the pressure of rising freight traffic and competitive railroad racing shook the company out of its lethargy in the 1890s.[151] While water was added to the capital of existing railroads during the amalgamation period, only the Midland, Sheffield and London (M. S. and L., or "Money Sunk and

[145] *Innovation*, pp. 14, 83.
[146] *Investment and Growth Policies* (1962), p. 48.
[147] See "Recollections" (1961).
[148] Court, *Concise Economic History* (1958), p. 167; Pollins, "Railway Shares" (1954).
[149] Cole, "Locomotive Replacement" (1955), part 2, p. 26.
[150] *Ibid.*, p. 31.
[151] *Ibid.*, p. 34. I return to this subject later in Chapter 7. Note that gross income of railroads grew fast from 1864 to 1874 — and only slowly thereafter to 1893, as the country adjusted to the use of railroads. Then came a sharp rise in the boom up to 1913. The figures for passenger and freight receipts in England and Wales, in millions of pounds sterling, are (Cole, pp. 26, 56):

Year	Passenger receipts	Freight receipts	Total
1864	n.a.	n.a.	24.5
1874	21.1	27.0	48.0
1893	30.5	34.3	64.8
1913	48.9	56.6	105.5

Lost") was constructed as a new main line, through towns already served by existing lines, at great expense.

The investment boom in the late sixties and early seventies produced large increases in capacity in cotton textiles, wool, coal, wrought iron, and Bessemer steel rails. Only in cotton and iron and steel did the organized market provide the capital. In other industries it was furnished by local capitalists and plowed-back profits. But however financed, overinvestment left overcapacity, creating a buyers' market. This inhibited standardization in cotton, led to attempts at pricefixing and restriction of output in coal and steel rails, and delayed the reorganization of the iron and steel industry. There were contributing factors — the drop in demand for worsteds, which had experienced the largest expansion in the woolen industry, and the successive losses of the American market, first for iron and then for Bessemer steel rails. New spinning companies, *de novo,* in cotton permitted operation at higher and more efficient scales.[152] But there were too many companies. Barrow, the most efficient steel plant in the world in 1873, built at peak costs and became too big.[153] Fifteen years after 1874 there were still no profits, and the Duke of Devonshire was still struggling to get the enterprise afloat.

Another speculative boom took place after World War I, as the prospect of wiping out German competition opened up entrancing vistas for the coal, steel, shipping, and textile industries. Substantial investment was undertaken in coal until the disastrous strike of April 1921.[154] But the major effort was mergers and recapitalization, assisted by bank loans. In cotton textiles, capacity which had cost and been capitalized at £1 a spindle before the war, and could have been replaced for £3, was capitalized at £4.[155] Two big steel combines were formed, and United Steel took on "heavy liabilities in annual interest and preference share dividends." [156] The postwar prospects were very bright: Germany would be knocked out and American costs were

[152] In the cotton mills of the 1840s, 1850s, and 1860s, investment had been undertaken by merchants, machine makers, architects, and other people associated with the venture. With limited liability, shares in new firms, with an appointed manager rather than a family owner-operator, were floated in £5 denominations that were partly paid up (Jeffrys, *Trends in Business Organization,* pp. 188ff and pp. 84–92). The average number of spindles per mill of 59 companies floated in Oldham between 1873 and 1875 was over 50,000, compared with a national average of 15,400 in 1871.

[153] See Pollard, "Barrow-in-Furness" (1955).

[154] Beacham, "The Coal Industry" (1958), p. 136.

[155] Robson, *Cotton Industry* (1957), p. 161.

[156] Andrews and Brunner, *Capital Investment in Steel* (1951), p. 117. These writers deny that United Steel was capitalized at inflated values in consequence of an orgy of financial speculation. They state that the businesses which formed the combine were paid a fair price for their shares (p. 362).

high.[157] Ships were among the assets which changed hands at fancy prices, and even houses rose sharply, to evade the rent control.[158]

High hopes did not last beyond the summer of 1920, but high capitalization persisted. In the immediate postwar era, pressure for quick extra output led to piecemeal extra capacity at existing works in existing centers; afterwards, the 1920s were dominated by a struggle for cash to pay fixed charges.[159] In a falling market, debentures found their way into the hands of banks, which also acquired an interest in industry through frozen overdrafts.[160]

The blame in either case can be put on the falling market. But overcapitalization and overbuilding through speculative excess can compound the difficulties. There is more here than merely the positive feedback of the cycle, even the eight- to nine-year cycle affecting industrial equipment, as contrasted with the cycles related to stocks. The first two occasions affected industries in the forefront of industrial investment, which later made comebacks only in response to exogenous changes in other variables — the coal, steel, and textile industries as far as railroads were concerned, and the electrical, mechanical, and chemical industries for coal, steel, and textiles. After World War I, renewed overcapitalization in coal, steel, textiles, and shipping imparted further delay to the readjustment of these industries, to which additional elements — particularly motor cars — had been added. Overcapitalization involved the banks deeply in declining industries and may thus have slowed down transformation by making capital scarcer for the new industrial leaders.[161]

THE BRITISH CAPITAL POSITION SUMMARIZED

We conclude, tentatively, that by any reasonable test the supply of British capital was sufficient in the period up to 1938; that the London capital market, while hardly favoring domestic investment, did not inhibit it, given its willingness to convert private to public companies, to raise large amounts of capital for new industries started large, and the availability of other capital for industry in the provinces; that the Macmillan gap existed in the 1920s, though bank loans were available for large-scale industry, and to a certain extent in the 1930s and 1950s, though the case is the same for all growing untested industries; and, finally, that the difficulties were compounded by speculative excesses

[157] *Ibid.*, p. 78.
[158] Pigou, *Aspects of British History* (1948), p. 194.
[159] Andrews and Brunner, pp. 77–78, 144.
[160] Burnham and Hoskins, *Iron and Steel in Britain*, p. 263; Robson, *Cotton Industry* (1957), p. 157.
[161] See Allen, *British Industries*, p. 281.

in the wrong industries at the wrong time. Speculative excesses in new and growing industries, like the railways in the 1840s, can be absorbed in growth. Coming as they did at the end of growth, they created a more difficult problem.

COMPARISON OF FRENCH AND BRITISH CAPITAL FORMATION

There are many similarities between the British and the French experiences — the regional banks in France and the provincial in London; the need for debentures for trustee investments and the *rentes* of the *père de famille;* the Macmillan gap and the absence of industrial banks, on the one hand, and the need for rediscounting industrial advances, on the other; the financial institutions channeling savings abroad, although after the 1870s French loans clung to the Continent, while British shifted overseas to the empire and areas of recent settlement, where capital could be combined with land. But there were important differences: those on the demand side remain to be explored. In supply, France saved more out of a given income, but had less income, as well as a smaller group of middle-class savers, a larger group of peasants, and fewer upper-class dissavers.

In neither instance, however, is the case convincing that economic development was held down in any critical way by lack of capital. More savings insistent upon finding an outlet in domestic industry would have been better than the existing amount or less, unless by some chance the reduction in demand for consumption goods would have blunted investment incentives. But this is true only in the sense that more of anything is better than less in a world of positive prices. In France, what was needed was an enormous increase in the demand for savings in domestic industry, which would have enabled more resources to be drawn out of low-productivity occupations into high. The supply of savings was adequate. It is possible to blame the greed of the financial community in France, though not in Britain, but it would still be necessary to explain why more opportunities for big profits were not forthcoming on the domestic front. By and large, it is very hard to make an argument that the supply of capital, or the fact of its export, was responsible for slowing down the British and French rates of growth.

CHAPTER 4

POPULATION

Moving from land and capital to labor, we should discuss not only the development of population in Britain and France, but its quality as a factor input — its skill, education, responsiveness to economic opportunity, and so on. This chapter, however, is limited to population growth. Other relevant aspects of the efficiency of labor will emerge in later chapters on the social aspects of growth, technology, agricultural transformation, and urbanization and regional balance. This chapter deals with numbers, and mostly with France where the belief persists that a low rate of population growth in the past has held back economic development.

Here is a paradox. Many countries today are concerned that too high a rate of population increase will handicap growth, diverting capital from industrial equipment to housing, for example, or reducing the ratio of land to labor to the point where diminishing returns bind. In France, on the other hand, too low a rate of expansion, and indeed population decline, has been thought to reduce the demand for investment and contribute to stagnation. The theory is one of long standing. Raudot in 1849 gave the low rate of population increase as the first of his five reasons for French economic decadence.[1] Today many writers find hope for future French growth in the fact that the birth rate, after mysteriously declining for almost two centuries, has equally mysteriously risen.[2] Alfred Sauvy, the distinguished French demographer, has expounded both views at length.

There is some statistical support for the view, but not much. Kuznets' data show high correlations between rate of population growth and growth of national product, and between rate of growth of national product and product per capita. The correlation between population growth and product per capita is positive, but not significantly so.[3] That France has had a population problem is suggested by the fact that the rate of population increase over the first fifty years of the

[1] Cited by Cameron, "Profit, croissance et stagnation" (1957), p. 442.
[2] See, e.g., Jeanneney, *Forces et faiblesses* (1956), p. 275; Fauvet, *La France dechirée* (1957), p. 150.
[3] Kuznets, "Rates of Growth" (1956), p. 30.

present century is the lowest of nineteen countries listed by Kuznets, save for Ireland, and significantly lower at 0.6 percent per decade than the third country, Britain, at 5.6 percent.[4] Over a still longer period, approaching the one hundred years in which we are interested, the discrepancy in rate of population increase is even wider, though the rate of growth in income per capita (on rather poor data) is of the same order of magnitude. The figures are given in Table 3.

Table 3. Percentage Change per Decade in Population, National Product, and Product per Capita in the United Kingdom and France

Country	Years	Population	National product	Product per capita
United Kingdom	1860–69 to 1949–53	8.0	21.5	12.5
France	1841–50 to 1949–53	1.3	15.3	13.8

Source. Kuznets, "Rates of Growth" (1956), table 2, p. 13.

The actual population increase in France is entirely accounted for by the increase in life expectancy, which has risen from thirty years in 1801 to forty-eight in 1936. Over this period Landry calculated that the gain from increased longevity amounted to 16,800,000, compared to a decline on a net reproduction basis of 5.3 million.[5] Increased life expectancy, of course, has been a normal accompaniment of increased real income; today, with improved public-health techniques, it can operate independently.

THE MODELS

The view that a low rate of population expansion slows down economic growth is based first of all upon a Keynesian employment model, rather than a Harrod-Domar growth model. Hansen and Higgins have tried to show how *ex ante* investment is a function not of the rate of interest but of exogenous variables like population growth, technological change, the availability of unutilized land, and so on. Their theory of secular stagnation relied significantly on the decline in the rate of population increase, producing a shift to the left in the investment de-

[4] *Ibid.*, table 1, p. 10. The comparison with Ireland raises the question of the natural increase plus or minus net migration. The slow French rate of increase took place with very limited emigration, whereas large-scale emigration took place from Ireland after the 1840s.

[5] Quoted by Morazé, *La France bourgeoise* (1945), p. 19, from Landry, *Traité de démographie* (1945).

mand for savings, lowering investment, capital formation, and employment. Goldenberg has tried to apply this theory to France, which he says it fits, despite capital exports.[6] Jacques Duvaux observes that demographic maturity can have effects on savings, which operate in the opposite or inflationary direction. An aging population may be expected to save less, consume more, and thus reduce the supply of savings along with the investment demand for them.[7]

With an ordinary Harrod-Domar model, a slower rate of population growth helps to increase income per capita, since less capital is needed for widening the stock and more is available for deepening or increasing the capital/labor ratio. This assumes unlimited investment opportunities, or an elastic demand for savings in response to any reduction in the rate of interest — a classical rather than a Keynesian system. Where investment is connected to income through an accelerator, or a positively sloped schedule, capital widening may lead to capital deepening along Hansen lines by maintaining fuller employment.

The Sauvy model is still different. Growth takes place in response to investment, on the one hand, and to technological change, on the other. Expanding markets for goods brought about by increasing population encourage investment by coming to the rescue of those who have overexpanded capacity; and they encourage cost reduction through technical change. A stationary population leads to Malthusianism[8] — in the peculiar French sense of that word — fears of overproduction and collapse of prices which limit risk taking, leading to production controls and price fixing. A stable population restricts the opportunity for youth in industry, produces old and unadventurous leadership; technical progress results in overproduction or the necessity to liquidate capacity. Since transformation occurs more readily at the margin than within it, an increasing population is more readily redirected into new industries, more effectively trained for new tasks. Two children per family, a boy and a girl, replace the father and mother and maintain the existing economic structure. With more children, there is the necessity to redirect resources and pressure to create more economic opportunities.[9]

Certainly Sauvy is right that the France of 1960 felt the pressure of population increase and the need for expanding schools, housing, hospitals, roads, and the rest of the infrastructure. But there is no necessary

[6] See Goldenberg, "Savings and a Stationary Population" (1946).
[7] Duvaux, *Maturité économique* (1958), p. 167. Reddaway, *Economics of a Declining Population* (1939), p. 114, cites six reasons why a smaller, older population will save less.
[8] Sauvy, *Richesse et population* (1943), chap. xi. See also United Nations, Economic Commission for Europe, *Europe in 1954* (1955), pp. 174–177.
[9] See also Reddaway, *Economics of a Declining Population*, pp. 58–67.

reason that the historical explanation must run from population decline to economic Malthusianism. It can just as well operate the other way, as the Le Play school has held — that is, from unwillingness to modify the economic structure to family limitation. More on this shortly.

Finally, of course, there is the true Ricardian model which says that economic growth is impossible because of the iron law of wages. Population grows up to the limits made possible by improvements in production. Accordingly, French population might have been slowed down by the law of diminishing returns. As crowding on the land increases, with a fairly static agricultural technology, income per capita in agriculture falls and with it the population, owing to a rise in the death rate. This model can be dismissed as inapplicable to France or Britain because the death rate kept falling. But, as we shall see, these conditions have been said to have brought about a decline in the birth rate — a result which Malthus advocated, though it may be doubted whether he thought his counsel would be honored.

French Birth and Death Rates

The rate of population increase in France turned downward before that of any other country, except possibly Ireland. Two schools of thought in France account for the decline: the one of Le Play, which is the larger, holds that the decline is attributable to the change from primogeniture in the inheritance of property under the monarchy to equal inheritance under the Napoleonic code. The other is that of Leroy-Beaulieu — "more in keeping with modern views" — that family limitation is a result of the whole complex of things called civilization: the growth of cities, the rise of the middle class, the spread of education and interest in material comfort, the extension of leisure, and the spread of individual and family ambition to rise in the social scale.[10]

A nondemographer is unhappy in having to choose between the views of two groups of experts. But the Le Play view has several deficiencies besides its failure to be modern. For one thing, the gross reproduction rate started to go off as early as 1780, when the revolution was preparing, well before the Napoleonic code.[11] Second, while equal inheritance is regarded in France as limiting the birth rate, in Germany it is thought that the single-heir system does so. Equal division may actually promote population growth. Under equal inheritance, marriage is encouraged — the individual children have prospects of creating a home — but there are small families. With a single heir, marriage is dis-

[10] Kirk, "Population" (1951), p. 315.
[11] Gravier, *Paris et le désert français* (1958), p. 33.

couraged, but there are larger families.[12] What equal inheritance inhibits is mobility. Seasonal mobility proceeds under both systems: under equal inheritance the possessor of an uneconomically small holding may have to earn cash to survive. But the younger children are tethered to the peasant society. This limits growth by attracting industry to dispersed labor, reducing the pressure to concentrate industrial location with consequent external economies.[13]

If there are difficulties in accepting the Le Play explanation, the Leroy-Beaulieu school scarcely fits the history of French population growth, especially the "deep gap dug by the crisis of 1847–1850 between two demographic periods in the nineteenth century." [14] Net reproduction-rate averages show a sharp discontinuity between 1841–1845 and 1851–1855, as Table 4 shows.

Table 4. French Net Reproduction Rates,
1806–1810 to 1851–1855

Years	Rate of reproduction
1806–1810	1.08
1816–1820	1.09
1826–1830	1.05
1836–1840	1.05
1841–1845	1.04
1846–1850	0.99
1851–1855	0.95

Source. Landry, *Traité de démographie* (1945), p. 332, cited by Pouthas, *Population française* (1956), p. 28.

There can hardly have been such a discontinuity in the progress of civilization. Moreover, the annual data show a high sensitivity to political disturbance, which, in turn, in mid-century is intimately connected to the harvest. The annual data from 1806 to 1955 are given in Table 5. The high variability in the net reproduction rate makes it difficult to connect it to such a sluggish concept as civilization; see, for

[12] Habakkuk, "Family Structure and Economic Change" (1955), p. 5. In "Basic Conditions of Economic Progress" (1955), p. 167, Habakkuk states that wide distribution of property coupled with equal division on inheritance provided a strong inducement to postpone marriage.

[13] Habakkuk, "Family Structure and Economic Change," pp. 7–10.

[14] Pouthas, *Population française* (1956), p. 29. The net reproduction rate, as is widely known, is measured by the rate at which women of child-bearing age are reproducing themselves by female babies at the birth rate of a given year. At 1.0 the female population is just maintaining itself.

Table 5. Net Reproduction Rate for 100 Women in France, 1806–1955

Year	Net rate	Year	Net rate	Year	Net rate	Year	Net rate
1806	105	1846	98	1886	100	1926	92
1807	104	1847	96	1887	101	1927	93
1808	107	1848	100	1888	101	1928	92
1809	110	1849	91	1889	102	1929	89
1810	111	1850	108	1890	93	1930	93
1811	106	1851	102	1891	98	1931	93
1812	108	1852	101	1892	95	1932	92
1813	107	1853	102	1893	98	1933	88
1814	108	1854	88	1894	99	1934	90
1815	109	1855	89	1895	95	1935	87
1816	119	1856	98	1896	101	1936	88
1817	111	1857	95	1897	102	1937	89
1818	103	1858	99	1898	97	1938	91
1819	104	1859	92	1899	96	1939	93
1820	109	1860	105	1900	95	1940	82
1821	109	1861	100	1901	100	1941	77
1822	104	1862	105	1902	101	1942	85
1823	110	1863	105	1903	98	1943	90
1824	108	1864	105	1904	97	1944	94
1825	102	1865	100	1905	97	1945	93
1826	101	1866	105	1906	95	1946	126
1827	109	1867	107	1907	93	1947	131
1828	101	1868	100	1908	96	1948	133
1829	109	1869	103	1909	95	1949	133
1830	107	1870	93	1910	96	1950	132
1831	108	1871	69	1911	87	1951	126
1832	97	1872	109	1912	94	1952	125
1833	105	1873	105	1913	92	1953	124
1834	92	1874	111	1914	88	1954	125
1835	108	1875	108	1915	57	1955	124
1836	111	1876	111	1916	45		
1837	103	1877	110	1917	48		
1838	102	1878	107	1918	46		
1839	105	1879	109	1919	58		
1840	103	1880	104	1920	98		
1841	104	1881	106	1921	98		
1842	103	1882	106	1922	97		
1843	102	1883	106	1923	94		
1844	105	1884	104	1924	93		
1845	109	1885	105	1925	94		

Source. INSEE, *Annuaire statistique, 1956*, part 2, p. 14, table 7.

example, the sharp declines in 1849 and 1871, which follow political disturbances with a brief lag. But Table 6 suggests that the index sensi-

Table 6. Agricultural Output and Prices Compared with
Net Reproduction Rate, 1841–1857

Year	Qa (1914 = 100)	Pa (1901–10 = 100)	PaQa/100	NRR
1841	66	115	76	104
1842	65	124	81	103
1843	66	114	75	102
1844	74	105	77	105
1845	62	108	67	109
1846	52	135	65	98
1847	89	159	137	96
1848	80	111	87	100
1849	72	80	58	91
1850	74	91	67	108
1851	58	96	66	102
1852	48	124	66	101
1853	44	131	58	102
1854	57	145	83	88
1855	50	150	75	89
1856	57	144	82	98
1857	74	133	98	95

Note. Qa = agricultural output; Pa = agricultural prices; NRR = net reproduction rate; PaQa/100, calculated.
Source. Net reproduction rate from Table 5; agricultural output and prices from Sirol, *Le Role de l'agriculture* (1942), Appendix 4.1.

tively reflected agricultural conditions. The drawbacks of Sirol's indexes of agricultural output have already been noted, including the uncertain results from matching the price index of one year with the volume index of the same year rather than the preceding one.[15] It is nonetheless suggestive that the price-times-quantity agriculture index, which provides a crude measure of agricultural income, seems to explain, with a lag, the further sharp drop in the net reproduction rate in 1854 and 1855, as well as the crisis of 1848.

The sharp drop in French fecundity which occurred in the middle of the nineteenth century was therefore rural in origin. The cities were not greatly affected.[16] Part of the cause was undoubtedly the equal division of inherited land.[17] But superimposed on this long-run influence

[15] See above, Chapter 1, note 8.
[16] Pouthas, p. 147, notes that the birth rate in Paris was higher than in the rest of France. See also Juillard, *Basse-Alsace* (1953), p. 299.
[17] Fouillée, *Psychologie du peuple français* (1903), cites a certain amount of

was the brusque effect of the violent agricultural crisis. The drop in
natality between 1846 and 1861 in the lower Rhine area of Alsace has
been called a last example of the direct influence of the state of subsistence on demography — a Ricardian view but not the Ricardian
mechanism.[18] The means of family limitation in the country are not
entirely clear; the movement of young people to Paris in the 1850s and
delayed marriages account for only part of the effect, since the year-to-
year changes are so sharp.[19] But whatever the means, the effect is
undeniable.

One hundred years later the position had changed, and the cities had
fewer children than the countryside, even after taking account of the
low fertility in certain rural areas like those of southeast and southwest
France.[20] The average number of children per family in 1946 — before
the effects of the demographic counterrevolution had been registered
— was 2.13 for France and 1.53 in Seine (Paris). But the French pattern
of high and low fertility did not follow that of other countries then —
nor had it ever.[21] Workers had more children per family than the petty

---

evidence in support of the Le Play view, though he backs Leroy-Beaulieu (pp.
310–313). Typical of this is that in areas where land worries are not strong, birth
rates are high. Examples are the fishermen of Brittany and the settlers in French
Canada.

[18] Juillard, p. 299.

[19] Most authorities agree that family limitation was achieved principally by
coitus interruptus. See Ariès, *Populations françaises* (1948), pp. 496, 497, 515;
Royal Commission on Population, *Report* (1949), p. 37, para. 93. Prior to about
1880, contraceptives were used exclusively by prostitutes and physicians. For a
fictional account, see Zola, *La Terre* (1887). Marcilhacy, "Emile Zola, historien
des paysans beaucerons" (1957), gives Zola high marks for the historical accuracy of his picture of peasant life and states (p. 585) that the peasants of the
Beauce have not forgotten 1848. Ariès states that the French practiced late marriages in the eighteenth century, but not in the nineteenth (p. 504). Some restriction was achieved by men marrying older women. For the residual uncertainty
over the means of limiting families, see Mendras, *Novis et Virgin* (1953), who
describes a remote village in southwest France where families are limited, where
there is no practice of contraception or abortion, and where initial sexual experiences take place at fourteen or fifteen.

[20] The lowest rates are those in Ariège, Drôme, Landes, Basses-Alpes, Creuse,
and Lot, but the rural rates are still 37 percent higher than the urban. See
Valarché, *Mobilité des ruraux* (1953), p. 122.

[21] See Fouillée, *Psychologie du peuple français*, p. 304, who states that the
extended family encourages large families, but not in France; and p. 309, that the
Catholic religion encourages large families, but not in France. Juillard compares
birth rates for Catholic and Protestant villages in Alsace (*Basse-Alsace*, appendix,
p. 527) and percentage of families with three or more children (text, p. 301).
The Catholic averages are somewhat higher than the Protestant. But what is
surprising is the wide variability of the Catholic averages, through both time and
space. Note, however, Royal Commission on Population, *Report*, pp. 29–30, para.
72, that the decline of family size in Britain has been slower among Roman
Catholics than among Protestants, "but the extent of the difference can easily be
overstated . . . Moreover Roman Catholics of different occupational groups seem
to differ in average family size in very much the same way as non-Catholics."

bourgeoisie, but the latter had fewer, not more, children than the upper middle class.[22] This was the result of "social capillarity," to use a phrase of Arsène Dumont that is popular in France. At the bottom of the social scale — in the north — there were larger families, but still family limitation,[23] and at the top there was no need to practice it. On the contrary, the rich bourgeoisie had large families to staff family concerns.[24] The pattern of the middle of the nineteenth century of limited rural fertility still applied, however, in the south if not in the north, especially not in Normandy and Brittany.[25]

Beginning in 1946 the French birth rate changed abruptly, as Table 5 demonstrates. There is a possibility that the net reproduction rate turned up in 1935–1939, before being set back again by the outbreak of war. The movement is regular and lasts five years. But from 87 to 93

[22] See Girard, "Aspects statistiques du problème familial" (1955), p. 56, who gives a table of the number of children surviving for 100 married men, aged 45 to 54 years, from the 1946 census:

Miners and terracers	272	Higher employees, liberal professions,	
Farmers	253	employers of more than 5 workers	170
Common laborers, foremen	189	Tradesmen, shopkeepers	165
Small employers, artisans	181	Office staff	162
		Sales clerks	139

[23] La Pière, *The Freudian Ethic* (1959), regards family limitation as a manifestation of the Puritan ethic of accepting responsibility for one's destiny, whereas the upsurge in the birth rate in the United States is the consequence of its replacement by the Freudian ethic of irresponsibility. But this applies very poorly to France, where the "irresponsible classes" — workers and farmers — did not have large families.

[24] See Pitts, *Bourgeois Family and French Retardation*, p. 260. Lambert Dansette, *Quelques familles du patronat textile* (1954), pp. 670ff, notes that the bourgeoisie had large families and not because of religion. Ariès, *Populations françaises*, points out (p. 486) that the de Wendel family moved down from eight children in the middle of the eighteenth century to four at the end of the eighteenth and beginning of the nineteenth, four and three in the middle of the nineteenth, five, four, three, and six at the end of the century, and four, four, and six in the twentieth. Cf. Sauvy who believes that it was the bourgeois class that led the way in family limitation (*Richesse et population*, p. 65). He cites some research of Bertillon, who found that the birth rates declined with wealth in Paris in 1897. Paris may not have been representative of the country. Or the distinction may run between the bourgeoise and the great dynasties, as Ariès refers to them, of the high bourgeoisie.

[25] See Pressat, "Population" in *Région Languedoc* (1957), p. 25, who states that the birth rate gives a surplus of population north of the Nantes-Geneva line, a deficiency south of it. The birth rate was much higher in the Moselle than in the Nord, and higher in the Nord than in France as a whole. See Nistri and Prêcheur, *La Région du Nord et Nord-Est* (1959), p. 7. For regional sketches, which justify the plural of his title, see Ariès, *Populations françaises* on Brittany, the Alpes, Aquitaine, the Nord mining country, and Paris by arrondissement. The high birth rate of the mining regions of the Nord, emanating from conditions described by Zola in *Germinal* (1885), dropped from 40 to 47 per thousand in 1891–1911 to 20 to 21 after the war. This was much later than in other parts of France.

is no great distance. The abrupt change occurs in 1946. There is a
fundamental difference of opinion in France as to the cause of this
change. To the demographers, it is owed to the Code de la Famille of
1939, which provided family allowances that increased as the size of
the family grew.[26] The code had its forerunners, which went back to
1913, but July 1939 marked the adoption of nationally uniform and
far-reaching allowances to encourage natality. These allowances were
raised in 1947: at that time the first child produced an allowance of
7.5 percent of the basic salary of 200,000 francs a year; two children,
22.4; three children, 38.3; four, 49.1; and five, 60.3. Large families became economically feasible.

Against this view, however, is the evidence that the rise in family
size cannot be attributed to economic phenomena. To prove that it
was, it would have to be shown that poorer families, to whom the
allowances made a larger contribution to income, had increased their
birth rate more than well-to-do.[27] Unfortunately there is yet no defini-
tive study on the point. But the evidence suggests that it is the
bourgeoisie which now has more children,[28] as well as the urban population.[29] The official government point of view is that the family allowances are "by no means the only reason for the increase in the birth
rate. There has been a change in the French outlook on life which
began during the darkest days of the German occupation . . . It is no
longer fashionable to have just one child."[30]

We can dispose briefly of the death rate. In the first half of the
century, the death rate and the birth rate fluctuated together in the
short run. In a country near the subsistence level, more deaths left
more room for more children. But in the second half of the century, the
rates move independently.[31] The death rate declined in every area but

[26] See Sauvy, *La Montée des jeunes* (1960). Jeanneney (*Forces et faiblesses*,
p. 20) agrees that the upturn in the birth rate is due to the family allowances.
Gravier (*Paris et le désert français*, p. 97) says this view cannot be contested.

[27] This assumes that both middle-income and poor families calculate. It may be
that the former do and the latter do not. But this is improbable in the French
context since the poorer classes did limit family size earlier.

[28] See Clement and Xydias, *Vienne* (1955), who state that the young bourgeois
families have the most children (p. 28); and Brams, *Sociologie comparée* (1955),
p. 180, who holds that after the change in population, voluntary sterility is greatest
among the petty bourgeoisie.

[29] See Mendras (*Novis et Virgin*, p. 69): "The third child [in a small rural
community] is a mistake for which the family allowances and the premiums are
never more than a consolation."

[30] See Centre de Diffusion Française, *The Young Face of France* (1959), p. 3.
Henry, in *Sociologie comparée* (1955), p. 67, supports the statement that the
"brusque" change occurred during the occupation, "in couples married in 1943,
and perhaps in couples married in 1941 and 1942."

[31] Morazé, *La France bourgeoise*, p. 17.

alcoholism, with its effects on tuberculosis in men. The rise in alcoholism occurred especially in the last quarter of the century, especially in the Midi.[32] The consumption of alcohol doubled per capita between 1855 and 1900 and started to decline only after that.[33] The problem remains serious to this day.

Emigration has not been important in France, in contrast with all other countries in Europe. The French are rooted in the soil. During the period 1846–1851, 275,000 emigrants left for overseas, 70 percent of the total emigration of the first half of the century.[34] Migration to Algeria was stimulated by the phylloxera; and recently, as a consequence of overcrowding, a few Bretons are leaving for abroad as well as for other parts of France. But the net movement has been one of immigration. Italians and Spaniards in the south, Poles in the coal mines of the Nord, Germans in the east, and North Africans everywhere, but especially in the low-end jobs of Lorraine and Paris, have amounted with their descendents to 5.5 million persons between 1801 and 1936.[35] In the boom period from 1921 to 1931, 1,340,000 immigrants entered France.[36] In 1930 there were three million foreigners employed. During the 1930s, 500,000 left or were expelled.[37] These immigrants were not assimilable. But in the absence of a willingness of French agricultural laborers to go into industrial occupations at any distance from their home villages, they were needed.

French war losses in World War I were enormous and serious: 1.3 million killed, 4.5 million wounded.[38] The net loss in the killed and natality loss from the depressed birth rate is estimated at 3.3 million. The qualitative loss is impossible to measure, but there is a high probability that war, like emigration in other countries, attracts first the most vigorous elements.

The comparative method helps here. It is hard to know how much economic stagnation can be ascribed to heavy war losses suffered by Britain in World War I, by Germany in both wars, or by France. Germany recovered its economic vigor both times; Britain suffered economic stagnation in the 1920s, but recovered fifteen years after the middle of the war, when it might have felt the loss most keenly. What counts may be not mere numbers but changes in density. Since territory did not change in Britain, density moved with war losses. But

[32] Fouillée, *Psychologie du peuple français,* pp. 354ff.
[33] Ariès, *Populations françaises,* p. 490.
[34] Pouthas, *Population française,* p. 198.
[35] Spengler, "Declining Demographic Growth" (1951), p. 405.
[36] Lorwin, *French Labor Movement* (1954), p. 66.
[37] *Ibid.,* p. 67.
[38] *Ibid.,* p. 51.

France, in this view, was hurt and Germany was helped by the territorial changes after the wars. Denmark grew vigorously after the loss of Schleswig-Holstein in 1864. Allowing a considerable time after 1871 for the discovery of iron and the financing of its development, France grew rapidly from 1896 to 1913, particularly in Lorraine which was the recipient of the "first large-scale migration of modern times." [39] In 1918 and 1945 the Germans were compressed into a smaller space, so that their war losses were less keenly felt. In 1918, on the other hand, France was handed back Alsace-Lorraine and had to fill it out. After the intensive period of reconstruction, the strain on the reduced manpower of leadership quality made itself felt.

POPULATION INCREASE AND GROWTH

Timing problems are serious for any theory about war losses, but much more so for any general view about stagnation based on the slow rate of population increase in France. If there had been only two periods of rapid economic expansion — in the 1850s and 1950 — there would still be difficulty. Stagnation set in *after* the big population increase in the first half of the nineteenth century had been achieved,[40] but recovery came *simultaneously* with the onset of the demographic counterrevolution. There were also the boom of 1896–1913 and that of 1919–1929, neither of which has a change in population trend to explain it, apart from the war losses and the war decline in natality that both operate in the wrong direction. Moreover, French growth in these periods was faster than in Britain, where the rate of population increase was declining only slowly.

Furthermore, the mechanism is as difficult to understand as the deep-seated causes of population change. The rapid economic growth of the 1850s was linked mainly to railroad construction. There was a housing boom, especially in Paris; but this had nothing to do with any natural rate of increase. It was occasioned by the movement to Paris on an enormous scale of discontented farmers, workers to take part in the building program of Haussmann, shopkeepers, politicians, lawyers, and so on. The city grew by 20 percent in five years at the

[39] Rideau, *Houillères et sidérurgie de Moselle,* p. 12. See also Blanc, Juillard, Ray, and Rochefort, *Les Régions de l'Est* (1960), p. 26: "The annexation of Alsace in 1871 upset the organization of markets of these new industries and definitely provoked progress.

[40] Spengler points out that 77 percent of the total increase in population between 1801 and 1936 had been achieved by 1866 ("Declining Demographic Growth," p. 403). Is the decline in the rate of population increase, by implication, responsible for the economic stagnation after 1871?

peak of the boom.[41] This increase and that of 1881 led to peak building in the subsequent five-year periods.[42]

In other cities, as in Paris, building was as much a function of inward migration as of the birth rate. Bettelheim and Frère and Wylie
have shown that there is more mobility in France than is generally
credited, and not all in the direction of Paris, important as that is.[43]
Much of this mobility is local, but this is equally true of Britain.[44]
Mobility will produce net building with a stable population, of course,
because houses are both durable and (as yet) immobile; new houses
needed to accommodate immigrants cannot be made good by those
abandoned.

Industrial workers always had a sort of mobility — partly seasonal,
partly cyclical. The masons of Limousin, the carpenters from Nièvre,
and the ditch diggers of the Auvergne are the best known.[45] A few
other trades went "tramping" in search of work in bad times.[46] But
French mobility, urbanization, and especially the readiness to drive
agricultural workers off the farm were far below the British trends, as
will be examined in detail below. Rather than saying that some exogenous change in the French birth rate produced economic slowdown, it seems much more realistic to cite the reverse for the early part
of the period of economic slowdown — in the crisis of 1848–1851,
again in the 1880s, and, at a still lower level, in the 1930s. The slow
falling away of the net reproduction rate (Table 5) from 1876 to
1896, apart from the dip in 1890, is suggestive. This intermediate trend,
to be sure, is superimposed on long-run declining fertility as the petty
bourgeois became discontented with his lot. But in the short run eco-

[41] Chevalier, *Population parisienne* (1949), pp. 40–41. The figures for the second
half of the century are of interest: in the five years ended 1856, 20.5 percent;
1861, 10.2 percent; 1866, 7.6 percent; 1872 (census lagged a year to escape the
war), 1.45 percent; 1876, 7.4 percent; 1881, 14.1 percent; 1886, 3.3 percent;
1891, 4.9 percent; 1896, 3.6 percent; 1901, 7.0 percent. These figures of course
allow for the change in administrative zone in 1858.

[42] Direction de la Statistique, *Logement à Paris* (1946), p. 108.

[43] Bettelheim and Frère, *Auxerre* (1950), p. 85. Only 25 percent of the population sampled was born in Auxerre; 35 percent was born in neighboring Yonne;
and 13 percent in other neighboring departments. In Vienne (Clement and
Xydias, *Vienne*, p. 32) the geographic origins of the population were 42 percent
local, 13 percent from neighboring Isère, 8 percent Rhone, 8 percent other nearby
departments, 13 percent the rest of France, and 10 percent abroad. But Vienne is
below its population peak of 1871 (p. 22).
Wylie, *Village in the Vaucluse* (1957), chap. ii.

[44] Redford, *Labour Migration in England* (1926), pp. 158–160. London was a
greater center of attraction than Lancashire and the northwest (p. 157).

[45] See Lamèyre, *Haussmann* (1958), pp. 146–151, 182; Chatelain, "La Main-
d'oeuvre" (1953), pp. 50–56; and Redford, p. 4.

[46] Hobsbawm, "Tramping Artisan" (1951), p. 304.

nomic recovery can lift the index, as in the early 1850s, the early 1860s, and the late 1870s.

The timing of the demographic counterrevolution is interesting in relation to economic recovery. The demographer's case embraced by Sauvy is that the change is a consequence of the Code de la Famille of 1939 and that it is responsible for the subsequent economic recovery. Having resisted the first part of this argument, we must deny the second. Detailed demonstration must wait. Admittedly the rising tide of youth has impressed the French — government and public alike — with the necessity to push economic growth, but it was not the only such stimulus. The humiliation of France in 1940 could have produced an equally strong resolve for more effective performance. The mechanism is lacking. To the extent that French growth since the war has depended upon improved technological performance, the change in the birth rate has had little to do with it. A steady expansion of capacity assists the application of a steady rate of technological change, but is irrelevant to a discontinuous one. And the necessity to provide housing and schools for the wave of youth could have diverted resources from investment in productive outlets in an inflationary period, rather than assisting in the maintenance of full employment during stagnation.

Therefore, French economic stagnation — when it existed only periodically — cannot be laid at the door of population decline,[47] nor can post–World War II recovery be ascribed to the change from the old to the young France. On the first score, we cannot even accept Morazé's watered-down statement that "demographic weakness was perhaps not the first cause of economic decline." [48] It was as much a result. Habakkuk's conclusion still holds: "Population growth and widening of the market, while not a basic condition of economic growth, certainly made the task of entrepreneurs easier." [49] But this is simply to say that growth is a positive feedback process in which more growth helps population expansion which in turn supports growth — if nothing interrupts.

And at the other end, the same forces which produced growth produced a change in attitude toward family size, or we can state it in-

[47] The issue is discussed on rare occasions in diametrically opposite terms. See Eliane Mossé, *Marx et la croissance* (1956), pp. 58–59, who holds that the strong French growth of the nineteenth century (presumably under the Second Empire) was not caused by demographic stagnation. She disputes a view of Maurice Dobb, who, regarding France as an exception to the general rule that economic growth engenders population expansion, is thought inferentially to believe that population slowdown assists growth.

[48] Morazé, *La France bourgeoise*, p. 25. Nor is Bettelheim accurate in calling it a symptom (*Bilan de l'économie française*, 1947, p. 141).

[49] Habakkuk, "Basic Conditions of Progress," p. 161.

versely. But this is different from assigning any causality to population, which may even have hindered the growth of this period by diverting capital, even though it reinforced the resolve to expand at all costs.

POPULATION AND ECONOMIC GROWTH IN BRITAIN

Not nearly the same attention is paid to population as a cause of faster or slower economic growth in Britain as in France. It is widely believed that the Industrial Revolution made possible the population explosion of the second half of the eighteenth and the first half of the nineteenth century, though this view is not totally unchallenged.[50] In the 1930s and again after the Second World War, much attention was given to the decline in the rate of population growth and to the possible problem of stagnation that this might present along the lines of a Keynes-Hansen model. But the general conclusion was an optimistic one. There were advantages and disadvantages for growth in an expanding population. The disadvantages were the pressure on land and the need to use capital for widening rather than deepening. The advantages were the stimulus to expanded output and technical change, the low average age of the population (if the expansion came through an increase in the birth rate), the increased flexibility of the economic system, and an increase in the country's international influence.[51]

The Royal Commission on Population considered that the disadvantages had been unimportant in the nineteenth century when the virgin territories of "areas of recent settlement" were opened to food production to relieve the pressure. In the twentieth century, however, the possibility was thought to exist that the terms of trade would turn against Britain so that feeding increased numbers would present difficulties.[52] After a careful analysis Reddaway was inclined to dismiss the economic arguments: the economic importance of population was exaggerated; and the economic problems involved in a declining population could be solved by such standard policies as taxation and government spending.[53] In the final analysis, moreover, the Royal Commission's recommendations for change are based on the importance of improving social conditions for the British population, and on the broad grounds of national identity. "A community . . . can only prosper or,

[50] See Deane and Habakkuk, "Take-off in Britain" (1960), who assert that the rise in population began as an independent phenomenon and helped to produce the Industrial Revolution.

[51] Royal Commission on Population, *Report*, pp. 101–102, para. 261.

[52] *Ibid.*, pp. 104ff.

[53] Reddaway, *Economics of a Declining Population* (1939), pp. 232–233.

in the long run, survive, if its members think it worthwhile to have families large enough to replace themselves." [54] The economic mechanism is only vaguely mentioned — the fourth in the list of advantages of growing numbers which "tend to increase the nation's international influence and so in various ways to strengthen its economic position." [55]

The connection between economic expansion and contraction and population change has been examined for the nineteenth century by a sociologist, T. H. Marshall, who has found a varied pattern.[56] Working with three variables, births, deaths, and international migration, he notes that the last is most nearly keyed to the broader movements in prosperity — a relationship supported by Brinley Thomas's findings.[57] Even here, however, the large-scale emigration movement of the decade of the Great Depression, 800,000 leaving England and Wales in 1881–1891, led to a further outward movement of 500,000 during the prosperous period 1901–1911; the earlier expulsive force started a process that continued on its own momentum.[58]

The death rate did not fall during the boom of the "golden years" from 1851 to 1873, but only in the depressed period that followed. This was owing to the lag of urban public-health measures behind the increase in urban concentration which that prosperity produced. Whereas today's demographers expect a decline in the death rate immediately to follow any increase in income per capita, this was not the case in mid-Victorian England because of the way the increase in income was spent — on things other than doctors, hospitals, housing, and drains.[59]

The birth rate is the most interesting variable. This was independent of business conditions, Marshall asserts, and especially since 1880 or

[54] Royal Commission on Population, *Report*, p. 232, para. 687. At an earlier point (p. 136, para. 360), the commission says that the decline in British population gave some reason for disquiet but did not justify alarm.

[55] *Ibid.*, p. 102, para. 261. Only half a paragraph (p. 103, para. 266) is devoted to this theme: "The environment of rapidly growing numbers helped to make possible the leading role, which Britain acquired at a formative time, in international trade, shipping and finance. It enabled the British people to make a large contribution through migration to the population of the expanding continents, and thus ensured that these populations would contain strong elements with personal attachments to Great Britain, and sympathetic to British ideas and British customs. These considerations were important even from a commercial standpoint. It is also manifest that, in addition to the military advantage of a large manpower, they contributed greatly to the national strength which has enabled us to emerge successfully from two world wars."

[56] Marshall, "The Population of England and Wales" (1935).

[57] Thomas, *Migration and Economic Growth* (1954).

[58] Marshall, p. 333. The figures for Great Britain are 817,000 and 756,000 (Royal Commission on Population, *Report*, p. 15, para. 40).

[59] Marshall, pp. 337–338. Ariès also observes that the sterility of cities is not automatic and that the great urbanization of Britain did not reduce the birth rate (*Populations françaises*, p. 363).

the mid-1870s.[60] Some writers note that World War I ended the Victorian family system.[61] The change is sometimes thought of as dating from the Bradlaugh-Besant trial of 1877, which spread public awareness of contraception.[62] Marshall, however, believes that the decline in fertility began prior to 1877, touched off by the depression which raised the average marrying age.[63] (One can also find the opinion that the new Poor Law of 1834 and the Factory Acts of 1847, prior to which children were a capital asset, started the trend.[64]) The birth rate fails to indicate the turning because it is affected by changes in total numbers; at its peak, in the decade 1871–1881, it shows an annual average of 35.4 per thousand before the decline set in to 24.6 in the census period 1910–1912; 23.1 in 1920–1922; and 16.3 in 1930–1932. The Fertility Census of 1911 and the Sample Census of Families taken for the Royal Commission on Population show the rapid decline in family size in different ways — by dates of the birth of women and dates of marriage, respectively, which makes the timing hard to pin down.[65] But whether the change occurred in the 1870s or at the end of that decade is relatively unimportant: the birth rate took off on its own independently of short-run or intermediate business conditions in Britain, unlike the 1848 divide in the demographic history of France. Marshall states that population as a factor in economic history must be regarded as a cause and not merely an effect;[66] but he does not say what the independent change in the birth rate caused.

As in France, where the net reproduction rate reached its low in 1933, the birth rate in Britain halted its decline in the same year and moved sideways to the outbreak of war.[67] A major contributing cause

[60] *Ibid.*, pp. 333, 336.
[61] See Cole and Postgate, *The British People* (1961), p. 534.
[62] See Royal Commission on Population, *Report*, chap. v, esp. p. 36, para. 90.
[63] Marshall, p. 336.
[64] Ariès, *Populations françaises*, p. 364. The Royal Commission (*Report*, p. 42, para. 107) notes that the Factory Acts and the Education Act of 1870 extended the period for which children were a burden on their families.
[65] See Royal Commission on Population, *Report*, pp. 24, 25, paras. 59, 61:

Period of birth of women	Average number of live births	Period of marriage	Average number of children
1841–45	5.71	1900–09	3.37
1846–50	5.63	1910–14	2.90
1851–55	5.40	1915–19	2.53
1856–60	5.08	1920–24	2.38
1861–65	4.66	1925–29	2.19

[66] Page 341.
[67] Royal Commission on Population, *Report*, p. 3, para. 11.

was a reduction in marriage age,[68] which in turn may have been a consequence of the fall in unemployment and the increase in housing.[69] But the similarity of timing as compared to France should not be allowed to cover the fact that economic conditions were very different in the two countries. It is perhaps not noteworthy that Britain should stabilize its birth rate after the depression and with the return of quasi-prosperity. What is remarkable is that the French rate should have leveled off during the deflation and subsequent economic unrest.

A further contrast follows World War II. The fundamental change in the French position has been noted. In Britain a demographic counterrevolution also occurred, but on an exiguous scale.[70] The postwar backlog peak of the birth rate reached a little over twenty per thousand in 1948. Thereafter the rate settled down just under sixteen per thousand, compared with fifteen in the 1930s. Here different demographic behavior is matched with different growth rates, in contrast with the similar demographic and diverse economic patterns of the 1930s.

For our period, then, there is no short-run link between economic growth and population change, nor any clear-cut model of the secular connections running between bigger population and greater prosperity. More prosperity led to more people, as death rates moved down faster than birth rates in France and in Britain. The French cut down on fertility first, though they had the lower income per capita, and they cut it especially in crisis and on the farm. The British reduced family size in about 1880, responding partly to the short-run influence of depression,[71] mainly to long-run prosperity, but with causal elements of publicity about birth control, changes in the net burden of children due to public enactments, and a simple change of taste spread through the system by social conformity.[72]

The causation running from population to growth remains elusive. The Royal Commission's emphasis on "leadership" and population growth as an "essential condition of the development of Britain as a

[68] *Ibid.*, p. 46ff, paras. 114–118.

[69] In discussing policy, the commission states (*ibid.*, p. 202, para. 561): "In modern conditions, the shortage of housing is the main deterrent to parenthood."

[70] *Ibid.*, p. 57, para. 137: "The extremely small family is no longer as 'fashionable' as it was in the early 1920's."

[71] *Ibid.*, p. 41, para. 104, and p. 220, para. 620. The depression is only mentioned among the myriad causes which add up to the Leroy-Beaulieu explanation in the earlier reference. In the second, it and the Bradlaugh-Besant trial are said to be likely in large measure to have been responsible for timing the turn at about 1880.

[72] *Ibid.*, p. 43, para. 109, "Once the movement for smaller families had gathered some way, social example and fashion no doubt helped to spread it."

rich and great nation" [73] goes beyond my terms of reference, since I am interested in the "rich" but not in the "great." The listed advantages and disadvantages lead, on balance, nowhere, since their importance changes in the world situation. And the notion that slow French population growth is ruinous on a Keynes-Hansen-Higgins model requires a statement, along Reddaway's analysis, about why full employment cannot be achieved by other means, with the redundant savings, if these are in fact produced with an aging population, used to deepen capital formation.

My hunch is that we are in the presence of collinearity, that population changes in response to other influences which also affect economic growth in the long run, with differential effects in the short. In particular, the discontinuous changes of 1880 in Britain and of 1942 in France are impressive, associated as they are with a decline in economic vigor in the first case and a resurgence in the second. But this does not mean that one can identify a declining birth rate with the waning of economic energy — witness the 1848 decline in France with the expansion that followed 1851, and so on.

[73] *Ibid.*, p. 8, para. 21.

CHAPTER 5

SOCIAL DETERMINANTS
OF GROWTH

The economist approaches the subject of this chapter with hesitation on more than one score. The disciplines to which it refers seem to him, in comparison to his own, undisciplined. To the extent that he can comprehend the jargon of social psychology, social anthropology, and sociology, their theorems seem to him either wildly overgeneralized or self-evident. He is distressed by the fact that quantification is impossible. And he recognizes, in most of his own profession, the lack of a felicitous prose style, with its possibilities for irony and paradox, which makes the subject so enjoyable in belles-lettres.

It cannot be helped, for the matter is important. It is entirely possible — many people think likely — that the economic growth of France and Britain has been determined by traits of individual character and social process, rather than by geography, demography, finance, and such.[1] Certainly it works the other way, that economic change affects the character of the individual, the family, the functional group, the social class. The subject is not only important: it is difficult. National character and class structure are full of contradictions;[2] averages conceal significant differences among individuals,

[1] See Christopher, "Dessication of the Bourgeois Spirit" (1951) who contrasts traditional or historical explanations on the one hand and the determinist on the other, including geographical, political, diplomatic, financial, educational, demographic, and Marxist. The traditional or historical explanation amounts to the dessication of the bourgeois spirit, an elusive concept which is not fully developed.

[2] Lorwin, *French Labor Movement* (1954), observes that the French are both emotional and logical, impulsive and practical, zealous and skeptical (p. 40). We have already seen that they like safe investments, such as the *rente*, and love to speculate. But perhaps the most extensive statement of this sort is from Anon., *An Estimate of the Manners and Principles of the Times* (1757), a century before our period opens: "The Character of the *French* Nation, tho' inconsistent, is respectable: They have found, or rather invented, the Art of uniting all Extremes: They have Virtue and Vices, Strengths and Weakness, seemingly incompatible. They are effeminate, yet brave; insincere, yet Honourable; hospitable, not benevolent; vain, yet subtile; splendid, not generous; warlike, yet polite; plausible, not virtuous; mercantile, yet not mean; In trifles serious, gay in Enterprize; Women at the toilet, Heroes in the Field; profligate in Heart, in Conduct decent; Divided in Opinion, in Action united; In Manners weak, but strong in Principle; *Con-*

classes, towns, and regions. It is virtually impossible to avoid over-generalization in describing a given aspect at a given time. Finally, and of great significance, national character and the social structure evolve over time, affecting and being affected by economic growth.

I write as an amateur who has examined only a small portion of the wide literature, and not always with comprehension. In particular, I have been unable to ascertain what the "best opinion" believes about the countries we are interested in or whether it finds national character or social structure to be pre-eminent in the social field. I divide the subject arbitrarily into values, personal characteristics, family, class, and social cohesion more generally. No attention is paid to the vulgar stereotype of the Frenchman as a man devoted to gaiety and pleasure, on the grounds that this, along with the comic-strip view of the Englishman, is no longer to be taken seriously.[3] Let us start with a description of the two societies as they existed in 1875, at the height of the Victorian era and early in the life of the Third Republic. If the description is unqualified in time it refers to these periods, even though the present tense is used.

VALUES

British thought is experimental, French theoretical; British behavior active, French intellectual; British communication in large measure silent, French vocal. But above all British leadership has been amateur, French professional.

The experimental nature of British thought is seen in its inventions, which came from all walks of life — from barbers, clergymen, gentlemen farmers, professional scientists, often from the shop floor.[4] Many of these inventors were Scots, where scientific training was rigorous. The Englishmen were frequently self-taught.[5] British inventions were

temptible in private Life, in public Formidable" (p. 141). In revenge, the French have the remark of Edmond de Goncourt, cited by Briffault, _Decline and Fall of the British Empire_ (1938): "The English, taken individually, are decent; while collectively they are scoundrels" (p. 120).

[3] This has not always been so. See Fouillée, _Psychologie du peuple français_ (1903), and Wendell, _France of Today_ (1907), for two books which devote attention to proving that Frenchmen are industrious and serious, rather than exclusively interested in frivolity and sex. On the opposite side of the question is Mourre, _Décadence économique de la France_ (1900), who explains French national character in terms of the climate which made his countrymen joyful and enthusiastic (p. 19), frivolous (p. 186), and excitable (p. 249).

[4] Ashton, _Industrial Revolution_ (1947), pp. 13ff, esp. p. 16.

[5] Halévy insists that Herschel, Dalton, Davy, and Thomas Young (optics) were self-taught, in the strict sense of the word (_History of the English People_, 1937, III, 199). Barker, "Perspective" (1947), adds Cavendish and Darwin (p. 565). Musson and Robinson assert that this view of the British inventor is exaggerated ("Science and Industry in the Eighteenth Century," 1960).

purposeful and practical, even though produced outside industry, as those of Bessemer, Siemens, and Gilchrist Thomas.[6] French scientists, on the other hand, excelled in the elucidation and occasional application of abstract principle, along lines taught in the École Polytechnique or the École des Mines. Training at these institutions was "general, theoretical, highly mathematical, intensive," followed a fixed curriculum.[7] The French engineer almost certainly required an apprenticeship on the job before he was ready for responsible work in the plant.[8] With his interest in deduction and logic, Descartes is the popular personification of French thought.[9] British concern for induction reveals itself not only in absorption in facts, but also in a well-known antipathy for formal constitutions and hypothetical questions.[10]

Silence and action go together,[11] as do verbalized thought and disagreement.[12] Renier regards the British silence as one of the charms of the British — also as a source of repressions.[13] But in France vocability

[6] Burn, "British Steelmaking and Foreign Competition" (1940), p. 221.

[7] Parker, "French and German Ore Mining" (1959), p. 209.

[8] *Ibid.*, p. 210. See also the question put by Tocqueville to the French consul at Liverpool: "Q. Have any French engineers come recently to look at the work [a passenger tunnel for the railroad]? A. Not so long ago M. Navier and several others came. They only wanted to stay three days; they visited the railway only, and when someone told them a fact, M. Navier, after making some calculations, often said: 'The thing is impossible, it does not fit at all with the theory!' Those gentlemen have not left the English greatly impressed with their ability, at least in practical matters" (*Journeys to England*, 1958, p. 113).

[9] Fourastié and Laleuf, *Révolution à l'ouest* (1957), p. 54, object to the widespread characterization of French thought as Cartesian on the grounds that Descartes was the last of the prescientific, not the first of the scientific, savants.

[10] See Fouillée, *Esquisse psychologique*, p. 201. The British are always collecting facts while the French intellectual often plays with notions and deductions that attract him independently of practical results. The British think to act. See also p. 466 for a discussion of the passionate French interest in logic which, John Stuart Mill is quoted as having stated, the French mistake for a proof. See further André Maurois, *Les Silences du Colonel Bramble* (1918), p. 36: "The Colonel adored numerical information to the great distress of Aurelle, who, incapable of recalling a figure, was each day interrogated on the number of inhabitants of a village, the effectives of the Serbian army, or the initial velocity of the French bullet." See also, Royal Commission on Population, *Report*, p. 166, para. 445: "New systems in Great Britain are seldom established by a single enactment. They usually develop gradually from comparatively small beginnings which can be modified as experience suggests and extended as circumstances permit and opinion enjoins."

[11] See not only Maurois, *Les Silences du Colonel Bramble*, but also Fouillée, *Esquisse psychologique*, p. 207.

[12] De Madariaga, *Englishmen, Frenchmen and Spaniards* (1951), p. 159: "In the English assembly, opinions are not the leading thing at all — the leading force is the conviction that things must get done. Now in the French Chamber and Senate the desirability of getting things done must wait on the all-important questions of how they are to be done, who is to do them, and in the name of which principles; and it is easy to see that while roads to action are bound to converge, roads to thought radiate in all the directions of the mind."

[13] Renier, *The English: Are They Human?* (1956), p. 15.

impedes action. "It is necessary to act; I will write an article for the *Revue des Deux Mondes*." [14] "Everyone said better methods: fertilizer, seed selection, irrigation, drains, roads, cheaper transport, and education. Immediately. But they did not do anything, even slowly." [15] Still, the amateur quality of British leadership, in contrast to French professionalism, goes widely into education, careers, and industry. In contrast to the French diplomé, an Oxford or Cambridge first in Greats or the Tripos was ready for anything. "The ambition of the ablest was to play a part in the political and parliamentary life of the country." [16] Politics was the field of the "ignorant, but the disinterested." [17] A bachelor degree in Greats during a somewhat earlier epoch (well before the establishment of Sandhurst in 1860) qualified the graduate equally for the church or the army.

The "vogue of the amateur" persists in England, despite the fact that the world has become more complex, and with it industry. Robert Graves observes that the word "pro" is a deadly insult among public-school soccer players and the greatest compliment in village or waste-ground football.[18] The amateur prevails among historians, in sport, politics, management of agriculture,[19] and especially industry.[20] Lord Balniel holds that the amateur tradition grows out of the varied duties expected of the ruling class — which in England never abandoned country life for militarism, as in Germany, or for the court, as in France — and is beneficial in maintaining a mutual esteem among professions which does not exist elsewhere.[21] The position is otherwise in France, so much so that the word "professional" is evoked.[22] The contrast has been especially striking in government. In Britain it is the amateur who rules, while the expert official is "on tap but not on top" and regarded somewhat contemptuously, frequently with the addition of a pejorative

[14] Fauvet, *La France dechirée* (1957), p. 35.
[15] Augé-Laribé, *Politique agricole* (1950), p. 80. See also Gravier, *Décentralisation* (1954), p. 332, on the thirteen years of "tergiversations" between the formation in 1934 of a company to build the dam at Génissiat — suggested in 1902 — and the first practical steps.
[16] Halévy, *History of the English People*, III, 178.
[17] Barker, "Perspective," p. 565. See also Table 7 below, Chapter 6.
[18] Graves, *Lars Porsena* (1927), p. 20.
[19] Barker, p. 565.
[20] Florence, *Logic of Industry* (1953), p. 330. Florence quotes André Siegfried, *England's Crisis* (1933), p. 147: "A gentleman, we must realize, never strives too much; it is not considered the thing. He does nothing too well; he leaves that to the professional and the champion."
[21] Balniel, "The Upper Class" (1960), pp. 430–31.
[22] Wendell, *France of Today*, p. 25: [Of French students] "Their spirit seems quite to lack the amateurish grace so engagingly characteristic of American undergraduates; in contrast they seem intensely professional." And p. 28: [Of French professors] "Serious . . . never relax . . . concentrated and unceasing intellectual activity. Nobody could imagine industry more unremitting, more intense. 'Professional' again is the word which comes to mind."

adjective, such as "petty" officialdom.[23] In France, on the other hand, it is government by amateurs, or parliamentarians, which is in disesteem, while it is felt that the technicians (professionals) should hold an essential role in national life.[24] The amateur spirit links business and sport. Business is a game with rules — like cricket.[25] The British expect to win, in the long run (the only way one can win in cricket).[26]

National characteristics and values differ, but these also differ from class to class. At one time the values of one class dominate; at another, those of another. This may account for some of the contradictions in national character and the changes that supervene. We can distinguish the aristocrat, the bourgeois, the town worker, and the countryman, each with separate attitudes and beliefs. In France the bourgeoisie is typically broken down into the *grand* and the *petit*, and sometimes further.[27]

The aristocracy in Britain was not above working.[28] The landed gentry not only lived on the soil, but interested themselves in it. Their central value or norm was duty. In particular, they embraced local service or stood for national office. In France, on the other hand, the aristocratic value par excellence has been called prowess, "the cult of the exceptional feat, its style, form, perfection — regardless of social utility, practical consequences or economic value." [29] "An aristocrat does not pick up his change or take cover." A *gentilhomme* gambles

---

[23] MacKenzie, "Technocracy and the Role of Experts in Government: United Kingdom" (1961), pp. 1, 2.

[24] Vedel, "Les Problèmes de la technocratie et le rôle des experts: Rapport sur la France" (1961), pp. 1, 2.

[25] Florence, *Logic of Industry.*

[26] See Brogan, *The English People* (1943), p. 210: "What the English expect in their hearts is a final victory when the more brilliant and professional armies have got tired and see by the rules of the game, as Ludendorff did in 1918 and Petain in 1940, that all is lost. It is then that the English soldier gets his unprofessional revenge."

[27] Leuillot, "Bourgeois et Bourgeoisie" (1956), pp. 86, 101, distinguishes out the *grande, haute, moyenne,* and *petite* bourgeoisie. The first belongs to the dynasties running steel and the great banks; the second to large-scale industry and deposit banking; the third to trade; and the fourth to petty trade.

[28] Bonnet quotes Voltaire that the son of a royal pair in England would not disdain to enter commerce (*Commercialisation* (1929), p. 31). See Mourre, *Décadence économique de la France,* p. 104. In Britain, sons of lords "accepted work in banks, industry and even commerce. And who would dare to blush at that when the nobles didn't blush!" But see Halévy, *History of the English People,* III, 163, that a manufacturer had to renounce commerce to enable his son to enter the upper classes via Eton. Noble families did not enter medicine, nor could a doctor obtain a peerage. Surgeons were below doctors, and still further down the scale were chemists (*ibid.,* p. 179).

[29] Pitts, "French Values and Their Implementation by Social Classes before World War II" (1959).

but does not work.[30] Manual labor was taboo and gloves were worn to preserve the delicacy of the hands, which is a sign of class.[31] The French love of quality and abhorrence of mass production have been widely noted, and are attributable to the dominance of prowess as a value in aristocratic consumption, affecting the output of all classes.[32]

Bourgeois values are strongly shaped by family structure, and here we may note several broad characteristics. While Britain is a nation of shopkeepers, Madariaga calls France one of *petit rentiers*.[33] The British gladly emigrate; the French stay at home in their corner of France, in the family. Adventure, which the British embrace as a game, is abhorrent to the French. "Risk and adventure were the two dreadful enemies that might, at one strike, deprive one of the bliss of living in France, or the modicum of well-being necessary to live in their comfort as the unluxurious French understand it." [34] Moderation is not altogether missing in Britain. The tinmasters of Wales, uninterested in conspicuous consumption, were unadventurous, easily satisfied.[35] But the French readiness to accept the security of the life of a functionary[36] was altogether absent in England, where government too was a game and not a business.

The literature on both countries is choked with references to the capacity to sell, generally domestically but in foreign markets as well. Toward the end of our period, the British were said to lack it, preferring a take-it-or-leave-it arrogant view toward the customer.[37] For the French, such difficulty in selling as may have existed — as claimed

---

[30] Pitts, "Bourgeois Family and French Retardation" (1957), p. 411. Selling a mass product, Pitts adds, is to subject the validation of one's worth to the change in taste of a Métro ticketseller.

[31] Goblot, *La Barrière et le niveau* (1925), p. 30.

[32] See, e.g., Cameron, "Profit, croissance et stagnation" (1957), including a quotation from Richard Cobden on the French superiority, at the Crystal Palace exposition, in products involving delicate manipulation, the best taste, and the rules of chemistry and manufacturing production. See also Dunham, *Industrial Revolution in France* (1955), pp. 357, 377, 398, 421; Hoselitz, "Entrepreneurship and Capital Formation" (1956), p. 304.

[33] *Englishmen, Frenchmen and Spaniards*, p. 132.

[34] Edith Wharton, *French Ways and Their Meaning* (1919), p. 88. Elsewhere she says that the French are unafraid of risks (p. 63), but these are physical. Compare Bigo, *Les Banques françaises* (1947), who quotes Courcelle-Seneuil (p. 45): "In France men readily risk their lives, with difficulty their fortunes."

[35] Minchenton, *British Tinplate Industry* (1957), pp. 105–107.

[36] Mourre, *Décadence économique de la France*, pp. 15, 102, 169, 245, 257.

[37] See Williams, *Made in Germany* (1896), who wants British industry to study the demands of customers, send out travelers who know the language, and cease to scorn the small order. See also Brogan, *The English People*, p. 217: "An old and justifiable complaint that the English business man is slow to learn to adapt his product to the foreign market, that he is reluctant to admit that his customer is always right."

by Duveau[38] or Pitts[39] — presumably rested on bases other than confident disdain, such as fear. The agricultural classes shared the views of the gentry in Britain and of the petty bourgeoisie in France. Finally, the working classes. Revolutionary at an early stage in Britain, in London, Birmingham,[40] and Peterloo — or at least violent — they settled down to a combination of practical collective bargaining and political Fabianism. In France the tradition remained revolutionary. There was little need to seek day-to-day improvement because the next revolution would produce the millennium.[41] The years 1789, 1848, 1871, and the intellectual tradition of Georges Sorel, in combination, produced a passion for complete solutions in contrast to the peasant's acceptance of reality and readiness to defend what was his.

RELIGION

The differences in values between France and Britain might be ascribed to religion. France is Catholic; Britain, Protestant. In each country, moreover, leading business and industrial groups at various times have been members of minorities — the Huguenots and the Jews, prominent in banking in France, in the industry of Alsace, and in the trade of Montpelier; the Nonconformists in Britain, who have been responsible for a disproportionate share of the innovations in enterprise and who have formed a surprising proportion of the industrial pioneers. The subject is complex and merits detailed discussion. Within the limits of the present treatment, the most that can be said is that the differences between Protestant and Catholic France, or between Nonconformist and Church of England industry in Britain, are not wide enough to account for either the growth of each country or the discrepancies between them.

The merchant banks and large-scale industry in France were dominated by Jews and Protestants, who were excluded from the liberal

---

[38] Duveau, *La Vie ouvrière* (1946), pp. 131ff, observes that English development has gone one better than the French because each producer is flanked by a merchant. Lhomme, who sides with Duveau against a disputant, Audiganne, notes that the British are also better at mass production (*La Grande bourgeoisie*, 1960, p. 177). But see Lambert Dansette, *Quelques familles du patronat textile* (1954), pp. 556ff, who remarks on the abundance of commercial spirit enjoyed by the textile industry, both in beating down the prices of materials and in selling, and particularly his account (p. 559) of the zest with which Lille salesmen pounced on the buyers from Paris as they came off the train.

[39] *Bourgeois Family and French Retardation.*

[40] Halévy, *History of the English People*, II, 99. Smelser, *Social Change in the Industrial Revolution* (1959), attributes the disorders less to tradition than to certain economic changes which threaten the family.

[41] Lorwin, *French Labor Movement*, pp. 36–38; Pitts, p. 365 calls the revolutionary movement a religion of salvation in which the faithful work for the hereafter rather than for the present.

professions; and when a single family divided between Catholicism and Protestantism, the Protestant side did better financially.[42] But Protestants in small business — in Nîmes or Alsace — suffered from indolence or from a sense of moderation that made them limit their piling up of fortunes.[43] The differences between Catholic Lille and Alsatian Mulhouse in textiles were much less than those between Catholic Lille and Catholic Rouen.[44] Catholics and Protestants combined to form the Crédit Lyonnais,[45] and Bouvier returns a verdict of "not proven" to the charge that the Catholic Union Générale was pulled down by the combined efforts of Jews and Protestants in the *haute banque* world.[46]

Religious issues have divided and continue to divide France. The extent of their relevance to economic matters is doubtful, however. The issues are largely political — education, for instance. But religious practice is perfunctory, at least on the part of men.[47] The church's influence has risen during the period since World War II; it has moved from spiritual to more practical matters.[48]

The part played by Nonconformism in the Industrial Revolution is well known. While innovation has not been the exclusive prerogative of the Nonconformists and Scots, their importance has been larger

[42] Duveau, *La Vie ouvrière*, p. 129.
[43] *Ibid.*
[44] Lambert Dansette, *Quelques familles du patronat textile*, p. 750, points out that the Catholic religion of the north was serious only in externals and basically lukewarm and touched with Voltairism. On the Normands of Rouen, see pp. 520ff, p. 581, etc. The Nord and Normandy had no interest in their workers, while Alsace was paternalistic (Fohlen, *L'Industrie textile*, 1956, pp. 86–87). The Alsatian manufacturer also borrowed from banks, as his Lille-Armentières did not (Lambert Dansette, p. 415), but note that the neighboring manufacturers in Roubaix-Tourcoing used bank credit, not without, in 1867, dire results (*ibid.*, p. 420). Fohlen stresses religious differences (pp. 83–84), but his evidence supports the view in the text that the Normand-Nord differences among the Catholics were wider than those between either and Protestant Alsace. For a further discussion of the differences between the *patronat alsacien* and the *patronat norman*, see the introduction by Eugène Dolléans to Duveau, *La Vie ouvrière*, p. xii.
[45] Bouvier, "Le Crédit Lyonnais" (1958), p. 136.
[46] Bouvier, *Le Krach de l'Union Générale* (1960), chap. v. The Pereire brothers and Mirès, both of whom incurred the enmity of the *hautes banques* and were perhaps destroyed by them, were also Jewish.
[47] Only 12.5 percent of the men attend church services regularly in Auxerre, as compared with 29 percent of the women (Bettelheim and Frère, *Auxerre*, 1950, p. 242). Clement and Xydias also report that religion is superficial and a facade in Vienne (*Vienne*, 1955, pp. 175ff). See also Wylie, *Village in the Vaucluse* (1957), pp. x, 290; Goblot, *La Barrière et le niveau*, p. 95. But there are regional differences, and religion plays a pivotal role in life in Avéyron (Mendras, *Novis et Virgin*, 1953, pp. 47, 55).
[48] Pitts has attached importance to the role of the new Catholicism emerging in the 1930s through such movements as the Bourgeoisie Chrétienne in Lille. See the discussion of "Adieu à la France de Papa?" (Center for International Affairs, Harvard University, 1959).

than their proportion in the population.[49] But the relationships between religion and economic growth are by no means simple. Nonconformism declined early in the eighteenth century, before the Industrial Revolution, and expanded most rapidly after 1788, whereas the bulk of the inventions occurred in the decade of the 1760s.[50] Nonconformism assisted the Industrial Revolution by spreading the demand for education, preaching the doctrine of responsibility, stressing the value of work and thrift, and excluding men of talent from the universities and hence from the professions. But it also worked vice versa. Wesley's great successes were in the cotton-mill towns — Oldham, Stockport, Rochdale, Preston[51] — where Nonconformism reached its peak in the 1820s. Smelser refuses to make a judgment about whether dissent caused the Industrial Revolution or incipient economic development revitalized Nonconformity by creating conditions in which its doctrines were required to stabilize values.[52] Halévy is equally eclectic: Protestant revival and the Industrial Revolution are two parallel forces. Where both existed, there was vitality and progress; where neither, stagnation.[53]

Moreover, the basis of the relationship between religion and entrepreneurship is in doubt. Whereas Weber and Tawney found the clue in the Protestant value system — the Puritan ethic — later investigators have believed the connection to be merely social. Hagen finds the Nonconformist seeking to fulfill his need for achievement because of his inferior status in the social hierarchy, as indeed the location of the Industrial Revolution in Britain can be said, by a long chain of relationships, to be regarded as compensation for the Norman Conquest.[54] A vigorous Swedish critic of Weber explains away Weber's evidence that the Protestant value system favored economic growth by saying that it was based on statements made by church leaders specifically for the purpose of winning support from the merchant class. Samuelsson is prepared to accept the view that the Puritans suffered a sense of rejection and estrangement and went into business because other roads to social approval were barred. But his general conclusion is that it is a hopeless undertaking to isolate one particular factor even from a limited sequence of events, in one country and over a very short period of time, with the object of determining the extent to which the factor

[49] See Hagen, *On the Theory of Social Change* (1962), pp. 294ff. Whereas Scots and Nonconformists constituted about 17 and 7 percent, respectively, of the population of Britain in 1770, they formed 24 and 41 percent of the entrepreneurs in a sample drawn from Ashton's *The Industrial Revolution* (1947).
[50] Smelser, *Social Change in the Industrial Revolution*, p. 69.
[51] *Ibid.*
[52] *Ibid.*, pp. 71–72.
[53] Halévy, *History of the English People*, III, 151.
[54] Hagen, chap. xiii.

evolved in harmony with the general process under consideration.[55]

In the later period of our interest, the economic impact of religion, if any, waned. Nonconformist schools were unimportant, whether in steel, which drew a large proportion of its upper executives from British public schools, or in hosiery, where most executives were drawn from the ranks of those who had left school at the age of ten.[56] Barker observes that both Anglicanism and Nonconformist religion have been modified by the English character, the former into compromise and imprecision, the latter into the voluntary, eccentric, amateur, and experimental.[57]

In Anglican Gosforth, as in Péyrane in the Vaucluse, "religion is of no importance." [58] In this it differs from the Welsh villages of religious revival. But the most interesting modern view is found in Banbury, where Anglicans and Nonconformists alike belong to the traditional life of the town. They differ: Anglicans drink, are sporty, and Conservative; Free Church members abstain, are concerned with cultural pursuits, and are Liberals. But both differ from the nontraditional, nonchurch-going people of all vertical classes who came to Banbury when the aluminum factory was established. And both have failed to expand their businesses, less from lack of capital than from lack of inclination, preferring, for all their expressed faith in competition, to compete in a controlled way among themselves and refusing to speak to a competitor who lets premises to a firm new to the town. Religious difference remains an undiscussed aspect of political and social life, largely irrelevant to the economic.[59]

This sketch is too brief to do more than lend support to the presumption that, whatever the complex role of religion in economic life prior to 1850, its importance declined over the ensuing century. Lack of space and knowledge precludes a deeper analysis. I claim to have gone far enough into the question, however, to be able to reject the hypothesis that changes in religious belief and practice played a major role in the course of British or French economic development after 1850.

INDIVIDUALISM

Britain and France are both regarded as countries of individualism. And so they are. In Britain, however, individualism refers to property;

[55] Samuelsson, *Religion and Economic Action* (1961), pp. 29, 99, 121, 124, 150. Samuelsson notes Ashton's alternative theory that their exclusion from schools and universities required the Nonconformists to establish their own institutions, which gave them a special capacity.
[56] Erickson, *British Industrialists*, pp. 33, 35, 110.
[57] "Perspective," p. 570.
[58] Williams, *Sociology of an English Village* (1956), p. 180.
[59] Stacey, *Tradition and Change* (1960), pp. 27-8, 30, 41, 168.

in France, to the person.[60] Politically, every Englishman is born liberal
or conservative. France is divided into 43 million Frenchmen. British
individualism leads to the defense of rights, usually property rights,
against the state or other individuals, including the poacher, and their
exercise at whatever social cost, as in the enclosure movement. French
individualism (until a few years ago) required a peasant to build a
high wall around his house within four years of its completion, to
separate himself and his family from outside contact.

Individualism coexists in Britain with "the spirit of association," regarded by the French "as an exotic importation from perfidious Al-
bion." [61] Tocqueville wondered at the mysterious combination in Britain
of the spirit of association and the preservation of individualism.[62] One
aspect of individualism, lack of sociability, was believed by Fouillée to
help the Englishman to associate with others. Coolness prevented meetings from turning into battles, and the Englishman could be contra-
dicted with sang-froid.[63] But a generation of young writers is persuaded
that, whatever the relationship earlier, today the spirit of association,
or conformity, has triumphed over the individualism.[64] There is face-
saving. The individual may get his way and merely appear to conform
— or conform and merely appear to get his way. Real individualism
exists in limited spheres, such as dress, as well as in property rights.
But the pressure to conform is relentless, as Lawrence, Orwell, Amis,
and Martin Green testify.

There is occasional reference to the inability to cooperate in Britain.
British capacity in this regard has been compared unfavorably to the
Danish, on the basis of the inability of an honorable secretary of a
Norfolk rat and sparrow society to get its members on with their
tasks.[65] The difficulties of collaborating for pumping groundwater in
Birmingham have been mentioned, and an official report notes a "riot
of individuality" that inhibits the adoption of standard railway equipment.[66] A description of a village in West Cumberland sounds French
down to the history of organized activities for the youth of the parish,
which "is one of short-lived associations which have failed through lack
of support or the inability of the organizers to discipline the mem-

[60] Miller and Miller, *The Giant of the Western World* (1930), p. 199.
[61] Dunham, *Industrial Revolution in France*, p. 225. The context is French fear
of companies.
[62] *Journeys to England and Ireland*, p. 88. Tocqueville insists that the spirit of
association exists side by side with the spirit of exclusion (pp. 15, 87), the British
organizing into associations of equals, like clubs, which rigorously exclude non-
members.
[63] Fouillée, *Esquisse psychologique*, p. 208.
[64] Birnbaum, " 'Empiricism' and British Politics" (1961).
[65] See Haggard, *Rural Denmark and Its Lessons* (1911).
[66] Ministry of Reconstruction, *Standardization of Railway Equipment* (1918).

bers." [67] But the evidence favors the spirit of association as a British trait, based on a "strong sense of collective entity." [68] And the opposite is true for France.

A clear correlation appears between secrecy and unprogressiveness in British firms.[69] Secrecy characterizes the French.[70] This is based on distrust, fear of getting involved, worries about what "they" will do to the narrowly defined "us." In contrast to the British sense of responsibility, the French have posed *incivisme*,[71] the failure to act as a good citizen, taking care of oneself, maintaining vested interests (*positions acquises*) no matter how petty, despite the public weal. *L'état, ce n'est pas moi*.[72] One observer is concerned with the lack of responsibility of the elite; another, with the need for discipline and respect for law among the vintners in the Midi; a third, with the absence of farsighted individuals and the poisoning of the atmosphere by parish quarrels, which hold back economic development; a fourth finds that cooperation, never high, has declined in rural Avéyron.[73]

This unwillingness to cooperate has been ascribed in southern Italy to low incomes, which afford too little margin to risk in public ventures.[74] This hardly seems the case in France. Edith Wharton qualifies the view that Anglo-Saxons are more generous than the French because they are richer by putting it in terms of confidence in the future: "We are more generous not because we are richer, but because we are so much less afraid of being poor; and if we are less afraid of being poor it is due to the fact that our ancestors found it easier to make money,

---

[67] Williams, *Sociology of an English Village* (1956), p. 61; Bettelheim and Frère, *Auxerre*, p. 247. Associations in Auxerre are numerous, varied but not very important; see also Wylie, *Village in the Vaucluse*, pp. 292ff. The villagers are unable to work together except on matters of great importance, like the cooperative.

[68] Renier, *The English: Are They Human?* p. 230.

[69] Carter and Williams, *Technical Progress* (1957), p. 117. See also the list of characteristics of good firms which puts high up, on a too-long list, quality of incoming information, deliberate survey of potential ideas, willingness to share knowledge, willingness to take new knowledge on license, readiness to look outside the firm (p. 179). See Marshall, *Industry and Trade* (1920), p. 563: insofar as "the Englishman's home is his castle" side of national character "induces a manufacturer or trader to shun associated action, on the grounds that it would enable his associates to penetrate into the secrets of his business, it may be a source of national weakness rather than strength."

[70] See Bigo, *Les Banques françaises*, p. 244, "the passion for the secret"; Pitts, *The Bourgeois Family and French Retardation*, pp. 343, 353, 406; Ehrmann, *Organized Business in France* (1957), p. 208 — "The passion and mania for secrecy corrupt all life. The Frenchman is not a chess player. He chooses games where one hides"; and Lorwin, *French Labor Movement*, p. 217.

[71] Ehrmann, p. 107.

[72] Baum, *The French Economy and the State* (1958), p. 357.

[73] See Sawyer, "Strains in the Social Structure" (1951), p. 303; Augé-Laribé, *Politique agricole*, p. 175; the review by Juillard of Chevalier, *La Vie humaine dans les Pyrenées ariègoises* (1956); Mendras, *Novis et Virgin*, pp. 52, 67.

[74] Banfield, *Moral Basis of a Backward Society* (1958).

not only because they were willing to take risks, but because opportunities came their way."[75] French children have been taught to distrust the group from earliest childhood.[76] The *brouille*, or long-standing quarrel, is an honored institution of the extended family, the village, the profession, and business.

But there is contradiction here, too. Most French historians and many economists believe that tariffs were imposed on wheat to maintain the agricultural sector and thus to preserve social stability.[77] In many industries, firms agree not to compete. "Group solidarity outweighs the competitive urge."[78] A modus vivendi has been worked out between the few powerful firms and the swarm of small units, as well as one between the few modern regions and the more or less backward sectors.[79] Cooperation exists in agriculture, despite the notorious independence of the peasant. Isaac Pereire claimed, "that which France possesses in the highest degree is the spirit of association, a genius for organization."[80] More recently, the French have learned some limits to individual action, according to Pitts, by the increasing difficulty of displaying prowess or hostility in driving an automobile in heavy traffic, and the high negative rewards to civic responsibility in this dangerous sphere.[81]

Conflict between innate hostility and the spirit of the cartel requires a distinction between positive and negative action. The trade association was an instrument of the firm against its enemies — government, customers, foreign suppliers, and upstart competition at home. Intense hostility was against other entrepreneurs who tried to change the rules.[82] And the trade association or cartel functioned without any effective pooling of information or even statistics until the wartime impositions from Vichy.[83]

There is, moreover, a further question of whether the hostility among Frenchmen is real or ritualistic, whether the antagonism has not been kept at the verbal level while groups remain deeply involved with

[75] Wharton, *French Ways*, p. 91.

[76] Wylie, *Village in the Vaucluse*, pp. 199ff. Ehrmann, *Organized Business in France*, p. 40, maintains the "Gallic inclination to be happy over a neighbor's misfortune," as if *Schadenfreude* were a French monopoly.

[77] See, e.g., Sée, *Histoire économique de la France* (1942), p. 366; Jeanneney, *Forces et faiblesses* (1956), p. 65.

[78] Ehrmann, p. 391; also Pitts, p. 347.

[79] Landes, "French Business and Businessmen" (1951), p. 340.

[80] See Cameron, *France and the Economic Development of Europe* (1961), p. 158. The French spirit of association is linked with Saint-Simonism (*ibid.*, p. 114).

[81] The parallel of a hundred years earlier is the timetable which, according to Young (*Portrait of an Age*, 1936, p. 50 note), "did much to discipline the people at large."

[82] Pitts, pp. 485, 488.

[83] Ehrmann, p. 280.

each other in reality.[84] French antagonism has largely been controlled. Physical aggression among children is threatened, not executed. French hostility gave way to violence in the riots of the 1930s and in the immediate postwar response to Vichyism. But feuds were normally kept in check and had their uses: they limited the range of personal involvement, with its costs, and they made life interesting.[85] For symmetry's sake, we may note that Birnbaum believes that the ostensible class harmony in Britain covers secret conflicts, prolonged and bitter, over power, property, and status.[86]

The Family

A major difference in French and British social behavior is found in the organization of the family and the education of the young. The relevance of this difference to the family firm is left to the next chapter; but the social aspects can be dealt with now. In brief overgeneralization, the French have, until recently, operated with the extended family, as contrasted with the British limited conjugal type. Relations between generations went deeper. Children stayed at home longer, seldom going away to school. Peasant farmers reaped the trees planted by their great-grandfathers and planted more for their great-grandchildren, certain in the knowledge that the family farm would remain in family hands. As in traditional societies, respect was shown for ancestors as well as for elders.[87] Migration was virtually unthinkable.

These national differences have been widely remarked upon and need little demonstration. Their economic significance, however, is not completely clear. The extended family system can induce a low rate of saving in societies where the young are committed to care for their parents in old age, so that the latter have no need to save; or it can lead to a very high rate, as in France, where value is placed on family status, large dowries and good marriages for daughters, and secure business prospects for sons. Conversely, the conjugal family in which

[84] See the inconclusive discussion among the experts at the Pitts seminar, "Adieu à la France de Papa?" It is possible that here is an area of change in which the forms of early real hostility have been kept as the content evaporated.

[85] Wylie, pp. 200, 204.

[86] "'Empiricism' and British Politics."

[87] Wylie notes (pp. 282–284) the number of migrants who revisit Péyrane on All Saints Day to pay their respects at the cemetery. Fauvet tells of a miner of the Midi, who was urged to move to the Nord after his pit had been closed but asked whether the cemetery would follow (*La France dechirée*, p. 26). Fourastié and Laleuf (*Révolution à l'ouest*, 1957, p. 66) have detected, however, a decisive rupture in the expulsion of the cemetery from the middle of the village — along with the disappearance of mourning — and date it from about 1935.

the young find their own place in the world, neither depending upon the family fortune nor responsible for parents, may yield a higher rate of saving in the older generation, left to provide its own security, or to capital consumption by the older group, relieved of the necessity to give offspring a running start.

Literate Americans are familiar with the picture of youth in upper-middle-class Victorian England: children left in charge of Nanny except for a half hour at tea, when they saw their parents (or at least Mummy), and put to bed at 7:30, when they were not living with an aunt in England while their parents were in India; prep school at the age of seven, eight, or nine; public school at thirteen. The parents dissociate themselves from the children early. Friends are preferred to relatives. Brothers are not very intimate in British families, nor cousins.[88] There are even indications that man and wife limit their associations. Sport, club, and pub have been masculine institutions, though changes in this are taking place today. Cricket and fishing provide little basis for masculine-feminine companionship.[89] A man's home is *his* castle, a very different concept from the family foyer.[90]

In France the child has always stayed at home. Americans and the British train children for maturity, which means to make their own way. This implies the greatest degree of experience within the range of safety. In France, on the other hand, children are trained to take their place in the world, which means giving them the greatest degree of protection within the range of prudence.[91] Freudian overtones have been detected in the French tendency to keep their children at home. The father fosters artificial incompetence in his sons, as in his company retainers, in order to prolong the parent-child relationship.[92] Or the same phenomenon can be a compulsion: "keeping one's children with one (an absolute necessity to the passionately tender French parent)." [93]

The tensions in the extended family, which make the *brouille* a neces-

[88] Fouillée, *Esquisse psychologique*, p. 210.
[89] See Henriques, "The Miner and His Lass" (1960). This is a summary of family relations in a Yorkshire mining village and parallels a fictional treatment of the same subject in Clancy Sigal's *Weekend in Dimlock* (London, 1960).
[90] Métraux and Mead, *Themes in French Culture* (1954), part 1. See also Wendell, *France Today* (1907), p. 121.
[91] Wendell, *ibid.*, p. 201.
[92] Pitts, *The Bourgeois Family and French Retardation*, pp. 352, 460. Note the further parallel with Gosforth, Williams, *Sociology of an English Village*, where parental authority is strict (p. 42), younger members of farm families accept dependence on parents without overt resentment (p. 43), and there is a long delay in maturity, with lack of responsibility in masculine youth (p. 44). Note also that Gosforth marriages are late (p. 45).
[93] Wharton, *French Ways*, p. 87.

sity, also produce what Pitts calls "the delinquent peer group." [94] The family is usually in charge of "tension management";[95] but when the family is its source, the tension must be managed outside. This is done by "pals" (copains) or the gang. This delinquent peer group is regarded as the forerunner of the trade association or cartel, committed to defend the interest of the insiders against those of the broader community. The playing fields of Eton prepare for business competition. But in France the delinquent peer group makes the firm a refuge from the complications of family and a conspiracy against order and progress.[96]

One more phenomenon related to French family life has had important effects for business. To the delinquent peer group Pitts adds the concept of the "faithful family retainer," the lifelong employee who inhibits technological change (especially of a labor-saving kind), economic rationality, spatial and occupational mobility. Members of the revolutionary parties in France refused to accept the role of the retainer, but there were enough such workers — with a broad and undefined relationship to the patron, aided with garden plots and housing, unwilling to bargain — to affect the total behavior of the plant. Promotion was from within, and hired executives became retainers.[97]

English economic literature has its equivalent of the faithful retainer late in the period being studied here. Earlier the remarkable fact was that family firms were prepared to take in friends on the basis of equality.[98] Twentieth-century observers, however, comment on the nepotism of the family firm, the frustration of able subordinates who are unable to marry into the family, and the necessity for capable working-class boys to accept subordinate routine positions.[99] In this capacity they become conservative;[100] as "department managers who came up the hard way," they resist innovation and the hiring of functional specialists;[101] workmen in steel or in engineering develop hereditary con-

[94] Pitts, chap. xii, esp. p. 338.

[95] Smelser, Social Change in the Industrial Revolution, p. 159.

[96] Note the contrast suggested by Pitts ("French Values," seminar, Center for International Affairs, Harvard University, October 5, 1959) between French life prior to World War II and that in the United States. In France the family is a source of tension from which children seek relaxation in school (and later on as adults, in the firm). In the United States, school and office are sources of tension from which children and adults seek relaxation at home. This is said to account for the widely observed contrast between the domestic manners of French and American children.

[97] Pitts, pp. 353–362, 418.

[98] See Landes, "The Structure of Enterprise" (1960), p. 111, and John, A Liverpool Merchant House (1959), pp. 30, 163.

[99] Florence, Logic of Industry, pp. 295, 324, 333.

[100] Marshall, Industry and Trade, p. 103.

[101] Carter and Williams, Innovation, p. 48. Contrast their statement that the firm has doubt and fear that if Joe, who knows the secret of the firm's process, goes,

nections with particular industries and become immobile.[102] But there is evidence to the contrary as well — an extraordinary adaptability of British craftsmen, especially for the earlier portion of the period.[103]

Family life has been changing in both France and England, and in somewhat different directions. While British middle-class families still regard prep school and public school as vital to the preservation of social class, the disappearance of Nanny has perforce increased the intimacy between generations. In France a similar host of factors has served to alter family life, decreasing the dependence of both wife and children on the man as head of the family, weakening the ties of youth to family.[104] Marriages of inclination substitute for dynastic alliances. The young marry early, choose careers independently of their parents, and so on.

The British delegation of raising the younger generation to paid help began in the nineteenth century, possibly as far as the nursery is concerned, certainly for the boarding schools. Renier claims that the latter had a profound influence on British character, inculcating in the leading class the "ritualistic way of life," with strong emphasis on what is done and not done. With emphasis on external behavior and repression of inner feelings, including the sexual, this ritualism has produced disorders resulting in pruriency and animal worship, according to this author, but compensating virtues of wistful charm and childlike delight in play and hobbies and the "truly remarkable capacity for organizing public life." [105] Renier ties the change in character to the Reform Bill of 1832, to the railroad, which made it possible to develop schools at a distance from home, and to the shadow of Thomas Arnold, which lay over all the schools established or developed after 1840.[106] British character is not ascribable, he insists, to climate, as so many other continentals would have it,[107] or to sport. This is important, if true, and the timing is right. A change in British character starting with the youth of

---

the firm will be helpless, with Pitts's (p. 353), that to change the industrial secrets of the firm, which have been taught to a few, is like withdrawing the sacraments from a communicant.

[102] Burnham and Hoskins, *Iron and Steel in Britain* (1943), p. 270. Burn, "American Engineering Competition" (1931), p. 297.

[103] See Allen, *Birmingham and the Black Country* (1929), p. 409, on the remarkable adaptability shown by certain trades.

[104] See CNRS, *Sociologie comparée* (1955), esp. the contributions by Lefèbvre (pp. 155ff) and Bourdet (pp. 188ff); also "Adieu à la France de Papa?" and Wylie, "Social Change in Rural France." On the second point, Dutourd (*Taxis of the Marne*, 1957) notes that the mother had become the head of the family in 1914 (p. 192).

[105] Renier, *The British: Are They Human?* chap. ix and p. 161.

[106] *Ibid.*, pp. 260–261. It is possible that the Anglican revival also had an influence in promoting the "ritualistic way of life."

[107] See, e.g., Fouillée, *Esquisse psychologique*, p. 198; and Mourre, *Décadence économique de la France*, note, pp. 416–420.

the 1840s could explain the substantial decline in the rate of growth a generation later.

But the old question arises. Is the public school responsible for Anglo-Saxon repression, or vice versa? Roger Thabault notes that the French father is much more deeply concerned than the American (one can read British) with the progress made by his children. This is partly the result of the store placed on intellectual values: the failing child runs the risk of debarment from the joys of paradise. But it is also rooted in the extended family and the nature of the social contract. Thabault states: "American fathers feel themselves less responsible, perhaps, than French fathers for the future of their children because they respect more their individuality and because, belonging to a stronger and richer collectivity, they have more confidence in the future." [108] The organization of the family and the social value system thus merge into one another.

CLASS STRUCTURE

Wide differences separate the class structures of Britain and France. Class hierarchies exist in each and are recognized to exist. In Britain it has been accepted. In France, on the contrary, the hierarchy is never accepted. "Each individual has a consciousness of belonging to a superior class and the firm resolve to maintain that superiority. But he refuses to recognize the superiority of those in higher classes." [109]

There has also been divergence between British and French social mobility. Tocqueville pointed out that the words "gentleman" and "gentilhomme" had very different meanings: the first was any well-educated man; the second, a nobleman by birth.[110] Entrance into the British aristocracy was possible through the royal power to create peers; exit was required by the law of primogeniture which reduced younger sons to the liberal professions or commerce. But the main avenue for upward mobility into the upper middle class was the public schools, open to those with the price.

In France the road to the ranks of the gentry was presumably blocked by the facts of birth. In reality, the vital "de" could be added to one's name by one means or another.[111] The upper middle classes were less accessible. Education was again the highway and the basis of selection,

[108] Thabault, "Les Institutions scolaires aux Etats-Unis" (1955), p. 6.
[109] Laroque, *Les Classes sociales* (1959), p. 111.
[110] Tocqueville, *Journeys to England and Ireland*, p. 67. But see Briffault, *Decline and Fall of the British Empire* (1938), p. 49, who states that a gentleman was originally one of gentle birth, but later anyone with an income of three thousand pounds a year.
[111] See duPuy de Clinchamps, *La Noblesse* (1959), pp. 108–114, on the recruitment of the "false nobility."

for education was intellectual, not financial. Ostensibly more egalitarian, the system in actuality proved more restrictive. The system was "exclusive, classical and rigid, especially at the upper levels, and uses a severe and savage system of examinations which excludes all but a select minority from the benefits of higher and technical education." [112] Children of superior intellectual capacity from lower-class homes did not pursue their studies in accordance with their opportunities because of lack of interest, the desire to work, and the high cost of studies even when free. The wealthy used the free educational system. [113] And the purpose of the educational system in France, as of proper speech and manners taught in British public schools, has been to maintain class distinctions. [114]

For these reasons it has been said that it took at least two or more generations [115] to rise from the lowest to the upper middle class in France, as contrasted with half a lifetime in the United States and a generation in Britain. [116] The statistical basis of these estimates is open to suspicion. But the qualitative difference remains.

The importance of the openness of the class structure has been emphasized by a sociologist attempting to analyze British and French politics by reference to the Parsonian structural/functional system of value-pattern variables. The major variables consist in how a society fills roles (membership), which may be done on the basis of particularist or universalist criteria; how it judges individuals, whether by ascription or achievement; and the nature of interpersonal relations and obligations, which may be diffuse or specific. [117] To this set of pattern variables Lipset has added the (overlapping) distinction between an elitist and an egalitarian society. [118]

The interesting point is that, while English society is found to be based on ascription, elitism, diffuseness, and particularism, the crucial areas of economics and politics are characterized by achievement, elitism, diffuseness, and universalism. Achievement and universalism

---

[112] Padover, *French Institutions* (1954), p. 86.

[113] See Bresard, "Mobilité sociale" (1950); Girard and Bastide, "Selection scolaires" (1955); Padover, p. 87.

[114] Goblot, *La Barrière et le niveau*, p. 128: "The unique function of the baccalaureat is to create a gap difficult to cross and to unite on the level of equality all who cross."

[115] Girard, "Mobilité sociale" (1951), p. 122; Fourastié and Laleuf, *Revolution à l'ouest*, p. 102. But note that Laroque does not believe that social mobility is less in France than in other countries (p. 108). He concedes, however, the existence of social sclerosis, caused by economic sclerosis of the first half of the twentieth century (p. 109), and then states that if there have been negligible social advances, descents have been rare (p. 110).

[116] Goblot, p. 126.

[117] See, e.g., Parsons, *The Social System* (1951), pp. 58–67.

[118] Lipset, "Democracy and the Social System" (1961), p. 5.

have been substituted in judgments and membership for ascription and particularism. A new economic class achieves high position, using methods which have traditionally been defined by the elite as inappropriate for those of high status. In France, on the other hand, the accepted pattern variables are achievement, egalitarianism, specificity, and universalism. They fail to provide substantial economic vigor and democratic stability, however, because these values are not shared sufficiently widely. Industry recruited Catholics of good family, based on personal recommendations, even though the Civil Service stressed formal academic criteria in accord with the value system; and instead of accepting new recruits, the elite insulated itself and reserved for itself privileged positions in government, the military, religion, and education.[119]

This demonstration may attest less to the importance of class than to the possibilities of incongruence between the value system on the one hand and economic performance on the other;[120] or to the possible divergence between professed and actual values; or to the existence of antithetical values not only in different classes but in the same class for different aspects of life.[121] As such it casts doubt on the major thesis being tested in this chapter, that economic capacity for growth is determined in a narrowly causal sense by social forces.

But however closely the social systems of France and Britain are linked to economic performance, it is interesting and important to note that these systems are in the process of change. In Britain there has been more interest in equality; in France, less. With the increase in equality comes perhaps more opportunity for upward social mobility, but less concern for it; with less leveling within the classes in France, there may be some reduction of the barriers between them. "Fair

[119] *Ibid.*, pp. 15, 25, 31, 52.

[120] *Ibid.*, pp. 88, 92. For reliance on the hypothesis of necessary congruence, see Harry Eckstein, *A Theory of Stable Democracy* (1961). Eckstein finds stable democracy incompatible with Catholicism, which needs more authoritarianism in government and less "principle," and ascribes the longevity of the Third Republic to a series of accidental circumstances (p. 34). He also believes that stable democracy is incompatible with an individualistic society in which associational life is not intense, and finds the instability of the Fourth and Fifth Republics in the combination of unmitigated democracy and weak association (p. 37).

[121] See, e.g., the sociological theories about France of Michel Crozier, who believes that the French love for equality is accompanied by the partly polar, partly parallel fear of face-to-face contacts, which give rise to insupportable tensions. This fear of confrontation, Crozier believes, has given rise to much of the centralization of authority and the reliance on objective standards for selection and promotion. Personal competition is abhorred, along with personal conflict and such confrontations as that between employer and unions; and decisions are either postponed, pushed up to a higher authority, or rendered impersonal in some such manner as objective examinations. See Crozier, "La France, terre de commandement" (1957), " Le Citoyen" (1961).

shares," the slogan of equality, limits the incentive to produce. In wartime this is provided by patriotism. But fair shares carried into peacetime restricts inputs of labor and personal savings.

The equalization of incomes in Britain is a symptom of interclass harmony, but there is doubt whether it has in turn contributed to it. It may even have disturbed the former British readiness to accept the hierarchical structure. In a series of lectures at the School of Industrial Management at Massachusets Institute of Technology in 1960, S. C. Leslie reported that British labor was currently less interested in increasing its pay than in narrowing the differences in privileges between it and management: hours of work, holidays, amenities, dismissal procedures, and so on. Equality within labor has not increased; the maintenance of traditional differentials remains a goal of the separate unions (and not wholly a device for inching up the general scale). As income equalization between classes has proceeded, however, the sense of social injustice has increased, and workers resent more deeply the social distances which persist.

In France, on the contrary, the fierce interest in equality has been lessened. In the French bureaucracy morale is low in bureaus with merely routine work, despite the opportunity thus afforded to avoid face-to-face contacts, to cultivate the aristocratic value of independence or petty-bourgeois safety.[122] But where uncertainty, crises, changing practical problems emerged, say, among the inspectors of finance, the prefects, or even maintenance engineers in the tobacco monopoly (who repaired breakdowns), morale is high. Bureaucracy illustrates the French overt insistence on equality, with promotion based on competitive examination from outside and significant decisions being passed to the top. But the satisfaction which equality and evasion once provided is ebbing, and prestige attaches increasingly to performance.

Social Cohesion

The picture that can be drawn from this series of disjointed sketches is one of two socially dissimilar countries moving in opposite directions — France quite rapidly and with a discontinuous change in World War II; Britain with its traditional Fabianism. In France the individual has been intellectual, verbal, professional, Catholic, hostile to all groups and families save his own, except when bound with delinquent peers in escape from the tensions of his environment. A rigid class structure has not been accepted, as members of each class try to gain a wider basis of equality. Increasingly, however, the hold of the family on the individual, and especially the young, has lightened; concern for status has

[122] Crozier, "French Bureaucracy" (1960).

given way to interest in performance, and so on. In Britain the contrary is broadly true. It would be tiresome to recapitulate details. But the most important change may be the weakening of the acceptance of the class system and of trust in the disinterestedness of others, including especially the amateur leaders, politicians, and businessmen.

The significance of these changing social forces for economic development must be faced. Part of this task waits until the next chapter, when I look at the family firm. Here it is appropriate to address the question of the impact on growth of French social disintegration and British cohesion, as they existed in the nineteenth century and in subsequent transmogrifications.

It is a familiar theme that French economic growth has been held back by social disharmony. To many writers there have been two Frances warring with one another — one aristocratic, one petty bourgeois; or two capitalisms; or three Frances; or the countryside against Paris;[123] or one class against another, raising wages, prices, and (the peasants) the cost of living in turn, and holding back development by price-wage inflation;[124] or merely warring tribes of bankers.[125] Class antagonism has been continuous, with even individuals persistently discontented.[126] Or the matter may be put more generally. The French

[123] See, e.g., Landes, "French Business and Businessmen," p. 336; Perroux, "Croissance de l'économie française" (1955) pp. 59–60; Sawyer, "Strains in the Social Structure of Modern France" (1951), p. 3. (The three conflicting Frances: traditional, bourgeois, and industrial.) In "France's New Horizons" (1959), Sawyer makes less of the conflicts and suggests that economic life was stabilized within a familiar pattern, except for the "new men" of the 1850s, who came to terms with the bourgeois establishment in the 1860s (pp. 163–164); Gravier, *Paris et 'le désert français* (1958), *passim*.

[124] See, e.g., Aujac, "Inflation as a Consequence of Social Groups" (1950).

[125] See Lefèvre, *Politique intérieure du Second Empire* (ca. 1953), p. 56: "The history of the Empire is illustrated for a good part by the struggles of rival financiers." The most famous quarrels are those between the Bank of France and the Pereires, between the house of Rothschild and the Pereires, and those of all the merchant and deposit banks against the Catholic banker Bontoux. A modern example is that the Banque Lazard was *brouillé*, both with the Bank of France and with Octave Homberg (Moreau, *Souvenirs*, 1954, pp. 13, 181). Much of the literature describes the origins and consequences of these feuds, and whether they were based on personalities (as Cameron claims for the Rothschild-Pereire, *France and the Economic Development of Europe*, p. 136) or because Pereire persuaded Louis Napoleon to break the Rothschild monopoly of *rente* issuance and move to competitive bidding (Lefèvre, p. 51). Similarly, Cameron traces the feud between the Pereires and the Bank of France back to 1830 (p. 117), in place of the more usual explanation related to the Pereires' acquisition of the Bank of Savoy and their desire to retain the note-issue privilege in the face of the Bank of France's pursuit of a monopoly (Lévy, *Histoire économique de la France*, 1951–52, p. 121).

[126] This is a recurrent theme: Clapham quotes d'Avenel who wrote in 1896 that the French people were never happier and never believed themselves more to be pitied. Their grievances grow with comfort (Clapham, *Development of France and Germany*, 1955, p. 406). Baum cites Raymond Aron that the low level of

have been unable to undertake the organization of large affairs that require cooperative work — as contrasted with hierarchical ones, such as the army[127] — because of a basic inability to cooperate.

The narrower explanations are better than the broader one when it is remembered that French economic growth was rapid in a number of periods. Growth could have gone on but broke down because of quarrels or incapacity to adapt institutions to new needs emerging over time. But a general incapacity to associate cooperatively or a general hostility to others is difficult to accept as an explanation of the particular periods of French slowdown, given the rapid periods of growth between. Perhaps best of all the pattern fits the 1930s, when the social cement seemed to dissolve. At other times the underlying decision to agree enabled the warring groups to tolerate the strong men who alternated politically with the periods of parliamentary stalemate: Louis Napoleon, Doumergue, Clemenceau, Poincaré. In the 1930s neither Laval nor Blum at the extremes and not Herriot or any other middle-of-the-road personality could achieve a consensus. Much of the present view of the French national character as essentially hostile goes back, in my judgment, to the experience of that decade. Differences over Dreyfus at the end of the nineteenth century or Catholic education or Algeria could readily coexist with economic growth. They were interesting, important, but did not structurally damage the need for making a living or the benefits from doing so efficiently. The analysis, then, fits the 1930s, but its relevance to the period from 1882 to 1896 seems doubtful.

A basic change seems to have occurred in France after its defeat by Germany in 1940.[128] We have seen its effect on the birth rate and on the family. Other aspects have been felt in the rate of technological change, examined below, in the expanded role of government, and so on. Essentially, this change was agreement — nationally — that economic backwardness was intolerable and that, whatever differences might divide France on other issues, economic progress must be made. Lalumière attributes the change to the Inspection des Finances, which discovered Keynes around 1942.[129] One can, however, find it elsewhere,

income of much of the French population would be more tolerable were it not for the universal suspicion that the system as a whole is unjust (*French Economy and the State*, 1958, p. 353).

[127] *Ibid.*, p. 232. Clapham does not accept the view that the French cannot organize large-scale enterprises.

[128] Some economic changes seem to go back to the German occupation. But Duroselle insists that it was defeat in 1940 which established a degree of French community, not the divisive German occupation (see "Changes in French Foreign Policy since 1945," 1963, p. 325).

[129] See Lalumière, *L'Inspection des Finances* (1959), pp. 179ff. The author recognizes how empirical the Inspection has been (pp. 185, 196, 198).

as among the geographers.[130] This was not general social cohesion: on religious education, Algeria, the atomic bomb, relations with the USSR, and so on, the French remained divided, at least for a time. The change in attitude, moreover, was not the sole cause; with growth came further changes. As population pressures increased, transport improved; the world of jets extended horizons beyond the corners of a French *pays*. Contributing also were some prewar changes, such as the family allowances.

One fundamental change occurred: while on other issues the French might operate intellectually, verbally, and theoretically, in economic reconstruction and growth there was a turn to empiricism, which made the British recovery efforts seem doctrinaire. There was talk of planning, but this noun was quickly modified by the addition of the adjective "flexible" (*souple*), which converts it into empiricism. If national character can change over night, and in particular respects, how far can it be used to explain historical events?

Basic British themes are two: one that empiricism brilliantly fitted the world before 1875 — a world of emerging mechanical invention — but was ineffective under subsequent conditions when chemicals, electricity, and, more recently, automation called for rigorous scientific professionalism. The other theme is that British growth to 1875 depended on the docility of workers, the capacity of business leaders to associate, and the problem-solving propensity of politicians. When all three ebbed, the brilliance of the British economic performance declined.

The amateur-professional explanation, though relevant, seems inadequate. Mass production was an empirical discovery from Eli Whitney to Henry Ford, not a scientific one — and, apart from cotton yarn, the British passed it by. The practical character of technological training was recognized and acted upon only slowly, and recognized faster than acted upon. British empiricism and practicality dried up, to a degree, rather than remaining constant despite a changing requirement.

The other hypothesis, that economic slowdown is the result of ebbing social cohesion, is equally difficult to credit. In Britain, social harmony reigns on most questions, despite the increasing irritation over social distances. The nuclear-disarmament group in the Labour Party and the jingoists in the Conservative, along with the angry young men on the one hand and the Edwardians on the other, cannot disguise the basic identity of point of view in the center. Party consensus has become more difficult to obtain than before, leaving more room for extreme views. But the differences even over Suez did not go deep; nor do they

---

[130] See their reports published in 1945 by the Ministère de l'Économie Nationale under the title *Rapports et travaux sur le décongestion des centres industriels.*

over the joining of the Common Market, which all factions regard as a question wherein there is much to be said on both sides.

What fits the British case better than modern social theory is the ancient formula of three generations from shirtsleeves to shirtsleeves. The society found a good set of practices and kept on applying them, without having institutionalized those habits of innovation, saving, and technical receptivity which build change into the system. And three generations rather than a change in national character provide the explanation why the empiricism that used to govern British thought and action has given way to doctrine on such questions as nationalization, government controls, and full employment.

There can be no doubt that differences in national character are real and have a significance for many aspects of life. Whether they shape the course of economic development, after the earliest beginnings and the break away from traditional society, is more doubtful. Claims are readily made and are disproved with difficulty. Few propositions are testable in ways that satisfy the statistician, and most can be turned inside out or found to be riddled with paradoxical exceptions. A sufficient case that individual psyches, family structure, or class behavior determines the rate of French and British economic development is hard to find in the evidence from the last hundred years.

CHAPTER 6

ENTREPRENEURSHIP

It is but a short step from national character to the role of entrepreneurship, and the extended if inconclusive discussion of the previous chapter can allow me to be brief here. This is especially so since two major aspects of the entrepreneurial function — technological change and readiness to compete — are dealt with in succeeding chapters.

The view that entrepreneurial behavior shapes economic growth goes back to Schumpeter or even to Cantillion. The idea is that in an environment established by factor endowments, with given tastes and incomes, differences in entrepreneurial vigor can yield strikingly variant results in economic activity. Entrepreneurship is especially critical when changes occur in the system, either on the supply side — through discovery, population growth, capital accumulation, or cost reduction, particularly in transport — or on the demand side — through the widening of the market or changes in taste. These changes require entrepreneurial responses.

A historical school has grown up to investigate this hypothesis, with a publication, *Explorations in Entrepreneurial History*; a locus, the Harvard Busines School; and, in a loose way, a thesis, that the differences between the economic growth of various countries, including Britain and France, can be explained by differences in the behavior of their national prototypical entrepreneurs. The outstanding member of this school which favors the entrepreneur-conditioned economic growth in France is David S. Landes. Considerable investigation has been made of the British entrepreneur in the Industrial Revolution; but he has received far less attention for the period of our interest, 1851–1950.

There are several difficulties with the model. First, there is the familiar question of timing. Two countries may differ in the total rate of growth because of national differences in entrepreneurial behavior; or a rate of growth may decline because of evolution in the national businessman's traits. It is conceivable, further, that with vigorous entrepreneurship a country will recover faster from depression, and maintain prosperity longer, than will another country with less business élan.

But when cycles or trends are roughly parallel in two countries, and periods of growth alternate with periods of stagnation, it is hard to ascribe differences in average growth rates to differences in entrepreneurial behavior without exploring more deeply into cycles or trends themselves.

The second question is also related to averages. Is there such a thing as an average businessman when a country that is not highly homogeneous can adduce varying prototypes for large business, medium business, and small business, for one industry and another, and for regions and even particular cities? Is the Welsh tinmaster representative of the British businessman, or Lord Nuffield of Morris Motors, or Lord Leverhulme of Unilever?

Third, and of major importance, it is evidently wrong to compare entrepreneurial behavior between countries without equalizing the conditions in which they operate; and this is impossible. The stimulus from the demand side may be much stronger in one case than in another and may produce a more substantial reaction from businessmen in one country who are in essence no different from those in the other. Or, to refer to the 1850s and 1860s when both countries were growing at satisfactory rates, the British businessman may differ in temperament and behavior from his French counterpart, but all the effects on economic growth may be offset by differences in an opposing direction between, say, the passive British government and the dynamic French. Differentiated entrepreneurial behavior is thus neither sufficient nor necessary to explain differences in growth patterns, and it may exist without affecting growth because of countervailing forces.

Fourth, the entrepreneurial function is many-sided and not merely innovational, as Schumpeter stressed. How effectively do firms in a given country not only innovate, but also recruit and train labor, accumulate capital, reduce costs within a given technology, market their wares, undertake expansion through market competition, and so on? Wide differences in entrepreneurial behavior may lead by different paths to the same result: a family firm, fearful of losing capital, and a bureaucratic firm, in which the hired managers are fearful of criticism by stockholders, may behave identically; or one firm weak at marketing may help growth no better than another weak at production.

Despite these ambiguities about the relevance of the question, it is necessary to examine several theses put forward about British and French entrepreneurship, including especially Landes' belief that the family firm held back growth in France and the view that, in Britain, the change from the family to the private company after 1875 had some connection with the loss of economic vitality in this period.

THE FRENCH FAMILY FIRM

The Landes thesis is set forth in two well-known articles and in his reply to Alexander Gerschenkron in *Explorations in Entrepreneurial History*. Two other articles by John E. Sawyer, and his reply to Gerschenkron, also occupy an important place in the literature. The sociological underpinning is the work of Talcott Parsons, and the special research on France of his student, Jesse Pitts.[1]

The theory is partly concerned with the role of entrepreneurs in society and partly with their behavior in that role. Sawyer in particular emphasizes the former; Landes, the latter. Pitts specifies that the dominance of aristocratic values, and especially that of "prowess," has left entrepreneurs with little social approval, but at the same time he elaborates the various ways in which the attempt to maintain a bourgeois dynasty produces uneconomic, or nonmaximizing, behavior in the family firm.

The family firm is said to have sinned against economic efficiency, and hence against growth, by limiting expansion — failing both to extend into new markets when finance was available from internal funds and to seek outside funds when these were required for expansion. Mergers were shunned so as not to get involved with "others." Public sale of stock was avoided.[2] When expansion was possible through inside funds, it frequently took the form of purchase of discrete units of limited size, with their markets, to provide an outlet for the energies of other scions of the family; or there would be vertical integration but without the cost accounting that might enable effective control of the various units.[3] Recruiting was undertaken from within the family, except for faithful retainers who assisted the firm against the revolutionary working force.

[1] Landes, "French Entrepreneurship" (1949), "French Business and Businessmen" (1951), and "Comment" (1954), answering Gerschenkron, "Social Attitudes" (1953). Sawyer, "The Entrepreneur and the Social Order" (1952); "Strains in Modern France" (1951), and "Defense" (1954). Parsons and Shils, eds., *Toward a General Theory of Action* (1954); Parsons, *The Social System* (1951); Parsons and Smelser, *Economy and Society* (1956). Pitts, "The Bourgeois Family and Economic Retardation" (1957).

[2] Lambert Dansette, *Quelques familles du patronat textile* (1954), p. 415, quotes the Lille industrialist, Scrive, who would not issue securities: "We do not wish to throw among dogs a name which already counts honorably among industrialists." But most observers regard the reluctance to convert family to public companies as the result of unwillingness to share authority rather than of aristocratic disdain. See, e.g., Pitts, p. 407, who adds that selling capital rights in a family firm is a confession of weakness.

[3] *Ibid.*, pp. 426, 431, 417, 423. For data from the textile industry, showing large firms but small plants, see below, Chapter 8.

Bankruptcy was regarded as a hereditary stain on a family's reputation, to be avoided at all costs.[4] Fraud could be forgiven, but not poverty.[5] The firm not only plowed back a large portion of profits in savings, but also remained liquid against possible emergency. Large-scale industry, where it existed, conspired with small industry to limit output and keep up prices. The firm is characterized in other respects by secrecy, suspicion, and fear of banks, government, and the consuming public. In these circumstances, industry expands slowly, investment is limited, innovation exiguous — all to the detriment of economic development.

The thesis is not without its logical difficulties. There will be occasions, as in speculation, when the aristocratic value of prowess clashes with perpetuation of the bourgeois dynasty. Moreover, the aristocratic way of life requires income. Pitts notes that when an aristocratic family loses its money by some misfortune, it abandons elegant consumption for a few years and buckles down in the shortest possible order to restore its fortunes. With sufficient mobility into the top class, the aristocratic value system could constitute a tremendous spur to the amassing of fortunes.

Similarly, dynastic fortunes must be established before they can be preserved by prudent tactics. The first rule of the bourgeois standard is that the wife shall not work; the second, that the education of the children shall be prolonged. The main motive in early capitalism is to divorce the wife from work and the man from manual labor.[6] There would thus seem to be room for attempts at income maximization and risk taking on the part of artisans and shopkeepers, who require manual labor or working wives in order to rise from the petty bourgeoisie to the middle class.

There is in fact considerable confusion in the discussion of the family firm as between the higher bourgeois family and the petty. Landes de-

---

[4] Landes, "French Business and Businessmen," p. 336. Note that Gerschenkron is interested in the social stigma attaching to bankruptcy (as also in the family farm and its effect on labor mobility — see below, Chapter 11). He makes a distinction between the settled and the migratory society. "In the former, bankruptcy is apt to end a businessman's career . . . In an immigration milieu, failure does not block the road to subsequent success" ("Soviet Novels," 1960, p. 171). His contrast is between tsarist Russia (and France) and the United States. It is not clear whether it would apply to an emigratory society such as Britain. But observe the "vital part" of the small capitalist in the development of the coal industry in South Wales, some of whom, bankrupt in one attempt, would return to try again (Morris and Williams, The South Wales Coal Industry, 1958, p. 141).

[5] Pitts, p. 101. But Pitts elsewhere cites that firms indulge in the aristocratic value of speculating in inventories (pp. 410–411), though this may risk bankruptcy.

[6] Goblot, La Barrière et le niveau (1925), pp. 34–35. Pitts, p. 385.

fends the family-firm thesis against Gerschenkron by statistics on the number of artisans and proprietors of small shops, which are relevant only to the static quality of the petty bourgeoisie. It is necessary to demonstrate not only why family firms acted the way they did, but also why more artisans and traders did not seek to push their way into the ranks of substantial family concerns.

Landes and Pitts in fact require certain theses: one, that bourgeois dynasties tried to preserve themselves and, two, that the chances of a bourgeois dynasty's graduating into the aristocracy, or an unknown's establishing a new bourgeois dynasty, were limited. If to this were added the insistence on independence and avoidance of salaried labor, which induced persons leaving the farm to go into independent ateliers or small shops, despite the lower rates of return there, the explanation of the slow rate of growth in France would be complete, apart from timing. If opportunities opened up by the railroads in the period from 1850 to 1870, by the new industries of electricity, chemicals, and automobiles in the late 1890s, and by the rebuilding of the devastated north and east in the 1920s are seen as pulling either family firms into expansion or small artisans into the vigorous drive needed to create a family enterprise, even the timing becomes accounted for.

There is substantial evidence in support of the Landes-Pitts thesis, as thus reformulated, but also evidence that fails to fit. In support we have the well-documented account of the textile industry, accounts of the mechanical industry in 1914, a limited amount of evidence from the automotive industry and from coal and steel. Casting doubt on the theory is the evidence of mergers in particular industries, as well as the disparate behavior of firms of the same size in the same industry and the parallel behavior of large-scale industry and small. A case can be made, further, that French firms acted rationally in, say, staying liquid, in a world where price changes could be sudden and sharp and where bankruptcy, however disesteemed, had been frequent.

In the Pitts model the firm is an extension of the family, the equivalent of a trust fund, whose function it is to perpetuate the family. But there is evidence that the family lived for the firm. Fohlen states that the family existed only as an extension of the enterprise and notes that when the wife of a textile magnate came to the office, he would take notice of her only to the extent of observing whether the material of her dress had been produced in his factory.[7] Bigo quotes Courcelle-

[7] Fohlen, *L'Industrie textile* (1956), pp. 84, 89. There is of course much evidence on the other side. Henri Coisne-Beghin, a Lille cotton manufacturer, writing in his journal of pleasures, said: "It is not like that that one makes a family." Lambert Dansette, *Quelques familles du patronat textile*, p. 354.

Seneuil: "Men are common, capital is rare. Man is the accessory of capital." Brogan at a later time states: "The rich were readier to sacrifice their sons than their savings for France." [8]

But in other respects the textile industry conformed to the Landes-Pitts picture, especially in the Lille-Tourcoing-Roubaix area and in Alsace. Dependence on banks was avoided.[9] Profits were plowed back and only small salaries were paid to the owners.[10] Protection was demanded from the state at home and for markets in the colonies.[11] Bankruptcies were said to be infrequent. Investment was cautious; firms cooperated to maintain prices, joined in hostility to the state and its demands for information, to unions, and to the higher ranks of outside employees.[12]

But this picture is perhaps insufficiently subtle. Textile dynasties were by no means stable — especially in flax, which prospered during the cotton famine and largely collapsed afterward.[13] Moreover, the size of cotton-spinning firms changed in the second half of the nineteenth century and numbers declined, as the capital required rose beyond the capacities of family financing.[14] It is not true to say that firms in the Lille-Tourcoing-Roubaix area go back to the Napoleonic era, as Beau de Loménie believed, or that established firms set up a single line of

[8] Bigo, Les Banques françaises (1947), p. 45. Brogan, France under the Republic (1940), p. 677.

[9] See Lambert Dansette, p. 415, on Lille-Armentières, as contrasted with Alsace. See also the instructive history of Méquillet-Noblot, recounted by Fohlen, Une Affaire de famille (1955). In its long history the firm got into serious difficulties in one of the few times it borrowed because the lender failed in the crisis of 1847 and the liquidator demanded repayment in the crisis (pp. 65–66). On another occasion the firm contemplated borrowing 100,000 francs out of a 200,000 franc modernization program in the late 1850s, but could obtain only a two-year credit amortized one eighth every three months. It forewent borrowing, stretched out the program, and finished it during the cotton famine.

[10] Capronnier, La Crise de l'industrie cotonnière (1959), p. 175; Fohlen, Une Affaire de famille, p. 20; Lambert Dansette, p. 583. The latter notes one concern where two associates drew 5 percent interest on their investment and above that no more than 3,000 francs each up to 1867, then 5,000 francs, and after 1893, 12,000 francs. On p. 626 he records that Scrive netted 113,856 francs in 1887–88, of which his family budget records expenditures of 21,832, including one item of 41 francs for what must have been a magnificent dessert.

[11] Lambert Dansette, p. 482. Capronnier, p. 41. Dunham, The Anglo-French Treaty, p. 126, notes that the 1,400 manufacturers protesting the treaty were mostly in cotton textiles. Rouen of course suffered more from British competition than Alsace, and it is noteworthy that Dollfuss in Alsace and Motte in Lille were free-traders.

[12] Capronnier, pp. 176, 178.

[13] See Lambert Dansette, p. 143n. Of the 164 firms established in flax spinning in the greater Lille area prior to that time, 36 were left in 1887. Of 105 firms in Lille itself, only 2 continued under the original organization. Others failed, shifted into cotton, merged. Between 1859 and 1869, 16 cotton mills were in liquidation (p. 499).

[14] See note 107, Chapter 3, above.

activity and clung to it.[15] The commercial spirit was not wholly missing;[16] mechanization took place,[16a] whether because of competition, as Morazé held, or because of the instinct of workmanship, as in the Lambert Dansette view. Finally, and most damaging of all, a few bourgeois retired at forty, bought chateaux and securities in other lines, and lived the lives of large landowners.[17] This sort of conduct was expected of the Normands, who loved exterior signs of wealth more than their work — to the evident displeasure of the historians of the textile industry.[18] But this was also the group that bore the brunt of British competition in gray goods.

It is possible from this evidence to construct a theory that the family firms were relatively or sufficiently effective in risk bearing at the start, ready to mechanize, if only slowly and without borrowed capital, and to expand their operations. Later, however, when the growth of the textile industry had reached its zenith in 1898–1913, the original Rouen industrialists got out — buying land and *rentes* in petty-bourgeois fashion; whereas the Flemish responded to the change in environment by maintaining liquidity, avoiding innovation, and so on. No new names appear in the industry for fifty years because demand was comparatively static, not because of the sociopsychological character of the family firm.

Evidence on the inertia and excessive prudence of the mechanical industry comes from the report of the Minister of Commerce study group of 1919, which tries to assess responsibility for the relative backwardness of the French in machinery as among too low tariffs, high prices of raw materials due to lack of coal, and inadequate entrepreneurship. The last is stressed as the most profound of the three causes. Here there was no question of demand limitations, since imports rose from 60 million francs to 297 million between 1895 and 1913, and exports only from 40 million francs to 102 million. The report insists that the leaders of the engineering industry were fearful of government or banking assistance, timid about the future, unwilling to expand, and hesitant

[15] Note that while perhaps half of the great names in Lille-Armentières were local families, many bourgeois had immigrated (*ibid.*, p. 83). Moreover, the entrepreneurs had a taste for risks, as suggested by the "rush" to spinning linen in 1862 (p. 536). Fortunes were made, but needed effort and audacity. (See also p. 366.) Lambert Dansette also says that one has to look hard to find a family which stuck to one fiber (pp. 578–579).

[16] See Chapter 5, note 38 above, and Fohlen, *Une Affaire de famille, passim,* which describes how the company gradually conquered the national market and specialized narrowly.

[16a] The modal number of spindles per firm was 5–10,000 in 1849, 10–20,000 in 1859, and 30–50,000 in 1899 (Lambert Dansette, p. 186).

[17] Lambert Dansette, pp. 532, 551, 628–635.

[18] *Ibid.*, pp. 520–521, 581; Fohlen, *L'Industrie textile*, p. 80, and on Laval, p. 169; Capronnier, pp. 44, 173.

about taking on new lines, and specializing on old, or even renewing
their equipment and revising their procedures. There was no awareness of what was going on abroad. The few successes were limited to
technical achievement and to perfection at whatever cost in the luxury
field.[19]

There is no faulting the technological record of the steel and automobile firms, where large families like de Wendel, Schneider, Renault, Citroën, and Peugeot stand out. Bauchet finds an important
weakness in automobiles in the financial policy which consisted in making only limited appeals to banks, whether because of the individualist
spirit of the firms or the repugnance of the banks for long-term loans.
The Peugeot story in particular indicates how a family business can
break up, split off, multiply, and diversify, although its historian is
exasperatingly discrete on finances and how the firm weathered the depression.[20]

In his attack on the theory of the family firm as responsible for
French economic growth at slower rates than German growth, Gerschenkron insists that the theory is forced to "overlook vast and significant fields of French entrepreneurial endeavor, such as railroads,
mines, iron and steel industry, automobile production, banks and department stores." [21] Gille puts his apparent opposition into positive
form, studying the origins of large-scale capitalist enterprise in France
in the eighteenth century for metallurgy and the first half of the nineteenth for the others.[22] Gille's thesis is that the evolution of banking
and the capital market were principally called for by the formation of
large-scale capitalist firms,[23] but he takes occasion to insist that the textile industry was essentially a family industry, that textiles were different from other industries, and that in other industries there were
sales of securities to the public, bank loans, mergers, and concentration — all the paraphernalia of the public company as contrasted with
the family concern.[24] Gille, moreover, is particularly interesting on the

[19] Ministère du Commerce, *Rapport générale*, I, 308–309, 312, 379, 455–458.
[20] Bauchet, "La Structure d'une branche d'industrie" (1952), p. 394. Sédillot,
Peugeot (1960), esp. pp. 84–95, 110. The Peugeot company did resist a British
offer to purchase it (p. 92). There was a separate firm for bicycles, and Japy in
typewriters were inlaws. But the impressive characteristic of the firm has been its
capacity to abandon dying industrial lines: cages for crinoline skirts, springs for
pince-nez, umbrella frames, corset ribs, phonograph springs (p. 115). "The
secret is adaptation" (p. 166).
[21] Gerschenkron, "Social Attitudes," p. 10.
[22] Gille, *La Grande industrie métallurgique* (1948?) and *Formation de la grande
entreprise* (1959).
[23] *Formation*, p. 8.
[24] *Ibid.*, pp. 69, 90, 93. Cf. Gignoux, *Une Entreprise française* (1955), who presents a picture of Pechiney, a pioneer in the chemical industry, as a model of the
careful, detail-minded entrepreneur who defended positions attained against
foreign innovators and preferred to improve existing processes rather than to de-

failures of large-scale integrated firms in textiles. Rich Parisian industrialists "frequently" tried to enter the linen business on an integrated
basis, spinning and weaving, in contrast to the normal specialized pattern of Amiens (and of Armentières). These firms "led difficult lives,"
with frequent crises in the market for raw materials, and had to be
liquidated.[25]

The fact is that the existence of textile firms with large inventories
was precarious, particularly those which were in the banks for support.
The crisis of 1848 shook out many cotton firms, especially in weaving.
The sharp credit crisis of 1867 in turn was hard on the newly established linen firms, particularly those in Roubaix-Tourcoing, which were
affected by two bank failures.[26] With wide fluctuations for raw-material
prices, a firm survived by staying liquid and plowing back extra-normal
profits. Hesitation about innovation, high rates of savings, and the maintenance of liquidity may have been manifestations less of the psychic
pattern of French entrepreneurs than of the conditions of Darwinian
survival.

This is, in fact, the Habakkuk view: that the character of the enterprise was primarily a product of the economic environment rather than
the reverse. This writer observes that foreign firms in France behave
much as French firms do, and large firms with professional management behave the same as family concerns. Both he and Hobsbawm
view the family firm not at all as a unique feature of the French economic scene, but as the common agent of nineteenth-century capitalism throughout Europe, especially Britain and Germany.[27] Habakkuk
goes further and states that the family firm in Britain was in fact not
only compatible with rapid progress but also its main agent — a view
to which, as we shall shortly see, objection has been taken.

Supporting Gille and Gerschenkron is some limited evidence on
mergers, which suggests that reluctance to share control with outsiders,
and the desire to preserve a family trust fund intact and under sole
control for future generations, is not proof against hard economic

velop new ones. The differences may be more by industry than by region. Labasse
(*Les Capitaux et la région*, 1955, p. 465) quotes a Maxime Perrine in a book,
Saint-Étienne et sa région économique (1937), to the effect that as of 1937 the
capital of only the ribbon industry and basic metallurgy (Schneider at Creusot?)
remained in the hands of the directing families, while the mines, electrical industry, and the finishing stages of the metallurgical industry were financed by
outsiders. Labasse adds that this generalization is debatable in 1955 and may
have been even in 1937.

[25] *Formation de la grande entreprise*, p. 92.

[26] Lambert Dansette, *Quelques familles du patronat textile*, p. 279, observes a
60 to 70 percent reduction of firms, including several notable families, especially
in weaving and especially in Armentières. See also p. 420.

[27] Habakkuk, "The Basic Conditions of Economic Progress" (1955), p. 159.
Hobsbawm, review of *Modern France*, in *Economic History* (1951).

fact. French economic literature is full of merger and concentration movements. One occurred in coal and metallurgy in the 1840s. The concentration of glass companies took place in the Second Empire, as well as gas companies, chemicals, breweries, and transport.[28] The number of breweries, flour-milling companies, and even textile mills in Alsace declined substantially from 1850 to 1914.[29] The same was true for sugar refineries in the North.[30] By 1914, and even as early as 1892, the process of industrial concentration was already far advanced.[31] Among the four biggest changes between 1913 and 1938 in the French economy was the process of industrial concentration.[32] Industrial concentration in France has been notable since 1946, but the number of mergers is only slightly higher than in 1929.[33]

There is also the regional evidence, cited above in this chapter and in that on capital formation. In textiles there are substantial differences in the temperament, character, and behavior of entrepreneurs from one area to another — between Alsace and the Nord, between both of these and Normandy and Laval, and among the entrepreneurs, as seen by the bankers of Lyon, Grenoble, Roanne, St. Étienne, and, of late, Annecy.[34] This evidence tends to support Landes and Pitts against Habakkuk, that entrepreneurial attitudes are more important than environmental factors, though Habakkuk might argue that subtle and critical differences existed among regional environments. But it also works against Landes and Pitts, especially the latter, insofar as it suggests that any general sociological explanation based upon generalizations about French family life and education must make room for plentiful exceptions. It is striking in the face of generalizations about family dynasties and faithful retainers to read that businessmen re-

[28] Gille, *Formation de la grande entreprise*, pp. 62, 65.
[29] Juillard, *Basse-Alsace* (1953), p. 293, gives figures for the rapid reduction in the number of firms in brewing (317 in 1872, 71 in 1902, 42 in 1914, 25 [of which 9 were large] in 1950). In flour milling the numbers decrease from 265 in 1895 to 80 in 1949, of which a few were large, many small (p. 292). Lévy, *Histoire de l'industrie cotonnière en Alsace* (1912), p. 166, gives the number of firms as declining from 40 in 1939, although he says that the largest decline from 1861 occurred after the evacuation of a number of firms to French territory when Alsace was German.
[30] See Gendarme, *La Région du Nord* (1954), p. 208, for a table showing the fairly rapid concentration of sugar refineries from 280 in 1870 to 19 in 1922. This was doubtless a reflection of an increase in the scale of efficient operation of such refineries and an inelastic demand, the hard economic facts against which social forces are frequently not immobile. An earlier period of concentration in the 1840s reduced the number of plants from 418 to 308 (Lhomme, *La Grande bourgeoisie au pouvoir*, 1960, p. 103).
[31] Perroux, "La Croissance de l'économie française" (1955), p. 59.
[32] Rist and Pirou, introduction, *De la France d'avant-guerre* (1939), pp. iiiff, and Auguy on "Structure industrielle" and Denuc, "Structure des entreprises," *ibid.*
[33] Houssiaux, *Le Pouvoir de monopole* (1958), table, p. 340.
[34] See Labasse, *Capitaux et région*, pp. 277ff, discussed above, Chapter 3.

tired when they had enough to buy a *rente,* that large-scale production is impossible because staff and workers change continuously, or that name and family continuity in business are rare.[35]

The environmental view stresses the level of profits, averaged out over long periods to take into account bankruptcies. Mourre, who emphasizes character, in answer to an objection concedes that profits have been low in industry and in commerce. The businessman earns less than a functionary or a lawyer.[36] To the environmentalist this is the explanation.[37] But the more enthusiastic supporters of entrepreneurial vigor as the source of growth demur: "Profits stimulate, but only on a mediocre scale. They give rise to the initiatives of merchants of cattle, butter and cheese, and the speculations of chestnut sellers. But they are absolutely impotent to stimulate great innovations which change the lot of people . . . To offer profits to these men [Renault, Citroën, de Lesseps, Curie, etc.] is to give bread to a baker." [38] It is difficult to obtain evidence on profits in the nineteenth century, given the secretive nature of French private business. Dansette has only a few pages on the subject, with very scrappy information. Fohlen's study of a single firm's experiences sets forth a record of profits over ninety-six years, from 1804 to 1900; but the data are in thousands of francs, which cannot be related to a figure for invested capital that grew through the period, and the method of computation is not clear. Nonetheless, they have some interest in that they show, for the sixty years from 1840 to 1900, losses in sixteen years and relatively good profits after 1884, except for 1897 to 1899, as contrasted with losses or low profits in the 1850s.[39]

There is great difficulty in establishing the net weight of the evidence amid so much contradiction and unsupported opinion. Admittedly, the position might be worse with more facts. But it is difficult to see that the Landes-Pitts thesis has been established. In textiles there is much to support it, and something against it. In other industries there have been inertia, secrecy, mistrust, failure to imitate or innovate, without the dynastic features sought by Pitts. And the theory needs, furthermore, to explain why large firms, when they existed side by side with family enterprises, failed to take advantage of their larger resources to run the small fry to the wall and why new runs of small fry did not elbow their way in to establish new dynasties.

[35] Bonnet, *Commercialisation* (1929), p. 32; Duveau, *La Vie ouvrière* (1946), p. 131.
[36] Mourre, *Décadence économique de la France?* (1900), p. 285.
[37] Cameron, "Profit, croissance et stagnation" (1957).
[38] Fourastié and Laleuf, *Révolution à l'ouest* (1957), p. 62.
[39] Lambert Dansette, *Quelques familles du patronat textile,* pp. 621ff. Fohlen, *Une Affaire de famille,* appendix 15, pp. 135–136.

THE BRITISH FAMILY FIRM

Habakkuk considers that the British family firm has been an important engine of economic progress. This is not the general view in Britain. Florence has stated the matter extremely: "It is possible that the relative decline in British industry between 1880 and 1930, when compared with that of other industrial countries, has been due to the large proportion of its output controlled by family heads reacting less keenly to higher profit and reinvesting less of that profit." Carter and Williams, who have much to say in criticism of the family firm, dissent from this judgment.[40] But Florence makes it clear that he is speaking less of the form of control than of "leadership by inheritance." In the early nineteenth century, businesses were controlled by a self-made entrepreneur who was a "regular hustler" and worked harder when increased returns were in sight. At the end of the century, when the sons or grandsons of the founder were in command, the supply curve of effort became less elastic and possibly even backward-bending. Some 4,000 or 5,000 pounds sufficed to send sons to public school and Oxford or Cambridge and to satisfy other conventional needs. After the family had held property for two generations, it became aristocratic in thought and interested in dynastic succession. People recruited for the business from outside the family circle were required to be of equally good family and breeding. Able subordinates who were not members of the family had no chance of advancement unless they married into it. And so on. Leadership by inheritance, moreover, applied in banking, steel and coal, even though these took the form of joint stock companies, as well as in pottery, carpets, boots and shoes, cocoa, brewing, sugar, and the older branches of engineering.[41]

Specific limitations of the family firm apply in its unwillingness to expand for fear of losing control, and a strong tendency to reduce entrepreneurial energy as the founder who emerged from poverty is replaced by the son or grandson "without exceptional energy" and "brought up to think life easy." [42] "The first obstacle is the desire for

---

[40] Florence, *The Logic of Industry* (1953), p. 320. Carter and Williams, *Innovation* (1958), pp. 40, 51, 83; and, by the same authors, *Science in Industry* (1959), pp. 90–92.

[41] Florence, pp. 295, 303–304, 320.

[42] Carter and Williams, *Innovation*, p. 40: "Many family firms will not expand their assets to grasp opportunities for profit because to do so would endanger family control by introducing outside capital." See also Cook, *Effect of Mergers* (1958), p. 342, for the case of Pilkingtons, a highly efficient family firm in glass, which sold a profitable subsidiary because it "did not wish to expand beyond the possibility of remaining a family firm." Marshall, *Industry and Trade* (1920), pp. 63, 87, 91–92.

the quiet life, or for public esteem." [43] The best chances of innovation in steel and hosiery in a family firm occurred in the founder's generation, and firms which started large as a result of stock promotion were conspicuously unsuccessful.[44] Along with the family director as a handicap to business is the absentee or outside director, chosen for prestige. Concern has also been expressed about the professional manager who may be given only limited powers of decision making by the shareholders or who may, in his own turn, be moved by the desire for the quiet life.[45] Bureaucratization of large firms is perhaps as great a danger as leadership by inheritance (occasionally merely another form of bureaucratization). The increasing age of company leadership is partly attributable to the increase in national life expectancy, but it may bespeak as well either failure to renew family leadership or the bureaucratic senescence of a public company.[46] Family firms of the French sort are not unknown in Britain, whether the auto-financing liquid type — exemplified by the hosiery industry;[47] the firms which are sold by their families when a sufficient fortune is reached — the Welsh tinplate manufacturer;[48] or the technological leader, such as Cadbury, Pilkington, or Wedgewood, comparable to Peugeot, Gouin, and so on.

One of the major changes which seems to have occurred in British entrepreneurship, whether family or corporate, is the decline in the attention paid to marketing. For the entrepreneurs of the Industrial Revolution, "commercial flair was basic." [49] In the American merger movement, marketing was the first function to be tackled as firms shifted from regional to national size.[50] But the advancing social status of the members of a British firm hurt sales efforts. Selling to the government or to industry exposed the family prestige to less risk of harm than selling to the public.[51] The commercial ability so crucial to the

[43] Carter and Williams, *Innovation*, p. 40.

[44] Erickson, *British Industrialists* (1959), p. 165.

[45] *Innovation*, p. 41; and Wilson, "The Entrepreneur" (1955), p. 143.

[46] Charlotte Erickson's study of steel executives shows that their average age rose over her five periods: (1865; 1875, 1885, and 1895; 1905, 1915, and 1925; 1935, and 1947; and 1953), as follows: 38, 46, 50, 54, and 55. Burn, *History of Steelmaking*, p. 216, is quoted on the prevalence of old men in the industry at the turn of the century. Erickson found that the lower limit of the third quartile rose between 1865 and 1895 from 54 to 65.

[47] Erickson, p. 124. Only three firms in the hosiery trade raised capital by selling shares before 1930.

[48] See Minchenton, *The British Tinplate Industry* (1957), pp. 105–107.

[49] Wilson, "The Entrepreneur," p. 138.

[50] Chandler, "Beginnings of 'Big Business' in American Industry" (1959), p. 26.

[51] See above, Chapter 5, and Pitts, "Bourgeois Family and French Retardation," p. 388, who states that the nearer the firm is to the general public, the lower is its prestige because the more easily can lower class buyers reject and refuse it. Com-

innovator — more important than technical capacity — was down-
graded as firms grew and became bureaucratic. Finance dominated
marketing and production.[52] Marketing was left with or turned over
to merchant houses — some functioning best in the semiprotected imperial markets — interposing a barrier between the firm and its customers and slowing down product changes. Marketing was still an avenue
for advancement in some industries, as Sir Thomas Lipton and Lord
Leverhulme proved, but not of much interest to those who had arrived.

A number of insights into the British entrepreneur of the eighteenth
and nineteenth centuries is furnished by three fat volumes, *Fortunes
Made in Business,* published in 1883. The articles are anonymous and
the tone eulogistic, but what stands out are the energy and interest in
money of the founders[53] and the concern of later generations for public life and charitable works. Table 7, prepared on fourteen families
for which the information is reasonably full, shows a marked diversity
in the religious and educational origins of the founders, but there is a
member of Parliament in all but one family and four or five in several.
(The table was compiled only from the information furnished by the
authors, with no attempt to fill in gaps from original sources.) A fuller
investigation would probably reveal a more uniform pattern of ownership of a country place and participation in public life, both locally and
on the national scene, together with charitable benefactions. The
authors make much of the expression, "new men and old acres." [54]

Writing in the early 1880s, the anonymous authors clearly reveal
the attitudes of the period: "Messrs Hird, Dawson and Hardy built up
immense fortunes of their own — fortunes which placed their families
in positions of affluence, and enabled their descendants to compete

---

pare the quotation from Laski by Barna (*Investment and Growth Policies,* 1962,
pp. 54–55): "A refusal to consider adequately the wants of the customer. He must
buy not the thing he wants but the thing you have to sell . . . A disbelief in the
necessity of large-scale production, just as a gentleman would rather lose his income than his uniqueness." Barna observes that managements which have been
successful in selling to government or industry may fail vis-à-vis the public; and
that three electrical companies withdrew after embarking on selling television sets
(pp. 55–56).

[52] Erickson, *British Industrialists,* pp. 187, 194.

[53] From *Fortunes Made in Business* (1883), I, 34: "He [Isaac Holden] sometimes
crossed the channel five times in a given week, attending courts in France [to
contend lawsuits over patents], and doing business in England." Page 57: "For
twenty years," said Mr. Lister on one occasion, "I was never in bed at half-past
five in the morning." Page 179: "How did he [Sir Josiah Mason] apply it [his
knowledge]? In the first place unquestionably to money-making . . . Even six-
pence had value in his eyes." Page 311: "Mr. Salt was a born worker, and could
not think of taking refuge in idleness as a young man."

[54] See, e.g., *ibid.,* II, 39. But sometimes, as when Horrocks contested a seat in
Parliament against Derby's man Hoghton of Hoghton Tower, "It was another case
of 'new men' against 'old acres' " (III, 22).

successfully for some of those offices of State and distinction which it is the highest ambition of an educated Englishman to fill." [55] The interest in political life had of course also affected the founders.[56] But interest in business by the descendants of the founder was rare. Mr. Gladstone at Liverpool in 1872 said: "I know not why commerce in England should not have its old families, rejoicing to be connected with commerce from generation to generation. It has been so in other countries; I trust it will be so in this country. I think it is a subject of sorrow, and almost of scandal, when those families who have either acquired or received station and wealth through commerce turn their backs upon it, and seem to be ashamed of it. It is certainly not so with my brother or with me." [57] And the authors regard it as "somewhat remarkable that the business instincts and great natural abilities of the founders of the [Low Moor Iron] works should have been inherited so fully by their descendants." [58]

It is of course true that French businessmen, particularly the bankers, held seats in the Chamber of Deputies. Henri Germain, for example, was able to combine the presidency of the Crédit Lyonnais with legislation, along with other representatives of high finance. The point is, however, that these men were bankers first and politicians second, whereas in Britain the descendants of the founder were typically statesmen first and businessmen second. Where this is not the case it is remarked: "Mr. Foster will talk of wools and yarns . . . with as great readiness at Burley and Bradford as he will talk in London of party tactics and national movements." [59] And in an expanding industry of the period — Welsh coal — only rarely did a colliery owner sit for Parliament. The industrialists chosen to represent South Wales in Westminster had their main interest in the already developed iron or copper industries.[60]

A striking paradigm of the family dynasty's gradual disenchantment with business is furnished by a recent account of a business which failed in the 1880s, *Marshall of Leeds, Flax-Spinners*. Most business history deals with survivors; to undertake an autopsy helps to correct bias in the sample. Moreover, the case mirrors in accentuated form the macrocosm of British economic slippage. From the world's outstanding flax spinner in 1846, the company fell behind as early as the fifties. One son of the founder tried to introduce technical improvements, but failed to make them work. Another had a passion for gathering statistics,

[55] *Ibid.*, I, 95–6.
[56] Titus Salt sought relaxation in public duties (*ibid.*, I, 311).
[57] *Ibid.*, II, 113.
[58] *Ibid.*, I, 127.
[59] *Ibid.*, I, 404.
[60] Morris and Williams, *The South Wales Coal Industry* (1958), p. 131.

Table 7. Selected Nineteenth-Century Business Dynasties in Britain

Family name	First name and relationship	Education	Religion	Business	Municipal public life	National public life	Charitable works
Bright	Jacob(f) (b 1796)	Quaker school, private tutor	Quaker	Cotton spinning	Magistrate	MP	
	John(s)					Minister	
	Thomas(s)			Family business	Mayor	MP	
	Jacob(s)			Family business			
Crossley	John(f)		Congrega-tionalist	Carpet manufacture			
	John(s)			Family business	Mayor	MP	Donations to religious and educational charities
	Joseph(s)			Family business			Donations to orphans' school
	Francis(s)			Family business		MP Baronetcy	Donations to park, almshouse
	Saville(g-s)					MP	Built Crossley Institute
	Edward(g-s)			Family business	Mayor	MP	
Fairbairn	William(f) (b. 1787)	Rudimentary	Anglican	Mechanical engineer		Baronetcy	
	Peter(f) (b.1799)	Rudimentary	Anglican	Flax spinning, Machinery	Town Council, alderman, mayor	Knighthood	Local patron of arts and sciences
	Thomas(s)	Tutor, Cambridge Univ.	Anglican	Machinery	Magistrate	Knighthood refused	Benefactor of art schools
	Andrew(s)			Railway director	Alderman, mayor	MP	Art patron
Fielden	Joshua(f)	Rudimentary	Quaker	Cotton spinning			
	John(s)		Unitarian	Cotton spinning		MP	

Family	Individual	Education	Religion	Occupation	Office	Honor	Notes
Foster	John(f) (b. 1798)	Grammar school, private school	Anglican	Worsted manufacture	Justice of peace		Active in church
	Jonas(s)		Anglican	Worsted manufacture			School trustee
	William(s)	Private schools	Anglican	Worsted manufacture	Justice of peace		
Gladstone	John(f) (b. 1763)		Anglican	Importing merchant		MP	
	William Swart(s)	Eton, Oxford	Anglican			Baronetcy; MP, Prime minister	
	Thomas(s)	Eton, Oxford	Anglican	Importing merchant		MP	
	Robertson(s)		Anglican				
	W. H.(g-s)		Anglican	Importing merchant	Alderman and Mayor	MP	
	Henry N.(g-s)			Importing merchant			
	Herbert(g-s)					MP	
Hardy	John(f)	Private school	Anglican	Mining		MP	
	John(s)				Recorder of Deeds	MP	
	Gathorne(g-s)	Shrewsbury, Oxford		Mining		MP, Minister, Viscount	
	Charles(g-s)		Anglican	Mining	Magistrate	MP; Baronetcy	Active in building churches
	John(g-s)			Mining		MP	
Henry	John(g-s)					MP	
	A. E.(g-s)					MP	
	Alexander(f) (b. 1766)		Presbyterian	Merchant			
	Alexander(s)		Presbyterian	Merchant			
	J. Snowdon(g-s)	Tutors, Univ. Coll., London				MP	
	Mitchell(g-s)					MP	

(table continued)

Table 7 (*continued*)

Family name	First name and relationship	Education	Religion	Business	Municipal public life	National public life	Charitable works
Hird	Richard(f)		Anglican	Mining	Magistrate		
	Lamplugh(s)	Grammar school, Oxford	Anglican	Mining	Magistrate	MP	
	Henry W.(g-s)			Mining			
	LamplughW.(g-s)		Anglican	Mining	Magistrate		
Holden	Isaac(f) (b. 1807)	Rudimentary and night school	Methodist	Wool combing		MP	Technical-school benefactor
	Angus(s)			Wool combing	Mayor		
Kitson	James(f)			Railway locomotives	TC, mayor Magistrate		Benefactor of hospital, education
	James(s)	Grammar school Univ. Coll.	Unitarian	Railway locomotives	Justice of peace	Defeated for MP; baronetcy	Benefactor of schools, workers' housing
	J. Hawthorne(s)			Railway locomotives			
	F. W.(s)			Railway locomotives			
Pease	Edward(f) (b. 1764)		Quaker	Wool, railways			
	Joseph(s)		Quaker	Wool, railways, collieries		MP	School benefactor
	Henry(s)			Wool, railways, collieries	Mayor	MP	Active pacifist
	Joseph(g-s)	Tutors	Quaker	Wool, railways, collieries		MP Baronetcy	Church benefactor

Family	Person	Education	Business	Local office	National	Other
	Arthur(g-s)			Alderman, mayor	MP	School governor
	Henry(g-s)			Alderman, mayor	Defeated for MP	
Platt	Henry(f) (b. 1792)					
	James(s)	Anglican	Cotton manufacture	Town Council	MP	Gave land to church
	John(s)	Rudimentary	Cotton manufacture	TC, mayor	MP	Benefactor to education, hospitals
Salt	Titus(f)(b.1803)	Grammar school	Alpaca wool	Mayor	MP	
	William(s)					
	George(s)		Alpaca wool	Magistrate	Baronetcy	
	Edward(s)		Alpaca wool			
	Titus(s)		Alpaca wool			

Source. *Fortunes Made in Business* (1883).

which it was found impossible to bring to bear upon the firm's problems. The American Civil War postponed the day of reckoning. The
third generation finally put the company into receivership, auctioned
off the plant, and lived off the income of investments, largely in railways and foreign bonds.

The case reveals every possible cause of morbidity. The firm stagnated technically after the death of the founder in 1846, and the efforts
of James Marshall to switch from hackling to mechanical combing, as
the French did with a Schumberger machine, and chemical retting
failed after 1858. Plant efficiency was low; marketing was unenterpris-
ing (using commission agents); the composition of output was unsuited
to the market; James and Henry drew more than the profits of the
enterprise, especially during the Civil War; James sat in Parliament
from 1846 to 1853, before resigning in an effort to revive the enterprise, and later moved to Italy; Henry immured himself in the country;
Richardson, the manager, clung to old ways of production and hired
his brother and friends in posts earning 300 to 500 pounds a year; the
brothers quarreled; a prolonged strike in 1872 was badly handled; and
where the founder's sons had neglected the enterprise, their own
despised it. The historian concludes that the sons could not share their
father's satisfaction in business as a way of life and lacked his overrid-
ing ambition to become rich and distinguished. In middle age they put
other interests ahead of the firm: politics, foreign travel, country life.
The business was sacrificed, and the verdict of the coroner is managerial paralysis.[61]

The passage of generations may often be the worst enemy of the
family firm.[62] If so, the means to correct this was incorporation and
conversion of a private into a public company. These changes frequently enabled the second generation, or the third, to withdraw from
active management. There were other reasons for incorporation: the
need for large amounts of capital first in railroads in the 1840s, and
then coal, especially in steel and textiles, shipping and banking in the
boom of 1866–1873, and later more general manufacturing and brewing. Some of the companies were public in name only,[63] but others
were designed to give the sons a seat on the board and their weekends
free.[64]

[61] Rimmer, *Marshall of Leeds* (1960), pp. 234–300.
[62] Landes, "Structure of Enterprise in the 19th Century" (1960), p. 115.
[63] Vaizey, *The Brewing Industry* (1960), p. 151 — in no industry is the family
structure of firms more established behind the mask of incorporation. Vaizey points
out that the monopolistic character of distribution, in which the tied-houses are
limited by law, has kept inefficient firms alive longer than in competitive industries
and given them a considerable value in mergers even when highly inefficient.
[64] Jeffrys, *Trends in Business Organization* (1938), p. 140.

This explanation does not go deep enough, however. Many large public companies became somnolent, and not only in general but department by department. Paid managers hesitated to take risks with stockholders' money, and stockholders, whether family or public, tolerated inefficiency and low profits over long periods of time. But what needs to be explained is not the behavior of old firms, public or private, but the absence of new firms that might force on the old greater attention to costs, technical performance, marketing, and the like. The competition which did in Marshall of Leeds came from Belfast and Belgium, not elsewhere in Britain.

Why did not new enterprises elbow their way to the forefront in Britain after 1880? Here it is impossible to do more than speculate, but it would appear that social values had the greatest effect. As business became more complex, the amateur ideal of British society became less sought through accumulation and more through the liberal professions, the civil service, and politics. The attention of people in business drew back from income maximization. Those outside either found themselves satisfied with social acceptance in a class structure which emphasized coziness or sought to achieve the upper-middle-class ideal in other ways. The hungry outsiders — immigrants, Quakers, Jews, and lower-class aspirants to wealth — diminished either in numbers or in the intensity of their drive.

Unlike France, since World War II Britain has not had an influx of new men into industry, spurred on by a revision in the value attached to economic expansion and progress. Technological training is more widespread and business is increasingly seeking recruits in the universities — Oxford and Cambridge as well as the red-brick — and at an earlier age in the public schools. Some firms, like Pilkingtons or I.C.I., of whatever size, remain technologically progressive and alert, from having built progressive habits into their structure. Others, like jute and paper, have awakened from years of technological sleep to revolutionize their attitudes, change over to new young managers, employ scientists and absorb them into management, and so on.[65] But these changes are by no means ubiquitous in Britain or France. And it remains to see how widely they will spread.

It is hard, then, to accept any simple explanation for economic growth which relies heavily on the role of entrepreneurship. The theory that ascribes overwhelming importance to this factor has been developed more fully for France; if anything, it fits better the facts of

[65] Carter and Williams, *Industry and Technical Progress,* appendix case studies on jute (pp. 220ff) and paper (pp. 230ff). Jute consists of many small firms; paper of a few large, which have seen most of the changes, and many small.

Britain, after it has been modified to account for great economic vigor in the founder's generation and less subsequently. For France the theory suffers from the existence of considerable local divergences in entrepreneurship and from the failure of a unitary explanation, such as the family firm, to account for alternate periods of rapid growth followed by stagnation. In Britain, moreover, the stagnation is seen to reach beyond the family firm as such and to embrace family enterprises, private companies, and public companies. The record in steel, which was incorporated, is no better than in unincorporated industries. And some family firms, like Pilkington, despite a reluctance to grow in certain directions, remained in the first rank of efficiency, like other large family firms in France.

Of greatest interest despite the similarity between French and British family firms — their sluggish technological push after the initial upsurge — are the differences. In Britain the family firm is milked for profit; in France it is kept intact. In Britain the family firm follows a life cycle from one generation to the next, rising, stabilizing, declining. In France it achieves a plateau of operations to which it hopes to cling. In Britain the character of the family firm is hard to distinguish from that of incorporated enterprise. In France, while there are many family firms that function like ordinary efficient large-scale business, the majority behave in different fashion.

But the greatest weakness in attaching first importance to the nature of entrepreneurship in shaping France's and Britain's economic development is that the model is incomplete. What needs to be explained is not why business behaved as it did but, taking this for granted, why other firms did not come along and challenge existing enterprise.

CHAPTER 7

TECHNOLOGY

The Harrod-Domar model is one in which growth gives rise to growth, as increased income leads to more savings, more investment, more income, more savings, and so on. The marginal propensity to save may fall in the long run and stabilize the process, or it may slow it down. But, as a rule, where investment is the key to growth, the front runner is likely to win. The head start opens up a gap that widens.

In models that depend on technological change for economic growth (called here for convenience the Abramovitz-Solow models, after two writers who have emphasized this feature in statistical investigations), the rate of growth is a function of the rate of technical change and its application in industry. Where technical change is indigenous, innovation is the key. With innovation elsewhere in the world, growth requires imitation.

The first question to ask about a leading country is whether the rate of technical change is independent of growth and, if so, whether it tends to move along at a constant rate or to vary in some systematic or random fashion. If technology is a dependent factor, on what does it depend — the overall demand for output, the age of a given industry or economy, the price of labor, or what? Second, there arises the question of how rapidly technological inventions developed at home in a leading industrial economy, or in others developed abroad, are applied. Here a particular question arises for Britain, the value of the head start. Technical progress leaves the pioneer with obsolescing equipment.[1] Gerschenkron believes in the value of starting last, shortcutting the technical stages at which earlier developers rest.[2] Long-lived equipment is said to be a particular handicap, whether in railroads, steel, canals, or early motor roads.

There is, however, dissent from this view: the existence of capital, however obsolete, is said to be a help or nothing — in any case, no hindrance. It is a free gift of the past, which the present has freedom

[1] Veblen, *Imperial Germany*, p. 128: "The British have not sinned against the canons of technology. It is only that they are paying the penalty for having been thrown into the lead and so having shown the way."
[2] Gerschenkron, "Economic Backwardness" (1952), p. 7.

to scrap or use, but the country is in no way worse off than if it has no capital stocks.[3] The issue is particularly relevant to Britain, which began as the innovator in 1760 and found itself after 1880 or so falling behind other countries, even in imitation.[4]

No such clear-cut issue exists for France, though there is a variety of smaller questions. There is the frequent allegation that the French are good at invention but poor at innovation, or that French inventions partake of a universal quality because of the scientific and deductive character of their thought, while those of Germany or Britain have a much more localized application.[5] The first part of this statement has also been applied to Britain.[6] And finally, the most impressive question to consider, there has been the high technological content in France's economic recovery after World War II, led by the government and nationalized agencies.

THE DEVELOPMENT OF TECHNOLOGY IN BRITAIN

The relations between technical change and growth are complex. Although it is true that technical change — increased productivity not accounted for by capital and labor inputs — has been found by Abramovitz and Solow to be responsible for perhaps two thirds of growth in the United States, and similar results have been obtained for other countries, it is also true that technical change depends in part on economic growth. Or it may. The growth may offer an opportunity to take advantage of new inventions — but the response must be forthcoming.

[3] See, e.g., Jervis, "The Handicap of Britain's Early Start" (1947).

[4] *The Economist*, "Rostow on Growth" (1959), p. 413, states: "Several factors combined to slow down the relative rate of Britain's development; but one is especially significant. It is one thing to be a mature economy, out at the margin of technology, having available each year only a rough approximation to the new technology created in, say, the previous year; it is quite a different thing to be a latecomer with a big unapplied backlog of technology available.

"Once the United States and continental western Europe had completed their take-off, much of the British lead was gone; for they could bring the backlog of technology to bear more rapidly than it had been created."

This is a possible model of relative growth, but one which does not apply. After 1875 British growth slowed down absolutely as well as relatively. In addition, the country was slow in applying existing technology as it developed at home and abroad, and in new industries. In these areas it had room to develop as rapidly as any country.

[5] Parker, "Comment," p. 189.

[6] Wilson, "Electronics" (1958), p. 143: "It is frequently said that the British are quick to invent but slow to develop. No doubt the French and many other people say the same of themselves!" A variety of writers, e.g., Carter and Williams, *Technical Progress*, p. 28, believe that the distinction between invention and innovation is virtually impossible to make today, since inventions represent continuous changes, largely realized in applications rather than in discontinuous steps.

Schumpeter's theory of economic development was connected with business cycles and rested on the observation that innovations occurred in the depth of business depression as business firms sought to cut costs.[7] In the early phases of Britain's growth, however, it was expansion that led to new processes. Two reasons account for this: in the first place, there is the pressure for additional supplies, which leads entrepreneurs to seek new and cheaper methods of production; second, the risk of loss is very much reduced with a briskly expanding demand.[8] Two outstanding waves of British innovation — in the cotton textile industry in the 1770s and in iron and steel in the 1850s and 1860s[9] — were supported by rapidly expanding markets, which happened to be for export.

One can go further and suggest that the decline in British inventive activity was associated with the Great Depression. Its timing is debatable, as noted in the discussion of the Climacteric in Chapter 1. Phelps Brown and Handsfield Jones attach it to the 1890s; Coppock, to the 1870s. These views derive from statistical examination. But the historian's view reaches back before the Great Depression. W. H. B. Court has noted that, whereas the Great Exhibition of 1851 demonstrated that Britain led the world, the Paris Exhibition of 1867 suggested that Britain was falling behind, a mere sixteen years later.[10] The timing is debatable, but the fact that it occurred is not.[11] The slowdown was experienced in cotton textiles, building, coal, steel, and, as we shall see, with some interruption in railroads.[12] But while the rate of technical progress slowed down during or after the depression, the most striking fact is that it did not pick up when business did after

[7] Schumpeter, *Theory of Economic Development* (1934), chap. vi; *Business Cycles* (1939), I, 159.

[8] See Sheahan, "Government Competition and the French Automobile Industry" (1960), who suggests that the structure of the market may be less important for technological change than its rate of growth.

[9] Smelser, *Social Change in the Industrial Revolution*, p. 62; Habakkuk, "Commercial Expansion," p. 802.

[10] See Young, *Portrait of an Age*, pp. 159–160: "After the age of the great producers, Armstrong, Whitworth, Brassey, comes the age of great shops and great advertisers. Famous names still kept our station in a world which had no naturalist to equal Darwin and no physicist to surpass Clerk Maxwell, but the springs of invention are failing, and, for the successors of the Arkwrights and the Stephensons we must look to America, to France and even to Italy."

[11] Saville notes ("Retarding Factors in the British Economy," 1961, p. 53) that a minor flurry of interest in scientific and technical education followed the Paris Exhibition and produced the Select Committee on Scientific Instruction, whereas a greater upheaval occurred in the 1880s and led to the Royal Commission on Technical Instruction.

[12] Jones, *Increasing Returns* (1933), parts 2, 3; Taylor, "Productivity and Innovation in British Coal" (1961); Burn, *History of British Steelmaking* (1940), chap. x. On the first four of these industries, see Dobb, *Development of Capitalism* (1947), p. 317.

1896. By this time invention and innovation abroad had made a variety of new processes available to the British in the industries just listed. These industries undertook impressive programs of expansion, especially in cotton textiles and steel, but without modernization. The challenge of demand met no response, even in the application of available technology.

According to this interpretation, there was a major slowdown in the rate of British technological progress in the last quarter of the nineteenth century. There is evidence in support of the contrary. R. S. Sayers has pointed out that technical progress during the 1920s and the growth of real income in Britain have been consistently understated because of the deflationary character of the period.[13] Monetary income did not grow markedly, but real income gained as a result of the application of foreign innovations — American and German, in particular — in new industries. British innovation was not needed to achieve a rapid rate of technological progress, in view of the backlog of existing innovations to be applied — in motor cars, airplanes, radios, electrical appliances, artificial silk, plastics, the internal-combustion engine, ball-bearings, metal alloys, stainless steel (especially), and the mechanical industries. The old industries — textiles, iron and steel, coal, and, to a lesser extent immediately after the war, shipbuilding — failed to share in this advance.[14] Their great weight in the production indexes held down the overall averages.

But I cannot accept the view that technical change proceeds at a pace of its own, or at two paces, in the older and the newer industries. The classic statement that technological change proceeds in fits and starts is that of Schumpeter in Volume One of *Business Cycles.* For our period the evidence of the railroad industry lends support. Cole notes that changes in locomotive design for the Great Western Railway were concentrated in the Brunel period of the 1830s and 1840s, and again in a brief span between 1891 and 1906, when new types of locomotives were produced under Churchward every three years. After 1906 there was no improvement in design until 1945.[15] Both periods happened to coincide with brisk demand. But it seems evident that it was more the personalities of the managing directors than economic conditions which determined the rate of technical progress. Saunders, the general secretary, retired in 1886; Tyrell, the superintendent of lines, in 1888; Gooch, the chairman, died in 1889. Between 1889 and 1893 ten out of nineteen directors remaining after the loss of the three officers listed either died

[13] Sayers, "Technical Progress" (1950).
[14] Kahn, *Great Britain in the World Economy* (1946), emphasizes the distinction between the expanding electrical, automobile, and chemical industries and the declining staple trades.
[15] Cole, "Locomotive Replacement," part 2, p. 38.

or retired.[16] The boom of 1885–1889 produced a shortage of locomotives, to be sure, but the extent and duration of the response were
matters of personality. Declining industries may fail to attract energetic
people and leave promotion to seniority.[17] When this happens, the industry will neither innovate nor invest in the inventions of others.

THE APPLICATION OF EXISTING TECHNOLOGY

The problem of the application of up-to-date technology is posed by
Frankel in terms of choice between an existing and a new technology,
when a substantial amount of capacity is needed to replace capital
stock that suddenly wears out, like the one-horse shay.[18] He has devised a formula involving, for each process, the rate of interest, the
ratio of fixed to variable cost, the amount of fixed cost, the durability
of capital, the elasticity of demand, and the number of components
which have to be altered. The impact of most of these variables is
obvious. The number of components, however, represents what he calls
"interrelatedness": the possibility that a change in one element in the
economic process — in production, transport, raw-material supply —
will entail other changes elsewhere in the system, because of complex
physical interrelations, and will require complementary capital changes.
In his view, this technological interrelatedness makes for difficulty of
technical progress in complex economies and represents one disadvantage of the head start.

A slightly different formulation is offered by Salter, who holds that the
decisions to scrap old capacity and invest in new are theoretically distinct.[19] An old technique using capital that wears out over time will
be scrapped when it is unable to cover variable costs. New investment
involving a new process will be undertaken only if it is able to earn
superprofits. In equilibrium, the price of an output will equal average
variable costs in the old method, which in turn are equal to average
full costs, including normal profits, on the new. Salter is not concerned
with interrelatedness. To him factor prices are the critical variables
determining when it is useful to undertake new investment using new
techniques. The existence of outmoded capital equipment is an indication not of inefficiency but of relatively cheap labor, which keeps variable costs low in the old technique (assumed to be labor-intensive),
or high interest rates, which make for high fixed costs in the new technique.[20]

[16] *Ibid.*, p. 33.
[17] Carter and Williams, *Technical Progress*, p. 157.
[18] Frankel, "Obsolescence and Technical Change" (1955).
[19] Salter, *Productivity and Technical Change* (1960), chap. iv, sec. 3, pp. 55ff.
[20] Note that wage rates influence the application of existing technology rather

A number of other economic factors are relevant. One is competition. Under less than perfect competition, old techniques can cover variable costs by means of high prices so long as entry is limited and the super-profits available to the new technique do not lead to expanded output. Another is the rate of gross investment, required either by a widening market as population grows or by high rates of physical depreciation, which would keep physical output falling and prices rising, with a stable population. A high rate of gross investment permits a choice among techniques along the lines of Frankel's model. When such choice is offered, the more efficient technique will be chosen without the margin in favor of the older one, since each process must cover fixed costs if capacity is to be sustained.

Still another factor is the secondhand value of old equipment, which can be regarded as a subtraction from the capital cost of the new technique or as an increase in variable cost — to the extent of interest and normal profit on the secondhand value — which the old technique must earn to be kept going.[21] Salter does not pay much attention to the secondhand value of old equipment; but in some markets, as in the automobile market in the United States today, it clearly plays an important part. The British shipping industry may have been enabled to maintain technological leadership longer than coal, textiles, steel, and locomotives by its brisk secondhand market in ships. At the peak of secondhand sales, in 1911, Britain built a million tons of new shipping, of which 93,000 tons were sold to foreign customers. Another 487,000 tons were sold abroad secondhand.[22] The net expansion of 215,000 tons was much smaller than the 487,000 modernized by selling off the old and building new.

Finally, there is the antieconomic possibility that investment decisions are taken, or are altogether evaded, by rote or habit. In economic terms it might be said that decision makers are a scarce input, decision making has a high cost, and the total return to the firm would be maximized in some sense under a standard other than economic calculation.

---

than, as in some analyses, the production of inventions. (See, e.g., Dobb, *Development of Capitalism*, p. 276.) In discussing the decline in growth in the British economy in the last quarter of the nineteenth century, which "unquestionably failed to provide incentives and encouragement" to transformation, Saville ("Retarding Factors in the British Economy," pp. 55–56) refers to a PEP report which mentions the weakness of incentives to economize labor and states that the British labor market was never in short supply, but without indicating what changes in relative wage rates occurred between the third and fourth quarters of the century. Salter (p. 45) states that the relative price of capital and labor is strongly affected by the cheapening of capital goods relative to wages as a consequence of technical progress in the capital-goods industries, which was occurring rapidly, at least abroad, in this period.

[21] Salter, *ibid.*, p. 54.

[22] *Statistical Abstract for the United Kingdom, 1911–1925*, p. 275.

This might be physical life of equipment, or an arbitrary accounting life as laid down in an office, or merely some traditional number. Frankel's and Salter's models may call for more rationality than the system is prepared to provide. Rules of thumb may substitute for calculation, and these rules of thumb may embody more or less technical change, favoring scrapping or retention of old equipment and adoption or rejection of new.

INTERRELATEDNESS

Frankel's discussion does not make it completely clear whether, by interrelatedness, he means merely physical input-output relations, involving the complementarity of investment decisions at different stages of production, or something more. That something more might be the lumpiness of investment in social-overhead capital, which would inhibit technical change if capital markets were imperfect and small investors had better access to capital than large investors. Or it may be the failure of the market to coordinate investment decisions in different firms — a form of external diseconomy.

Let us take the size of British freight cars on which Frankel quotes Veblen's remarks of 1915 (he could have cited the 1885 authority of Hadley).[23] It has long been understood that small cars are inefficient. To enlarge them from 10 to 20 tons' capacity would raise earning capacity 100 percent, but tare weight only 33 to 50 percent and capital cost only 50 percent. Current maintenance could be reduced 25 percent per ton mile, shunting requirements would fall, and locomotives could haul payloads up to 25 percent greater.[24] The most efficient size for coal wagons has been estimated at 24.5 tons capacity (plus 10.5 tons tare), which would stay within the critical limitations of size — 9 feet in width, 12 feet 10 inches in height, and two axles, limited to 17.5 tons of load per axle.[25]

Two reasons have been advanced for the failure of British railroads under private ownership to move to a more efficient freightcar size. I restrict the discussion to coal cars, since there is the further complication with miscellaneous merchandise that the average load per car has been well below capacity; haul has been short; and, in the absence of an organization like the American Railway Express Agency, speed for numerous small retail shipments has been furnished by the railroads themselves, often assigning a whole car to a single relatively small

---

[23] Mentioned by Savage, *An Economic History of Transport* (1959), pp. 76–77.
[24] Fenelon, *Railway Economics* (1932), p. 172.
[25] Parkhouse, "Railway Freight Rolling Stock" (1951), p. 214.

shipment.[26] In coal, the retention of the ten-ton car is sometimes said to have been due to the impossibility of changing it without also modifying "terminal facilities, tracks and shunting facilities," [27] which made the cost prohibitive. On the other hand, the major impediment is said to have been the fact that the coal wagons were owned by the coal mines and not by the railroad companies.[28]

The technical aspects of interrelatedness do not seem to have held up the movement to more efficient size, either through making such a change uneconomic because of the enormity of the investment required or by adding amounts too great for any one firm to borrow. The sums involved were not large, and railway finance was rarely a limiting factor in the period up to 1914.[29] Private ownership of the coal cars by

[26] Sherrington, *Economics of Rail Transport* (1937), I, 214; Williams, *Economics of Railway Transport* (1909), p. 134. The question is debatable. British average loads run about 50 percent of capacity, but so do those of other countries with larger wagons.

[27] Veblen, *Imperial Germany,* pp. 126–127. It is wrong to mention track, since there is no necessity to strengthen roadbeds or bridges or to modify tunnels, so long as car size is kept within the limits cited in the text. With bogies or trolleys, much heavier cars are possible with increased construction cost. Fenelon in 1932 mentioned a 70-ton transformer wagon and a London and Northeastern Railway wall-trolley wagon built to carry 110 or, in special circumstances, 150 tons (*Railway Economics,* p. 56). The primary problem for coal would be to re-equip collieries and ports to take larger wagons, and in particular to modify coal screens, weigh-bridges, and sidings (where curves have to be altered to accommodate the greater length of wagon) in collieries, and hoists and tips at ports, along with the work sidings of certain large-scale coal consumers (*ibid.,* p. 172). Fenelon estimated the cost of all alterations at about £8,750,000 in 1932, and the net saving at £2 million per annum.

[28] Of the 1,320,000 freight cars in Britain in 1930, 630,000 were privately owned and 90 percent of these were used for coal. The advantage of direct ownership of cars by a colliery was that it could be assured a supply of cars. The overall economic loss to the country, apart from any inhibition of technical change, was the necessity to haul empty cars back to their owner, rather than to pool them, with an increase in shunting and in empty running. Pearson points out that the change from private to National Coal Board ownership has raised the proportion of productive to total miles from 66.8 percent in 1938 to 71.3 percent in 1952 ("Developments in British Transport," 1953 p. 123).

[29] The problem of inefficient freight-car size may have been affected by an old Railway Clearing House specification for private wagons, forbidding carrying capacities above 10 tons, which was modified "belatedly" in 1902 (Williams, *Economics of Railway Transport,* p. 136). But it was not likely that such prohibitions, which did not bind the railways themselves, were very powerful. The adoption of the Gauge Act by Parliament in 1846 induced the Great Western Railway to abandon its 7-foot gauge only in 1892, under the pressure of competition. Three major conversions took place in 1869, 1872 and 1874, but a new merger in 1876 raised the broad-gauge track from 8 to 293 miles. This was worked down to 183 miles by 1889 and finally converted in 1892. (See Cole, "Locomotive Replacement," part 2, pp. 14–15, 28.) This slow move to modernize and standardize provides an instance of technical interrelatedness. The necessity for new or reluctance to scrap old rolling stock was the main cost of the conversion, apart from labor to shift the rails, since new track was needed only at bends, points and crossings, and very little roadbed. Locomotives had long been built on a convertible basis,

the collieries, on the other hand, posed a type of interrelatedness that was institutional rather than technical.

A decision to change the size of rolling stock involves investment by the railroads, on the one hand, and by the collieries, on the other. Even if the rolling stock had been owned by the railroads, there might have been reluctance on the part of the collieries to alter their screens, weigh-bridges, and sidings. They could insist that they were under no obligation to undertake investment to benefit the railroads. And the railroads in turn would have difficulty in effecting an adequate distribution of the gains from the new investment, especially with uncertainty as to what those benefits would be.

For the railroads to guarantee new low rates on larger wagons would have been to take all the risk of the new investment, and that of the collieries, on themselves. To indicate that they would consider new and lower rates only if these were justified by operating economies would assign the risk to the collieries. An attempt to apportion the risk between the two would have been equitable but not likely to arouse much enthusiasm. The Great Western and the Great Eastern railways adopted twenty-ton wagons for their own use for locomotive coal as early as 1897;[30] and the Northeastern had used twenty-ton bottom-discharge mineral wagons for iron ore and forty-ton bogie coal wagons since the beginning of the century.[31] These wagons were all owned by the railroads, not the coal or iron companies. The Great Western Railway failed, however, to persuade colliery owners to change to a larger wagon when it offered a rebate of 5 percent on freight cars for coal in fully loaded twenty-ton wagons in 1923 and, in 1925, reduced charges on tipping and weighing these wagons. Only 100 came into use.[32] Colliery owners gave the excuse that the bigger wagons resulted in increased coal breakage. But neither ancient example, rebate, nor exhortation by Royal Commission[33] proved of avail until nationalization of the collieries.

---

with wheels outside the frame for broad-gauge work brought in for standard. Part of the slowness was due not to the investment problem, nor to reluctance to scrap rolling stock and traction that could not be converted, but to management's firm belief that the broad gauge was superior to the standard. In Australia the standardization of gauge is held back partly by the lumpiness of the investment problem involved and partly, despite frequent Royal Commissions, by the difficulty of getting agreement among the states. But interstate traffic is more in passengers than in goods.

[30] Sherrington, *Economics of Rail Transport*, p. 214.

[31] Fenelon, *Railway Economics*, p. 171. The London, Midland and Scottish Railway also used 40-ton bogie wagons to carry coal to its own power station.

[32] Sherrington, p. 218.

[33] The Reid Report recommended the establishment of a Standing Committee on Mineral Transport. In its report this latter characterized the system of private wagons as defective and recommended that the railroads ultimately take over the

Institutional interrelatedness inhibiting technical change can be compared to pecuniary economies that are external to the firm. Investment is required of two or more firms. Uncertainty attaches to the yield. A commitment as to the division of the benefits may create such a skewness in the distribution of risk and benefit, or such uncertainty, that one or more parties refuses to participate. An investment is not undertaken because of the possibility that the return will accrue to others. Where the railroad owns the cars and serves its own purposes — locomotive fuel, fuel for power, or even the delivery of iron ore for hire — the more efficient technology is used. Like Rosenstein-Rodan's classic example of external economies in production in underdeveloped countries, vertical integration converts the external to an internal profit and makes the technical change feasible.

The same analysis applies to the equipment of freight cars with automatic brakes. These were fitted to passenger cars after 1878 in response to public and governmental demands for safety, on the one hand, and the need for higher speeds, on the other.[34] Higher speed was partly a response to pressure of competition for passengers.[35] But it was also economical, permitting more traffic to move over a given way. Required were bigger and more powerful locomotives and automatic brakes; these were forthcoming for passenger trains and for a few special commodities which rode in special cars on passenger trains, like flowers and fish. But not for general or coal goods-traffic. In 1903 the Great Western Railway fitted some freight cars with automatic brakes and designed a special locomotive, the Mogul, to pull them — such a nuisance was the short, slow freight train. By and large, however, little was done to fit automatic brakes to freight wagons, and the question of whether to do so, and to what extent, is still under debate.[36] After

wagons. In the meantime it recommended pooling. The Report of the Royal Commission on Transport (Cmd 3751, 1931) scolded the railways, except the Great Western, for not having moved to larger wagons. Sherrington attacks the Act of 1921, consolidating the 130 prewar lines into four major companies, for its failure, *inter alia*, to eliminate private traders' wagons (p. 262).

[34] See Eversley, "The Great Western Railway" (1957), p. 177; Cole, "Locomotive Replacement," part 2, p. 41.

[35] Eversley, *ibid*. It is misleading to think of the railroads as monopolists in this period, since there was intense competition for passengers to different resorts, as well as alternative company facilities on a number of main routes, such as Birmingham to London.

[36] See Hunter, "Freight Rolling Stock" (1954), who claims that fitting brakes to 500,000 cars would be too costly and who would limit them to the new 24.5-ton cars and to mainline wagons. Parkhouse criticizes this limitation and comes out in favor of all cars (p. 364). In rebuttal Hunter suggests that Parkhouse has oversimplified the problem and neglected the extra costs of shunting in marshaling yards, what with all the coupling and uncoupling of vacuum hoses. While this seems absurd to people acquainted with the practice elsewhere, it may not be for Britain, given its greater volume of shunting per ton-mile because of the shortness of average haul.

setting forth estimates of cost and benefits which favor the adoption of brakes on British freight cars, to match those of every other major country, S. E. Parkhouse expresses the opinion that the government would have directed the equipment of freight trains with brakes long ago — "probably before the beginning of this century" — had it not been for the existence of a large fleet of privately owned wagons.[37]

This is where wholesale destruction would have helped — and why a country that loses a large proportion of its capital equipment in a war may thereby gain over the enemy, which emerges with its fixed capital relatively intact. Destruction permits a fresh start. No nation normally has the option of destroying or scrapping existing equipment and starting again. Private owners clinging to their privileges inhibited the railroads from acting as if the old cars, or freight cars without brakes, had no value. Until the coal wagons were nationalized, the British railroads were handicapped by the fact that in the 1830s they had the example of canals and roads in mind, and sought to act as common carriers on which individual traders would provide both rolling stock and motive power.[38] This early proved unworkable for locomotives; but, when it came to freight cars, the unsatisfactory results in inhibiting technical change were recognized too late or were blocked by the tradition of laissez faire. Sherrington says that the policy of private ownership of wagons would have been tolerated in no other country.[39] A later start, governmental intervention of great authority, or wholesale destruction permitting a fresh start would have been required to achieve a more workable basis. In the end it was nationalization.

The same historical issue of the difficulty of change in industries which may be called disintegrated, with separate firms responsible for separate processes or components, can be found elsewhere in Britain. Frankel mentions steel, with its separate stages of smelting, rolling, blast-furnace size, and so on, all technologically interrelated; and cotton textiles, where the adoption of ring spindles and automatic looms was held back by the separation of firms for separate processes and the fact that automatic looms require yarn spun a slightly different way.[40] Frankel discusses the externality of the interrelatedness only for cotton textiles and puts his faith in the purely technical indivisibility of

[37] Parkhouse, "Railway Freight Rolling Stock," pp. 216–218, 242. A truly technological indivisibility is that many private wagons are unsuitable for accelerated running, especially those with grease lubrication instead of oil. For a discussion of lack of standardization in freight cars, see Ministry of Reconstruction, *Standardization of Railway Equipment*, which mentions that there were at least 200 different types of axle boxes and 40 different types of hand brakes.
[38] Sherrington, *Economics of Rail Transport*, p. 213.
[39] *Ibid.*, p. 214.
[40] Frankel, "Obsolescence and Technical Change."

technological change in steel. But the retention of beehive coke ovens
for so long in Britain, when the far more efficient by-product recovery
oven had come into use in 1880, may well have been due to the separate character at that time of coal and coke firms, on the one hand, and
iron and steel, on the other.[41] Other possible reasons for the retention
of beehive ovens: Frankel's interrelatedness; Salter's cheap labor and
high capital cost;[42] simple economic irrationality, which made steel
mills incapable of taking advantage of profit opportunities. But it is
likely that steel firms were both uncertain of the costs and profits of
the existing beehive ovens and fearful that a lower price might reduce
the profitability of by-product ovens if they invested in them. Later,
when vertical integration occurred, by-product coke ovens came into
general use.[43]

A further striking example is furnished by shipbuilding. This industry grew to world supremacy between about 1870 and 1900 on the basis
of a highly disintegrated and specialized industry. There were separate
industries for shipbuilding, marine engineering, marine hardware, and
so on; and big ships were built in big yards, little in little. A host of
distinct innovations was developed, largely by trial and error, and
fitted into ships by the market mechanism. British efficiency was higher
than anywhere else in the world: in 1890 its productivity was 12.5 tons
per man employed, compared with 1.8 tons in French shipyards. This
lead was achieved through the great craftsmanship of the British
worker, through an enormous amount of specialization, and in spite
of comparatively backward equipment. Shipyards lacked electric light-
ing on the ways, electric motors, pneumatic tools. But the degree of
specialization was carried much further than anywhere else.

After World War II, however, the industry could be held up by
Andrew Shonfield as an outstanding example of what was wrong with
British industry — its failure to grow or to adopt new methods.[44] Shonfield blasts the industry for its failure to keep up with the changes that
had taken place in Germany, for example, or in Japan. But he does not
consider the notion that the organization of the industry into separate
firms dealing with each other at arm's length may have impeded tech-

[41] Burnham and Hoskins, *Iron and Steel in Britain*, p. 39, point out that by 1900
no one of the steel companies was fully integrated.

[42] See Burn, *Economic History of Steelmaking*, pp. 250ff, who believes that inadequate access to capital handicapped the British steel industry. See above,
Chapter 3, note 124.

[43] See Andrews and Brunner, *Capital Development in Steel*, p. 146. Just before
the big amalgamations of 1929–1931, pig-iron producers controlled 54 percent of
their coke needs.

[44] Shonfield, *British Economic Policy since the War* (1958), pp. 41ff.

nological change because of the possibility that part of the benefits of that change would have been external to the separate firms.[45]

There is of course no magic in vertical integration. It can lead to a "false sense of balance."[46] More important, it may fail to be combined with sufficient cost accounting and thereby perpetuate inefficient operations. The Ministry of Reconstruction was convinced of the necessity of investigating the costs of construction of locomotives and rolling stock by the separate railways in Britain, persuaded that the companies were making inadequate provision in their costs for rates and taxes, ground rent, and depreciation, though they might save a private builder's profits and advertising costs.[47] But it seems likely that technological change can proceed faster under vertical integration, unless the separate departments seek a quiet life.[48] Integration of the technological changes in one component into the process of another unit can be effectively organized and supervised in many ways which the market alone cannot effect.[49]

[45] Carter and Williams, *Technical Progress*, also fail to test technical change against the degree of integration. They furnish, however, an excellent example of external economies in citing shell moldings as an example of product-user reluctance to accept an innovation (p. 78). Accurate casting of these moldings saved machining, which used to be done by the buyer. The producer hesitated to introduce the casting process, however, because of concern over whether the buyer would be willing to pay the higher price for an improved product.

[46] Jewkes, "Is British Industry Inefficient?" Jewkes believes that the advantages of integration are normally very limited, and that the firms equipped with automatic looms suffered a heavy mortality during the war (p. 7, note). In general, the answer he gives to his question is no.

[47] Ministry of Reconstruction, *Standardization of Railway Equipment*.

[48] Cole observes that in the Great Western Railway there was no interdepartmental pressure for innovation during the superintendency of Tyrell from 1864 to 1888, with his interest in safety and in slowing down trains ("Locomotive Replacement," part 2, p. 30).

[49] This is an inadequate treatment of a complex problem, and it may be that the only effective means of maintaining interest in technical change is to alternate the organization between smaller separate independent units, dealing at arm's length through a market, and a larger integrated entity, subject to central direction. This would be analogous to a discovery made during my own government experience: there is no single system of organization of a bureau designed to keep up with what is going on in the world — whether by geographical units with functional subgroups or by functional units with geographic components. The only guarantee of alertness is the periodic reorganization which shifts to the other system. By the same token, Burton H. Klein of RAND has recently concluded that the organization of weapon development by "systems" (single companies responsible for the design of an entire weapon, with its component systems and subgroups) may be inherently (or currently?) inferior to a disintegrated system under which there is competition among producers of separate components to develop the most efficient possible subunits, and only at the end does an assembler undertake to produce a finished weapon out of competitively improved components. The analogy with the British shipbuilding industry of 1890 is striking.

THE MERCHANT SYSTEM

A particular form of disintegration is the division of functions of producing and selling between separate firms. This is clearly an efficient system under a fixed state of the arts, allowing separate managements to concentrate on essentially different tasks and to obtain the benefits of specialization and exchange. This is the basis on which Alfred Marshall defends it as the best system for advancing British export trade, despite an occasional yielding by merchants to the temptation to sell non-British goods to their customers.[50] But the separation of selling from production may have the drawback of slowing down technical change by interposing barriers of communication between the ultimate customer and the producer;[51] it may render external to consumer, merchant, or producer the benefits of changed products, or a changed process entailing some alteration in product, or merely increase the possibility that the benefit of change will be external to the firm. In the cotton-textile trade the merchant was partly responsible for the unnecessarily high number of separate qualities of product, since he lacked incentive to induce the customer to change the specifications, however arbitrarily fixed, and had the power to transfer orders from one manufacturer to another. Robson cites a case of fifty-four orders for thirty different varieties of low-grade poplins, differences among which were unimportant to the ultimate user, who could distinguish at best three grades.[52] The advantages of standardization were lost by preventing the producer from sharing his benefits with the customer. It may be significant that the woolen industry, which did much better than cotton in maintaining its rate of technical change (with the help of French competition), moved to direct trading.[53]

Beeseley and Throup point out that in machine tools the selling agents are more concentrated than the producers, which inhibits entry by the latter into new fields. The agents want noncompeting products, and to add a new line, a producing firm may have to change agents — which occurs infrequently.[54] Moreover, the merchant system lacks the capacity to develop new tools through close liaison between producer

[50] Marshall, *Industry and Trade,* pp. 616–618.

[51] Cf. Nicholas Kaldor's defense of advertising as a means of enabling the producer to overcome the stultifying effects of the wholesaler on product change in "Economic Aspects of Advertising" (1950–51), pp. 17–18.

[52] Robson, *Cotton Industry,* pp. 92–95. Robson concludes, however, that the advantage of longer runs of standardized specifications were not of great consequence (p. 100).

[53] Allen, *British Industries,* p. 260. Allen notes that woolens were not sold in the tropics, but only in countries with cultures and legal systems akin to the British, which may have eased the task of replacing the merchant system.

[54] Beeseley and Throup, "The Machine-Tool Industry" (1958), pp. 380ff.

and consumer. After nationalization, for example, Renault established its own machine-tool plant to effect the changes in design it wanted — there were no competent firms at that time in France — and owes the brilliant tooling of its Flins plant to vertical integration.[55]

It is difficult to know how far the merchant system inhibited technical change in tinplate production, where no major change in technology took place for two hundred years.[56] It probably had little to do with it, given the readily satisfied character of the Welsh manufacturers. Complaints leveled by the manufacturers against the merchants dealt with upgrading of produce, passing off seconds as standard sheets, and earning the difference in addition to normal brokerage, all of which hurt the long-run interests of the industry.[57] But it may be significant that when bigger companies emerged from the mass of small producers — Richard Thomas, Stewart and Lloyds, Guest, Keen and Nettlefolds, and Baldwins — they set up their own sales agencies.[58]

The institutional literature on foreign trade devotes a great deal of attention to the choice between direct selling by the manufacturer and indirect selling through merchants. Writers like Allen attribute British losses in foreign trade to the established position of the merchant, in particular to the fact that merchants occasionally substituted cheaper foreign products for British goods.[59] Lewis puts it that the merchant system is fitted to sell consumer goods to agricultural countries, not capital equipment to industrial.[60] But there is the distinct possibility, whose complete demonstration would require a separate book, that the merchant system bears a significant share of the responsibility for slowing down technical change because it renders a large proportion of the benefits of technical change external to the firms that must effect or sell it.

STANDARDIZATION, TECHNICAL EDUCATION

A special form of external economy in technology exists in standardization. Where a single firm has several types of equipment for the same job, it pays to scrap the nonstandard ones first, especially since these are limited in number. In locomotives and buses, odd types acquired in mergers are eliminated ahead of older standard models to save the

---

[55] See the quotation from Pierre Bézier, *ibid.*, p. 386.

[56] Minchenton, *British Tinplate Industry*, p. 35.

[57] *Ibid.*, pp. 105–107, 148ff.

[58] *Ibid.*, p. 246. See also Chandler, " 'Big Business' in American Industry," p. 26, where the shift from regional to national companies is said to involve above all the assumption of the marketing function.

[59] See Allen, *British Industries*, pp. 18–19, 311. See also Burnham and Hoskins, *Iron and Steel in Britain*, pp. 210–211.

[60] Lewis, "International Competition in Manufactures" (1957), p. 578.

bers took place; but they are difficult to specify precisely because of changes in classification and a late start (plus doubtful accuracy) on animal numbers.[29]

The period from 1900 to 1914 brought further transformations. Perhaps the major increase in efficiency was in agriculture north of the Loire, especially in sugar beets.[30] But there were others. Acreage devoted to pasture increased, but changes in classification make it difficult to say by how much. Arable declined, especially. in industrial crops where flax, hemp, and oil seeds were hurt by imports. The decline in wool was also sharp, partly owing to imports, partly to the suppression of the fallow. Wine made a comeback in volume after the phylloxera; with the shift from the hillsides to the irrigated valleys and to the Aramon grape, the average yield per hectare increased as well as the acreage. But quality was off. With wide variations in production and destabilizing speculation, moreover, prices and income

---

the work of Brousse in "La Productivité du travail" (1953), which gives an enormous increase in output per capita per active person in agriculture for this period, from an index of 23 in 1852 to 126 in 1882 based on 1914 = 100 (p. 638) and calculated from net revenues (= gross revenues at 1914 prices less costs of production at 1914 prices). The rise in the cost of production from 10.1 billion francs to 10.7 billion seems small, in the light of the increased use of capital, though the cost of the equipment and supplies may have fallen owing to more efficient transport. The decline in active population also seems small, however, from 100 in 1852 to only 95 in 1882. I am therefore disposed to suspend acceptance of Brousse's striking results until they have been evaluated by the experts.

[29] The allocation of acreage among crops, and animal numbers, can be given for selected dates (from *Annuaire statistique, 1958*, pp. 25, 27, 28). Acreage is in thousands of hectares, animals in thousands:

Year	Arable	Pasture and meadow	Vineyards	Woods and forest	Unculti- vated	Not classified
1840	25,227	4,198+	1,972	8,805	9,191	3,635
1852	26,139	5,057+	2,191	n.a.	6,580	12,760
1862	26,569	5,021+	2,321	9,317	6,546	4,032
1882	25,588	5,237+	2,197	9,445	6,253	2,555
1913	23,651	8,048	1,617	9,887	3,793	2,730
1929	21,768	9,990	1,585	10,406	5,086	3,682
1938	20,196	11,775	1,605	10,728	5,680	4,176
1946	17,964	12,224	1,530	10,879	6,699	5,198
1957	18,735	13,243	1,467	11,396	4,328	4,846

Year	Horses	Cattle	Sheep	Pigs
1890	2,862	13,562	21,658	6,017
1913	3,222	14,778	16,131	7,036
1929	2,936	15,631	10,452	6,102
1938	2,692	15,662	9,872	7,127
1946	2,354	15,100	7,259	5,334
1957	1,986	17,928	8,575	8,063

[30] Dumont, *Voyages en France d'un agronome*, as quoted by Valarché, *L'Économie rurale*, p. 176.

zoomed and slumped, culminating in rioting in 1907, when the price reached 1.75 francs per hectolitre with no takers, after having averaged 7 francs in 1900.[31] The industry became demoralized. Elsewhere pastures were extended to meet the increasing demand for milk, butter, cheese. Demand grew for table wine, fruit, vegetables. And technical progress picked up again as workers left the farms for industry, to be replaced by machinery.[32]

It is not, then, correct to say that French agriculture was entirely static. Adjusting in turn to new crops, the railroad, agricultural machinery, and to changing product prices, it also experienced a considerable change in labor inputs and in land tenure. Paid farmhands quit for two reasons: to join the children of farmers in going into trade or industry, or to acquire land themselves. Lévy notes that a million rural wage earners disappeared between the agricultural census of 1862 and 1882; 250,000 had become farmers and 750,000 had been absorbed into cities and towns.[33] Railroad construction attracted rural workers after 1848, and again under the Freycinet Plan.[34] Between 1882 and 1892, 400,000 more daily workers left, 150,000 to take on their own farms and 250,000 for the city. Finally, between 1906 and 1911 there was another rural exodus.[35]

It is difficult to find these movements sharply defined in the figures for France as a whole. The total active population engaged in agriculture, fishing, and forestry continued to rise until 1911, even though men engaged declined from 1876.[36] Outward migration occurred, of

[31] See Carrère and Dugrand, *La Région meditérranéenne*, p. 78; Warner, *Winegrowers of France* (1960), p. 17.

[32] Augé-Laribé, *Politique agricole* (1950), pp. 156, 157.

[33] Lévy, *Histoire économique de la France*, p. 138.

[34] Chatelain, "La main-d'oeuvre et la construction des chemins de fer"; Augé-Laribé, *Politique agricole*, p. 53.

[35] Lévy, *Histoire économique de la France*, pp. 209, 218. Faucher, *Le Paysan et la machine*, says that the decline was particularly rapid after 1890 and above all after 1900 (p. 218).

[36] Estimates of active population for selected years are in millions (from *Annuaire statistique*, 1957, p. 3):

Year	Engaged in agriculture, fishing, forests	Percent of total	Number of men
1856	7.31	51.4	5.15
1876	7.99	49.3	5.78
1896	8.46	45.3	5.71
1911	8.64	41.7	5.40
1931	7.69	36.4	4.50
1946	7.48	36.6	4.22
1954	5.21	27.4	3.39

Brousse ("La Productivité du travail," p. 636) notes that the 1851 census is particularly wrong on the proportion of women in the active labor force, and the 1946 census full of mistakes.

to specify basic steel, so much cheaper than acid.[70] The conversion from coal to oil was delayed, moreover, by an (intentionally?) ill-designed experiment in which an oil-burner naval vessel emitted large clouds of black smoke to make itself unduly conspicuous.[71]

A more familiar type of external economy relevant to technical change, and widely discussed in the development literature, is the provision of technical education — whether by the state, other governmental bodies, or private institutions. Much has been made of the comparative neglect of technical education in Britain,[72] after an early flowering of scientific societies in the course of the Industrial Revolution. The weakness of Oxford and Cambridge in science has been mentioned, as well as the lack of people with scientific education in business. Although there is some skepticism toward all generalizations about technical change,[73] including the one that progress could be made for a time by empiricists and amateurs but that late in the nineteenth century it required trained technical personnel, there seems to

[70] Andrews and Brunner, *Capital Development in Steel*, p. 77, state that with World War I "even buyers so notoriously conservative as the Admiralty had to accept basic steel." This, however, was basic open-hearth steel, not basic Bessemer, which Andrews and Brunner regard as good only for tube and strip (p. 98). Acid Bessemer was largely used for rails, but declined because of the dwindling of hematite iron ore (see above, Chapter 2). All basic steel was distrusted initially, because of the difficulties of controlling its quality and its consequent variability. In 1878 Lloyds Institute of Insurance Underwriters withdrew a 20 percent reduction in premiums accorded to steel ships over iron from Bessemer steel. But with the basic process, German and French metallurgists learned how to control the quality of basic Bessemer. In time, the demand favored basic steel. To what extent the British industry remained more dependent on acid than on basic, and on open-hearth than on Bessemer, because of conservatism on the part of consumers, slowness of the industry to achieve the appropriate skills, or unwillingness to adapt, is a question on which it is difficult to make judgments. Burnham and Hoskins attach importance to the consumer predilection against basic steel, but note that European supplies were imported (*Iron and Steel in Britain*, pp. 35, 118). Contrast the French enthusiasm for Bessemer which, after its invention in 1856 was demonstrated at the London exhibition of 1862 and said by Michel Chevalier to be the greatest thing since the discovery of steel (Labrousse, *L'Évolution économique*, III, 89). For a contemporary account of Bessemer's encouragement by Napoleon III and discouragement by Woolwich arsenal, "the enemy of inventors," see *Fortunes Made in Business* (1883), I, 226. This source also comments ironically on shipbuilding with Bessemer steel in 1862 as follows: "Few will be surprised to learn that this made no impression whatsoever on the Lords of the Admiralty" (I, 233).

[71] Seminar, Nuffield College, November 28, 1960.

[72] See, e.g., Cotgrove, *Technical Education and Social Change* (1958). The general historian puts it much along the following lines: "It was becoming doubtful how long the personal energy of the manufacturer, even the high quality of his wares, would make up for an ignorance of chemistry and the metric system and a lordly indifference to the tastes and requirements of his customers. The age of pioneers was over, and for an age of close cultivation we were imperfectly equipped" (Young, *Portrait of an Age*, p. 164).

[73] Jewkes, Sawers, and Stillerman, *The Sources of Invention* (1958).

be little doubt that British universities and public bodies were slow in responding to the widely recognized need for more technological education.[74] A big push in science began after the Crystal Palace exhibition, under the patronage of the prince consort, with the establishment of the South Kensington museums, the Cavendish laboratory in 1860, and the practical provincial universities. But the National Laboratories for standards were not begun until 1900, and the Division of Scientific and Industrial Research not until 1915. After World War I, a number of industries formed research associations, with government prodding. The failure in higher technical education was matched on the lower levels: technical colleges for artisans were not started until after 1900.

Sponsored research and scientific education are not enough to induce rapid technological progress. There must be general acceptance of the value of the scientific approach to industrial problems at all levels. Education must be widespread instead of just for the elite, and education plus intelligence must be accorded some prestige in business, along with experience on the shop floor.[75] Business leadership must make room for technically competent people. Government cannot provide technical education until the value system is ready to accord it place. When the public is ready to receive it, moreover, there will be a lag before science and technology can be taught, while teachers are being readied.[76]

This interest in technical change and the readiness to take chances on new processes are emphasized by Carter and Williams, especially when they write of a firm's lack of secrecy and willingness to communicate with the outside world and within the plant.[77] In the early phases of the Industrial Revolution, continuous interest and excitement were felt over solutions to technical problems; and work took place on them by people outside of industry. This implies communication. In the third quarter of the nineteenth century, the three major inventions in the steel industry came from nonindustrial sources. By the end of the century, however, interest had turned away from the rapid advance

[74] Carter and Williams, *Technical Progress*, p. 100. Cotgrove (p. 27) believes that the need was not widely recognized, despite the Royal Commission on Technical Instruction of 1882, and he stresses the complacency of the Commission on the Depression of Trade and Industry, in 1885, and the neglect of science and apathy toward technical education bred by fifty years of industrial pre-eminence. Marshall, *Industry and Trade*, p. 95, states that British businessmen awoke to the need for improved education for technical efficiency in 1904.

[75] See Erickson, *British Industrialists*, p. 43: "Workshop training produced men with a supreme contempt for theory and science."

[76] The point was made by Faraday before the Royal Commission (Young, *Portrait of an Age*, p. 97). Young adds that the reason for the classical curriculum was that classically trained teachers were available.

[77] *Technical Progress, passim,* esp. pp. 7, 117, 179.

has sped up when industrial growth has picked up — under the Second Empire, after 1890, 1900, or 1910, and again after World War II, though not in the 1920s — it has been slow.

But this simple averaging is a trivial cause of retardation. No one assigns significance to the slow growth of productivity of the services sector in overall economic development, though if this part were to proceed more rapidly, the total would also, other things being equal. The most important effect of French agriculture in slowing down economic development in France may be merely its effect on the average. But the authorities quoted, Nicholls, Lewis, Gerschenkron, Rostow, intended to say something more interesting.

AGRICULTURAL DEMAND

Lewis has talked of French agriculture as a drag on demand and hence on growth. The point is also made by others.[46] A rapid rate of growth of income in agriculture can stimulate industry if demand for industrial products grows rapidly.

Here, however, in contrast to the previous section, it is impossible to be simple-minded. One must specify the conditions under which the increase in productivity would have resulted in an increase in income and how this would have contributed to growth. Or, inversely, given a lack of productivity, what other changes in the system, such as a push for foreign markets, could have contributed the demand that agriculture failed to provide? It is necessary to specify at least the supply and demand conditions under which the incremental output is sold, the marginal propensities to consume and save in agriculture, whether the economy is open or closed, and why the initiative should be left to the agricultural sector. And probably more. These general-equilibrium models, including both income and price, are very difficult to cope with, especially when they are open. It is particularly trying that so many theorists are prepared to dismiss the subject in a sentence.

Something of the difficulty in saying anything sensible on this score can be illustrated by the rather waspish controversy between David Landes and André Danière over the effect of crop fluctuations on business cycles in eighteenth-century France.[47] Landes was attacking the Labrousse thesis that crop failures led to depression because of cutting the demand for commodities by tenant farmers. Landlord income

[46] See Nicholls, "Agriculture in Economic Development," p. 2; Rostow, "Leading Sectors and the Take-off," p. 20.
[47] Landes, "The Statistical Study of French Crises" (1950), and Danière, "Feudal Incomes and Demand Elasticity for Bread," plus a reply, a rejoinder, and a second reply.

might have increased, as rent was paid in kind and prices rose. This increased savings. But after rent had been paid, the decline in marketable grain was greater than the price increase, according to Labrousse, which reduced farm money income and spending. Inelasticity of demand for bread of the workers in the city further caused a diversion of their income from consumer goods other than food to bread, reinforcing the decline in peasant spending.

Landes agreed with the Labrousse thesis for acute crises, such as that of 1848.[48] For more usual cycles he was unpersuaded, believing that the demand for bread was inelastic, when bread was 50 percent of the consumers' budget, and that on this account agricultural income and spending should rise during crop failures, rather than fall. Danière suggested that the data indicated that the demand for wheat was elastic, which would support the Labrousse thesis on the side of agricultural spending, but would hurt it insofar as it relied upon the diversion of urban spending from industrial products to food.

The controversy dealt mainly with the eighteenth century. In the nineteenth there are two important changes. The role of rent is cut down, though it is still sizable relative to farm income.[49] And the economy is much more open. An open economy makes it possible for urban demand for all grain to be inelastic at the same time that the demand for French grain is elastic. In crises the price will not rise as high as it otherwise would because of imports; whereas in bumper harvests, some support will be found for price, and income, through export sales.[50]

There can be little doubt but that the 1846–1848 crisis was of the Labrousse sort, modified for these two factors. The scarce crop first hurt urban real income greatly and agricultural income considerably. Next, the bumper crop failed to make good the loss of farm income because exports could not be organized as rapidly as imports. But

[48] Contrast the curious position of Cameron, referred to in Chapter 1, note 3.

[49] Latil quotes the ISEA estimates of rent as 31 percent of agricultural income in 1788, 24 percent in 1845, and 28 percent in 1890 (*Revenu agricole*, p. 202). Valarché, *L'Économie rurale*, p. 140, gives very different figures, of different trend: 50 percent under the Second Empire, 39 percent in 1900, and 26 percent in 1930, calling them gross rather than net. The difference is depreciation on farm buildings and equipment.

[50] There is in this discussion no hint of the mechanism in factor markets by which Chambers thinks (referring to Britain about this period) that agriculture transmitted crises to industry: "A good harvest . . . stimulated industry by increasing the demand for labor and so raising wages at the same time as the means of life became more abundant; and a bad harvest diminished the demand for labor and lowered wages while causing the price of necessities to rise" (*The Workshop of the World*, 1961, p. 152). This provides a splendid illustration of the difficulty of general-equilibrium analysis in history, with one set of observers focusing on goods market, another on factors.

Excellent reasons exist to reduce replacement and process decisions to a habit. Decision making is expensive; but habits can differ, as well as the approach to technological innovation. The response to suggestions for change can be either "What does it save?" or "What does it cost?" [84] Excess of either courage or caution can lead to disaster, the former more rapidly. Still, habits of receptivity to change, to write-offs, to new processes and new products, can, with appropriate safeguards, yield income and ultimately economize even the most painful decision making.

FRENCH INNOVATION

After this long disquisition on technical change in Britain, I shall make only a few points about France. First, we should note the more prominent role of government in technical change, in the early efforts of Napoleon I for spurring on French adoption of machinery by loans, subsidies, and orders, on the one hand, and expositions, competitions, and prizes, on the other.[85] Second, there is the importance of technical assistance from Britain, whether through British entrepreneurs and workers in France or visits of French industrialists to Britain.[86] Third, there is the Cartesian and scientific quality of French inventions,[87]

[84] Burn, *Economic History of Steelmaking*, p. 208. See also p. 296 for the comment to the young men making suggestions, who were told to teach their grandmothers to suck eggs, and that that was tried fifty years ago. See, finally, Minchenton, *British Tinplate Industry*, p. 195, for the Welsh tinmaker's response, "Has any other fool tried it yet?"

[85] Ballot, *Introduction du machinisme* (1923), *passim*. Ballot contrasts British and French mechanization in the Industrial Revolution, the former spontaneous, the latter a response to British competition; the former, on private initiative, the latter, government-spurred.

[86] Henderson, *Britain and Industrial Europe* (1954). See also Gille, *Formation de la grande entreprise*, pp. 24–27; Duveau, *La Vie ouvrière*, pp. 126–127. For a detailed account of one ironmaster who visited England, see Thuillier, *Georges Dufaud*, esp. the diaries in the appendix.

[87] See, e.g., Pollard, "Laissez-Faire and Shipbuilding," p. 99, where it is noted that British shipbuilding in 1800 was experimental and that each ship was an empirical venture, except when a French ship had been captured and could be taken apart and copied for its mathematical design. French innovations in steel, especially ship plate, were copied in Britain in the period from 1875 to 1900 (see Burn, "British Steelmaking and Foreign Competition," p. 221).
In chemicals, broadly simultaneous British (Perkins, 1856) and French (Verguin, 1859) inventions in synthetic dyes failed to hold the field against German innovative capacity, but France did particularly well in aluminum (Allais-Camargues), glass (St. Gobain), automobiles (Citroën), and locomotives (the steel companies, Five-Lille, and Gouin). David Landes warns me that there is some doubt about the order for fifteen locomotives which Schneider-Creusot claimed to have taken away from British competition (Lhomme, *La Grande bourgeoisie au pouvoir*, p. 235); but evidence from Rist ("Le Traité de 1860," 1956, p. 932), who says that French locomotives were as cheap as or cheaper than British because of specialized production, and Cameron (*France and the Development of Europe*, p. 100), who

although still other innovations, like the department store, seem far more appropriate to a nation of shopkeepers than they do to a country with the aristocratic value of "prowess in consumption." [88] Finally, and most important, we have the scattered and occasional character of French innovations, except for the revival of technocratic vigor, again with governmental leadership, after World War II.

There are those who claim that the French are not good at science because they favor literary over scientific studies.[89] On the other side of the argument are Clapham, who regards the French as "unusually" inventive; Simiand, who has turned out a long list of inventions to prove that the rhythm of industrial change cannot be used to account for changes in industrial output; and Cameron, who believes that French science was pre-eminent and that French engineers developed European industry.[90]

There can be little doubt that France had a strong history of technical and scientific education, in contrast with Britain. Moreover, the increasing complexity of modern industry fitted well with the French tradition of pure science, as contrasted with British empiricism. But the French flair for technology did not operate in a vacuum. Government support was sporadic — emerging under Napoleon I and Napoleon III. Bourgeois opposition was fairly continuous. The French tradition of technical virtuosity is embodied in the heritage of Saint-Simon,

---

discusses the fuel economies of the Schneider locomotive, suggests that it was possible. Cole records an instance of the Great Western Railway's ordering a French locomotive before 1900, as it contemplated changing its design (see "Locomotive Replacement" for its scrapping in 1922 and 1926). In the end, Churchward did not adopt the principles of the French design. Saul, *British Overseas Trade* (1960), notes that French productivity in soda ash increased markedly and more rapidly than British in the years after 1860 (p. 162). Other French competitive gains at British expense were recorded after 1880, particularly in woolen cloth where there was a change of taste against British worsted and in favor of the softer French cloth, more suitable for dress goods. Here was a commodity in which the French interest in quality, and in such questions as which manufacturer could cover the biggest area with a given amount of wool, paid off. See Duveau, *La Vie ouvrière*, pp. 136–137.

[88] For a discussion of the founding and expansion of the department stores see above, Chapter 3. For a fictionalized account of their operation by a near contemporary, see Zola, *Au Bonheur des Dames* (1883).

[89] Aron, *Le Développement de la société industrielle* (1955–56), p. 129.

[90] Clapham, *Development of France and Germany* (1936), p. 232. Simiand, *Le Salaire* (1932), II, 22–23 — Simiand's candidate for responsibility for the fluctuations is gold discoveries (Marjolin, *Prix, monnaie et production*, 1941, p. 180, says that Simiand's views are "too categorical" and that technical progress was important in the upswing from 1895 to 1914). Cameron, *France and the Development of Europe*, chap. iii, esp. p. 43. But Cameron exaggerates the impact of French engineering on European industry and neglects the extent to which French technical contributions outside of France were confined to public works, including railroads, and mining. British technical work in France, on the other hand, had included both railroads and industry.

Doubt has been expressed in the appendix about the value of these estimates for measuring short periods of growth. There is further doubt over the agricultural estimates of 1872 and 1882, relative to one another, since the Sirol index, admittedly faulty, shows a decline in volume while price remained steady. Volume fell from 86 in 1872 to 75, or by 13 percent. Measuring from the agricultural peak in 1874, however, income would have certainly shown a decline to 1882 and thereafter, since the volume index for that year was 95 and the price 137, against 75 and 115 in 1882 and 70 and 93 in 1892 (1914 = 100). Perroux's technique of including linear estimates of growth for meat and forage crops, and a lump-sum estimate for gardens which jumps from 500 million francs in 1872 to a billion in 1882,[63] limits the short-term accuracy of his sectoral estimate.

The only item in the detailed ISEA estimates of agricultural income which declined between 1872 and 1882, apart from a decrease in industrial crops from 306 million francs to 290 million, was wine. From 1882 to 1892 there were small declines in a number of items, such as dried vegetables, wood, and industrial animal products, along with industrial crops; but large declines in wheat and wine. Over the two decades the decline in income in grains amounted to 650 million francs; that in wine to a billion. These compare with a net gain for all of agriculture of 300 million francs in the twenty years and a setback of 1.1 billion between 1882 and 1892.

There is reason, however, to think that this decline is somewhat underestimated, not only because of the biases already mentioned. Augé-Laribé had put the gross value of wine production at 2 billion francs in 1869.[64] An 1875 peak figure — with the all-time record output and steady prices — would have been higher, the resulting fall greater. Second, the structure of French farms of this period made the fall in cash income larger than indicated by the total grain figures. Wheat was only 30 percent of total grain, but it was the major cash crop. Oats, barley, and corn were grown largely for feed. The price of wheat fell more than that of other grains. Forced sales of wheat in twelve representative departments doubled by 1889 from the 1873–1879 base.[65] As farmers needed cash to meet their commitments, whether rentals or interest on mortgages, wheat was sold in competition with imports, bringing down their cash income more than income in kind. Total income therefore underestimates the decline in money income.

Cash income was needed for farm and household expenses. The

[63] ISEA, *Le Revenu national* (1952), p. 76.
[64] *Politique agricole*, p. 67.
[65] Golob, *Méline Tariff*, pp. 77ff.

specialized farm discussed earlier was not on a subsistence basis, and Augé-Laribé is misleading when he says the farmer was self-sufficient at this time, needing only some wine, salt, clothes, and tools. Moreover, there is agricultural debt. It is hard to form any precise idea of the burden of debt. Gille comments that in 1848 land was high-priced — it yielded only a 3 percent return, but had to bear burdens of 5 to 12, 15, 20, and even 22 percent.[66] After that time the price of land rose much further, but the information is only qualitative.[67] It is likely that large farms were less indebted; small holders, relatively more so. With the depression, the price of land fell. The burden became heavier on old debts. The lower rate of interest may have permitted some refunding. But that agricultural debt was a problem is illustrated by the agitation to establish the Crédit Agricole and to get the Crédit Foncier active in the field, as discussed in Chapter 3.

Sharp and persistent depression in agriculture spread through demand to other sectors, especially after the building boom had burst and the stock market and speculative bubble collapsed. The loss in farm income in grains and wine was in the vicinity of 2 billion francs, or 8 percent of national income. Deflation in the south led to widespread bank failure in the Hérault.[68] The weak state of agriculture, followed by a stock-market boom and collapse, is strongly reminiscent of 1925–1929 in the United States.

There are several lines of argument against attributing this much significance in the stagnation after 1882 to agricultural depression. It can be argued, first, that apart from the deflationary impact of imports, loss in money income of the farm sector is offset by the gain in real income of consumers. Such was the case in Britain, for example, where worker real income increased throughout the Great De-

[66] Gille, *La Banque et le crédit*, p. 136. See also the other references in note 35, Chapter 3 above.

[67] Fauchon, *Agriculture française*, p. 118, merely says that the value of land rose from 1840 to 1880, during the golden age, and fell by one third after 1880. (See also Valarché, *Mobilité des ruraux*, 1953, p. 116.) Bernard notes that the price of land was steady in Seine-et-Marne (a region of specialized rented farms) between 1851 and 1879, though its rental value rose, and fell sharply to 1908 — except when expressed in terms of wheat, in which coin its price was steady (*Seine-et-Marne*, p. 71). The difference between the sale value and the rental value is due to the declining share of rent. Bernard observes further that the price of land in Brittany went steadily up (p. 72), but deprecates this by saying that price of land is a secondary consideration compared with the need for capital to farm it. There may be some question of whether these regional figures are representative of national trends, for in Britain disparities occur in rents owing to differences in crop. But wheat is grown everywhere, as I have noted. Golob (*Méline Tariff*, p. 72) has the price of wheat land falling less than the price of wheat between 1879 and 1884, but much further to 1892, when it reaches 73 (1879 = 100).

[68] Carrère and Dugrand, *La Région meditérranéene*, p. 80.

change was pervasive and spread to private industry. To indicate that nationalization is not sufficient to bring about technological progress, it is necessary only to compare the experiences of France and Britain — whether in railroads or coal. In France after World War II, rapid increases took place in labor productivity in coal output and in ton-miles and passenger-miles. This was in part because of large-scale investment. In Britain, a similar substantial investment occurred, but without the same increase in labor productivity, at least immediately.[94]

There appear to have been two kinks in British and French technological history — one for the worse in Britain about 1880; one for the better in France immediately after World War II. But these can hardly be regarded as parametric shifts. The styles of the two countries were very different, British pragmatism contrasting with French theoretical and scientific elegance. There is something to the view that the former became less and less appropriate to the world of che istry and electricity after 1880, but it is also likely that the pragmatic flair drooped under the impact of prosperity. In France, on the other hand, the Cartesian tradition remained vigorous, occasionally smothered by conservatism and business distrust. When it gained ascendency after World War II, it added to itself the effective ingredient of empiricism.

In neither case can technological change be said to have determined the course of growth. Although a conditioning influence of great importance, it can act only as part of a complex social, economic, and political matrix.

[94] A British friend believes that a distinction should be made between the nationalized railways, which were ultra conservative and fought hard for steam against diesel and electric, and the Coal Board, which faces a long delay in payout from its mechanization of mining.

CHAPTER 8

SCALE AND COMPETITION

Two aspects of industrial organization remain to be discussed in more detail: the size of firm (or plant) and the degree of competition. In particular, we must examine the theses that French economic growth has been held back by the small size of French *plants,* thus losing economies of scale in production; and, second, that growth has been slowed down by monopolies, usually large firms, which have held up prices, restricted output, inhibited technical change, and so on. These theses need not be contradictory or inconsistent. Small firms can act monopolistically in small markets. But other reconciliations are possible. The large firm can consist of many small plants.[1] Different conditions can exist side by side in different industries. Or a single industry can contain a few large firms, which hold an umbrella over the many small enterprises in the rest of the industry, making a large profit at monopoly prices and concerned not to destroy the small firms for reasons of social and political stability.

As in others of these complex relationships, the slowness of French economic growth may have been the result of limited scale and lack of competition, or the other way around: industry may have acted defensively for lack of expanding markets. In particular, the question arises after 1950: did competition both with the Common Market and internally stimulate French growth, or was competition made possible by growth otherwise achieved?

The British literature on economic development has much less reference to size of plant or market control. There is some expression of the view that imperfections of competition slowed down development, but also the contrary: that too much competition, especially dumping from abroad, prevented needed steps. Since World War II there has been some move to break up restrictive trade practices in order to stimulate competition and expansion. On the whole, however, the consensus is that market control was unimportant up to World War I because of the difficulties of organizing industries in the face of import

---

[1] Gendarme, *La Région du Nord* (1954), p. 56, describes a *clouterie* (nail manufacturer) in Maubeuge which has 300 workers who are all engaged in isolated workshops, having often no more than 1 master and 2 companions.

refuses to move because of its attachment to the soil. On this showing one would expect to find a wide gap between earnings in industry and agriculture, which would increase in periods of industrial expansion. An opposite formulation would run in terms of very low supply elasticity in agriculture and low demand elasticity for agricultural products. Increased demand for the output of the agricultural sector, in this circumstance, or a small decline in output resulting from the transfer of resources to industry, would quickly lead to an increase in the price of foodstuffs and increases in the return to factors engaged in agriculture, thus holding labor on the farm. Returns, then, would be equal in agriculture and industry. A compromise is of course possible: there is normally a gap between returns to agriculture and industry; this narrows in periods of expanding industry so that rising industrial wages or the absolute scarcity of labor cut off the possibilities of continued growth.

A third formulation emphasizes less the high wages in urban locations than the cheap labor available in rural areas. This attracts industry into dispersed locations, thus losing the external economies of the agglomerative process in urbanization and slowing down growth in a roundabout way.[73]

The first two versions of the theory rely on the rise of industrial wages to halt industrial expansion. This might help to explain timing, and why periods of growth like that under the Second Empire came to an end. But it stands opposite to those theories about French growth which stress that labor was too cheap and so failed to encourage the employment of machinery. And it is also possible to develop models in which the block to growth comes from too low wages and too little demand.

Direct evidence to enable one to choose the most likely theory is difficult to come by. For the period before 1850, Gille and Dunham have amassed a certain amount of material, without pointing to a definite conclusion. Gille notes that the textile industry used labor complementary to agriculture and did not emerge into large firms until the middle of the century. Mining and metallurgy, however, suffered from needing large groups of workers, held by the land through the system of equal inheritance. The evidence is meager. A thesis is required on the subject, Gille admits, citing seven cases of labor shortage in coal, numerous ones in metallurgy, but then he goes on to say that the major lack was qualitative. Labor was unskilled and ignorant. A company like d'Anzin built housing for workers and

---

[73] Habakkuk, "Family Structure and Economic Change" (1955); Juillard, *Basse-Alsace;* and Dobb, *Development of Capitalism* (1947), pp. 230–231 — "clinging to soil means primitive capitalism."

arranged adult courses at night. For the most part, however, workers lacked the instruction which was general in England and which enabled them to adapt to factory work.[74] Dunham gives much the same picture: labor supply was adequate but not overabundant. There was no crowding in the cities because of the attraction of agriculture. Labor retained its connection with agriculture, was industrially untrained. It was cheap in price but costly. Industry was small-scale because labor was untrained, and labor was untrained because industry was small-scale. The peasant resisted the factory system. An abundant supply of cheap rural labor made the domestic system strong. The rural worker's passion for the land inhibited the development of a labor force.[75] When the rhetoric of these statements is dismissed, the argument has shifted, at least part way, from the price of labor in industry to the labor cost of production.[76]

From 1850 on, with the advent of the railroad, conflicting tendencies operated. Over wide parts of the country,[77] rural industry and inefficient agriculture were destroyed by the competition from more efficiently organized producers. Peasants moved from the hills to the

[74] Gille, *Formation de la grande entreprise* (1959), pp. 39ff. But compare the view of Isaac Holden with extensive interests in wool combing in France: at Rheims, Croix near Roubaix, and St. Denis in the first half of the nineteenth century. He found French workers to be "active and industrious, working contentedly and earnestly, and easy and agreeable to manage when treated with respect and firmness" (Anon., *Fortunes Made in Business*, I, 42).

[75] Dunham, *Industrial Revolution in France* (1951), pp. 182, 184, 243, 306, 434.

[76] Cameron, *France and the Development of Europe,* p. 27, discusses the effect of the Junker organization of agriculture in eastern Germany which drove landless peasants into cities, where they became the backbone of the cheap, docile industrial labor force. The question here is how much to emphasize the word "docile." Paul Hohenburg has studied the labor force in chemical plants in France at the end of the nineteenth century, noting that there was no difficulty in getting enough workers, despite unattractive working conditions, but that it was no place for craftsmen. He cites Baud (*Les Industries chimiques régionales de la France,* 1922, p. 3) as attributing German success to the absence of tradition and handed-down skills. The migrating peasants were willing and docile. Löffl (*Die Chemische Industrie Frankreichs,* pp. 12–13) also observes the conflict between following exactly the incomprehensible instructions of a laboratory and the traditions of *liberté* and *egalité* of the artisan.

[77] See Coutin, "La Décongestion des centres industriels et la vie agricole" (1945), p. 62. In Picardy and Normandy industry moved into cities; in the Bas-Maine and Middle Garonne, it disappeared. Armengaud, "Les Débuts de la dépopulation touloussaine" (1951), ascribes the local depopulation after 1850 to the collapse of rural industry and the opportunity to escape afforded by railroads, big public works, the embellishment of cities, and the expansion of wine in Bas-Languedoc. Dion notes that different localities exhibited different times for starting their population decrease in the Loire Valley, depending upon the specialty crop; thus localities specializing in fruits and onions started down in 1831, field crops in 1851, and wine in 1851, but with a specially sharp break after 1866 when the plow was introduced among the vines (*Le Val du Loire,* pp. 674–675). Juillard observes that the vigorous rural industry of Basse-Alsace partly disappeared and partly moved to the city after 1850 (*Basse-Alsace,* p. 288).

measure, or less accurately the value of output, this long tail does not count for a great deal because of its low productivity. The uncertainty in establishing the limit of the industry, then, is of no great consequence. With manpower, however, this long tail may count for much more. Any measure couched in terms of a percentage of an industry or its average when the industry is measured in workers is accordingly suspect.

A choice between plant and firm as a unit of measure turns on whether one is interested in scale of production or control of the market. For production, size of plant is relevant; for market control, the firm. The same division is required between the two main measures: average size and indexes of concentration. The average size of firm is unimportant for production, in industries where firms may have more than one plant. It is true that economies and diseconomies of administration must be approached by numbers of plants per firm; but for the most part my interest lies in technological economies of scale found within the plant, not the firm. For market control, however, the index of concentration should relate to the selling unit, the firm. Such indexes typically seek to establish the existence of market control by specifying the percentage of output (or assets or employees) of the leading firms in the industry, as given by the census of production. It is an error to equate an industry with the firms listed on the Stock Exchange, for example, or to measure their size by the market quotation of their quoted capital, as do P. E. Hart and S. J. Prais in an article covering the period from 1885 to 1956.[5] Their conclusion that business concentration in the British economy as a whole has not changed much is invalidated by what they recognize as an unrepresentative sample, on the one hand, and by an inappropriate measure, on the other.[6]

It is necessary to add that market shares of firms give no necessary indication of market control, since there are many forms of association for control of markets that are distinct from the organization of the firm. The possibility exists that the separate branches of a firm will compete freely in the market against one another, as two branches

the British government does not require firms of less than ten workers to fill out a Census of Production form, with the result that very little is known about this scale of business. But since the vast majority of the working force is employed in firms of more than ten workers, the missing numbers can be taken to be small.

[5] "Business Concentration" (1956).

[6] It is unnecessary to indicate why quoted firms are not representative of all firms, given the changing status of private companies in this period. It may be worth mentioning, however, that the market valuation of quoted capital may differ from total assets by (1) bank borrowing; (2) privately placed securities; (3) differences in earning power per unit of asset between companies; and (4) differences in the optimistic or pessimistic bias of the market with respect to the earning power of particular companies. There may be some reason to take the third of these discrepancies into account, but not the others.

of General Motors, Buick and Chevrolet, are said to have competed. But, typically, degree of concentration by firms is a minimum. Nistri and Prêcheur observe that the formation of Sidelor, Sollac, and Lorraine-Escaut in 1946 did not represent a significant change in industrial organization, since Sidelor consisted of the entente Mar-Mich-Pont, formed in 1919; Sollac is de Wendel; and Lorraine-Escaut is a mere extension of Aciéries de Longwy into the Moselle area.[7]

Of the variety of data which could be presented, I offer only a limited selection. Table 8 compares firms of more than ten employees in

Table 8. Average Size of Firms (with More than 10 Workers) in Selected French and British Industries, about 1954

	Great Britain			France		
Industrial area	Firms	Workers (000)	Average	Firms	Workers (000)	Average
Metals and primary transformation	1,915	552	289	2,778	426	153
Machinery, electrical industry, shipbuilding	8,886	1,856	209	5,742	549	95
Textiles	6,210	862	139	7,031	630	90
Paper, cardboard, printing	4,334	481	111	3,504	207	57

Source. Calculated by Passe, *Economies comparées* (1957), p. 20; from Central Statistical Office, *Annual Abstract of Statistics, 1956*; INSEE, *Les Établissements industriels, 1954.*

France and Britain in about 1954 by broad classes of industry. Table 9 gives the change in size distribution by numbers of salaried workers in France from 1896 to 1936 by establishments. (Establishments are parts of a firm located in a single geographical locale. They are therefore smaller than a firm, but may be larger than a plant when a firm has two or more plants in the same location.) This table omits the self-employed worker. Table 10 furnishes British figures for firms by number, net output, and employment, distributed by firm size, arranged by numbers of workers, in 1935. This is not comparable with the French

[7] Nistri and Prêcheur, *La Région du Nord et Nord-Est* (1959), p. 124. Sollac in fact grouped La Société de Wendel et Cie., the Lorraine properties of Sidelor and the Aciéries de Longwy, Forges et Aciéries de Dolling, UCMPI, Etablissements J. J. Carnaud, and Forges de Basse-Indres. But de Wendel was the biggest subscriber and the offices were established on its property (Sédillot, *La Maison de Wendel*, 1958, p. 390).

sale prices. Finally, one can net out more or less of the income of a given sector. This seems to be the main problem posed by Clark's calculations.[83] The second and third editions of his *Conditions of Economic Progress* give relative figures for the agricultural sector and absolute figures for agricultural and total income that permit other relative figures to be calculated. The results are very different, as we may see in Table 17. The difference between the direct percentage

Table 17. Percentage of National Income Produced by French Agriculture, According to Clark

			Calculated from absolute figures	
Date	Percentage figures (1)	Date	With imputed income (2)	Without imputed income (3)
1861–65	63[a]	1860–64	30	23
1911	32	1910–13	17	11
1930	19	1934–38	13	8.5

[a] This figure appears to be a gross error.

Source. Column 1 is from the second edition of *Conditions of Economic Progress* (1951), p. 444; it is with imputed income. Columns 2 and 3 have been calculated from the third edition (1957), pp. 123–125, 262.

figures and the calculated goes back to the attempt to make a more restricted definition of agricultural output, excluding double counting of grain and other foodstuffs used as fodder or as seed,[84] as well as purchases of fertilizer, equipment, and "all other expenses of production." [85]

Bellerby also concludes that France is different from the rest of the world in the proportions of income earned in agriculture and in industry. He works with a limited concept of "aggregate incentive

[83] *Ibid.*, p. 110n, states that the work of Clark requires a patient exegesis which is not always rewarded.

[84] The ISEA estimates for agricultural net output in Table 14 involve, for 1872, a gross output of 13,167 million francs, and deductions of 600 million francs for seed, 3,080 million for animal feed. It seems curious that the deduction for animal feed should have risen since 1862 by 1,060 million, when the gross value of forage crops had increased only 200 million, that of cereals 400 million, that of meat 175 million, and that of other animal products 383 million. On this showing, there seems to have been a reduction in grains available for human consumption, on the one hand, and either a loss on meat output or a substantial increase in animal draft work, on the other.

[85] *Conditions of Economic Progress*, 3rd ed. (1955), p. 256.

income" of the farmer-entrepreneur group, which is net factor income in agriculture less net rent, interest, wages of agricultural workers, and the income of any independent agricultural personnel not ordinarily classed as farmers. He derives this by per-man equivalents of labor, including women and youths as fractions of adult men, and compares it with the ratio of all persons actively engaged in the labor force to all nonfarm income less rent and interest. He finds that this ratio is approximately 100 percent in France, compared to figures normally 30 to 60 and reaching as high as 70 in Britain.[86] But no one is able to control his figures, since they rest on some unpublished estimates of French farm income by Proctor Thompson.[87]

Adjusting Clark's higher result in any one or more of three ways — cutting down imputed income, which is high, adding women to the labor force, or moving as he does in the absolute figures to a more net and less gross definition of income — will alter the conclusion that per capita income in agriculture is as high as in industry. If one also dismisses the Bellerby figure for France, which he says is "probably above the incentive ratio," [88] one must conclude that the majority of observers are right and that the average income in agriculture has been below that in the rest of the economy by some substantial fraction, ranging from one third to one half.[89] After a most careful examination of the figures, Latil concludes for the twentieth century that average income in agriculture per person is one third to two thirds lower than in the rest of the economy and that the lag is growing — that is, relative income is declining as the rural exodus lags behind the rate needed to equalize incomes.[90]

But average income in agriculture is relatively meaningless. Agricultural workers, leaving the sector, compare their wages with what they can earn in industry. Here there is general agreement that agri-

[86] Bellerby, *Agriculture and Industry* (1956), table 33, p. 201.
[87] In a thesis at the University of Chicago. A summary was published in *Journal of Farm Economics* in 1952.
[88] Bellerby, *Agriculture and Industry*, pp. 191–192.
[89] As a further illustration of the difficulties in this area, note that income per person may differ from income per household, which is the relevant unit for some purposes. Personal income per household in agriculture before taxes was 106.7 percent of the national average in 1952, as contrasted with income per capita of 81.6 percent (calculated from figures from the Ministère des Finances, *Rapport sur les comptes de la nation*, 1955, vol. 2, set out in Peterson, *The Welfare State in France*, 1960, pp. 76ff). This is 108 percent and 78 percent, respectively, of the nonagricultural sectoral averages. Since both direct and indirect tax burdens are heavier on nonagriculture than on farmers, the figures after tax should move still further in favor of agriculture. The difference between household and per capita figures, of course, is the result of larger households, with more income earners, in agriculture than outside it. Note further that the results are altered again, but only slightly, if one changes from personal income, including transfers, to income from production.
[90] Latil, *Revenu agricole*, p. 115.

Table 12. Degree of Concentration in British Industry,
by Major Industrial Classification, 1935

Industry	Total employment (000)	Number of trades[a]	Employ- ment in "units" (000)	Aggregate employ- ment in 3 largest units (000)	Degree of concen- tration of em- ployment (percent)
Chemicals	194.0	16	184.5	89.0	48
Miscellaneous	182.6	16	123.5	57.6	47
Public utilities	698.1	7	565.2	251.3	44
Engineering and vehicles	1,104.1	36	793.1	338.0	43
Iron and steel	539.3	32	416.8	164.4	39
Food, drink, tobacco	520.7	27	474.6	151.6	32
Nonferrous metals	122.1	10	117.0	30.4	26
Textiles	1,054.9	41	981.6	222.6	23
Paper, printing, etc.	409.0	15	362.6	79.0	22
Clay and build- ing materials	249.4	12	211.8	47.5	22
Leather	50.5	5	47.4	7.0	15
Clothing	535.9	15	474.3	60.9	13
Mines and quarries	845.1	5	845.1	84.2	10
Timber	194.9	8	150.9	14.4	10
Building and contracting	502.3	4	418.7	17.5	4
Total	7,203.2	249	6,167.0	1,615.4	26

[a] The measures of concentration are higher for trades.
Source. Leak and Maizels, "Structure of British Industry" (1945), p. 157.

showing the decline in agricultural workers. The table shows the slow
pace of increase in plant size, in spite of the frequent discovery that a
wave of concentration had taken place.

It is impossible to go back of the 1935 census of manufactures in
Britain if one is interested in firms. These results have been carefully
studied by Leak and Maizels, in terms both of "firms," defined as an
aggregate of establishments trading under the same name, and "units,"
defined as a single firm or an aggregate of firms owned or controlled
by a single company and employing 500 persons or more. Table 12
measures the degree of concentration in units rather than firms. But
Table 10 suggests that three fifths of the firms in number, below 50
employees, had only one tenth of the output and 11 percent of the

total employees in British industry in 1935, whereas those firms with above 500 employees, 2,300 in number, or little more than 4 percent, had more than half the net output and half the workers.

The September 1954 article in *Études et conjoncture* offers similar percentages for France but only for establishments and employees. Eliminating the establishments of 10 workers and less gives the results shown in Table 13 for 1906 and 1936. The latter are incomparable with

Table 13. Establishments of More than 10 Workers by Size Group and Number of Employees, France, 1906 and 1936

Size of establishment	Number of establish- ments	Percent	Number of workers	Percent
1906				
11–50 workers	51,600	84	1,074,800	34
51–100	5,600	9	394,400	12
101–500	4,400	7	888,800	28
Over 500	700	1	811,900	26
Total	61,300	100	3,169,900	100
1936				
11–50 workers	64,800	80	1,369,300	30
51–100	7,900	10	554,400	12
101–500	6,500	8	1,279,900	28
Over 500	1,000	1	1,328,800	29
Total	80,200	100	4,532,400	100

the British, not only because of the difference between firms and establishments but also because they relate to industry and commerce rather than to industry alone. They indicate, however, not much increase in concentration of establishments between 1906 and 1936 and many fewer workers in large establishments than in the United Kingdom.

Certain industries are concentrated in France as in Great Britain, as shown in Tables 11 and 12, although perhaps a little less so. If the top three firms are taken, the French figures are consistently lower than the British, 32 against 39 percent in steel, 15 against 43 percent in metal manufacturing (engineering and vehicles in Britain), 36 and 40 percent in chemicals and fuel, apart from coal (largely petroleum), against 48 percent in chemicals including petroleum. These large industrial classifications lower the concentration indexes. Among the "trades" the degree of concentration reached at least 90 percent for manufactured fuel and wallpaper, between 80 and 90 percent for

land continued to be broken up and some agricultural workers bought or inherited farms.

Recall that industrial demands for labor will narrow the gap between industrial and agricultural wages (after perhaps an initial widening), while a supply push from the side of agriculture will widen it. The former seems to have been what happened from about 1850 to sometime in the 1860s, when agricultural wages rose faster than industrial. Thereafter, all the way to World War I, industrial rates kept rising, but agricultural wages, while they followed the same curve, had feebler rises and more marked declines.[95] This was the period of the rural exodus.

Further light can finally be thrown on the various theories by measuring changing wage dispersions. This has been done to a limited extent. According to Institut National figures, the geographic dispersion of agricultural wages widened between 1862 and 1892, the coefficient of variation going from 0.285 to 0.368, and declining thereafter to 0.1 in 1949.[96] The latter figure is relatively uninteresting because of the wage control, with its limited regional differentials. But the widening of agricultural disparities may coincide with a narrowing of industrial wages geographically. Madinier shows that the disparity in wages of qualified workers declines from 172 in 1853 (representing the average of the relatives of the first to the ninth decile, and the second to the eighth, expressed in percent) to 139 in 1892 and 128 in 1935.[97]

But these overall measures are of doubtful value in supporting broad generalizations. They suggest perhaps that in the second half of the nineteenth century the movement of the workers to industry was more important than the movement of industry to workers, which had been dominant in the first half. Beyond this they cannot go far because the interaction between industry and agriculture differed from locality to locality.

Paris was able to draw labor off the farm, particularly from the environs, the southwest, and the center, which had a tradition of seasonal travel and even of a "tour de France." [98] Moreover, the south

---

percent. If one moves to the level of the commune, a small industrial city like Albi had 34 percent of its population born outside the commune as early as 1837, and 56 percent by 1931 (George, *La Ville*, 1952, p. 93).

[95] Latil, *Revenu agricole*, p. 224.

[96] INSEE, "Les Migrations agricoles," p. 331.

[97] Madinier, *Les Disparités géographiques de salaire* (1959), p. 41. For all workers, however, his figures suggest some widening in geographic wage disparities for men from 1840–1845 to 1860–1865, a steady position to 1892, and a decline to 1954. See table, *ibid.*, p. 68, and statement, p. 82.

[98] Estienne and Joly, *La Région du centre* (1961), p. 131.

and west provided recruits for the army and civil service, including the gendarmerie, the Postes, Téléphones et Télégraphes (PTT), and the railroads, not to mention the tobacco monopoly. Outside of this, most movement if it occurred at all was of limited distance. In the north, where industry developed earliest and to the greatest extent, the wages of agriculture and industry probably narrowed. In the south and west, rural industry was destroyed; the gap between agricultural and industrial wages widened and led to rural exodus. In Brittany and Alsace, there was little industry and substantial excess population on the farm. Finally in a few places, notably Lorraine, the Clermont-Ferrand plant of Michelin in the Center, and to lesser extent in the Alps, there was modern industry surrounded by backward agriculture, with industry forced to rely on immigrants because of the reluctance of local peasants to leave the soil. When peasants did go to work in the factories, they remained part-time farmers, "doing double work." [99] The system has been described at length for Alsace, Lorraine, the Montbéliard area, the Alps, and Clermont-Ferrand.[100] The peasant is tired when he gets to the plant and inefficient there. He is not dependent on his income from farming, so there is no spur to efficiency at home. Industry and agriculture mutually handicap rather than stimulate one another.

It may be said that the labor shortages in industrial plants could have been made good by surpluses from Aquitaine and Brittany. Some companies attempted long-distance recruiting.[101] But long-range mobility did not exist for France, any more than for England, as noted earlier. While only 25 percent of the population of Auxerre had been born there, 50 percent more came from Yonne or the neighboring departments. In Vienne, 42 percent were born locally, 13 percent more from Isère, 8 percent from Rhône, 8.5 percent from other fairly nearby departments.[102] Valarché has found the same result in abandoned villages.[103] Departures proceed by stages: first, from farm to village; then, to the neighboring town; and ultimately possibly to Paris. Where there are neighboring towns to absorb farmers in industry, the result

[99] Mossé, *Localisation dans l'industrie automobile* (1956), p. 91.

[100] Juillard, *Basse-Alsace;* Blanc, Juillard, Ray, and Rochefort, *Les Régions de l'Est* (1960), pp. 35, 51, 104; Sédillot, *Peugeot* (1960), pp. 131–132; Lebréton, "Une Expérience de la dispersion industrielle dans l'électrochimie" (1946); Estienne and Joly, *La Région du centre,* esp. chap. ii.

[101] *Ibid.,* p. 98. Michelin brought in whole villages from Brittany in 1923 and transplanted both Perpignanais and their native game, rugby. But the area was still one where farms needed hands rather than hands farms (p. 70).

[102] See note 43, Chapter 4, above.

[103] Valarché, *La Mobilité des ruraux,* pp. 55, 60, 108. See also Mendras, *Novis et Virgin* (1953), p. 71.

was recorded.[13] But the process was slow — far slower than the hand nailer and the handloom weaver in England, who went out of business in the twenty- or thirty-year periods after 1815 and 1830, respectively; the small textile handicraft worker lingered on in France.[14] The railroad enabled Paris to extend its supply area from 50 kilometers in 1830 to 250 in 1855.[15] There were national firms like Schneider, whose workers at Le Creusot increased from 2,500 in 1845 to 6,000 in 1860, to 10,000 in 1870, and to 15,000 in 1878.[16] But large parts of the west and southwest were not closely linked to the north and east, and even the heavy industry of the east was cut off from parts of the national market. Transport, as we have noted earlier, was less than ubiquitous and cheap. Specialization was incomplete.

There were, moreover, limitations on the demand side. The French insistence on quality has been discussed. It contrasted with Britain, where increasing homogeneity of demand of the lower middle classes assisted the spread of the department store and multiple shop (chain store). A more tangible factor limiting specialization in distribution was the lag in urbanization in France, shown in Table 14 and discussed more fully in Chapter 11. The English figures would be reduced, of course, if the United Kingdom were taken as a whole. Morazé points out that of the 38,000 towns in France of more than 5,000 population,

---

milieu de XIXe siècle" p. 60. The wood and leather firms started to go in 1890, the latter especially hit by a strike in 1905. See Lefèbvre, *L'Évolution des localisations industrielles* (1960), pp. 23–24 on the destruction of the woolen industry in the Alps, the survival of the hemp, and the wiping out of the high furnaces of iron forge masters, some of whom managed to convert to metalworking.

[13] Sée, *Histoire économique de la France* (1942), p. 303, places the decline in the artisan as taking place from 1870. Bettelheim, *Bilan de l'économie française* (1947), p. 40, puts it after 1906. Clapham comments that the shift from the putting out system to the factory took place in France about 1895 (*Development of France and Germany*, 1936, p. 240).

[14] For the view that the speed of the elimination of the handloom weaver can be exaggerated, see below, Chapter 13. Chevalier comments that the influence of Paris on northern Picardy of Beauvais was not much stronger in 1944 than in the middle of the nineteenth century (p. 92). But see Pinchemel, *Structure sociale et dépopulation rurale* (1957), who uses detailed enumerations for three communes near Amiens to demonstrate that industrial depopulation in northern Picardy was greater even than agricultural. The number of artisans and factory workers fell from 6,400 in 1836 to 3,460 in 1872, to 2,569 in 1911, and to 1,143 by 1936 (p. 107). This decline is initially rapid, partly under the influence of the Revolution of 1848, then slowed down, then sped.

Juillard (*Basse-Alsace*, 1953, pp. 288ff) observes that the vigorous rural industry born of overpopulation in 1830–1850 was affected by the railroads over the forty years to 1890. Some disappeared, some moved to the cities, but some was enabled to survive through concentration with the help of railroad commutation, which preserved the rural population in place and left women in the countryside as a small-scale industrial workforce.

[15] See Chapter 2, note 61, and the related discussion.

[16] Lhomme, *La Grande bourgeoisie* (1960), p. 183.

Table 14. Percentage of Population Living in Cities of
Specified Size in France and England, 1851 and 1891

City	England		France	
	1851	1891	1851	1891
London	13.2	14.5	—	—
Other cities				
above 100,000	9.4	17.3	4.6	12.0
20–100,000	12.4	21.8	6.0	9.1
10–20,000	4.5	8.0	3.8	4.8
All cities				
above 10,000	39.5	61.6	14.4	25.9

Source. Weber, *Growth of Cities* (1899), pp. 37, 43, 71.

37,000 are in the 5,000–6,000 class. This and state regulation, in his
view, account for the vast number of small specialized shops.[17]

Size of Plant and Firm

The specialized firm, of course, need not be large — as in French
retail distribution — nor the large firm specialized — United Steel.[18]
But there remains a presumption that when markets fuse, through
cheap transport, standardization, and homogeneity of taste, internal
economies of scale with competition will raise the size of efficient
plant. Declining markets at the same time will offer efficient managements opportunities to increase the size of firms through merger and
takeover. Whether plant size will increase as firms do turns on whether
economies of scale remain to be exploited.

It is difficult to find comparable data on plant size in Britain and
France. A useful comparison has been made for steel, but the dates do
not fit completely. This shows that in 1929, and perhaps before World
War I, French steel plants were on the whole larger than British.[19] In
cotton spinning the reverse was clearly the case. The five largest firms

[17] Morazé, *La France bourgeoise* (1952), p. 192.

[18] Compare the small size of the *boucherie, charcuterie,* and *chevaline boutique*
and the *crèmerie, épicerie,* and green grocer. See also Duncan Burn, "Steel"
(1958)," p. 287: "The United Steel Company, the largest of all, variegated, foot
in many trades. . . . In a sense this combine was the antithesis of both the popular
principles of rationalization, regional and product specialization." Lack of specialization may lead to increased firm size: Morris Motors was obliged to make automobile components in its own shops (and import from the United States) for lack
of a specialized engineering industry which could produce a large supply of components to order in a short space of time. See Maxcy and Silberston, *The Motor
Industry* (1959), p. 13.

[19] Svennilson, *Growth and Stagnation in the European Economy* (1954), p. 126,

is no dynamic in soaring wages which brings booms to an end. The condition is interesting, but it explains little.

THE RURAL EXODUS

Having spent so much time on the opposite contention, we need not dwell long on the single-valued argument that the pull of industry ruined agriculture by robbing it of its labor supply. Economists say that people leave poor regions; it is demographers who insist that the regions are poor because people leave. It is true that there have been economies of scale; as a village declines in size it becomes too small for one doctor or one justice of the peace, not to mention the school [108] and various more mundane services.[109] This consideration has become less important since the spread of private transport. But the rural exodus is both inevitable and necessary: inevitable, as the rural community insists on narrowing the income gap between them and urban dwellers and escaping the life of monotony, harder work, and social inferiority;[110] necessary, since a rise in rural wages is an important stimulus to the modernization of agriculture. We have seen this in France, where the increase in agricultural productivity has been greatest under the Second Empire and prior to World War I, when industrial activity was rising. It is equally true of Britain.[111]

The backwardness of French agriculture cannot be blamed on the rural exodus. More education, which is a necessary condition of more effective agriculture — and of more effective use in industry and trade of those who leave it — will stimulate migration.[112] It is understand-

[108] Valarché, La Mobilité des ruraux, p. 63; Saville, Rural Depopulation in England and Wales, p. 246.

[109] Williams, Sociology of Gosforth (1956), p. 135, notes that Gosforth's nine inns in 1857 had now become four public houses, but ascribes it also to the rise of the price of beer and spirits and the decline in the popularity of excess drinking. Saville, p. 23, notes that villages under 500 had lost one of two inns between 1850 and 1920, along with thatchers, carpenters, shoemakers, tailors, and ascribes it to the decline of rural industry in competition with the factory.

[110] See Gautier, Pourquoi les Bretons s'en vont, vols. I and II (1950); Valarché, p. 101; Mendras, p. 72. All say that it is not income, but the hard work and lack of distraction which produce emigration. An important role is played by the female of the species. She leaves in greater numbers (Valarché, p. 103; Saville, p. 33); and she frequently propels the male. See Faucher, Le Paysan et la machine, p. 217: "Many a marriage was concluded on the condition of departure to the city."

[111] Saville, pp. 140–141.

[112] Martin, The Secret People (1954), p. 275, discusses how farmers and their children sabotaged the School Boards Act of 1870 in Britain; also the general rural view that education corrupted children's willingness to work in agriculture and was responsible for the rural exodus. Augé-Laribé, Politique agricole, p. 123, notes that the French Education Law of 1881 was equally not obeyed, as well as the existence of the same question of whether school made the peasants or ruined them. Contrast Danish rural education.

able that agricultural economists should be unhappy about the loss of numbers: Augé-Laribé calls the rural exodus "excessive" in 1880; Fauchon claims that the southwest has been "devastated" by rural exodus.[113] No one feels comfortable when his object of concern is shrinking. But it is inevitable. And the proof has been the rapid increase in French agricultural efficiency, with rapidly shrinking numbers, since World War II. Pockets of overpopulation remain, but outward transfers have been on a large scale — 1,100,000 between 1946 and 1954[114] and more since. French economic growth has been more rapid after World War II than it would have been if agriculture had not been so backward, and this on the same averaging principle that led agriculture to slow down growth prior to 1939. The transfer of men from jobs of low productivity to those of high does more than produce a higher rate of national growth in comparison with simple structural transfers between sectors of equal efficiency. It also stimulates increased efficiency in the sector left.

In conclusion, then, French agriculture has not been efficient, and its low productivity has held back average overall growth. Further, the deflation in French agriculture, until interrupted by tariffs, exercised a depressing effect on the economy as a whole, which slowed down the rate of growth between 1882 and 1896. But too slow a rate of transfer of resources to other sectors did not have a harmful effect on industrial expansion; nor did too rapid a transfer hurt agricultural efficiency. There were drags, perhaps, on industry from the independent and uneducated character of the emigrants from agriculture. Those who did not come, could not, because they were too far away, regardless of how much they would have been helpful if they had.

THE FAILURE OF BRITISH AGRICULTURE TO TRANSFORM

Our interest in British agriculture is unrelated to the question of overall economic growth, since the sector shrank rapidly in relative size after 1880. It concerns a more limited question: Why did this agriculture, as efficient as any in the world in the 1850s, lose its lead, not so much in wheat, where the answer is clear, as in the animal

[113] Augé-Laribé, ibid., p. 14; Fauchon, Économie de l'agriculture française, p. 23.

[114] See Annuaire statistique, 1961, p. 86, where the numbers engaged in agriculture are given on the basis of the new and the old definitions. The foregoing calculation uses the old definitions, which put the farm population in the labor force at 6,371,000. On the new definitions, the numbers are only 5,196,000. Most of the change (all but 225,000) is in women.

necessity to maintain family control of a business inhibited both sales of equity securities and the mixing of the interests of more than one family through merger.[26]

In Britain, on the contrary, a number of merger movements have occurred in textiles. Three were of private origin: in the late 1890s, at the end of World War I, and during the depression of the 1930s. A fourth has taken place since World War II at government behest. The first occurred in the finishing end of the industry, as the result of a wave of failures in the depression of the early 1890s. By the turn of the century, the Calico Printing Association, Bradford Dyers Association, the Bleachers Association (with self-evident functions), and J. and P. Coats in thread occupied dominant positions in their specialties.[27] The movement at the end of World War I, which resulted in Amalgamated Cotton Mills Trust, Crosses and Heatons, and Joshua Hoyle and Sons, Ltd., was the result of financial speculation.[28] During the depression, the banks with frozen loans insisted on an attempted rationalization. After World War II, redundant capacity was bought up and shut down at a salvage price.

Experience in steel was broadly similar, but mergers went further. Around the end of the nineteenth century, a number of firms began to extend vertically forward to products and backward to coal and iron.[29] Richard Thomas emerged from the depression in the tinplate industry, caused by the McKinley tariff.[30] Guest, Keen in steel merged with Nettleford in 1902, and in the same year J. Stewarts and Menzies of Scotland merged with Lloyd and Lloyd of Birmingham to constitute Stewart and Lloyd.[31] After the war, United Steel was formed out of a number of companies scattered about Britain and the English Steel Corporation Group. The next set of mergers occurred at the end of the 1920s, rather than in the 1930s, amalgamating South Durham and the Cargo Fleet, Ltd.; Blochow, Vaughn with Dorman Long; Beardmore with Colville in Scotland; and so on.[32] Finally, after the war, there was a new round.

---

dition of access to government capital, price increases, export subsidies, and the like.

   [26] See Chapter 5 above. See also Chapter 6 on the fact that the number of firms did shrink in many lines.

   [27] Macrosty, *Trust Movement in British Industry* (1907), pp. 125–126, 141, 144–145, 156.

   [28] See above, Chapter 3, and the references to Robson, *Cotton Industry*, in note 21, this chapter.

   [29] Burnham and Hoskins, *Iron and Steel in Britain* (1943), p. 208.

   [30] Minchenton, *British Tinplate Industry* (1957), p. 78.

   [31] Allen, *Birmingham and the Black Country* (1929), p. 357.

   [32] Burnham and Hoskins, pp. 209–210.

Similar movements were taking place in many other industries in Britain. Where the private movement lost force, the government enforced consolidation of 130 railroad lines into 4 companies in the Railways Act of 1921. In some industries, a single giant company like Lever, with 70 percent of total production and 55 percent of the British consumption, existed side by side with 230 firms. Only one other had importance: the Cooperative Wholesale Society. In the mid-1930s, however, Proctor and Gamble, with the backing of its parent American company, entered the market and quickly became the second largest firm.[33] The merger movement in beer has continued steadily from the start of the temperance movement at the end of the nineteenth century, as licensing of public houses provides monopoly profits in retailing which, with economies of scale in production and shrinking demand, lead inevitably to first vertical, then horizontal, integration. Three firms control one fourth of the national output in Britain; and 30 or 40 more local brewers are large, regional, and expanding. Only Guinness is not integrated forward.[34]

There were few mergers or amalgamations in coal. In 1911 there were 1,784 colliery businesses in the British Isles.[35] Entry was easy, with numerous shallow unworked seams, which could be attacked from the surface and needed little capital. By 1924 there were 2,481 mines belonging to 1,400 separate undertakings, although 98 percent of the coal was produced by 715 firms and 84 percent by 323. Allen finds this in striking contrast with the Ruhr, where 12 firms produced nine tenths of the output. He further explains that, with diminishing returns to scale, there was little incentive to amalgamate.[36] It is interesting to observe, however, that the nationalized industry put great emphasis on increasing investment but not much, so far as most accounts go, on shutting down small pits.[37] In France, Charbonnages de France increased productivity by closing some high-cost pits and joining others, thereby reducing the total number of mines from 220 to 140 and suggesting the possibility of cost reductions through amalgamations.[38] In this industry the failure to achieve a higher scale of output per mine before nationalization may have been due to failure to maximize rather than to diminishing returns.

Finally, there are the other industries, like hosiery, shoes, clothing, leather, building, and such, at the bottom of the list in Table 12, where

[33] Evely and Little, *Concentration in British Industry* (1960), pp. 261–262.
[34] Vaizey, *Brewing Industry* (1960), *passim*, pp. xiv, xviii.
[35] Chapman and Ashton, "Sizes of Businesses," p. 548.
[36] Allen, *British Industries*, pp. 57, 70.
[37] See Baldwin, *Beyond Nationalization* (1955), chap. x.
[38] Gordon, *Coal Pricing in the European Community* (1960), p. 12.

remained profitable.[124] In the absence of adequate data on either prices or costs, it is not clear that fruits and vegetables were also a profitable occupation during the depression. Acreage figures are available for fruit during the depression only from 1888, and not for green vegetables. The trend of this acreage, and of imports, however, suggests that here was another opportunity, and one which might have retained on the farm the agricultural workers who were leaving so precipitously.[125]

British agriculture changed to some extent in the face of these incentives. Wheat acreage fell in half between 1875 and 1908, barley by a third. Olson and Harris argue that the data for wheat show a much higher elasticity of supply than is normally found in the United States, and they find it "probable that the substitution between wheat and other products was easier in Great Britain than in many other wheat growing areas, such as the American Great Plains." [126] But there is a serious question about whether supply elasticity is the appropriate concept to apply to what was taking place in Britain in this period. It is true that oats for feed rose about 450,000 acres while wheat was declining 1,600,000 and barley 650,000; and that permanent pasture expanded from 10.5 million acres to 13.9 million. But was the increase in pasture a deliberate move or a consequence of the farmer's discouragement and lack of capital? [127] They simply let it "tumble down" to grass.[128] In these circumstances, there may have been an irreversible exit from the sector over a long period, and the concept of supply elasticity, appropriate for small changes in a limited time compass, is not applicable.

Animal numbers rose, though less than the population. Between 1870 and 1908, cows increased from 3,700,000 to 4,400,000, but declined from 118 per 1,000 inhabitants to 98.[129] Other cattle increased

---

ported meat except as a very last resort (Jeffrys, *Retail Trading in Britain*, 1954, p. 129).

[124] Trow-Smith, *British Livestock Husbandry* (1959), p. 234.

[125] This was not due to the enclosures, the last wave of which was over by 1845, but to first, High Farming, which released 300,000 men from 1850 to 1870, because of increased productivity; and second, to the decline in the price of wheat after 1879. The number of agricultural workers fell 400,000 from 1871 to 1901, or from 996,000 to 597,000. (There is the view, expressed in a seminar at Nuffield College, that High Farming did not so much release agricultural workers as an independent force as it constituted a response to the loss of workers pulled by industry and not pushed by the repeal of the Corn Laws. Here again, as in so much of the analysis, it is virtually impossible to sort out cause and effect.)

[126] Olson and Harris, "Free Trade in 'Corn'" (1959), p. 165.

[127] Bear, *English Farmer and His Competitors* (1888), p. 29; and Channing, *Agricultural Depression* (1897), pp. 4–5; 324.

[128] Stearns, "Agricultural Adaptation in England," p. 90.

[129] Besse, *L'Agriculture en Angleterre*, pp. 358–359.

somewhat more proportionately, from 5,500,000 to 7,400,000 over the same period. These figures are somewhat misleading, however. If the data are put on a more solid basis to distinguish dairy herds from beef, it can be seen that between 1873–1882 and 1902–1912 the number of cows and heifers in milk or calf increased by one quarter — from 2,240,000 to 2,740,000 — while the number of other cattle over two years old declined slightly — from 1,480,000 to 1,380,000.[130]

On the whole, however, the most striking fact that emerges from the British agricultural record after 1850 is the fact that it did not respond in the pattern of output to the changed conditions of grain supply abroad and the demand for animal foods at home. In the end, it was left for Denmark, the Netherlands, and New Zealand to provide the bacon, eggs, ham, and cheese in which the British worker and middle-class member chose to take such a large proportion of their increased productivity. These countries did transform under the pressure of British demand. The question is why was it they and not the more strategically located British agriculture.

The list of reasons is a long one and tends to explain more than 100 percent of the problem. Pride of place doubtless goes to the system of land tenure, ideal for grain on large farms, but poorly suited for more labor-intensive animal husbandry. Lesser considerations include the ignorance of the average farmer, despite the interest in agronomy of the leaders of British agriculture, particularly in matters of producing and marketing animal products; the laissez-faire attitude of government and the public; and bad weather. Let us dispose of the less important causes first.

Bad weather had the effect of disguising for a time what was taking place — the troubles of agriculture were blamed on nature rather than on the flood of imports, thus inhibiting the will to seek remedies.[131] But the effects were wider. Topsoils were physically affected and became deficient in minerals. Moreover, through discouraging the farmer, the bad weather led to capital consumption, which tends to become cumulative because poorly maintained land leads to decreased yields and more pressure to take from the land without putting back.

There were other long-run effects of the natural endowment. The heavy clay lands of East Anglia and Essex were splendid for producing wheat with proper drainage, but far less satisfactory for grass. It was possible to make a living from dairying, as was demonstrated by the invasion of Scotsmen with a knowledge of milk production after

---

[130] Cohen, *History of Milk Prices* (1936), p. 26.
[131] Ernle, *English Farming, Past and Present*, p. 380.

imports, new entry, and economies of scale that enable one or more firms to grow large at the expense of the others. Import tariffs, and quotas in the 1930s, met the first danger. New entry had to be tolerated and resulted in a rather precarious existence for the small shop and small factory. Potential competition of the efficient large-scale plant was held in check by many measures: the bias of tax and social legislation against bigness, which was exposed to both in a way that small business was not;[48] direct legislation, particularly in restricting chain and department stores;[49] cartels, both voluntary and compulsory;[50] and above all self-restraint on the part of the large firms.[51] This self-restraint is variously attributed to "group solidarity," to the closely related concern of large business for social stability, and to the high profits available to the efficient producer through keeping his high cost competitor barely alive.[52] It is important not to exaggerate: the euthanasia of the small producer had been carried through to its conclusion in a number of fields where cartels among large producers existed because of fear of price cutting based on the high ratio of overhead to total costs — in steel, salt,[53] electrical equipment, chemicals.

Once again, however, it seems inappropriate to attribute important causal significance to size or competition. Size does not confer initiative, as Sheahan points out in his study of the French automobile industry.[54] Nor does vigorous competition much recommend itself

[48] See Baum, *The French Economy and the State* (1958), pp. 157–158, and Chapter 9 below. Pitts, "Bourgeois Family and French Retardation," p. 436, calls the tax system a bribe to business to stay small. Prior to 1920, tax legislation imposed severe penalties on business mergers, ownership of subsidiaries and increases in capital (*ibid.*, p. 237).

[49] *Ibid.*, and Aubert-Krier, "Monopolistic Competition in Retail Trade in France" (1954), pp. 297–300.

[50] See Ehrmann, *Organized Business in France* (1957), pp. 370ff, who estimates that 30 percent of activities are bound by cartels (p. 372) and that 80 percent of the suppliers of the nationalized railroads are cartelized (p. 375).

[51] See, e.g., Landes, "French Business and Businessmen" (1951), p. 340; Pitts, p. 437.

[52] Pitts, p. 437, and Ehrmann, pp. 304–305, 391. The argument is put less in terms of solidarity between the high and petty bourgeoisie than between big business and workers. Business, it is said, argues that the efficiency required for exporting involves cruel concentration which means unemployment and other social upheavals. Ehrmann cites the one concrete case I have found — the alcohol lobby, which is interested in the survival of the marginal firm, possible only at prices which imply high profits for the efficient large producer (p. 244).

[53] Nistri and Prêcheur, *La Région du Nord et Nord-Est*, p. 111, state of this interesting industry, which is divided between the mines of Lorraine (Solvay and Kuhlmann) and the evaporation beds of the Mediterranean at Aigues-Morte (Pechiney and Ugine): "It is necessary to underline the prudence of this industry, so often on the edge of deficit. No adventures possible in this narrow market, threatened by overproduction and competition."

[54] "Government Competition and the French Automobile Industry," p. 215.

when demand is static or declining. There will be firms which respond positively in these circumstances, just as some generals attack when their wings and center crumble. But the standard of performance is too high to be generalized. Competition benefits from growth, perhaps more than the other way round. And although mergers and increased size of firms may be a useful defense against stagnation, they are not the only one; nor need they lead to vigorous investment and innovation.

This is an easy field in which to generalize.[55] But the generalizations are not worth much. Small firms and large can be competitive and vigorous. Small firms and large can be torpid. Growth will usually make all firms larger, but one successful way to grow is to have new firms formed from cadres created by the old.[56] Once growth starts, the risks of competition are reduced.

One argument, however, seems of doubtful historical validity: that big corporations withheld their competition out of a sense of social cohesion with the smaller employers, or through worries about structural unemployment among workers. When the growth of the market did occur after World War II, and the national emphasis on economic expansion began to erode the habit pattern of the family firm, leading industrial firms showed little hesitation in girding themselves for a competitive showdown with foreigners and with the domestic industry, regardless of consequences. Much of the Malthusian behavior of French firms, large and small, between 1882 and 1939 — with appropriate exceptions for the 1900s and 1920s — can be ascribed to simple defensive tactics of an unsophisticated type. Narrow markets made it possible for small firms to act monopolistically in a limited area, with big markups and small turnover. But any rapid period of growth — as in the economy as a whole in the 1850s and 1860s, and in steel, chemicals, automobiles, and electricity after 1896 — shook out the little firms and let big and small compete.

Restraint of competition is thus little different from the other factors that are said to limit French and British growth. First, the timing is wrong: it is impossible to make a case for restraint of competition as a proximate cause of the slow periods of growth, because one cannot explain changes in a way that would at the same time allow for the periods of expansion. Second, it is as much an effect as it is a cause, if

---

[55] Observe the contrast in the broader generalizations of de Riencourt, *The Coming Caesars* (1957), who believes that progress is only made through coalescence, and Kohr, *The Breakdown of Nations* (1957), who believes that man-made institutions, political and economic, collapse of their own weight in time by becoming too big. Another relevant generalization is that of Brooks Adams, that cartelization leads ineluctably to economic decline (*Law of Civilisation and Decay*, 1951). But he thought this applied to the United States in the 1890s.

[56] The one recommendation for this approach that I have found in the French literature is in Gravier, *Paris et le désert français* (1958), p. 165.

not more. When growth slows down, the temptation to stabilize market shares intensifies and, if competition is limited, the possibilities of an upsurge of growth are reinforced. Third, the causality could work out in the exactly opposite way: monopoly can lead to profits which are plowed back into investment and technical capacity. Accordingly, there is little basis for the view that restraint of competition in Britain or France has been a major cause of economic slowdown.

CHAPTER 9

GOVERNMENT

There is no general theory of how government behaves in the course of national economic growth, unless there is a cynical "law of expanding governmental intervention" to parallel the "law of declining foreign trade." [1] John Stuart Mill called on government only to establish law and order and to provide general education. This accords with the British conception of laissez faire. Today's theorists of economic growth, like Rosenstein-Rodan, believe that government should seek economies external to the firm through social-overhead capital — roads, ports, education, public health — standards for industry, and even occasional industrial investment, unprofitable in itself but needed to make related private investment profitable. The social-overhead aspect of this theory did not apply in Britain, where canals, roads, and railroads were initially built by private capital with the minimum of state direction. [2] It fits France in the nineteenth century, under Napoleon I and even more spectacularly under the Second Empire, when Louis Napoleon interested himself in the railroad network, roads, ports, canals, drainage, and irrigation.

Government has other functions connected with growth: it makes general rules governing economic life; modifies these rules to encourage some activities and restrain others; raises taxes to pursue its own particular tasks, and in so doing affects the distribution of income. It may go further and deliberately seek to redistribute income, providing welfare subsidies to its less unfortunate citizens even at the cost of savings and growth. This last is a view of government which finds confirmation particularly in Britain after 1930. A strongly negative view can be adopted of government as an instrument by which one or

[1] See Hicks, *British Public Finances* (1954). Government expenditure was never more than 15 percent of national income up to the First World War, hit 30 percent between the wars, and settled down at 40 percent after the war. For a table of the size of the French budget historically, see Baum, *The French Economy and the State* (1958), p. 113. The pre- and post-1914 figures cannot be compared, of course, because of the change in the value of the franc, but the upward march is relentless.

[2] The road system was not taken over by the state until the turnpike trusts went bankrupt after the railroads. See Savage, *Economic History of Transport* (1959), pp. 25, 33.

more classes of society exploit the rest. Government here is an ulcer rather than a motor,[3] or a factor of production.[4] This has long been a French attitude.

There is next the possibility that government takes on a life of its own. Political science has many theories of the relation between French politics and growth. Foremost among them perhaps is the view that the French government veers between alternating periods of a "strong man" —Napoleon, Louis Napoleon, Doumergue, Poincaré, De Gaulle — and of the parliamentary "game" of stalemate and frustration among vested interests.[5] The periods of growth during the Second Empire, the 1920s, and the Fifth Republic suggest the possibility that the strong man brings progress, while the parliamentary game — an attempt to restore "order" among various groups in the society — halts it. On the other hand, the history of the Third Republic before World War I lends little support to this notion. Growth occurred in the 1870s, when government was weak, and from 1896 to 1913, when it was not much stronger.[6] Other theories of French politics have been enumerated by J. B. Duroselle[7] as (1) the catastrophe theory: one revolution succeeded, others may. This possibility creates anxiety and hope. (2) The theory of movement and resistance, again centered on revolutions. Some groups are satisfied after each revolution, including those that fail; other groups are frustrated. The outcome of the struggle draws the lines of political battle for the next period of struggle. (3) The theory of Beau de Loménie, of bourgeois dynasties, that business and financial leaders under Napoleon I acquired power which they maintained, regardless of surface changes in government and constitution, until the nationalizations of 1944 and 1945.[8] (4) The theory of universal suffrage, which explains French economic conservatism by the fact that suffrage was achieved in 1848 prior to industrialization, whereas in other countries industrialization came first.

This list fails to exhaust the possibilities. Eckstein, for example, asserts that France of the Third and Fourth Republics was an unstable democracy because of the incongruence between the authoritarian

[3] The contrary view was expressed by Louis Napoleon in 1839. See Lefèvre, *Politique intérieure du Second Empire* (ca. 1953), p. 38.

[4] Abramovitz, "Economics of Growth," in Haley, *Survey of Contemporary Economics* (1952), II, 163.

[5] Hoffman, "Lasting Elements in the French Political Tradition" (1959).

[6] Eckstein in *A Theory of Stable Democracy* (1961), p. 34, asserts that the longevity of the Third Republic was the consequence of a long series of accidental circumstances. Explanations at this level are not very satisfactory in social science.

[7] Listed in the discussion of the Hoffman paper cited in note 5.

[8] Apart from brief intervals such as that between February and July 1848. For a parallel view of the survival of the Junkers to 1945 under all conditions and circumstances, see Gerschenkron, *Bread and Democracy in Germany* (1943).

nature of a Catholic country and the unmitigated democracy of French institutions.[9] Or still another possibility, of great importance, is that the course of governmental intervention can be explained less by historical determinism or social-science theorems than as a random process of confusion, muddle, error, and accident, alleviated by occasional lucid periods of effective action and by serendipity. This view is clearly set forth in W. C. Baum's *The French Economy and the State,* covering the post-World War II period, in which it is suggested that in contrast to the House of Lords in the Napoleonic wars, the French government did everything in general and very badly.[10]

GOVERNMENT AND GROWTH

The role of government in French growth is debated. One view is that the government promoted industrialization, which was responsible for growth.[11] The other opinion is that French governments redistributed rather than created.[12] The two sides of the debate can perhaps be reconciled historically. Under the July Monarchy, and especially during the Second Empire, the government played an important role in building the social-overhead capital on which economic growth — not just industrialization — rested. After the defeat of the Freycinet Plan in 1883, and until the Monnet Plan of 1945, the role of government, except in rebuilding the eastern region after World War I, was limited to redistribution.

Ostensibly liberal in economic doctrine, the July Monarchy of 1830 struggled to overcome the sluggishness of the progress toward development by pushing transport. The canal program of Ponts et Chaussées, elaborated in 1821–1822, finally got under way in 1844.[13] The Le Grand Plan of 1832 was presented to the Chamber in 1838 and adopted, after changes, in 1842. After interruption in the crisis of 1847, it was resumed in 1849, to be taken over by Louis Napoleon and finished in 1857. At this stage, the length of railroad in France was 6,820 kilometers. A new program was immediately set in motion to continue the old and was undertaken after the conventions of 1859. This lifted the system to

[9] *A Theory of Stable Democracy,* p. 37. Eckstein ascribes the theory that Catholic democracies are unstable to André Gide and Raymond Aron (p. 34). The stability of government in France, despite its Catholic population and unmitigated democratic institutions, may have been a consequence of the authoritarian character of such administrative arrangements as the prefectural system. See below, esp. note 64.

[10] *French Economy and the State,* p. 348.

[11] Léon, "L'Industrialisation en France" (1960).

[12] Morazé, *La France bourgeoise* (1952), p. 179.

[13] Girard, *Travaux publics* (1951), p. 27.

17,200 kilometers in 1870.[14] The "average length of track exploited" rose from 15,632 kilometers in 1871, after the loss of Alsace-Lorraine, to 23,089 in 1880. Thereafter the Freycinet Plan of 1879 under the Third Republic, as amended in the conventions of 1883, brought the length of the network in 1900 to 38,109 kilometers.[15]

Governmental spending was limited during the Second Empire. Total expenses for extraordinary works in fact surpassed the average level of 1845–1848 only during the war of 1870.[16] As noted in Chapter 3, government support took the form of planning the lines, furnishing loans, guaranteeing interest on bonds sold (under the conventions of 1859) and amortization (after 1883). Canal transportation was hurt during the Second Empire by the special rates favoring the railroads and by the inability of canals (also roads and ports) to issue their own bonds and obtain state support directly.[17] Canal traffic grew but 18 percent during the period from 1851 to 1875, and road traffic 19 percent, or 0.5 percent a year each, compared with 11 percent annually for railroads. The Freycinet Plan provided for the construction of 1,300 kilometers of canals and the deepening of 4,000 kilometers more, to enable them to take Flemish barges of 300 tons.[18] An attempt was made to put across a further Baudin plan in 1903 with emphasis on port construction, but Parliament cut the credits for ports from 163 to 87 millions.[19] Later, in the 1920s, the state canal system was developed still further, including at the end of the decade the important canal from Metz to Thionville.[20]

Louis Napoleon drew heavily on the inspiration of Saint-Simon and had a sweeping vision of planning and state action.[21] But the plans

[14] Renouard, Le Transport de la marchandise (1960), p. 11.

[15] Levasseur, Questions ouvrières (1907), p. 203.

[16] Block, Statistique de la France (1867), p. 505: the 1845–1849 average was over 125 million francs a year because of the construction of the fortifications of Paris as well as direct expenditure and subventions for railroads. The highest subsequent figures to 1870 were 107 million francs for 1862 and 122 million francs in 1866.

[17] Lefèvre, Politique intérieure du Second Empire, p. 65; Renouard, p. 12; Lévy, Histoire économique de la France (1951–52), p. 155; Girard, p. 103.

[18] Renouard, pp. 12, 39.

[19] Hersent, "Notre outillage maritime" (1921), p. 26. This essay makes the point that ports were neglected in French public works, receiving only 1,370 million francs of public spending in a century, compared with 40 billions for roads, 18 billions for railroads, and 2 billions for canals. The expenditure at Le Havre in 100 years amounted to 225 millions, compared with 250 millions at Antwerp in 35 years (p. 28).

[20] Burn, Economic History of Steelmaking (1940), p. 414.

[21] See Lefèvre, pp. 39–40, and the well-known speech of Louis Napoleon at Bordeaux in 1851: "We have immense uncultivated territories to clear, roads to open up, ports to dredge, rivers to render navigable, canals to complete, a railroad system to finish" (Lamèyre, Haussmann, 1958, p. 27). Note also the letter to Fould, published in the Moniteur industriel on January 15, 1860, eight days before

of Ponts et Chaussées had an orientation that was more national than Saint-Simonian European and industrial.[22] And while Haussmann, Magne, and Rouher[23] were impressive in action, some of the semi-monopolies to which essential branches of industry had been turned over undertook too much.[24] Other goals were simply not carried out.[25] Special interests were served, both in what was done and what omitted.[26] Occasionally governmental bodies, such as the Bank of France, operated from vengeful motives, rather than in the public interest.[27] In many matters, as in underdeveloped countries today, it was easy to plan, difficult to translate plans into action.

The technological role of government, large under Napoleon I with the establishment or expansion of the École Polytechnique, the École des Mines, the prizes and competitions for inventions and technical

the Anglo-French Treaty of Commerce was promulgated, calling for a full economic program: competition for industry, freedom of raw materials from import duties, development capital, loans to industry, improvement of the communications network (Dunham, The Anglo-French Treaty, 1930, pp. 83–84.)

[22] Lévy, Histoire économique de la France, pp. 145ff, contrasts the Legrand star centered on Paris with the Saint-Simonian conception of an industrial system linking Marseilles to Bordeaux and Antwerp or Calais, with its center at Saint Dizier. In any event, the Ponts et Chaussées Plan left Brittany, the Massif Central, and the Haute Marne regions isolated.

[23] It was said that France has a Rouherment instead of a government (Lhomme, La Grande bourgeoisie, 1960, p. 155).

[24] Lévy (p. 155) emphasizes that Paulin Talabot had been given the fief of Marseilles but was unable to prevent the harbor and the railroad stations from becoming choked. Talabot was interested at the same time in many other affairs in the north, Belgium, Algiers, and in railroads in France, Austria, Italy, and Spain. See Gille, Formation de la grande entreprise capitaliste (1959), pp. 96–112, and Cameron, France and the Development of Europe (1961), chaps. viii-x.

[25] See, e.g., Dunham, pp. 327–328. The Commission on Textiles reported in the summer of 1876 recommending duty-free admission of coal, machinery, tools; improvement of railroad equipment; and equipment of the ports. Dunham comments that there was no statesman of the caliber of Michel Chevalier to receive and act on this report.

[26] See the testimony of the Consul at Nantes in the Report of the Commission on the Depression of Trade and Industry (1885), p. 154: "The era of railway extension in this part of France is now over, all the lines which may be considered of any utility having been already completed, as well as some, I may add, of no utility whatever, and facetiously termed 'lignes electorales.'" Gignoux, L'Industrie française (1952), p. 108, asserts that the lines constructed under the Freycinet Plan are today largely an embarrassment to the national railway system.

[27] The literature is full of accusations of partiality and vindictiveness on the part of the Bank of France. See, e.g., the refusal to lend on mortgages in Le Havre in 1848 (Gille, La Banque et le crédit, 1959, p. 367), the "guerrilla war" with the Pereire brothers (Cameron, p. 191), and the strict attitude toward the Charpenay bank (Chapter 3 above). See also the insinuations against Magne, the Minister of Finance, who refused to help the Union Générale in 1881, but advanced 140 millions to the Comptoir d'Escompte in 1889 (Dauphin-Meunier, La Banque de France, 1936, p. 123). Bouvier (Le Krach de l'Union Générale, 1960) examines carefully the accusations of favoritism in assisting banks and returns a Scotch verdict of "not proven."

progress, declined under the Second Empire. The task was not to invent or to apply foreign inventions, but to bring French industry as a whole up to the standard of the best. In this the government could do little directly. It chose instead tariff reduction.

Prior to World War I, government influence on the economy widened through the increase in armament expenditure, but it was strategically less important. Large-scale government spending for the reconstruction of the devastated territories after World War I continued the same tendency. During the 1930s, government intervention took the form of first disengagement — the Laval deflation — and thereafter the disastrous forty-hour week of the Front Populaire. Not until 1944 and 1945 with the Monnet Plan did positive governmental intervention for growth assume the proportions of the Second Empire. The deep current of Saint-Simonian thought, with its emphasis on economic expansion, surfaced again in an atmosphere altered by two doctrines — socialist planning, on the one hand, and Keynesian pinning of responsibility for full employment and growth on government, on the other.

Although the Monnet Plan thus represented an ancient tradition, the vigor with which it and the successor Hirch and Massé plans were carried out, along with the empiricism, were new in French governmental annals. The planning was far from orthodox socialism at one extreme and simple projections of the private economy at the other. The Commissariat au Plan invited industry to assist it in formulating objectives, and then used a variety of prodding tactics and powers — pressures to merge, invest, modernize, and export; provision of government credit; restriction of bank credit; power to alter excise and operating taxes, to guarantee export prices, and to control or raise domestic prices.[28] The nationalized industries — railroads, coal, electricity, gas, aviation, and Renault — had privileged access to capital for investment from the government and the nationalized banks, and goals in amount were set. But the particular directions that investment took, and the technical emphasis, were left to the determination of the separate enterprises under rules which made them differ only slightly from profit-maximizing enterprises with a strong technological bias. The operation was called planning, but it resembled nothing so much as empirical direction of the economy of a continuous sort.

In Britain, the doctrine of laissez faire in the nineteenth century prevented substantial interference in the allocation of resources, except in the exercise of the police powers of the state to protect the general safety and welfare. In fact the drift was the other way — to remove the Navigation Acts, the Corn Laws, the prohibition on the export of

[28] See Lubell, *The French Investment Program* (1951) and Sheahan, "Government Competition and the French Automobile Industry" (1960).

machinery. Parliament, rather than a technical body like Ponts et Chaussées, granted the charters and rights of way of railroads, laid down standards, set rates. Government affected the allocation of resources in positive ways — through armament purchases, especially in buying superdreadnoughts, and in mail contracts. It was also ready to take negative action, such as the 1893 repeal, needed for the automobile industry, of the Red Flag legislation of the 1840s, which required any machine moving on the road at speeds in excess of fifteen miles an hour to be preceded by a man carrying a red flag. Occasional significant intervention occurred, such as the governmental guarantee of interest on the Indian railroad bonds in 1858.[29] But it was rare.

After the disastrous experience of the 1920s, government intervention went much further. The price of coal was regulated; town and country planning was instituted, with its requirement of permission before undertaking physical investment. Richard Thomas was pressured into building his tinplate strip mill at Ebbw Vale, a distressed area, rather than at a cheaper location in Lincolnshire.[30] And after the war a full panoply of nationalized industries, social security, agricultural controls and subsidies, import quotas, export set-asides, and state trading was put into effect.

The Labour Party subscribed to nationalization as a tenet of faith longer than it did to rationing, price controls, and state trading. The Conservatives were prepared to concede the practicality of nationalizing coal, which had had a miserable interwar record and showed no sign of improvement. But in steel the country faced a dilemma. There was some sentiment for nationalization based upon the view of the industry as "merchants of death," and some who regarded the industry as strategic for the planning and control of the economy as a whole, but the major charge against it was that it had failed to keep up with the times and to adapt to the evolving technical world. Threatened with nationalization after the war, the industry undertook a program of reform and modernization, which, though not rated very high in every quarter,[31] was a long step forward from its interwar performance. Should it be punished for ancient wrongs or reprieved for recent good behavior? Is nationalization a doctrine or a pragmatic device for coping with laggard industries? In any event, the nationalized industries were

[29] Overt intervention may have been limited in this field, because tacit intervention made it unnecessary. All colonial securities qualified for trustee investment and were in effect gilt-edge. Moreover the government would have acted to prevent any default, so that an implicit guarantee may be said to have existed. The overt action was taken in India, prior to its incorporation in the empire, because of possible ambiguity in its position.

[30] Minchenton, *British Tinplate Industry* (1957), p. 194.

[31] Burn, "Steel" (1958), p. 290. But Burn notes an increase in productivity per man in 1955 over 1937 of 41 percent.

given relatively free access to capital for investment without much
control over the economic criteria which they used to select their investments or to price their output. The result was originally judged on
the basis of personal predilection.[32] More recently there has been
general agreement among all but the most confirmed socialists that
the performance of the socialized sector of the economy has fallen
short of original hopes. Investment in nationalized industry was high
in both France and Britain, but increases in productivity, technical
achievements, and positive effects on the rest of industry were far
higher in France.

STABILITY

French governments were concerned less with economic than with
social stability. They were relatively uninterested in the average level
of income as contrasted with the dispersion about the average. Full
employment was not a significant problem, as in Britain, because of
the number of independent workers and tradesmen, the access of some
workers to garden plots, the possibility for others to return to the village, and the cutting off of new immigration, accompanied by gradual
expulsion of half a million foreigners already employed in France. The
government coped with the balance of payments when it had to, and
to a limited degree, ineffectually, with inflation. But up to 1939 its
major interest was in the distribution of income. And here it was
unable to use direct means of income redistribution, such as progressive
taxation, but indirect means which ensured that economic change did
not hurt: tariffs, price supports, subsidies, limitations on competition.

After 1945 the government looked to growth rather than stability or
distribution. When the French government could break the farmers'
monopoly after the big crop in 1951, it let the share going to farmers
drop from 25 percent of national income in 1948 to 14 percent in 1952.
And it took the small shopkeeper, the artisan, and the civil servant into
account only to the least extent made necessary by strikes and civil
commotion.

British experience is broadly the contrary. An intense interest was
felt in stability, much less in the equitability of distribution, up to about
1930. Thereafter concern was with full employment and fair shares.
In an open economy, and with substantial short-term debts owed
abroad, the balance of payments was inevitably a basic worry.

[32] See Brady, *Crisis in Britain* (1950), for a strong negative view; Hutchison,
The Decline and Fall of British Capitalism (1950), emphasizes the durability of
government intervention. Lewis, *British Planning and Nationalization* (1952),
offers a more judicious and factual balance.

Governmental action on stability prior to 1930 was by and large limited to banking measures and the appointment of royal commissions.[33] Thereafter unemployment, distressed areas, and the evolution of the Keynesian doctrine of income determination led to elaborate use of monetary and fiscal policy — initially fiscal policy but, with rediscovery of money, both. Each annual budget contained changes in tax and expenditure measures designed to restore the economy to an even keel. Special budgets were occasionally adopted between times. Some increased stability may have been imparted to the economies of both England and France by high levels of governmental expenditure and taxation after World War II, governmental expenditure being more stable than private investment. But the major difficulty rested in the fact that in Britain, in contrast with France after 1953, periods of rapid economic growth gave rise to balance-of-payments deficits, which required the application of restraint in the interest of stability. The reasons for the national difference were two: the reserves of labor which France, but not Britain, could draw from its underemployed agricultural sector and the different emphasis in the manner of growth in the two countries. In Britain, growth proceeded more through a Harrod-Domar type of expansion — investment leading to increased income, which spilled over into imports. French expansion had a strong element of technological change, which provided at the same time incremental exports and substitutes for imports. In 1956–1957 French involvement in Indochina, Suez, and Algiers led to a rapid drain on international reserves that was virtually ignored in the eagerness to protect the sources of domestic expansion. In the end, because of its large technological content and after the trimming operations in exchange devaluation and the Rueff measures of 1958, the expansion righted the balance of payments.

GOVERNMENT AS UMPIRE AND REDISTRIBUTOR

At the height of laissez faire in the middle of the nineteenth century, the British government was continuously interfering in the operation of the economic system by granting charters to private companies before ultimately providing for incorporation; by increasingly regulating the banking system; by laying down standards for railroads; by undertaking factory legislation; by limiting hours and conditions of work. One area in which government did not intervene was the pro-

[33] Especially the Royal Commission on the Depression of Trade and Industry in 1885 and the Balfour Committee on Industry and Trade, neither of which produced positive legislation. Is the royal commission, rather more developed in Britain than elsewhere in the world, a manifestation of the British love of facts for their own sake? See above, Chapter 5.

tection of agricultural workers — from the enclosure movement in the first half of the nineteenth century, from the increase in farm productivity during high farming, or from the collapse of wheat prices under the impact of imports after 1879. This last forbearance may have been due partly to doctrinal reasons — noninterference with the property rights of the landowners — but mainly, perhaps, to inattention. A succession of bad summers and plant and animal diseases distracted observers from the remedial character of an increase in imports.[34] Adherence to free trade had become an article of faith by the 1880s, but property rights in factories were continuously affected by inspection and regulation, under pressure from the nascent labor movement and intellectual agitation. British tradition in the poor laws involved intervention in behalf of the distressed classes of society — although the Speenhamland system cannot be said to have been effective.[35]

After the turn of the century, British government moved to even out inequities in the distribution of income. The social-security program of 1911 constituted the beginning. An increase in the income tax from its nominal prewar level followed the war. Rates were raised still higher during World War II, when interest rates and rents fell relative to wages; and the Beveridge Plan for the welfare state provided socialized medicine, unemployment, old-age, and other benefits on a far larger scale. Cartter has calculated that an index of income inequality, measuring the percentage of income that would have to be redistributed from higher-income recipients to lower to achieve equality, declined from .42 before tax and .41 after tax in 1880, to almost identical figures in 1913, to .38 and .30 in 1928, to .27 and .23 in 1937, and to .24 and .16 in 1948–1949.[36] Poverty, defined as a level of subsistence insufficient for the maintenance of continuing physical efficiency, was wiped out. Seebohm Rowntree followed up his 1900 investigation in York fifty years later and found that primary poverty — an absolutely insufficient income — had fallen from 15.5 percent of families in 1899 to 7 percent in 1936 and to 0.4 percent in 1950; whereas secondary poverty — a level of income barely sufficient for the maintenance of efficiency if optimally used, but which falls below when subject to the ravages of illness, drink, unemployment, or other economic disaster — went from 33.5 percent in 1899 to 31 percent in 1936 and to 2.8 percent in 1950.[37]

[34] See Kindleberger, "Group Behavior and International Trade" (1951), p. 32. Souchon devotes an article in 1904 to an attempt to explain why the British rejected protection as a solution to their agricultural problem ("L'Agriculture anglaise et la protectionisme").

[35] See Polanyi, The Great Transformation (1944).

[36] Cartter, Redistribution of Income in Prewar Britain (1955), pp. 74–75.

[37] See Rowntree, Poverty (1901); Rowntree, Poverty and Progress (1941), p. 460; and Rowntree and Lavers, Poverty and the Welfare State (1951), pp. 30, 31.

The British doctrine of fair shares, which gradually evolved and obtained universal acceptance during the twentieth century, had its roots in the social cohesion of all classes of society and the leading class's readiness to take responsibility. As noted in Chapter 5, this acceptance may be wearing thin, partly perhaps because so much of it has been achieved by full employment and the income tax. The working class is increasingly discontented with economic democratization, where class lines are as sharply drawn as ever; the middle class finds that it wants relative differentiation from the working class, as well as absolute standards of education, housing, medical attention, domestic service, holidays, and an opportunity to transmit some property by inheritance without a legal "fiddle." [38] And increasingly there is wonder whether fair shares, emphasizing consumption, are compatible with growth, which requires differential inputs into production.

The relationships among French social and economic groups and government are more complex, as viewed by sociologists, as well as different from the British. In the abstract, the French love order, the motherland, and the state. They despise merely government and the embodiment of authority.[39] These attitudes have undergone change since 1940, and the picture drawn here is of prewar vintage. Love of order is revealed in the need for norms, established and given from above: the Napoleonic Code and the Academy. But authority is different.[40] One must obey without love, never accept, never give in. In contrast with the German, who takes for granted the fact that he is incompetent and his boss is competent, the individual Frenchman always assumes that he knows better than the legitimate authority and does not hesitate to change blueprints or plans without notice, saying that he is carrying out orders. Rules are needed but little obeyed. Authority enforces rules on those with whom it does not sympathize but not on others. Government is a collectivity with the task of arbitrating among "delinquent communities," whose main purpose is to avoid change and to gratify the short-run demands of the individual against the general good.[41]

---

[38] Lewis and Maude, *The English Middle Classes* (1949), p. 262. There is also a question of whether the originally high standards of British morality in payment of income taxes may not have weakened in the course of time.

[39] Gorer, *Exploring British Character* (1955), appendix I, observes that the policeman is the benign father-figure in Britain (or has been until recent revelations of previously unheard-of corruption among them). Wylie in a seminar ("Criteria for Good Government," 1960) notes that the gendarme enjoys no respect and always gets put upon in French movies.

[40] Note the sharp distinction in popular opinion in France between the respected De Gaulle, who represents the state, and the detested Debré, who embodied the government.

[41] This paragraph is based on the seminars of Wylie, referred to above, and of Pitts on "The Role of the Citizen in France" (1960), Center for International Affairs, Harvard University, May 13, 1960.

French historians support this view of the relations between government and economic groups. The government was corrupt in the interest of business under the July Monarchy.[42] Under the Second Empire, before the interest of Louis Napoleon turned exclusively to foreign adventure, pseudo-liberal government supported big business, took care of business losses, and provided public works for the unemployed.[43] Morazé asserts that it is economic laziness which leads all classes to claim the assistance of the state, thus giving the state, when conflicting claims arise, the role of initiator.[44] But others are impressed that the state responded to conflicting demands by conflicting acts. The best example is the tariff policy after 1881, which provided tariffs for all groups — producers of foodstuffs, raw materials, and manufactures — in an effort to inhibit any and all change. Various economists have tried to make the case that industry or agriculture was favored over the other, as each feared that it had been left behind.[45]

But the general view is that government protected every group. Some industries got higher tariffs for outputs at the same time that they paid higher prices for raw-material inputs.[46] In the same fashion, inflation since World War I has been an effect of the government's giving way to separate groups as each tried to protect itself against rises in the cost of living or wages or industrial prices. The memoirs of Moreau, the governor of the Bank of France, are revealing in this regard: during the stabilization of the franc in 1926, attention was paid to the effects on commerce, industry, agriculture, and the middle classes with capital and fixed revenues.[47] More recently, Baum has attacked the inconsistencies and contradictions in governmental policy, trying

[42] Lhomme, La Grande bourgeoisie, p. 79.
[43] Lévy, Histoire économique, pp. 159, 167.
[44] Morazé, La France bourgeoise, p. 204.
[45] See Augé-Laribé, Politique agricole (1950), pp. 225ff; Golob, Méline Tariff (1944), p. 8; Léon, "L'Industrialisation en France," p. 182. Léon states that the government favored industry through subtle manipulation of the most-favored-nation clause. See the discussion, Chapter 12 below. Note also Wylie's inversion of the Golden Rule (Village in the Vaucluse): "Fear that others will do to you what you would do to them if you had the authority."
[46] Latil, Revenu agricole (1956), p. 287; and Weiller, "Économie française, échanges extérieurs et structures internationales" (1957), p. 59.
[47] Moreau, Souvenirs (1954), pp. 74, 170. For the fact of purchasing-power-parity calculations, see Rueff, introduction to Moreau, p. viii, and again "Le Niveau de la stabilisation Poincaré" (1959). In the end pressure from the export industry (pp. 66, 162, 163, 175, 177, 178, 184) brought about the stabilization at the undervalued level of 125 to the pound sterling, although Rueff insists that the intervention of Jouhaux of the CGT was decisive (introduction, p. viii, and "Le Niveau de la stabilisation Poincaré," p. 172). After he had given up the return to par as a moral obligation (Rueff, introduction, p. vi), Poincaré, the politician, showed himself more farsighted in his concern for a high rate of 100 to the pound (Souvenirs, p. 60) instead of 125 (p. 184) than the economists or bankers. Rueff defends the 125 rate to this day, using the argument that the decision, made on his calculations after Poincaré had asked him to look into

to improve efficiency while maintaining inefficient firms and farms; to stimulate building while maintaining rent control; hoping for vigorous action by large firms while penalizing firm growth through capital and corporate income taxes.[48] These activities led a number of observers, neglecting the history of the Second Empire when Louis Napoleon used his decree powers to lower tariffs in the Anglo-French Treaty of Commerce of 1860, to conclude that the French government "redistributes rather than enriches" and "protects more than it directs." [49]

An underlying lack of cohesion and agreement explains the character of French finances — so often the subject of wry comment[50] — both the deficits and the regressive system of budgetary and social-security taxation. Since the citizen found government oppressive, and operating in the interest of other groups than his own, he felt justified in evading progressive direct taxes. In consequence, the heavy burdens left to the state had to be met by taxes on employment and goods, brilliantly adapted to the prejudice against mergers by being levied against value added rather than on total sales, which would have provided an incentive to vertical integration. Lower-income groups provide their own social security, to the extent that the incidence of employment taxes for social security fall back on the workers, in sharp contrast to the English system, wherein the government contribution to social security amounts to one third of the total and is paid for out of general revenue, raised in largest part by progressive income taxes.[51] It is perhaps not the case that this regressive tax system in France con-

---

salaries, had saved France from the permanent unemployment which ravaged England. This echoes a theme of the Committee of Experts of 1926, among whom Rueff had sat, who feared as a consequence of the stabilization of the franc a deflation comparable to that in the United Kingdom, ruinous for industry, commerce, and agriculture (Lalumière, *L'Inspection des Finances*, 1959, p. 184n).

[48] *The French Economy and the State.* For an earlier illustration, see Dunham, *The Industrial Revolution in France* (1951), p. 394: the government tried to improve methods in metallurgy but at the same time to maintain the use and the price of wood.

[49] Morazé, *La France bourgeoise*, p. 202; Ehrmann, *Organized Business in France* (1957), p. 301. Ehrmann also emphasizes that the various groups are stronger in coalition than the government (p. 275) but divided generally (pp. 475ff).

[50] See, e.g., the remarks of Poincaré: "France — a land of excessive taxation, tempered by fraud" — quoted by Ehrmann, *Organized Business in France*, p. 314. Myrdal: "France, the land of the best public finance theorists and the worst public finances." André Siegfried: "The Frenchman usually contrived to make both ends meet, even if the state budget may show a deficit. This is in striking contrast to the English community where the private budget may show a deficit, while the state finances will be majestically balanced" (*France*, 1930, p. 7). The Myrdal dictum is generalized by Pussort, who regarded France as having the best laws and the worst government (quoted by Dunham, *Industrial Revolution in France*, p. 199).

[51] Baum, *The French Economy and the State*, pp. 351ff; Lorwin, *French Labor Movement* (1954), p. 22; Passe, *Economies comparées* (1957), chap. xi.

stitutes a separate engine of inflation, through its effect in raising prices and worsening the balance of payments.[52] The exchange rate can be adjusted to the level of prices as effected by direct or indirect taxes.[53] But the necessity for regressive taxes and budget deficits has been a symptom of the underlying and inflationary lack of cohesion, as one group after another refuses to bear a substantial share of the national burdens of war and investment, and the attempt to balance the budget with indirect taxes leads quickly to strikes, higher cost of living, higher wages, further higher prices, and a renewed governmental deficit.[54]

I have referred above to the widespread view that all French groups have been conscious of the need for social stability and, therefore, desirous of preserving both the countryside and the small artisan and shopkeeper.[55] The view seems idyllic and out of character. In agriculture, as in industry, the interests of the small were primarily a banner under which the large-scale agriculturist advanced. Zolla notes that the small farms consume most of their wheat at home, and even buy some, and that the price of wheat and hence the tariff were much more important questions for the large specialized farms.[56]

General agreement after 1945 on the importance of expansion did not automatically produce readiness of any group to sacrifice itself for development. An increase in individualism, and a reduction in the strength of the "delinquent groups," strengthened the hands of government in making bargains. When recalcitrant groups like the Poujadists or the wine lobby became obstreperous, government cracked down. The constitutional reform of 1958 has helped, but the social scientists detect a fundamental transformation of values and institutions.

---

[52] See, e.g., Peterson, *Welfare State in France* (1960), pp. 32, 52, 63.

[53] This was the view of the Tinbergen Committee, appointed by the European Coal and Steel Committee to look into the French claim that economic integration required other countries to shift from a direct system of social security to an indirect, like the French.

[54] As analyzed by Aujac, "Inflation as a Consequence of Social Groups" (1950).

[55] See above, Chapter 8. Sée is one historian who finds this theory attractive: "France remains at the beginning of the twentieth century a rich agricultural nation which does not have to sell the products of its factories, like England, to live. It has lost relatively to the rest of Europe since the end of the eighteenth century, when it was the richest and most populated country, distanced by Germany. But the equilibrium which it has maintained at home between agriculture and industry, this sort of harmony, assures it a strong stability and an enviable situation. It is this equilibrium which renders the class struggle less bitter" (*Histoire économique de la France*, 1942, II, 366). But see Hunter, *Peasantry and Crisis* (1948), p. 103: "It is difficult to resist the conclusion that the much-vaunted stability of French rural society does not bear close examination.

[56] Quoted by Golob, *Méline Tariff*, p. 81. Golob observes that the alliance between industry and agriculture over the tariffs broke down continuously over the question of tariffs on oil seeds, raw silk, hides, and similar farm-produced raw materials.

GOVERNMENT AS AN ULCER

It is a gentle transition from the view of government as a weak and arbitrary judge among groups to regarding it as a monster or an excrescence. This opinion does not apply in Britain, except perhaps in extreme Conservative circles after World War II. From the time of Louis XIV, however, government in France has been regarded as excessive, both in size and in centralization, and as a parasite fattening on the commonweal. Cordier worried about the centralization of public works in 1843, and Raudot lists excessive government centralization as one of his five causes of French decadence.[57] Earlier mention has been made to the concern of Mourre at the end of the nineteenth century, who attacked "functionarism," the form of government, intervention of the state, and so on.[58] Cameron notes that France had a million fonctionaires in 1913, or 2.5 percent of the total population and 5 percent of the active population.[59] Figures of this sort are difficult to interpret, since not only the post, telephone and telegraph systems, and some railroads were government-operated at that time, but the school system and much local administration and police were run from Paris. In emphasizing centralization, employees of the national government should be compared. But if the question is one of total government, national and local employees must be combined.[60]

One aspect of the practical character of government is size; another, centralization. Chapter 11 is devoted to regional aspects of French and British economic growth, where the dominant role of Paris and the central government is discussed. Here it is appropriate to say only that in France, unlike Britain, local responsibility has been limited at all levels of governmental and private initiative. Rarely does one find a

[57] Cordier, *Recherches sur les causes de la prosperité et les chances de décadence de la France et de l'Angleterre*, quoted by de Tapiès, *La France et l'Angleterre* (1845), p. 597; Raudot, quoted by Cameron, "Profit, croissance et stagnation en France" (1957), p. 442.

[58] Mourre, *D'où vient la décadence économique?* (1900), pp. 177, 189, 257. Mourre quotes from Leroy-Beaulieu, *L'État moderne* (1890), and Deschanel, *La Décentralisation* (1895), who share the view that the state is too big and takes on too much.

[59] Cameron, p. 438.

[60] The "established complements" of the Civil Service amounted to 167,000 in 1914 (Campbell, *Civil Service in Britain*, 1955, p. 73), but Abramovitz and Eliasberg give 718,000 for central government employment, including 395,000 armed forces and 190,000 post office employees (*The Growth of Public Employment in Great Britain*, 1957, p. 63). To these should be added local government staffs, including unemployed, given for 1911 as 660,000 (p. 70). A fair comparison for the period is virtually impossible. In 1955, Passe puts the French and British totals in "administrative services" as 1,556,000 and 1,959,000, respectively (*Économies comparées*, p. 26).

remark such as that quoted by Girard from the Conseil Générale of the Ponts et Chaussées, that the contribution of social-overhead capital by the national government waited on local investment and initiative.[61] For the most part it is the reverse: large-scale public works were important, but the Ponts et Chaussées planned them by itself.[62] Until recently local taxpayers would neither raise taxes beyond the inelastic *octroi* levied on goods entering the commune nor contract debt, with the result that local services were poor. This has been satirized by Chevallier in *Clochemerle*. In growing suburbs the problem has been more serious; and only the Communist Party in some communities has been prepared to face up to the task of providing sewers, roads, streetlights.[63]

The sociologist Crozier, who has studied the prefectural corps, goes further. He suggests that the role of Paris through the prefect is to control, rather than to produce change. Of the two principles of the prefect, order and the general interest, the first dominates. The French administrative system has a panic fear of disorder. It can contribute to development through the preservation of law and order, but it is never the motor.[64]

Government can harm economic development by seeking power and glory. On his deathbed Louis XIV admitted to having involved France in "too many palaces and too many wars." Nationalism has been used in France alternatively to extend French sovereignty and to consolidate national security at home.[65] During most of our period, these forces were relatively moderate, compared with the France of Louis XIV and Napoleon. But Louis Napoleon was "wasteful, reckless and incompetent," [66] bringing humiliation to France in his Mexican adventure and disaster in 1870 against Germany. The Third Republic under Ferry undertook colonial adventure — Tunis in 1881, Tonkin in 1883, Madagascar in 1895, Morocco in 1905 — before retreating after 1919 to drive for national security. France has been scolded for neglecting the colonies.[67] The usual view, however, is that they added nothing but problems in the form of more wheat and more wine.[68] The question

[61] Girard, *Travaux publics*, p. 105.
[62] Léon, *La Grande industrie en Dauphiné* (1954), pp. 464ff.
[63] Brogan, *France under the Republic* (1940), p. 638.
[64] Crozier, "Le Corps prefectoral en action" (1961), pp. 17, 18: "Public order is imposed from the top. It requires constant reference to the majesty of the state, a decorum, a prestige and personal power which make the prefect a mysterious and solitary person."
[65] Duroselle, "French Foreign Policy" (1959).
[66] Dunham, *Anglo-French Treaty*, p. 367.
[67] Dunham, *Industrial Revolution in France*, p. 356.
[68] Augé-Laribé, *Politique agricole*, p. 10. Bettelheim, *Bilan de l'économie française* (1947), p. 145, complains that the colonies did not make good the gaps in French resources. But if they had, the peasants would not have settled in them.

is asked whether colonial adventure did not divert manpower and investment from domestic growth in significant degree. But the answer is no. Metropolitan France had no alternative occupations to offer the peasants who were driven to Algiers in the 1880s by the phylloxera and the low price of wheat.

The colonial budget grew from 1885 to 1912 — from 42.6 million francs to 104 million.[69] These figures were not substantial as compared with a total budget of 3 to 4 billion francs. Investment in the colonies, including Algeria and Tunis, amounted to 3 or 4 billion out of total foreign investments of more than 50 billion.[70] Three billion were also invested by France in Africa outside the colonies.[71] Far more capital was wasted in Eastern Europe, both without and with the blessing of a government that was interested in financial support for its foreign policy. French colonial policy, as Brunschwig shows, was never economic, having been born of nationalism after the humiliation of 1871 — "the secret wound, the incurable plague of Alsace and Lorraine." [72] It did not cost a great deal. Nor, unlike Mexico, can it be regarded as an operation in prestige in which the French public took no interest. "Public opinion was very sensitive to the nationalist argument." [73]

The government exploited the individual less after 1850 than before. Under Napoleon I the state had made greater demands on its people longer than virtually any other state in modern times, both in taxation and in conscription. The gendarme was hated as the agent of the conscripting army. The central authority of the king had represented a counter to the local oppression of the seigneur under feudalism. Imperceptibly, however, the state slipped into the role of oppressor. And when the French people suffered another twenty years of war, from 1940 to 1960, it is not surprising that echoes of this view of government persist.[74]

The British tradition was diametrically opposite. Dr. Bowring said to Alexis de Tocqueville in August 1833: "England is the country of decentralization. We have got a government, but we have not got a central administration. Each county, each town, each parish looks after its own interests. Industry is left to itself." [75] And Lord Minto told him

[69] Brunschwig, *Impérialisme colonial français* (1960), p. 139.

[70] Germain Martin, *Problèmes du crédit en France* (1919), p. 96; Brunschwig, p. 140.

[71] Brunschwig, p. 141.

[72] *Ibid.*, p. 176. Luethy, *France against Herself* (1955), p. 216, says that France offered her colonial empire nothing and demanded nothing from it except soldiers.

[73] Brunschwig, p. 149.

[74] Based on remarks of Paul Henri, Center for International Affairs, seminar, Harvard University, March 25, 1960.

[75] Tocqueville, *Journeys to England* (1958), pp. 61, 62.

in 1835: "Up to now centralization has been the thing most foreign to the English temperament." [76] John Stuart Mill explained:

> Our habits or the nature of our temperament do not in the least draw us toward general ideas; but centralization is based on general ideas; that is the desire for power to attend, in a uniform and general way, to the present and future needs of society. We have never considered government from such a lofty point of view. So we have divided administrative functions up infinitely, and made them independent of one another. We have not done this deliberately, but from our sheer inability to comprehend general ideas on the subject of government or anything else.[77]

The result is that upper and middle classes participate in government, accept responsibility, and identify themselves with the government or the opposition.[78] The masses tend to ignore it: Westminster is irrelevant to a Cumberland village, in contrast with Péyrane in the Vaucluse where the entire populace talks about government all the time.[79] Britons are ruled by "our" government; French by "les autres."

The British may well have overdone it. I have already suggested that government was needed to lead the way in setting standards or in providing technical education. Bagehot said that an age of great cities required strong government,[80] which the British provided only after the energy of the private sector was beginning to flag and the task was less to direct than to replace.

GOVERNMENT AS AN INDEPENDENT FORCE

Moving from the position that every people has the government it deserves, we may usefully consider the possibility that government is an independent variable that affects economic growth by independent policy decisions, which may turn out to be better or worse. This is a position that appeals to the social scientist — to the political scientist, who believes that the words in the constitution (or the unwritten words) make a difference; and to the economist, who believes in a range for choice of commercial policy or a quantity of money or an exchange rate, and regards the choice as important for growth.

A long list of questions could be analyzed under this heading, on which whole books have been written. For France, we might examine

[76] *Ibid.*, p. 80.
[77] *Ibid.*, p. 81.
[78] See Halévy, *History of the English People* (1924), III, 220: " 'England is a free country'; this means at bottom that England is a country of voluntary obedience, of an organization freely initiated and freely accepted."
[79] Williams, *Sociology of Gosforth* (1956), p. 175. Wylie, *Village in the Vaucluse*, chap. x.
[80] Quoted by Young, *Portrait of an Age* (1936), p. 150.

the Anglo-French Treaty of Commerce of 1860, imposed on France by Louis Napoleon (and Michel Chevalier) against the will of the *corps législatif;* the reparation experiences after 1870 and 1919; rent control; the undervaluation of the franc in 1926; the 1934 deflation of Laval; the Front Populaire and its forty-hour week; monetary and debt policy in the 1920s and again after 1945. For Britain, similar questions arise over the revaluation of sterling in 1925; empire preference; the conversion of the national debt, making good on sterling liabilities contracted during World War II to the colonies and dependent countries; the nationalization of steel; the capital outflow to Australia and South Africa for nonessential investment; the importance attached to full employment. Decisions taken on these and other questions were important for the course of economic growth. Substantial doubt remains, however, about whether government was free to exercise much choice in the decisions taken or whether ignorance, cultural lag, political constraint, and so on, did not narrow down the range for leadership and choice to one little wider than simple historical determinism.

Mistakes and confusion are easy to find, especially cultural lag — the Maginot Line psychology by which economists no less than generals fought the last war. The French paid reparations, therefore the French can collect reparations: "Germany will pay." The prestige of the prewar structure of 1913 led all leaders to try to restore 1913 prices, exchange parities, resource allocation, and international economic relations, despite new circumstances.[81] After World War II, it was the obverse: the world, and especially Britain, resolved to cure the unemployment of the interwar periods, no matter what the consequences for inflation or the balance of payments.

Effective economic policies are often born of accident.[82] And effective critics — Churchill in the military field, Keynes in the economic, Reynaud in both — may take advantage of hindsight,[83] lack of re-

[81] Weiller, "Long-run Tendencies in Foreign Trade" (1943), p. 33.

[82] See Iversen, "The Importance of the International Margin" (1936), who contends that Sweden's successful experience during the 1930s was the result of the British building boom and buoyant exports, rather than domestic anticyclical policy. Schacht is similarly given credit for having devised a brilliant method of conducting foreign trade without gold reserves, when he merely permitted the system to evolve.

[83] Reynaud, *Thick of the Fight* (1955), sets out his superb record for advocacy of constructive and sensible policies: advocating reparations in kind after World War I, linking French and German heavy industry to prevent war in the early 1920s, recommending an offensive army (1924), urging France to cut its commitments (1930), predicting the success of the Popular Front (August, 1934), urging devaluation (1934), predicting that the forty-hour week would ruin the 1936 devaluation, and leading the fourteenth and only successful recovery plan in November 1938 (pp. 1, 2). He disagreed with the Bank of France over monetary policy, with the Quai d'Orsay over foreign policy, and with the General Staff over military policy (p. 3). But he was also the author of the slogan, "We will win

sponsibility in meeting political pressures,[84] or an erroneous reputation for prescience.[85] Criticism may even justify itself by making the intended course of action impossible.[86] Space does not permit analysis of much of this record, but perhaps three incidents may be taken: the collection of German reparations; the forty-hour week in France; and the restoration of the pound to par in 1925. In each, our interest is in seeing how far the policy adopted was the result of the lack of an analytical framework, errors of application of a valid analysis, or a lack of choice in the political context. It is also appropriate to decide how important the episodes were in slowing down growth.

French success in paying off the Prussian indemnity in 1872 astounded the Germans, the world, and the French. There was strong determination to pay, to rid the country of German troops. The transfer was initially made in gold and foreign securities bought with the proceeds of a massive internal loan; but these were repurchased with a real capital outflow by 1877 or 1878. At the time, and ever later, it was not realized how much the inadvertent German inflation of 1873 had contributed to the result — an inflation initiated in part by the receipt of 500 million francs in gold and the shift from the bimetallic to the gold standard.

For France in 1919, the problem was simple. It had won this war and the Germans had started it. Therefore they should pay. Keynes's arguments about the capacity to raise a surplus, and the later discussion of transfer, were sophistry. What one could do, another could. And the demonstration of Germany's capacity to pay, as Mantoux noted, was the country's feats in expanding coal production during the 1926 British strike or in rearmament in the 1930s. Viner and Mach-

---

because we are stronger," which Dutourd found so absurd (*Taxis of the Marne,* 1957). And he does not discuss his failures.

[84] The most celebrated example is Keynes's *Economic Consequences of the Peace* (1920), in which the economist was profoundly ironic at the expense of the four statesmen and politicians and, on many matters of substance and color, wrong. See, e.g., Mantoux, *The Carthaginian Peace* (1952), although much of his argument cannot be accepted. For a mature view that Keynes erred on many points, see Duroselle, *De Wilson à Roosevelt* (1960), p. 115.

[85] It is widely understood, for example, that Keynes was strongly opposed to the return to the gold standard at par in 1925, as he had been in 1923. See, e.g., Harrod, *Life of Keynes* (1951), p. 362, and the acceptance of the view, though he argues it was wrong, by Youngson, *British Economy* (1960), p. 234. But Keynes enthusiastically approved the return to gold in the *Nation* of May 2, 1925, changing his mind a week later, in the May 9 issue, only to reproach Churchill later for not having fixed certain conditions for it. Perrot, *La Monnaie et l'opinion* (1955), p. 32.

[86] See, again, *Economic Consequences of the Peace.* After its publication, as Mantoux points out, the collection of reparations was impossible, whether it was before or not. The parallel in physics, I am told, is that every observation modifies what is observed.

lup have cited the rapid change in the German balance of payments on current account after 1928, when American lending ceased, as proof that balances of payments do adjust readily to changes in capital movements,[87] although the fact that this was followed by large-scale unemployment, and ultimately the success of the Nazi movement, may cast doubt on the success of the experiment. The strong positive balance of payments of Germany after World War II, with reparations paid to Israel and repayment of debts to Britain and the United States, can also be noted.

But the difference remains between reparation payments by a country that wants to discharge its obligation and one that does not. This is particularly in point where the recipient is unwilling or unable successfully to levy its due with physical force. France remained determined to collect reparations in full in a world which was ready for the return of Germany to the trading community as a full partner and was unwilling to assist vengeful (as it thought) efforts to collect reparations through occupation of the Ruhr. It may be true that if *The Economic Consequences of the Peace* had not been written, Germany would have paid up like a sportsman losing a bet — but it had been written. In 1922, Germany needed a breathing spell and a possible reduction of reparations. The Bankers Committee recommended such a reduction. But the French remained obdurate in the Reparations Committee. There followed the occupation of the Ruhr and German sabotage of production, which ensured the collapse of the mark.

The French position is easy to understand. If the Germans had acted as France had; or if Britain had stood by France; or if the United States had canceled the war debts . . . But where was French realism? None of these things was true and, in the circumstances, German reparations were uncollectable. After 1924, the French were more realistic and collaborated in the Dawes Plan, the Young Plan, and the Hoover Moratorium. But the damage to the French budget and the franc, from spending freely on reconstruction in the expectation that the Germans would pay, had already been done.

The results were not bad for economic development in the short run. High levels of income and employment were maintained; the steel and cotton textile industries were rebuilt; government expenditure in northern and eastern France for social-overhead capital was maintained on a high level. But the subsequent stabilization of the franc at an undervalued level, which the monetary expansion made possible in the absence of knowledge of the techniques of exchange control,

[87] See Viner, *International Economics* (1951), p. 182; Machlup, "Three Concepts of the Balance of Payments" (1950), p. 59n.

put critical pressure on the international monetary mechanism, especially on the overvalued pound. The destruction of four fifths of the assets of owners of government *rentes*, after the blows the rentier had already submitted to in the repudiation of tsarist and Eastern European bonds, may have had some relation to the social disorders of the 1930s that definitely slowed down growth. If it did, economists and politicians were far from ready, without the experience of one major inflation, to adopt the highly sophisticated measures for the equalization of war losses put into effect in Germany after World War II; nor is there any indication that the French social structure, with its lack of cohesion, would have been willing to adopt them.

The forty-hour week of the Blum government is also readily understood. The country suffered from an overvalued currency after the adjustment of the pound and the dollar, and the experts joined the politicians in refusing to correct it.[88] Deflationary pressure from abroad was severe. Stopgap measures of various sorts were tried: restriction of immigration, quotas on imports. In 1933, Daladier tried deflation with a 6 percent cut in government salaries. He promised nationalization of arms plants and insurance and a forty-hour week, which the socialists rejected. Chautemps was defeated by the Stavisky scandals in December 1933. In February 1934 came right-wing riots, followed by left-wing, and a general strike. The Confédération Général de Travail proposed unemployment insurance, a forty-hour week, paid vacations, large-scale public works to fight unemployment, nationalization of key industries, national economic planning using credit as the lever for expansion through the nationalized Bank of France. (Lorwin notes that this is the program finally adopted after the liberation — except for the forty-hour week.[89]) In January 1935 Flandin tried to raise prices by contracting output, along with limitation of hours of work and collective bargaining with the Front Populaire. This was patterned after the National Recovery Administration in the United States and was equally successful. When Flandin resigned in May 1935, Laval tried deflation (instead of devaluation) or delavaluation.[90] Finally came the sit-down strikes[91] and the Front Populaire, with

[88] The undervaluation of the 1920s and its effect on the rentier led Flandin, for example, to think that renewed devaluation was both immoral and threatened social disorder (Brogan, *France under the Republic*, p. 674). Charles Rist, with rare candor, wrote on August 1, 1952: "I willingly admit that I was one of those most strongly in favor of maintaining the rate at which, after much hard work and many difficulties, the franc had just been stabilized . . . I made the mistake of not rallying to his [Reynaud's] support . . . until some time later . . . in 1936" (Reynaud, *Thick of the Fight*, pp. 22–23).

[89] Lorwin, *French Labor Movement*, pp. 71, 102.

[90] Thompson, *Two Frenchmen* (1951), p. 44.

[91] Ehrmann, *Organized Business in France*, p. 13, notes that the sit-down strikes frightened big business and humiliated the family firm.

the Matignon agreement of June 1936 — a thorough defeat for the employers after fifty years of struggling — and its forty-hour week, paid vacations, but no devaluation. Devaluation came in September 1936, but insufficiently. Costs and prices continued to rise. More devaluation in 1938. Cost inflation wiped out the effects of devaluation; capital went on strike; even finance ministers speculated against the franc. Finally, after Munich, the Reynaud government stepped into the moral and economic bankruptcy with freer prices, higher taxes, armament expenditure, the end of the five-day week — and, until the war, some recovery.

The Blum government has been attacked for economic illiteracy and for lack of economic realism.[92] But ideas were not lacking, and in a different setting the same ideas, more or less, produced an entirely different result. This was not a failure of policy but of social cohesion. Reynaud believes that his success after November 13, 1938, was a triumph for correct policies. Perhaps. The United States tried some of the same policies — deflation in 1932 and pegging the prices of output through the NRA of 1933. It may have been pure luck that an election happened to fall in 1932, that the Supreme Court killed the NRA, and that Roosevelt was a pragmatic experimentalist who would keep changing advice or advisers until he found something that worked. But it is likely that French immobility and American readiness to keep searching for an effective solution go further to explain the disparate conduct of the 1930s in the two countries than the quality of advice available to either. It is true that French economists, with their legal training, were not available in large numbers for government work on economic problems. Even if they had been, the result would hardly have been different. The popular-front program collapsed, like the right-wing programs, partly because it was intrinsically inappropriate, but mainly because the social cement fell out of the system. None of the conditions of success was present: a strong responsible labor movement, employer acceptance of limitations on authority, continuity of governmental policy, or international security.[93]

British cohesion would not have permitted the situation to deteriorate to the same extent as it did in France, and the failure of the general strike of 1926 left no heritage of bitterness comparable to the experience of the Front Populaire. Moreover, there was no lack of economic opinion. But most of it was rationalization for action to restore the pound to the prewar level. Part of the reason was nostalgia for this period; more of it was prestige, a need to "look the dollar in

[92] Aron, seminar at Harvard Center for International Affairs, October 1961; Luethy, *France against Herself*, p. 81.

[93] Lorwin, *French Labor Movement*, p. 81.

the eye." Marguerite Perrot calls the return to gold an affair of wounded amour-propre, rather than monetary policy.[94] Industrialists hoped to get back their export markets by encouraging capital exports; the City thought of invisible earnings. The public approved of the return to gold but was basically disinterested, "passive but optimistic." [95] The Establishment never wavered in its insistence on parity.[96] And after the Anglo-American debt settlement of December 1922 paved the way, and the German inflation showed the treacherous path of countries straying from the gold standard, even the heretics, Keynes and McKenna, joined Pigou, Hawtrey, Gregory, and the others in approval.

There is some English opinion today that the fault lay elsewhere. "What wrecked the gold standard was the self-regarding unwisdom of French and American monetary policies." [97] An equilibrium exchange rate would not have corrected structural unemployment in export industries of the 1914 size that were too large for 1924. It was not the pound that was set too high, but the franc too low.[98]

After World War II prestige revealed itself in another monetary guise: the refusal of the British to scale down their debts to colonies and dependent countries contracted during the war under provisional and arbitrary arrangements for financing the war in these areas. "A gentleman never counts his change or takes cover." There was no hesitation in asking for reductions of obligations contracted to countries of equal status — the dominions and the United States. A policy of prestige made it impossible to ask for such consideration from an inferior, even at the insistence of the United States during the negotiations over the British loan.

In retrospect, the stabilization of the pound at par seems to have been inevitable, given the history of one hundred years of the pre-eminence of sterling. Economic discussion had little to do with it. The independent roles of government, and of economic analysis, were in

---

[94] Perrot, *La Monnaie et l'opinion*, p. 35.

[95] *Ibid.*, p. 56.

[96] See Chandler, *Benjamin Strong* (1958), p. 252, on Norman's view.

[97] Youngson, *British Economy*, pp. 233–234. This seems a little severe on the United States, after the 1927 reduction of the discount rate in an effort to assist the pound. French-British financial relations during the period were exacerbated by domestic preoccupations, on the one hand, and rather petty central-bank rivalry over spheres of influence in Europe, on the other. See Moreau, *Souvenirs*, pp. 49ff, and Chandler, pp. 365ff.

[98] Youngson, p. 237. Norman viewed the French rate as "fortuitous." But we have seen above (note 47) that the rate was chosen after much thought. Strong had made calculations for the pound, but admitted that he underestimated its overvaluation (Chandler, pp. 282ff, 330). It is interesting to note that in their discussions of the stabilization with Moreau, neither Norman nor Strong mentioned the ultimate rate at which the franc would be stabilized, or he did not record it.

reality narrow. As on so many occasions, the task of economic analysis was a priestly one, to justify what was taking place for deep-seated reasons rather than to determine the direction of movement.

The episode was important for economic growth. There can be no certainty that a proper level of the pound would have enabled a government to tackle sooner the structural changes required by the war — the prewar obsolescence of British industrial equipment and the transformation from coal, cotton textiles, ships, rails, and galvanized iron to the products of engineering industry. Sayers is persuaded that much progress was made in technological modernization, and Youngson insists that the building boom dates not from the devaluation of sterling but from 1924.[99] Neither point is impressive, compared with the necessity to turn the economy away from the heavy concentration of employment in staple industries and distressed areas, a result achieved only during World War II. An equilibrium rate may not have been sufficient, but, in light of the vain effort to defend a disequilibrium rate, it was necessary.

The view of government as an entity independent of the body politic, badly trained in economics, interfering, making mistakes, acting in contradictory ways, and aiding or impeding growth, is insufficiently subtle. One needs a better theory of government in relation to social and political forces. Baum may be right that the French government really had no idea of what it was doing, and allowed itself to be pushed about in various ways; but this should not be attributed to a fault of leadership if there is no followership to choose, inspire, and support the leaders. Where followers lack a sense of direction, this can sometimes be supplied. But where all have strong senses of direction, which fail to converge, the fault is not in economic policy or government. And the opposite view is also wrong: that it is all planned, or that all stems from the resolve of government officials to achieve growth at whatever cost.[100]

Government is a reflection of the polity, accurate or distorted. When the British people after World War I yearned for the late Victorian era, the government made mistakes of exchange policy. When all social groups are unwilling to sacrifice for the common purpose, government policy will be inflationary. And when all are resolved to grow,

[99] Sayers, "Springs of Technical Progress" (1950); Youngson, *British Economy*, pp. 49, 63–64.
[100] See Lalumière, *L'Inspection des Finances*, p. 221. His theory is that the Inspection imbibed its views of expansion from Keynes (p. 179) and that it — "an active group which participates dynamically in national life — was alone or almost alone in the middle of the general inertia in representing an element of progress."

however much they disagree on political issues, government policies will be conducive to growth, although not necessarily in the manner foreseen in governmental plans. The proof: the Monnet Plan is based on a Harrod-Domar model of growth through investment. Growth in France after World War II has rested fundamentally on technical change, for which the plans made only incidental provision.

CHAPTER 10

AGRICULTURAL
TRANSFORMATION

Agriculture is frequently blamed for the slow economic development in France, not always for the same reason. Various theories relating the pace of development in agriculture to overall growth are possible, and most find expression in the discussion of French growth. This chapter will try to sort them out. The effort takes so much time and space that room will be left only for a brief discussion of the rapid progress of British agriculture to 1870 or 1880 and its failure to adapt to cheap food imports thereafter.

An increase in productivity in agriculture can be used in various ways in economic development: to expand exports or reduce imports, in an open economy; or to cheapen the price of food or of raw-material inputs in industry. Or the increase in productivity can be used to shrink the size of the sector and to free labor for employment elsewhere. The same increase in productivity, while it can be divided, cannot be used more than once. How it is used will affect the level of production and the terms of trade between agriculture and the rest of the economy. These, in turn, imply a level of income in agriculture which may be larger, the same, or smaller than before. If an increase in agricultural income occurs, it can be spent — on foodstuffs or industrial output — or saved. If saved, it may be invested in the agricultural sector, elsewhere in the economy, or loaned abroad. But again the same increase in income, if it occurs, cannot both furnish savings to other sectors and increase demand, though it may do some of both.

It follows that the same failure of agriculture to increase its productivity cannot be responsible, at the same time and to the extent of the missing increase, for a lack of capital formation, a failure of demand to increase, the high price of industrial materials from agriculture, and the failure of industrial recruits to come forward.

Nor is there any necessary reason, once economic development has gone a certain distance, why it should be agriculture which leads industry in expanding output and increasing productivity rather than the other way round. In a closed economy, with minimal capital, increased agricultural productivity may be a "precondition" of economic growth.[1] Without foreign borrowing, agriculture must expand its output and save in order to free labor for capital formation. In an open economy this is not so important. Capital can be borrowed from abroad. Savings of the industrial sector can be transformed by means of international trade into consumption goods for labor engaged in capital formation. In the long run, the industrial sector must grow and the agricultural shrink, relative to one another, as Engel's law shifts consumption proportionately from foodstuffs to industrial products. But agriculture can shrink without increasing its productivity — if industrial exports expand in exchange for food imports. Agricultural savings are important in the early stages because the sector is large in relation to industry. After a time, there is just as much reason for industry to furnish demand and savings to agriculture as vice versa. Historically, industrial growth may have been held back by agriculture; but it can also happen historically that lack of industrial expansion limits demand for agricultural products and opportunity for workers to shift into industry, which would give rise to increased investment in agriculture; or that industry fails to produce the capital needed in the modernization of the countryside.

It is neither possible nor necessary to deal with all types of interrelations between agriculture and the rest of the French economy. I limit myself to four: the analytically trivial but arithmetically sound view that agriculture held back the total growth of France by growing at a slower rate than industry;[2] the view that agriculture held back French development through failing to produce sufficient demand for industrial products;[3] the view that it failed to release sufficient manpower to industry;[4] and, finally, a contrary view which exists in both

[1] See Nicholls, "Agriculture in Economic Development" (1960), pp. 25–26. Nicholls adds (p. 13): "Even given initially favorable agricultural conditions, too long a neglect of policies promoting increased agricultural productivity may have serious repercussions on the rate of general economic progress [France and Russia]." The mechanism referred to in French experience is not made explicit.

[2] Lewis, *The Theory of Economic Growth* (1955), p. 279: "Of all the explanations offered for the relative stagnation of France, compared with Great Britain, the relatively slow growth of agricultural productivity seems to this author the most fundamental. France still needs a quarter of her population to feed herself, compared with 12 to 15 percent in the most advanced countries." The second sentence quoted implies the "averaging theory," but in the context an efficient agriculture is expected to provide demand for other sectors and furnish them with capital.

[3] *Ibid.*, p. 282: "This transition [of the dynamic role from foreign trade to home investment] may be long delayed, as in France, if the agricultural sector fails to be revolutionized on capitalistic lines, and therefore continues to be a drag on demand and the labor supply.

[4] Gerschenkron, "Social Attitudes, Entrepreneurship and Economic Development" (1953), p. 11: "Some of the factors which must in large measure have accounted

Britain and France that industry drew men too fast from agriculture — a rural exodus — thereby reducing its productivity.[5]

AGRICULTURAL PRODUCTIVITY IN FRANCE

The widely accepted view among nonspecialists is that French agriculture has been technologically very stagnant. In part, this idea has been disseminated by the early editions of Colin Clark's *Economic Conditions of Progress*. Later editions, as we shall see, have spread another inadequately qualified idea, that earnings per capita are as high in agriculture as in industry. The fact is that the greater part of France participated in some degree in the agricultural revolution of the eighteenth century, and much of this part — especially in the Paris basin, the north, and the east — shared in the further transformation wrought by the railroad, by fertilizer, and by machinery. Certain inefficient overpopulated areas remain — notably Brittany and Alsace — and certain stagnant though not overpopulated areas — Lorraine, the center, and the south. But it is incorrect to describe French agriculture as altogether stagnant. There are three French agricultures: one relatively modern, one backward, and one, until before World War II, archaic.

Data to measure French agricultural progress are scanty. Some of the obstacles are mentioned in the appendix — lack of consistency in the agricultural censuses, inaccuracy of peasant reports, and manipulation of the primary data by subsequent studies, not always with complete explanation. I therefore eschew an overall statistical view. But the qualitative picture is relatively clear, and some data will emerge as it is set out.

The late eighteenth century produced an agricultural revolution which, through the enclosure system, contributed to the political revolution.[6] The revolution in agriculture was based on new products, mostly imported from the United States, and not associated with the Indus-

---

for the difference of the speed of growth [between France and Germany] are obvious. The lack of a coal basis comparable to the Ruhr . . . The prevalence of the family farm with its unfavorable effects on the flow of labor to industry is another." See also W. W. Rostow. "Leading Sectors and the Take-Off" (1960), p. 18: "Some part of the low growth rate of France after 1848 relative to Germany is to be explained by the relatively light pressure on land caused by the damped population increase, and the consequently lesser flow of rural men to the cities." On the following page Rostow discusses further the possible interrelations between agriculture and economic development, preceded by the comment: "An increase in agricultural production and productivity plays a multiple role in economic development which can hardly be overestimated."

[5] The foremost French economist who believes in the rural exodus is Gravier.

[6] Lévy, *Histoire économique de la France* (1951–52), p. 132.

trial Revolution.[7] Its chief chronicler is Marc Bloch.[8] The potato, introduced from 1740 to 1770, ended periodic famines.[9] Clover and other forage crops came in between 1770 and 1790. Indian corn got a start at this time, as well as the sugar beet under the continental system. These new crops, especially corn in the south and sugar beets in the north, were "cleaning" crops and rested the land. They required change in the rotation but enabled the fallow to be suppressed. Forage crops, including beets and sugar-beet pulp, permitted a substantial change to stall feeding of cattle and expansion of the arable.

One writer states that this agricultural revolution had ended by 1825, although the period of expansion of sugar beets — largely for feed — went on in the Nivernais until 1880.[10] A more usual view is that it continued to 1850.[11] This was when agricultural expansion ended, and with it the "dynamism of the peasant who made the agricultural revolution." [12]

But there was a pickup under the Second Empire. Dumont places the agricultural revolution of the nineteenth century right in the period of the Second Empire,[13] which would make it coincide with the golden age of British farming. And except for the crisis of 1848, itself important, the countryside was prosperous from 1840 to 1870.[14] Fertilizer was introduced and, with the spread of the railroad, liming.[15] In large farms around Paris and Lyon, draining was undertaken privately, following British techniques, in addition to government projects.[16] Wheat yields rose 50 percent between 1850 and 1880.[17] Reapers were introduced, stimulated by the London exhibition, and freed an enormous number of workers who had been needed for the harvest. The Brabant plow for deep furrows dated from 1856, but was

[7] Faucher, *Le Paysan et la machine* (1954), p. 52.

[8] See his *L'Histoire rurale française* (1931).

[9] Juillard, *Basse-Alsace* (1953), p. 215. Danière points out ("Feudal Incomes and Demand Elasticity for Bread," 1958, p. 330) that potato production, which was an inferior substitute for bread, rose from 1.6 million metric tons in 1815 to 5 million in 1830, 7 million in 1860, and 12 million in 1900.

[10] Dion, *Le Val du Loire* (1933), p. 546.

[11] Faucher, *Le Paysan et la machine*, p. 8.

[12] Juillard, *Basse-Alsace*, p. 277.

[13] This is the summary of Valarché (*L'Économie rurale*, 1960, pp. 176, 236) of the observations of Dumont on particular agricultural areas in France in *Voyages en France d'un agronome* (1951). See, e.g., the latter, p. 424.

[14] Lévy, *Histoire économique de la France*, p. 140.

[15] *Ibid.*, p. 138. See also the review by Bouloiseau of two studies of agriculture in Auvergne. He dates the agricultural revolution and the rural exodus in that province from 1836 and states in passing: "From 1870, above all, the land was limed."

[16] Lévy, p. 140. See also Bernard, *Seine-et-Marne* (1953), p. 25. Bernard notes that the transformation of agricultural technique in Seine-et-Marne was continuous and without governmental pressure.

[17] Golob, *Méline Tariff* (1944), p. 28: output per hectare rose in quintals from 12.45 in 1840 to 17.98 in 1882; rye, from 10.79 to 16.38.

a long time in coming into general use. Combines come in about 1880, according to Faucher,[18] but perhaps a more fundamental change, though less spectacular, was that from the sickle to the scythe in harvesting, which took place under the Second Empire.[19] Lefèvre says that the increase in technical efficiency came largely after 1860.[20] As already noted, the railroad brought a golden age of prosperity in wine to the Midi until 1875.[21] The area supplying Paris spread from 50 to 250 kilometers between 1830 and 1855.[22] The Loire Valley, for example, shifted to young cattle, which now could be spared the grueling trip to Paris by road.[23] The peasant began to produce for the market and to buy his consumption. Wheat and white bread replaced rye.[24] Meat consumption increased throughout the century. There was a virtual revolution in food consumption.[25]

Farm income in this period was rising rapidly. The Institut de Science Economique Appliquée estimates that it rose 1.8 percent a year from 1850 to 1880, following a rise of only 1 percent a year from 1788 to 1850.[26] Thereafter it shows no rise to the end of the century. The best real-output figures consist in Sirol's index, which omits meat and fresh vegetables and understates total output.[27] Moreover, short-term variability makes it difficult to summarize the trend. A moving average suggests that the index ran from 65 in the early 1840s and 70 in the early 1850s, to 90 in the middle 1870s, before slumping in the late 1880s to 70. The peak of the index in 1913 at 111 is not much above the record of 89 in 1847.[28] But the picture is one of growth throughout the Second Empire, even omitting the record low of 44 in 1853 (and of setback later). Changes in acreage and animal num-

---

[18] Faucher, *Le Paysan et la machine*, pp. 77, 78, 93. The increase in yield per hectare is not representative of total efficiency, of course, since one would have to measure inputs of other factors. Faucher notes that with the combine, rather than the reaper, the harvest time per hectare was reduced from 16 man-days to 5 or 6 (p. 102).

[19] Chatelain, "La Lente progression de la faux" (1956). The writer notes that the spread of the scythe was slow and very uneven and that in the Limagne there was still a considerable distrust of the innovation in 1913.

[20] Lefèvre, *Politique intérieure du Second Empire* (ca. 1953), p. 84.

[21] Carrère and Dugrand, *La Région meditérranéenne* (1960), p. 64.

[22] Renouard, *Le Transport de la marchandise* (1960), p. 44.

[23] Dion, *Le Val du Loire*, p. 550.

[24] Lefèvre, *Politique intérieure du Second Empire*, p. 88.

[25] Laurent, "Les Archives d'octroi" (1957), p. 203. Lévy, *Histoire économique de la France*, p. 166, notes that the workers were not better off with rising money incomes because of the increase in the cost of meat, which was an increasing part of the dietary! He gives three fifths of worker income as spent for food. In 1848, in Lille, the textile worker spent normally 55 percent of his income on food, 90 percent of this amount for bread. See Lasserre, *La Situation des ouvriers* (1952), chap. vi, esp. pp. 124–125.

[26] ISEA, *Le Revenu national* (1952), p. 60.

[27] See above, Chapter 1, note 8.

[28] Sirol, *Le Rôle de l'agriculture* (1942), appendix 4. I am unable to evaluate

bers took place; but they are difficult to specify precisely because of changes in classification and a late start (plus doubtful accuracy) on animal numbers.[29]

The period from 1900 to 1914 brought further transformations. Perhaps the major increase in efficiency was in agriculture north of the Loire, especially in sugar beets.[30] But there were others. Acreage devoted to pasture increased, but changes in classification make it difficult to say by how much. Arable declined, especially. in industrial crops where flax, hemp, and oil seeds were hurt by imports. The decline in wool was also sharp, partly owing to imports, partly to the suppression of the fallow. Wine made a comeback in volume after the phylloxera; with the shift from the hillsides to the irrigated valleys and to the Aramon grape, the average yield per hectare increased as well as the acreage. But quality was off. With wide variations in production and destabilizing speculation, moreover, prices and income

---

the work of Brousse in "La Productivité du travail" (1953), which gives an enormous increase in output per capita per active person in agriculture for this period, from an index of 23 in 1852 to 126 in 1882 based on 1914 = 100 (p. 638) and calculated from net revenues (= gross revenues at 1914 prices less costs of production at 1914 prices). The rise in the cost of production from 10.1 billion francs to 10.7 billion seems small, in the light of the increased use of capital, though the cost of the equipment and supplies may have fallen owing to more efficient transport. The decline in active population also seems small, however, from 100 in 1852 to only 95 in 1882. I am therefore disposed to suspend acceptance of Brousse's striking results until they have been evaluated by the experts.

[29] The allocation of acreage among crops, and animal numbers, can be given for selected dates (from *Annuaire statistique, 1958*, pp. 25, 27, 28). Acreage is in thousands of hectares, animals in thousands:

Year	Arable	Pasture and meadow	Vineyards	Woods and forest	Unculti- vated	Not classified
1840	25,227	4,198+	1,972	8,805	9,191	3,635
1852	26,139	5,057+	2,191	n.a.	6,580	12,760
1862	26,569	5,021+	2,321	9,317	6,546	4,032
1882	25,588	5,237+	2,197	9,445	6,253	2,555
1913	23,651	8,048	1,617	9,887	3,793	2,730
1929	21,768	9,990	1,585	10,406	5,086	3,682
1938	20,196	11,775	1,605	10,728	5,680	4,176
1946	17,964	12,224	1,530	10,879	6,699	5,198
1957	18,735	13,243	1,467	11,396	4,328	4,846

Year	Horses	Cattle	Sheep	Pigs
1890	2,862	13,562	21,658	6,017
1913	3,222	14,778	16,131	7,036
1929	2,936	15,631	10,452	6,102
1938	2,692	15,662	9,872	7,127
1946	2,354	15,100	7,259	5,334
1957	1,986	17,928	8,575	8,063

[30] Dumont, *Voyages en France d'un agronome,* as quoted by Valarché, *L'Économie rurale*, p. 176.

zoomed and slumped, culminating in rioting in 1907, when the price reached 1.75 francs per hectolitre with no takers, after having averaged 7 francs in 1900.[31] The industry became demoralized. Elsewhere pastures were extended to meet the increasing demand for milk, butter, cheese. Demand grew for table wine, fruit, vegetables. And technical progress picked up again as workers left the farms for industry, to be replaced by machinery.[32]

It is not, then, correct to say that French agriculture was entirely static. Adjusting in turn to new crops, the railroad, agricultural machinery, and to changing product prices, it also experienced a considerable change in labor inputs and in land tenure. Paid farmhands quit for two reasons: to join the children of farmers in going into trade or industry, or to acquire land themselves. Lévy notes that a million rural wage earners disappeared between the agricultural census of 1862 and 1882; 250,000 had become farmers and 750,000 had been absorbed into cities and towns.[33] Railroad construction attracted rural workers after 1848, and again under the Freycinet Plan.[34] Between 1882 and 1892, 400,000 more daily workers left, 150,000 to take on their own farms and 250,000 for the city. Finally, between 1906 and 1911 there was another rural exodus.[35]

It is difficult to find these movements sharply defined in the figures for France as a whole. The total active population engaged in agriculture, fishing, and forestry continued to rise until 1911, even though men engaged declined from 1876.[36] Outward migration occurred, of

[31] See Carrère and Dugrand, *La Région meditérranéenne*, p. 78; Warner, *Winegrowers of France* (1960), p. 17.

[32] Augé-Laribé, *Politique agricole* (1950), pp. 156, 157.

[33] Lévy, *Histoire économique de la France*, p. 138.

[34] Chatelain, "La main-d'oeuvre et la construction des chemins de fer"; Augé-Laribé, *Politique agricole*, p. 53.

[35] Lévy, *Histoire économique de la France*, pp. 209, 218. Faucher, *Le Paysan et la machine*, says that the decline was particularly rapid after 1890 and above all after 1900 (p. 218).

[36] Estimates of active population for selected years are in millions (from *Annuaire statistique*, 1957, p. 3):

Year	Engaged in agriculture, fishing, forests	Percent of total	Number of men
1856	7.31	51.4	5.15
1876	7.99	49.3	5.78
1896	8.46	45.3	5.71
1911	8.64	41.7	5.40
1931	7.69	36.4	4.50
1946	7.48	36.6	4.22
1954	5.21	27.4	3.39

Brousse ("La Productivité du travail," p. 636) notes that the 1851 census is particularly wrong on the proportion of women in the active labor force, and the 1946 census full of mistakes.

course, to the extent that there was a natural increase in population
in the sector which was larger than the recorded increase. If one
changes from active population engaged to members of the labor
force, one runs into the serious problem of estimating what proportion of rural women are employed in agriculture.[37]

There is considerable doubt over the distribution of farms by size
because of the difficulty at the small end in separating a garden allotment from a farm. In 1929, for example, there were four million farms
by one way of looking at it; but only two and one-half million real
farms.[38] Nonetheless, there seems little doubt that farm numbers have
declined and farm average size has increased. The medial farm in
France, or the average size at that point in the distribution where
half the land is owned by smaller and half by bigger farms, rose from
25 hectares in 1892 to 81 in 1929.[39] In the 1942 census, which went by
exploitation rather than ownership, it was set at 28 hectares.[40]

There have in fact been two tendencies, one for farms to get smaller
in densely populated areas and another for more efficient land use in
the north, east-center, and around Paris. Averages in these circumstances are meaningless. This is accentuated by the fact that for some
labor-intensive crops, such as quality wines, the efficient exploitation
is a small one.[41] Some of the land used in small holdings is productive

---

[37] Clark excludes women from agriculture because the proportion of women to
total population varied widely from census to census (86 percent in 1851, 31 percent in 1866, and 50 percent in 1896), suggesting gross errors. Most writers
regard it as a greater error to leave them out. Thus the percentage of the French
labor force in agriculture is widely different between Clark and Bénard:

Year	Clark (excluding women)		Bénard
1866	43.0		52.0
1901	33.0	(1906)	43.0
1921	29.0		42.0
1931	24.0		36.0
1946	21.0		25.5

The above figures are from Kuznets, "Industrial Distribution of National Product
and Labor Force" (1957), p. 84. The Bénard figures are from Vue sur l'économie
(1953), p. 224. The 1866 figure including women is not from Bénard but from
de Foville. The 1946 estimate is that carefully worked out by Latil, Revenu
agricole (1956), p. 80. Latil further calculates that labor made up 34 percent of
the work force, in terms of hours of work; expressed in adult-man equivalents, the
percentage came to 28; excluding women, 22. This is for about 1954, when his
overall estimate was 25 percent.

[38] Latil, Revenu agricole, p. 250.

[39] Bernard, Seine-et-Marne, p. 53.

[40] Latil, Revenu agricole, p. 248.

[41] The land needed to support a family is 1.5 hectares in the champagne country,
4.5 in vintage wine, 10–12 in ordinary wine, and 10–12 in milk and meat in
Normandy, and 55 to 80 in the mixed farming of the Oise (Fauchon, Agriculture

but overcrowded.[42] All of it lacks capital. While the medium-size holdings produced the savings that were invested abroad, or later in gold, the small holder was saving or borrowing, often at usurious rates, to buy more land or to buy out his brothers.[43] The averages are of little meaning in France, when the Soissonas has 363 enterprises of more than 80 hectares, averaging 210 hectares, covering 78 percent of the land, and hiring 19 workers to each exploitation.[44] The division between the efficient and the inefficient agriculture is partly regional: along a line from Bordeaux to Metz, as it is sometimes drawn. But even within such a region as the southeast, there have come to exist two agricultures side by side: one a polyculture based on cereals, the other specialized in sheep, fruit, or vegetables, the second having progressed to the point in recent years where it fertilizes its pastures and raises feed crops.[45]

Having said all this, I must admit that French agriculture is backward compared to that in other countries — at every level, as well as on the average. If French agriculture as a whole has been held down by the peculiar backwardness of the small-scale branch of the sector, French economic growth as a whole has been held back by the slowness of advance in agriculture. The reasons may be analytical. But, at a minimum, the slow sector brings down the average of the fast. If industry grows at 3 percent a year, and agriculture at 1 percent, the total economy will grow at 2 percent a year if there are only two sectors of equal importance. Since productivity in services is notoriously sluggish, the economy average will be higher or lower, for a given rate of industrial advance, depending upon whether agriculture has been fast or slow. And, despite the fact that agricultural productivity

---

française, 1954, p. 33). Currently 1.7 million farmers produce wine; 1.8 million, wheat (*ibid.*, p. 64).

[42] Juillard, *Basse-Alsace*, p. 372, notes that while the Bas-Rhin earns a higher return than the French average per hectare (3,600 francs against 2,200), its gross revenue per man is lower (7,100 against 7,400) because it has 510 men per 1,000 hectares instead of the French average of 295.

[43] Latil, *Revenu agricole*, p. 172.

[44] See Juillard's review of Fauchon. Latil, on the other hand, believes that the average farm is a meaningful concept, at least in income, since there is a central tendency (p. 263). He notes that inequality of farm income is much less than in the United States (p. 274) and that two thirds of farm income goes to farms with incomes between 650,000 and 4 million francs (1952–1953). Brousse's table on landholdings ("La Productivité du travail," p. 640) points in the same direction: if one eliminates the part-time proprietors with 27 percent of the farms and 3 percent of the income from agricultural farming, and the large exploitations with 1.7 and 21.9 percent respectively, 71 percent of the farms have 72 percent of the farm families and 75 percent of the income from commercial farming. But of course it is possible to add the 200 hectare farms to those larger and get 9 percent of the farms and 45 percent of the income, as compared with the two smallest classes with 43 percent of the farms and 7.5 percent of the income.

[45] Carrère and Dugrand, *La Région mediterrànéenne*, pp. 57–58.

has sped up when industrial growth has picked up — under the Second Empire, after 1890, 1900, or 1910, and again after World War II, though not in the 1920s — it has been slow.

But this simple averaging is a trivial cause of retardation. No one assigns significance to the slow growth of productivity of the services sector in overall economic development, though if this part were to proceed more rapidly, the total would also, other things being equal. The most important effect of French agriculture in slowing down economic development in France may be merely its effect on the average. But the authorities quoted, Nicholls, Lewis, Gerschenkron, Rostow, intended to say something more interesting.

AGRICULTURAL DEMAND

Lewis has talked of French agriculture as a drag on demand and hence on growth. The point is also made by others.[46] A rapid rate of growth of income in agriculture can stimulate industry if demand for industrial products grows rapidly.

Here, however, in contrast to the previous section, it is impossible to be simple-minded. One must specify the conditions under which the increase in productivity would have resulted in an increase in income and how this would have contributed to growth. Or, inversely, given a lack of productivity, what other changes in the system, such as a push for foreign markets, could have contributed the demand that agriculture failed to provide? It is necessary to specify at least the supply and demand conditions under which the incremental output is sold, the marginal propensities to consume and save in agriculture, whether the economy is open or closed, and why the initiative should be left to the agricultural sector. And probably more. These general-equilibrium models, including both income and price, are very difficult to cope with, especially when they are open. It is particularly trying that so many theorists are prepared to dismiss the subject in a sentence.

Something of the difficulty in saying anything sensible on this score can be illustrated by the rather waspish controversy between David Landes and André Danière over the effect of crop fluctuations on business cycles in eighteenth-century France.[47] Landes was attacking the Labrousse thesis that crop failures led to depression because of cutting the demand for commodities by tenant farmers. Landlord income

---

[46] See Nicholls, "Agriculture in Economic Development," p. 2; Rostow, "Leading Sectors and the Take-off," p. 20.

[47] Landes, "The Statistical Study of French Crises" (1950), and Danière, "Feudal Incomes and Demand Elasticity for Bread," plus a reply, a rejoinder, and a second reply.

might have increased, as rent was paid in kind and prices rose. This increased savings. But after rent had been paid, the decline in marketable grain was greater than the price increase, according to Labrousse, which reduced farm money income and spending. Inelasticity of demand for bread of the workers in the city further caused a diversion of their income from consumer goods other than food to bread, reinforcing the decline in peasant spending.

Landes agreed with the Labrousse thesis for acute crises, such as that of 1848.[48] For more usual cycles he was unpersuaded, believing that the demand for bread was inelastic, when bread was 50 percent of the consumers' budget, and that on this account agricultural income and spending should rise during crop failures, rather than fall. Danière suggested that the data indicated that the demand for wheat was elastic, which would support the Labrousse thesis on the side of agricultural spending, but would hurt it insofar as it relied upon the diversion of urban spending from industrial products to food.

The controversy dealt mainly with the eighteenth century. In the nineteenth there are two important changes. The role of rent is cut down, though it is still sizable relative to farm income.[49] And the economy is much more open. An open economy makes it possible for urban demand for all grain to be inelastic at the same time that the demand for French grain is elastic. In crises the price will not rise as high as it otherwise would because of imports; whereas in bumper harvests, some support will be found for price, and income, through export sales.[50]

There can be little doubt but that the 1846–1848 crisis was of the Labrousse sort, modified for these two factors. The scarce crop first hurt urban real income greatly and agricultural income considerably. Next, the bumper crop failed to make good the loss of farm income because exports could not be organized as rapidly as imports. But

[48] Contrast the curious position of Cameron, referred to in Chapter 1, note 3.

[49] Latil quotes the ISEA estimates of rent as 31 percent of agricultural income in 1788, 24 percent in 1845, and 28 percent in 1890 (*Revenu agricole*, p. 202). Valarché, *L'Économie rurale*, p. 140, gives very different figures, of different trend: 50 percent under the Second Empire, 39 percent in 1900, and 26 percent in 1930, calling them gross rather than net. The difference is depreciation on farm buildings and equipment.

[50] There is in this discussion no hint of the mechanism in factor markets by which Chambers thinks (referring to Britain about this period) that agriculture transmitted crises to industry: "A good harvest . . . stimulated industry by increasing the demand for labor and so raising wages at the same time as the means of life became more abundant; and a bad harvest diminished the demand for labor and lowered wages while causing the price of necessities to rise" (*The Workshop of the World*, 1961, p. 152). This provides a splendid illustration of the difficulty of general-equilibrium analysis in history, with one set of observers focusing on goods market, another on factors.

1848 was a remarkable combination of circumstances, a unique one.[51]

In the middle of the nineteenth century, then, there was fairly general agreement that the "yield of agriculture" was the measure of the cycle.[52] Fohlen describes the attention paid by Méquillet-Noblot, producers of work clothes, to the harvest, which determined sales. Traveling members of the family would comment on the state of the crop, hoping for an abundance of wheat and a low price of bread. This interest remained. A letter of 1867 stated: "It is the question of the harvest which seems for the moment the delicate and essential point." Fohlen continues: "The harvest, the price of bread, even the abundance of wine, are the essential givens for the perspectives of manufacturing.[53]

Labrousse has described how the crisis in textiles, with its origin in agriculture, spreads to building.[54] And the cycles can move from agriculture to textiles, and thence to iron and coal.[55] When did the agriculture-initiated cycle change? Akerman states that the crisis of 1857 was the first truly international crisis in France, that is, the first which did not have a domestic agricultural origin.[56] Lefèvre says the same thing somewhat differently: the crisis of 1853 was the last of agricultural origin; the later ones started with finance and, in particular, that of 1857 was imported from abroad.[57] Labrousse picks 1867–68 for the last crisis of the old type, and Zarka picks 1869, with the qualification that the pure agricultural crises lasted only to 1832, the purely industrial began after 1869, and the intervening period experienced complex cycles compounded of the two types.[58] But Fohlen chooses 1878 as the end. In that year there had been the failure of the Bank of Glasgow in Britain, but wine and wheat were bad.[59] By 1885 cotton textiles no longer depended on the harvest. Consumption per head rose from 2.8 kilograms in 1885, at which level it had been stagnant since 1871, to 4 kilograms in 1890, despite a

[51] Labrousse, "Panorama de la crise" (1956). Lasserre notes (*La Situation des ouvriers*, p. 99) that the workers were naked by 1848, having bought no clothes for two years.

[52] Akerman, *Economic Progress and Economic Crises* (1932), p. 107.

[53] Fohlen, *Une Affaire de famille* (1955), pp. 53, 54. It is interesting to note a hint of the inverse causation in Gille, *La Banque et le crédit* (1959), p. 375n, referred to above, Chapter 3. He cites a contemporary observer of 1856 who blamed the crop failure on speculation, which diverted capital away from agriculture that would normally have been used to maintain productivity.

[54] Labrousse, *L'Évolution économique et sociale de la France et du Royaume Uni* (1954), p. 26.

[55] Zarka, "Un Exemple de pôle de croissance" (1958), pp. 92–93.

[56] Akerman, *Structures et cycles économiques*, II (1957), 311.

[57] Lefèvre, *Politique intérieure*, p. 96.

[58] Labrousse, p. 27; Zarka, pp. 90–91.

[59] *Une Affaire de famille*, p. 98.

slight decline in agricultural output.[60] Moreover, the boom from 1879 to 1881 took place in the face of the disastrous crop failure of 1879, with only limited recovery in 1880 and 1881.[61]

There is a possibility, however, that agriculture was responsible for an important part of the stagnation in French growth after 1881, through a somewhat different mechanism than that involved in the "oldtime cycle." The mechanism was not short crops, high prices, and cutting of urban consumption, with or without a reduction of agricultural consumption. After the expansion of 1875, volume declined, owing to bad weather and phylloxera; prices failed to improve in the early stages and then declined, owing to imports. Real consumption of urban dwellers with fixed money incomes could be initially maintained; afterwards it could increase. But deflation in the agricultural sector was substantial, and it combined after 1882 with the collapse of building. This was sufficient to give the country a prolonged depression of the Keynesian type, because of lack of sufficient spending in the economy. This could be the explanation of the Rostovian "trend-period." It was clearly no ordinary cycle or a crisis in the cyclical sense. It was a sort of general depression, as Sée put it, but one which affected above all agriculture.[62]

An idea of the size of agriculture relative to the rest of the economy can be gained from the estimates of Perroux in current francs, as shown in Table 15.

Table 15. National Product (in billions of current francs)

Sector	1847	1859	1872	1882	1892	1898	1908–10
Agriculture, net	6.1	8.7	9.5	10.9	9.8	11.2	13.4
Industry, net	3.9	5.8	6.8	8.0	8.4	10.1	13.9
Commerce	1.0	1.4	1.6	1.9	1.8	2.1	2.7
Liberal professions	.3	.4	.5	.6	.7	.9	1.1
Rent from built-up property	.7	.9	1.1	1.3	2.0	2.3	2.7
State	1.6	2.2	2.7	3.7	3.4	3.5	4.0
Total	13.6	19.4	22.2	26.4	26.1	30.1	37.8

Source. Perroux, "La Croissance de l'économie française" (1955), p. 61.

[60] Rabeil, L'Industrie cotonnière française (1955), p. 140. Sirol's index of agricultural output, omitting meat and vegetables, goes from 75 (1914 = 100) in 1882 and 1883 to 73 in 1885, 71 in the two following years and 67 in 1888, before a brief recovery and renewed slump to 65 at the bottom in 1893.

[61] Sirol's index dropped from 74 in 1878 to 54 in 1879 before recovering to 68 in 1880 and 1881. The 1874 high was 94.

[62] Golob, Méline Tariff, p. 82; Sée, Histoire économique de la France, p. 247.

Doubt has been expressed in the appendix about the value of these estimates for measuring short periods of growth. There is further doubt over the agricultural estimates of 1872 and 1882, relative to one another, since the Sirol index, admittedly faulty, shows a decline in volume while price remained steady. Volume fell from 86 in 1872 to 75, or by 13 percent. Measuring from the agricultural peak in 1874, however, income would have certainly shown a decline to 1882 and thereafter, since the volume index for that year was 95 and the price 137, against 75 and 115 in 1882 and 70 and 93 in 1892 (1914 = 100). Perroux's technique of including linear estimates of growth for meat and forage crops, and a lump-sum estimate for gardens which jumps from 500 million francs in 1872 to a billion in 1882,[63] limits the short-term accuracy of his sectoral estimate.

The only item in the detailed ISEA estimates of agricultural income which declined between 1872 and 1882, apart from a decrease in industrial crops from 306 million francs to 290 million, was wine. From 1882 to 1892 there were small declines in a number of items, such as dried vegetables, wood, and industrial animal products, along with industrial crops; but large declines in wheat and wine. Over the two decades the decline in income in grains amounted to 650 million francs; that in wine to a billion. These compare with a net gain for all of agriculture of 300 million francs in the twenty years and a setback of 1.1 billion between 1882 and 1892.

There is reason, however, to think that this decline is somewhat underestimated, not only because of the biases already mentioned. Augé-Laribé had put the gross value of wine production at 2 billion francs in 1869.[64] An 1875 peak figure — with the all-time record output and steady prices — would have been higher, the resulting fall greater. Second, the structure of French farms of this period made the fall in cash income larger than indicated by the total grain figures. Wheat was only 30 percent of total grain, but it was the major cash crop. Oats, barley, and corn were grown largely for feed. The price of wheat fell more than that of other grains. Forced sales of wheat in twelve representative departments doubled by 1889 from the 1873–1879 base.[65] As farmers needed cash to meet their commitments, whether rentals or interest on mortgages, wheat was sold in competition with imports, bringing down their cash income more than income in kind. Total income therefore underestimates the decline in money income.

Cash income was needed for farm and household expenses. The

[63] ISEA, *Le Revenu national* (1952), p. 76.
[64] *Politique agricole*, p. 67.
[65] Golob, *Méline Tariff*, pp. 77ff.

specialized farm discussed earlier was not on a subsistence basis, and Augé-Laribé is misleading when he says the farmer was self-sufficient at this time, needing only some wine, salt, clothes, and tools. Moreover, there is agricultural debt. It is hard to form any precise idea of the burden of debt. Gille comments that in 1848 land was high-priced — it yielded only a 3 percent return, but had to bear burdens of 5 to 12, 15, 20, and even 22 percent.[66] After that time the price of land rose much further, but the information is only qualitative.[67] It is likely that large farms were less indebted; small holders, relatively more so. With the depression, the price of land fell. The burden became heavier on old debts. The lower rate of interest may have permitted some refunding. But that agricultural debt was a problem is illustrated by the agitation to establish the Crédit Agricole and to get the Crédit Foncier active in the field, as discussed in Chapter 3.

Sharp and persistent depression in agriculture spread through demand to other sectors, especially after the building boom had burst and the stock market and speculative bubble collapsed. The loss in farm income in grains and wine was in the vicinity of 2 billion francs, or 8 percent of national income. Deflation in the south led to widespread bank failure in the Hérault.[68] The weak state of agriculture, followed by a stock-market boom and collapse, is strongly reminiscent of 1925–1929 in the United States.

There are several lines of argument against attributing this much significance in the stagnation after 1882 to agricultural depression. It can be argued, first, that apart from the deflationary impact of imports, loss in money income of the farm sector is offset by the gain in real income of consumers. Such was the case in Britain, for example, where worker real income increased throughout the Great De-

[66] Gille, *La Banque et le crédit*, p. 136. See also the other references in note 35, Chapter 3 above.

[67] Fauchon, *Agriculture française*, p. 118, merely says that the value of land rose from 1840 to 1880, during the golden age, and fell by one third after 1880. (See also Valarché, *Mobilité des ruraux*, 1953, p. 116.) Bernard notes that the price of land was steady in Seine-et-Marne (a region of specialized rented farms) between 1851 and 1879, though its rental value rose, and fell sharply to 1908 — except when expressed in terms of wheat, in which coin its price was steady (*Seine-et-Marne*, p. 71). The difference between the sale value and the rental value is due to the declining share of rent. Bernard observes further that the price of land in Brittany went steadily up (p. 72), but deprecates this by saying that price of land is a secondary consideration compared with the need for capital to farm it. There may be some question of whether these regional figures are representative of national trends, for in Britain disparities occur in rents owing to differences in crop. But wheat is grown everywhere, as I have noted. Golob (*Méline Tariff*, p. 72) has the price of wheat land falling less than the price of wheat between 1879 and 1884, but much further to 1892, when it reaches 73 (1879 = 100).

[68] Carrère and Dugrand, *La Région meditérranéene*, p. 80.

pression because of the decline in prices. Thus the loss in farmer spending could be offset by increases in urban spending.

Two or three points in rejoinder. First, the terms of trade of Britain improved, so that much of the offset to the worker gains in real income was felt abroad, not at home. In fact, since most of the decline in price was due to the reduction in transport costs through increasing efficiency, there was no offset. The agricultural sector hurt by import competition was very small relative to industry and to that in France.

Second, money illusion sometimes takes a hand in these questions. During the 1929 depression in the United States, the collapse of farm prices produced net internal deflation, since the loss in farm spending due to lower cash income was not offset by increased spending by urban consumers due to cheaper food. Worker spending in a crisis may be held down by consideration of money rather than real income. Moreover, the collapse of farm income can bring down banks and create a spiral of deflation. The coincidence of the collapse of the Union Générale, unrelated to the farm depression but to increasing peasant mistrust, reduced urban bank lending as well. "Spreading collapse" began in commerce, hit building especially, and only last reached heavy industry.[69]

The loss in agricultural income may be regarded as too small to be held responsible for the prolonged depression. It operated, however, with other factors — the end of railroad expansion, stock-market excesses, and a halt to the building boom. Moreover, deflationary pressure in wheat prices was relentless. Given weak expansionary forces elsewhere, after the check to the Freycinet Plan in the conventions of 1883, deflationary pressure in agriculture had to be relieved to let those other forces bring about recovery.

Finally, there is the argument that a loss of real output is inflationary, rather than deflationary, since it will necessarily lead people to spend idle balances.[70] This strikes me as irresponsible use of the Keynesian analysis in a situation where almost any other banking theory would be superior — Hawtrey, Phillips, and so on — and confuses changes in average propensities to spend with changes in spending. For, by this theory, depressions can hardly occur. The initial unemployment is inflationary. There will admittedly be occasions when the analysis does apply: after war, with destruction and inelastic output, people dissave to produce inflation. But the loss of real income from phylloxera necessarily reduces vintner spending gross, even though the average propensity to spend may rise.

---

[69] Bouvier, *Le Krach de l'Union Générale* (1960), pp. 231, 270.
[70] This point was put to me in a seminar at Nuffield College in 1930.

It is hardly any proof that recovery in France took place after farm income had increased again, and with the assistance of the Méline tariff. The long-run implications of this tariff were harmful to growth, as will be discussed in the next chapter. Here, however, we may note that some action was needed to break the deflationary impact of the cheap imports, much as the devaluation of the United States in 1933 can be defended for the same purpose. In a world of fixed exchange rates, the only possible means was the tariff. And farm and industrial income made a comeback together.

Accordingly, the price of imports was important, since it governed the prices of wheat and wine. Here is an area of controversy. Sée, for example, says that it was not gold but imports that hurt French agriculture, whereas Zolla, the agricultural economist, says the problem was gold, not imports.[71] Zolla's reasoning is unacceptable. He exonerates imports because the price rose between 1862 and 1881, when the import surplus in wheat tripled, and fell between 1881 and 1886, when imports dropped by a third. But the price of imports is critical, not the volume. The crop failure of 1879 established the connection. In that year food imports rose to 1,900 million from 1 billion francs two years before. Freight rates were then relatively high. But they fell sharply.[72]

AGRICULTURE'S RELEASE OF LABOR

The most interesting and widely held view of the relation between agriculture and industry in France blames the slow rate of industrial expansion, or its occasional slowdown, on the failure of agriculture to release labor to industry in sufficient numbers. Thus Nicholls, Lewis, Gerschenkron, and Rostow, as quoted in previous notes, lay stress on an inadequate increase in productivity (or population growth) which would permit such release, or on insufficient willingness of excess numbers of persons attached to the agricultural sector to move.

The theory is seldom precisely formulated. One possible version would depend on the imperfection of the labor market: labor could earn more in industry or in the tertiary sector than in agriculture, but

[71] *Histoire économique de la France*, p. 322. Note that Sée takes a favorable view of French agriculture after 1896, approving the "economic harmony" between agriculture and industry (see Chapter 9, note 56) and saying that with the benefit of protection, agriculture was fine after 1896, except for a few problems like the rural exodus. Most observers would disagree. The view of Zolla is quoted by Valarché, *L'Économie rurale*, p. 24.

[72] An index of freight rates on wheat from New York to Liverpool quoted by Golob (*Méline Tariff*, p. 77) from the U.S. Department of Commerce and Labor in 1909 gives five-year averages as follows: 1866–1870, 100; 1871–1875, 148; 1876–1880, 117; 1881–1885, 64; 1886–1890, 50.

refuses to move because of its attachment to the soil. On this showing one would expect to find a wide gap between earnings in industry and agriculture, which would increase in periods of industrial expansion. An opposite formulation would run in terms of very low supply elasticity in agriculture and low demand elasticity for agricultural products. Increased demand for the output of the agricultural sector, in this circumstance, or a small decline in output resulting from the transfer of resources to industry, would quickly lead to an increase in the price of foodstuffs and increases in the return to factors engaged in agriculture, thus holding labor on the farm. Returns, then, would be equal in agriculture and industry. A compromise is of course possible: there is normally a gap between returns to agriculture and industry; this narrows in periods of expanding industry so that rising industrial wages or the absolute scarcity of labor cut off the possibilities of continued growth.

A third formulation emphasizes less the high wages in urban locations than the cheap labor available in rural areas. This attracts industry into dispersed locations, thus losing the external economies of the agglomerative process in urbanization and slowing down growth in a roundabout way.[73]

The first two versions of the theory rely on the rise of industrial wages to halt industrial expansion. This might help to explain timing, and why periods of growth like that under the Second Empire came to an end. But it stands opposite to those theories about French growth which stress that labor was too cheap and so failed to encourage the employment of machinery. And it is also possible to develop models in which the block to growth comes from too low wages and too little demand.

Direct evidence to enable one to choose the most likely theory is difficult to come by. For the period before 1850, Gille and Dunham have amassed a certain amount of material, without pointing to a definite conclusion. Gille notes that the textile industry used labor complementary to agriculture and did not emerge into large firms until the middle of the century. Mining and metallurgy, however, suffered from needing large groups of workers, held by the land through the system of equal inheritance. The evidence is meager. A thesis is required on the subject, Gille admits, citing seven cases of labor shortage in coal, numerous ones in metallurgy, but then he goes on to say that the major lack was qualitative. Labor was unskilled and ignorant. A company like d'Anzin built housing for workers and

---

[73] Habakkuk, "Family Structure and Economic Change" (1955); Juillard, *Basse-Alsace;* and Dobb, *Development of Capitalism* (1947), pp. 230–231 — "clinging to soil means primitive capitalism."

arranged adult courses at night. For the most part, however, workers lacked the instruction which was general in England and which enabled them to adapt to factory work.[74] Dunham gives much the same picture: labor supply was adequate but not overabundant. There was no crowding in the cities because of the attraction of agriculture. Labor retained its connection with agriculture, was industrially untrained. It was cheap in price but costly. Industry was small-scale because labor was untrained, and labor was untrained because industry was small-scale. The peasant resisted the factory system. An abundant supply of cheap rural labor made the domestic system strong. The rural worker's passion for the land inhibited the development of a labor force.[75] When the rhetoric of these statements is dismissed, the argument has shifted, at least part way, from the price of labor in industry to the labor cost of production.[76]

From 1850 on, with the advent of the railroad, conflicting tendencies operated. Over wide parts of the country,[77] rural industry and inefficient agriculture were destroyed by the competition from more efficiently organized producers. Peasants moved from the hills to the

[74] Gille, *Formation de la grande entreprise* (1959), pp. 39ff. But compare the view of Isaac Holden with extensive interests in wool combing in France: at Rheims, Croix near Roubaix, and St. Denis in the first half of the nineteenth century. He found French workers to be "active and industrious, working contentedly and earnestly, and easy and agreeable to manage when treated with respect and firmness" (Anon., *Fortunes Made in Business*, I, 42).

[75] Dunham, *Industrial Revolution in France* (1951), pp. 182, 184, 243, 306, 434.

[76] Cameron, *France and the Development of Europe*, p. 27, discusses the effect of the Junker organization of agriculture in eastern Germany which drove landless peasants into cities, where they became the backbone of the cheap, docile industrial labor force. The question here is how much to emphasize the word "docile." Paul Hohenburg has studied the labor force in chemical plants in France at the end of the nineteenth century, noting that there was no difficulty in getting enough workers, despite unattractive working conditions, but that it was no place for craftsmen. He cites Baud (*Les Industries chimiques régionales de la France*, 1922, p. 3) as attributing German success to the absence of tradition and handed-down skills. The migrating peasants were willing and docile. Löffl (*Die Chemische Industrie Frankreichs*, pp. 12–13) also observes the conflict between following exactly the incomprehensible instructions of a laboratory and the traditions of *liberté* and *egalité* of the artisan.

[77] See Coutin, "La Décongestion des centres industriels et la vie agricole" (1945), p. 62. In Picardy and Normandy industry moved into cities; in the Bas-Maine and Middle Garonne, it disappeared. Armengaud, "Les Débuts de la dépopulation touloussaine" (1951), ascribes the local depopulation after 1850 to the collapse of rural industry and the opportunity to escape afforded by railroads, big public works, the embellishment of cities, and the expansion of wine in Bas-Languedoc. Dion notes that different localities exhibited different times for starting their population decrease in the Loire Valley, depending upon the specialty crop; thus localities specializing in fruits and onions started down in 1831, field crops in 1851, and wine in 1851, but with a specially sharp break after 1866 when the plow was introduced among the vines (*Le Val du Loire*, pp. 674–675). Juillard observes that the vigorous rural industry of Basse-Alsace partly disappeared and partly moved to the city after 1850 (*Basse-Alsace*, p. 288).

plains[78] and on into town, or to Paris. This was the beginning of the rural exodus, connected with increasing specialization in agriculture and in industry.[79] At the same time, however, some rural industries and much of agriculture resisted liquidation.[80] Movements of industry to rural sites occurred, and rural industries were founded or flourished.[81] The first of these tendencies operated to lower wages in industry and to raise them in agriculture, or to reduce inequalities. The third movement supported this tendency. Only the second — resistance on the part of agriculture and rural industry — would widen the disparities, since an enlarged demand would be created for labor in cities and a reduced demand in the country, owing to the deflation of rural industry. Such a disparity could also take place, however, if agriculture tried to rid itself of wage earners and industry refused to take them fast enough.

Before touching upon the history of wage movements, I should mention the peculiar muddle in which overall per capita earnings in French agriculture and industry find themselves. Much statistical work has been done on this problem, without producing an agreed-on result. Colin Clark and J. H. Bellerby conclude that French income per capita has been as high in agriculture as in industry — this would

---

[78] Sauvy in INED, *Région Languedoc Roussillon* (1957), p. 13; Léon, *Naissance de la grande industrie en Dauphiné* (1954), p. 634.

[79] See the useful table of Leroy, *Exode* (1958), pp. 18–19, which shows the number of departments reaching population peaks at given census dates:

1836	2	1851	15	1866	6	1891	7	1911	6
1841	4	1856	1	1881	1	1896	1	1926	1
1846	11	1861	5	1886	9	1906	2	1931	6

The areas that lost population after 1846 and 1851 included those in the southwest, Normandy, and the Alps, whereas the departments in Brittany and Alsace did not fall off until after 1900.

[80] Chevalier, "L'Évolution de la main-d'oeuvre industrielle dans l'Oise" (1930–39), notes that, despite the strong movement of peasants from the interior areas to the valleys, especially the valley of the Oise (p. 75), and the generally strong impact of industrialization on the south, the north of the department and especially Beauvais and Picardy have resisted. Textiles in the rural areas held up better than clothing.

[81] The most striking case is the Michelin plant at Clermont-Ferrand, discussed by Coutin ("Le Développement industriel à Clermont-Ferrand," 1945), which is hardly rural but whose workers almost all retain small farms or allotments. The expansion of this plant and town occurred mainly after 1870. But note the Peugeot plant at Sochaux, whose workers are only now gradually giving up farming (Coutin, "La Décongestion des centres industriels," p. 63; Lebréton, "Une Expérience de la dispersion industrielle dans l'électrochimie" (1946); and the move of Lyon silk factories to the countryside in search of cheaper labor (Laferrère, *Lyon, ville industrielle*, 1960, pp. 131ff). Labasse notes in *Les Capitaux et la région* (1955), p. 31, that the banks expected the railroad to make the wealth of a town grow or stagnate, and waited before opening branches to see which way it would go. Compare the effects of the European Common Market.

seem to indicate an equilibrium situation in which there was no need to move, or in which movement was so free that it kept returns in line. The work of other writers and some of the figures of Clark in other connections lead to the expected conclusion that earnings in industry were higher on the average.

The normal way of doing this is to take figures for the proportion of income produced in agriculture, such as can be derived from Table 15, and divide them through by figures for the proportion of the labor force engaged in agriculture, as, for example, those given in note 36 of this chapter. This gives output per worker in agriculture as a percentage of output per worker (including entrepreneurs, landlords, and rentiers) in the country as a whole. This relative income per head in agriculture can be compared with the industrial sector, or with all nonagriculture, to give the return to agriculture relative to the rest of the economy or to industry. Thus, if we fill in an estimate for the 1930s of 21 percent of income produced in agriculture,[82] we should arrive at the figures shown in Table 16.

Table 16. Income Per Capita in French Agriculture Relative to the Rest of the Economy

Date	Percentage of income produced in agriculture (1)	Date	Percentage of labor engaged in agriculture (2)	Relative income in agriculture (1) ÷ (2) (3)	Relative income in nonagriculture[a] (4)	Income in agriculture relative to income in nonagriculture (3) ÷ (4) (5)
1859	42	1866	52	87	120	72
1898	37	1901	43	86	117	74
1930	21	1931	36	58	122	41

[a] Calculated from dividing 100 minus column 1 by 100 minus column 2.

The possibilities for adjusting these estimates are endless. What, if any, proportion of the women in agriculture to include has already been discussed. It makes a considerable difference whether one includes all, none, one half, or two thirds. The income figure is also subject to wide variation. It may or may not include forestry and fishing. It may or may not include "imputed income," that is, an allowance for income in kind on the farm at retail rather than whole-

[82] Latil, *Revenu agricole*, p. 16. The estimate is from Dugé de Bernonville.

sale prices. Finally, one can net out more or less of the income of a given sector. This seems to be the main problem posed by Clark's calculations.[83] The second and third editions of his *Conditions of Economic Progress* give relative figures for the agricultural sector and absolute figures for agricultural and total income that permit other relative figures to be calculated. The results are very different, as we may see in Table 17. The difference between the direct percentage

Table 17. Percentage of National Income Produced by
French Agriculture, According to Clark

| | | | Calculated from absolute figures | |
| | | | With imputed income | Without imputed income |
Date	Percentage figures (1)	Date	(2)	(3)
1861–65	63[a]	1860–64	30	23
1911	32	1910–13	17	11
1930	19	1934–38	13	8.5

[a] This figure appears to be a gross error.

Source. Column 1 is from the second edition of *Conditions of Economic Progress* (1951), p. 444; it is with imputed income. Columns 2 and 3 have been calculated from the third edition (1957), pp. 123–125, 262.

figures and the calculated goes back to the attempt to make a more restricted definition of agricultural output, excluding double counting of grain and other foodstuffs used as fodder or as seed,[84] as well as purchases of fertilizer, equipment, and "all other expenses of production." [85]

Bellerby also concludes that France is different from the rest of the world in the proportions of income earned in agriculture and in industry. He works with a limited concept of "aggregate incentive

[83] *Ibid.*, p. 110n, states that the work of Clark requires a patient exegesis which is not always rewarded.

[84] The ISEA estimates for agricultural net output in Table 14 involve, for 1872, a gross output of 13,167 million francs, and deductions of 600 million francs for seed, 3,080 million for animal feed. It seems curious that the deduction for animal feed should have risen since 1862 by 1,060 million, when the gross value of forage crops had increased only 200 million, that of cereals 400 million, that of meat 175 million, and that of other animal products 383 million. On this showing, there seems to have been a reduction in grains available for human consumption, on the one hand, and either a loss on meat output or a substantial increase in animal draft work, on the other.

[85] *Conditions of Economic Progress*, 3rd ed. (1955), p. 256.

income" of the farmer-entrepreneur group, which is net factor income in agriculture less net rent, interest, wages of agricultural workers, and the income of any independent agricultural personnel not ordinarily classed as farmers. He derives this by per-man equivalents of labor, including women and youths as fractions of adult men, and compares it with the ratio of all persons actively engaged in the labor force to all nonfarm income less rent and interest. He finds that this ratio is approximately 100 percent in France, compared to figures normally 30 to 60 and reaching as high as 70 in Britain.[86] But no one is able to control his figures, since they rest on some unpublished estimates of French farm income by Proctor Thompson.[87]

Adjusting Clark's higher result in any one or more of three ways — cutting down imputed income, which is high, adding women to the labor force, or moving as he does in the absolute figures to a more net and less gross definition of income — will alter the conclusion that per capita income in agriculture is as high as in industry. If one also dismisses the Bellerby figure for France, which he says is "probably above the incentive ratio," [88] one must conclude that the majority of observers are right and that the average income in agriculture has been below that in the rest of the economy by some substantial fraction, ranging from one third to one half.[89] After a most careful examination of the figures, Latil concludes for the twentieth century that average income in agriculture per person is one third to two thirds lower than in the rest of the economy and that the lag is growing — that is, relative income is declining as the rural exodus lags behind the rate needed to equalize incomes.[90]

But average income in agriculture is relatively meaningless. Agricultural workers, leaving the sector, compare their wages with what they can earn in industry. Here there is general agreement that agri-

[86] Bellerby, *Agriculture and Industry* (1956), table 33, p. 201.
[87] In a thesis at the University of Chicago. A summary was published in *Journal of Farm Economics* in 1952.
[88] Bellerby, *Agriculture and Industry*, pp. 191–192.
[89] As a further illustration of the difficulties in this area, note that income per person may differ from income per household, which is the relevant unit for some purposes. Personal income per household in agriculture before taxes was 106.7 percent of the national average in 1952, as contrasted with income per capita of 81.6 percent (calculated from figures from the Ministère des Finances, *Rapport sur les comptes de la nation*, 1955, vol. 2, set out in Peterson, *The Welfare State in France*, 1960, pp. 76ff). This is 108 percent and 78 percent, respectively, of the nonagricultural sectoral averages. Since both direct and indirect tax burdens are heavier on nonagriculture than on farmers, the figures after tax should move still further in favor of agriculture. The difference between household and per capita figures, of course, is the result of larger households, with more income earners, in agriculture than outside it. Note further that the results are altered again, but only slightly, if one changes from personal income, including transfers, to income from production.
[90] Latil, *Revenu agricole*, p. 115.

cultural laborers, even after provision for payments in kind, earned considerably less than industrial.[91]

National averages are worth very little in a country like France in the middle of the nineteenth century, when it was "disarticulated." One can use Simiand's figures, however, to get a rough idea of what happened (though it is distressing not to have figures for identical years at the middle of the nineteenth century when annual movements were substantial), and these are set out in Table 18. If one wants a

Table 18. Relative Wages in Industry and Agriculture (1892 = 100)

Date	Agri-culture	Date	Mines	Industry Textiles	Sugar		Alsace	Angers
1852	67	1850	50	47		n.a.	54	57
1862	89	1868	70	74	(1864)	59?	68	62
1882	106	1882	86	100		108	(1875) 92	n.a.
1892	100	1892	100	100		100	100	100
1910	129	1913	127	n.a.		124	n.a.	n.a.

Source. Simiand, *Le Salaire* (1932), vol. 3, inset table.

benchmark, Latil quotes estimates by Simiand that the average daily wage in current francs was 2.30 for agriculture and 3.80 in the city in 1892.[92] With mines as the representative wage in industry — al-

[91] Again there are opportunities to compare one of several measures of one variable, with one of several measures of the other, producing a spectrum of possible results. But Clark (*Conditions of Economic Progress*, 3rd ed., p. 526) and Bellerby (*Agriculture and Industry*, p. 240, from Thompson's thesis) both give ratios of less than 100:

	Clark		Thompson
	Agricultural wages against unskilled urban	*Agricultural wages against skilled*	*Labor earnings in agriculture compared with industry*
Date			
1892	81	64	1901, 1906, 1911 70
1911	89	75	1924–1928 68
1928	88	80	1932, 1943 65

[92] Latil, *Revenu agricole*, p. 223. Souchon, *La Crise de main-d'oeuvre agricole* (1914), pp. 357ff, gives detailed figures for men and women, with and without meals, summer and winter, which show broadly the same trend. Wages for men, in francs per day, are:

	With meals		Without meals	
Year	*Winter*	*Summer*	*Winter*	*Summer*
1852	0.82	—	1.10	—
1862	1.08	1.82	1.85	2.77
1882	1.31	1.98	2.22	3.11
1892	1.30	1.85	2.04	2.94

He comments (p. 358) that the quality of the meals improved greatly during the 1850s.

though the figure may be low in 1882 on the showing of Table 18 —
ⅉ schematic picture of wages is presented in Table 19. An absolute

Table 19. Money Wages in Agriculture and Industry (francs per day)

Date	Agriculture (1)	Industry (2)	Relative (percent) (1) ÷ (2)
1852	1.50	1.90	79
1862	2.05	(1868) 2.65	75
1882	2.45	3.25	75
1892	2.30	3.80	60
1910	2.95	4.85	61

figure of 2.30 francs in other industry in 1862 from Simiand produces
a relative of 92 percent for that year, probably nearer the mark than
the 75 percent derived from comparing figures six years apart. This
was a period of rising wages. The general picture which emerges is
that relative wages narrowed considerably during the Second Empire[93] and widened after that. The timing of the widening is uncertain — whether in the early 1860s or 1870s. But the movement off
the farm did take place, and largely from the class of agricultural
workers.[94] Farm numbers increased for a time, as estates of bottom

[93] The table may not start at an early enough point referring to the period 1847–
1853. Girard notes (*Travaux publics*, 1951, p. 143) that "labor has become
dear."

[94] Statistical information is available for the number of people born in one department, living in another, from which migration can be estimated, but only from
1862. This misses out on short-run migration within a department, such as that
which led 35 percent of Auxerre to have been born in the department Yonne
(Bettelheim and Frère, *Auxerre*, 1950, p. 85). The figures are of some interest,
however (taken from INSEE, "Les Migrations agricoles, 1956, p. 331):

Percentage of people born in one department,
living in another

1862	11.3	1911	21.0
1872	15.0	1921	23.7
1881	15.0	1931	25.0
1891	16.8	1936	25.5
1901	19.6		

It is noted that the 1872 figure is unduly high because of the war, overstating
migration in the 1860s and understating it in the 1870s.
    Working from the departments of immigration, Chevalier notes (*Population
parisienne*, 1949, p. 61) that as of 1861 the percentage of persons born outside
the department reached 30 only for Paris, 20–30 for Seine-et-Oise and Rhône, and
15 to 20 for Seine-et-Marne, Bouches du Rhône and Var. By 1901, however,
Paris, Seine-et-Oise, and Lyon were above 30 percent; Calvados, Eure, Eure-et-
Loire, Oise, Seine-et-Marne, Meuse, Merthe-et-Moselle, Maine-et-Loire, Gironde,
Herault, Bouches du Rhône, Var, and Basses-Alpes were all between 20 and 30

land continued to be broken up and some agricultural workers bought or inherited farms.

Recall that industrial demands for labor will narrow the gap between industrial and agricultural wages (after perhaps an initial widening), while a supply push from the side of agriculture will widen it. The former seems to have been what happened from about 1850 to sometime in the 1860s, when agricultural wages rose faster than industrial. Thereafter, all the way to World War I, industrial rates kept rising, but agricultural wages, while they followed the same curve, had feebler rises and more marked declines.[95] This was the period of the rural exodus.

Further light can finally be thrown on the various theories by measuring changing wage dispersions. This has been done to a limited extent. According to Institut National figures, the geographic dispersion of agricultural wages widened between 1862 and 1892, the coefficient of variation going from 0.285 to 0.368, and declining thereafter to 0.1 in 1949.[96] The latter figure is relatively uninteresting because of the wage control, with its limited regional differentials. But the widening of agricultural disparities may coincide with a narrowing of industrial wages geographically. Madinier shows that the disparity in wages of qualified workers declines from 172 in 1853 (representing the average of the relatives of the first to the ninth decile, and the second to the eighth, expressed in percent) to 139 in 1892 and 128 in 1935.[97]

But these overall measures are of doubtful value in supporting broad generalizations. They suggest perhaps that in the second half of the nineteenth century the movement of the workers to industry was more important than the movement of industry to workers, which had been dominant in the first half. Beyond this they cannot go far because the interaction between industry and agriculture differed from locality to locality.

Paris was able to draw labor off the farm, particularly from the environs, the southwest, and the center, which had a tradition of seasonal travel and even of a "tour de France."[98] Moreover, the south

---

percent. If one moves to the level of the commune, a small industrial city like Albi had 34 percent of its population born outside the commune as early as 1837, and 56 percent by 1931 (George, *La Ville*, 1952, p. 93).

[95] Latil, *Revenu agricole*, p. 224.

[96] INSEE, "Les Migrations agricoles," p. 331.

[97] Madinier, *Les Disparités géographiques de salaire* (1959), p. 41. For all workers, however, his figures suggest some widening in geographic wage disparities for men from 1840–1845 to 1860–1865, a steady position to 1892, and a decline to 1954. See table, *ibid.*, p. 68, and statement, p. 82.

[98] Estienne and Joly, *La Région du centre* (1961), p. 131.

and west provided recruits for the army and civil service, including the gendarmerie, the Postes, Téléphones et Télégraphes (PTT), and the railroads, not to mention the tobacco monopoly. Outside of this, most movement if it occurred at all was of limited distance. In the north, where industry developed earliest and to the greatest extent, the wages of agriculture and industry probably narrowed. In the south and west, rural industry was destroyed; the gap between agricultural and industrial wages widened and led to rural exodus. In Brittany and Alsace, there was little industry and substantial excess population on the farm. Finally in a few places, notably Lorraine, the Clermont-Ferrand plant of Michelin in the Center, and to lesser extent in the Alps, there was modern industry surrounded by backward agriculture, with industry forced to rely on immigrants because of the reluctance of local peasants to leave the soil. When peasants did go to work in the factories, they remained part-time farmers, "doing double work." [99] The system has been described at length for Alsace, Lorraine, the Montbéliard area, the Alps, and Clermont-Ferrand.[100] The peasant is tired when he gets to the plant and inefficient there. He is not dependent on his income from farming, so there is no spur to efficiency at home. Industry and agriculture mutually handicap rather than stimulate one another.

It may be said that the labor shortages in industrial plants could have been made good by surpluses from Aquitaine and Brittany. Some companies attempted long-distance recruiting.[101] But long-range mobility did not exist for France, any more than for England, as noted earlier. While only 25 percent of the population of Auxerre had been born there, 50 percent more came from Yonne or the neighboring departments. In Vienne, 42 percent were born locally, 13 percent more from Isère, 8 percent from Rhône, 8.5 percent from other fairly nearby departments.[102] Valarché has found the same result in abandoned villages.[103] Departures proceed by stages: first, from farm to village; then, to the neighboring town; and ultimately possibly to Paris. Where there are neighboring towns to absorb farmers in industry, the result

[99] Mossé, *Localisation dans l'industrie automobile* (1956), p. 91.

[100] Juillard, *Basse-Alsace;* Blanc, Juillard, Ray, and Rochefort, *Les Régions de l'Est* (1960), pp. 35, 51, 104; Sédillot, *Peugeot* (1960), pp. 131–132; Lebréton, "Une Expérience de la dispersion industrielle dans l'électrochimie" (1946); Estienne and Joly, *La Région du centre,* esp. chap. ii.

[101] *Ibid.,* p. 98. Michelin brought in whole villages from Brittany in 1923 and transplanted both Perpignanais and their native game, rugby. But the area was still one where farms needed hands rather than hands farms (p. 70).

[102] See note 43, Chapter 4, above.

[103] Valarché, *La Mobilité des ruraux,* pp. 55, 60, 108. See also Mendras, *Novis et Virgin* (1953), p. 71.

(or sometimes the cause) is an improvement in agricultural efficiency.[104] But they must leave the farm entirely.

People leave the farm, but they do not all go into industry. A large-scale investigation was made in 1951 by INSEE, examining both rural origins of people in various occupations and the distribution of rural migrants by age and occupation. On the first score, recruitment of the farm population was highest among domestics, with 50 percent of them from the country, army and police (38 percent), common workers (32 percent), artisans (28 percent), commerce (26 percent), industrial workers (24 percent), and higher employees — functionaries, office workers, technical staff, and the liberal professions — stretching down from 14 to 8 percent. It is notable that people of rural origin were twice as many in building construction as in metallurgy. On the second score, two thirds of the migrants left as children. The average age of migration was twenty for women, eighteen for men. Of the males, the farmers or sons of farmers became storekeepers or artisans because they had a little capital: 23 percent of all migrants became small businessmen, comprising 30 percent of the farmers and their sons and 15 percent of the farm labor; whereas 58 percent of the workers became common workers or industrial workers, and only 38 percent of the farmers and their sons.[105]

This contributes something, but not very much, to the argument that French industry was held back by the family farm, at least after 1850. One can perhaps make the case for the 1830–1850 period, although even then the problem was more one of the worker's temperament than of his willingness to leave the farm. For the Second Empire, it is true that wages tightened, but this encouraged rationalization, both in industry and agriculture, and could be regarded as a strength. After 1875, the movement off the farm continued, espe-

---

[104] Valarché, p. 61. The Nivernais is a department of great rural exodus, losing 15,000 men between 1906 and 1911. In the commune of Asman there were only four agricultural workers left in 1946. But the farmer peasants remain prosperous, on a three-crop rotation, with above all lucerne, which makes cattle raising profitable. Dion, *Le Val du Loire*, p. 550, on the other hand, argues that the railroad and the loss of manpower produced the shift to cattle.

[105] Quoted by Latil, *Revenu agricole*, pp. 82, 148. The reference is to the *Bulletin mensuel des statistiques*, suppl., April–June 1952. Valarché gives some figures on a slightly different basis for two French towns: of 227 persons leaving an island village in Brittany (157 of whom had been agriculturists), 40 went into agriculture or fishing, 27 into industry or artisanry, 113 into commerce or administrative services, 3 into liberal professions, 44 unknown. Of 67 leaving a village in the Nivernais, over the same time (the middle of the twentieth century), 28 went into other agriculture, 9 into industry or artisanry, 40 into services, commerce, administration (*La Mobilité des ruraux*, pp. 55, 60). Mendras gives a different picture for Novis in Avéyron near Lozère: between 1929 and 1951, 74 had left the town — 39 percent for other agriculture, 56 percent to become workers or employees, 5 percent as artisans or commercants (*Novis et Virgin*, p. 71).

cially in the south. There was no labor scarcity up to 1895. Thereafter local labor scarcities in the north and east were met by immigration, at the same time that the rural exodus in the south and west provided France with functionaries, both civil and military,[106] and rather more small shopkeepers than were needed. Except in a few areas, there was readiness to leave the farm: if anything is to be blamed, it is the insistence on the independent life of an artisan or shopkeeper by a people too bound up in *egalité* and too conscious of their individual worth to be happily engaged in factory work.

The position, then, is more complicated than most people think. The labor supply has been adequate in Paris, and surplus labor moves freely out of some regions like the southwest. Other industrial areas also appear to have been served in satisfactory fashion, particularly Marseilles, Lyon, and most of the north. And where workers have been pulled readily into the city, the remaining agriculture has been improved by the stimulus to technological change given by shortages and the high price of labor. There is, however, no evidence that the pull of labor into industry has at any time been so intense and met such resistance that rising wages have cut down industrial expansion. On the contrary, opinion abounds to the effect that rising wage rates stimulated further industrial expansion, along the same lines as in agriculture, by encouraging the substitution of machines for unskilled labor.

Side by side with those areas in which intersectoral expansion worked effectively and in mutually supporting fashion, there have been large sections of France where labor has been short in industry and redundant on the farm. Some well-managed plants, such as Michelin and Peugeot, have operated efficiently and expanded, despite the use of some double-duty peasants. These plants have sought labor over wide commuting areas and attracted foreign immigrants. But neighboring agriculture has failed to be stimulated (until after World War II). There are other areas, however — especially in the Vosges valleys of Alsace and in Brittany — where industry and agriculture mutually retard each other. The new Citroën plant in Rennes has been a failure (at least to 1956) because the city lacked housing; the men farmed, commuted long distances, and were exhausted. Productivity per worker was less than half that of the main Paris plant.[107]

But there is great difficulty in making a case that this condition inhibited total French growth, in some regular way, apart from the averaging effect of lower productivity in agriculture. It has no connection with the periods of stagnation — the 1880s and the 1930s. There

[106] Sauvy in INED, *Région Languedoc Roussillon*, p. 15.
[107] Mossé, *Localisation dans l'industrie automobile*, pp. 83–85.

is no dynamic in soaring wages which brings booms to an end. The condition is interesting, but it explains little.

THE RURAL EXODUS

Having spent so much time on the opposite contention, we need not dwell long on the single-valued argument that the pull of industry ruined agriculture by robbing it of its labor supply. Economists say that people leave poor regions; it is demographers who insist that the regions are poor because people leave. It is true that there have been economies of scale; as a village declines in size it becomes too small for one doctor or one justice of the peace, not to mention the school [108] and various more mundane services.[109] This consideration has become less important since the spread of private transport. But the rural exodus is both inevitable and necessary: inevitable, as the rural community insists on narrowing the income gap between them and urban dwellers and escaping the life of monotony, harder work, and social inferiority;[110] necessary, since a rise in rural wages is an important stimulus to the modernization of agriculture. We have seen this in France, where the increase in agricultural productivity has been greatest under the Second Empire and prior to World War I, when industrial activity was rising. It is equally true of Britain.[111]

The backwardness of French agriculture cannot be blamed on the rural exodus. More education, which is a necessary condition of more effective agriculture — and of more effective use in industry and trade of those who leave it — will stimulate migration.[112] It is understand-

[108] Valarché, *La Mobilité des ruraux*, p. 63; Saville, *Rural Depopulation in England and Wales*, p. 246.
[109] Williams, *Sociology of Gosforth* (1956), p. 135, notes that Gosforth's nine inns in 1857 had now become four public houses, but ascribes it also to the rise of the price of beer and spirits and the decline in the popularity of excess drinking. Saville, p. 23, notes that villages under 500 had lost one of two inns between 1850 and 1920, along with thatchers, carpenters, shoemakers, tailors, and ascribes it to the decline of rural industry in competition with the factory.
[110] See Gautier, *Pourquoi les Bretons s'en vont*, vols. I and II (1950); Valarché, p. 101; Mendras, p. 72. All say that it is not income, but the hard work and lack of distraction which produce emigration. An important role is played by the female of the species. She leaves in greater numbers (Valarché, p. 103; Saville, p. 33); and she frequently propels the male. See Faucher, *Le Paysan et la machine*, p. 217: "Many a marriage was concluded on the condition of departure to the city."
[111] Saville, pp. 140–141.
[112] Martin, *The Secret People* (1954), p. 275, discusses how farmers and their children sabotaged the School Boards Act of 1870 in Britain; also the general rural view that education corrupted children's willingness to work in agriculture and was responsible for the rural exodus. Augé-Laribé, *Politique agricole*, p. 123, notes that the French Education Law of 1881 was equally not obeyed, as well as the existence of the same question of whether school made the peasants or ruined them. Contrast Danish rural education.

able that agricultural economists should be unhappy about the loss of numbers: Augé-Laribé calls the rural exodus "excessive" in 1880; Fauchon claims that the southwest has been "devastated" by rural exodus.[113] No one feels comfortable when his object of concern is shrinking. But it is inevitable. And the proof has been the rapid increase in French agricultural efficiency, with rapidly shrinking numbers, since World War II. Pockets of overpopulation remain, but outward transfers have been on a large scale — 1,100,000 between 1946 and 1954[114] and more since. French economic growth has been more rapid after World War II than it would have been if agriculture had not been so backward, and this on the same averaging principle that led agriculture to slow down growth prior to 1939. The transfer of men from jobs of low productivity to those of high does more than produce a higher rate of national growth in comparison with simple structural transfers between sectors of equal efficiency. It also stimulates increased efficiency in the sector left.

In conclusion, then, French agriculture has not been efficient, and its low productivity has held back average overall growth. Further, the deflation in French agriculture, until interrupted by tariffs, exercised a depressing effect on the economy as a whole, which slowed down the rate of growth between 1882 and 1896. But too slow a rate of transfer of resources to other sectors did not have a harmful effect on industrial expansion; nor did too rapid a transfer hurt agricultural efficiency. There were drags, perhaps, on industry from the independent and uneducated character of the emigrants from agriculture. Those who did not come, could not, because they were too far away, regardless of how much they would have been helpful if they had.

THE FAILURE OF BRITISH AGRICULTURE TO TRANSFORM

Our interest in British agriculture is unrelated to the question of overall economic growth, since the sector shrank rapidly in relative size after 1880. It concerns a more limited question: Why did this agriculture, as efficient as any in the world in the 1850s, lose its lead, not so much in wheat, where the answer is clear, as in the animal

[113] Augé-Laribé, ibid., p. 14; Fauchon, Économie de l'agriculture française, p. 23.

[114] See Annuaire statistique, 1961, p. 86, where the numbers engaged in agriculture are given on the basis of the new and the old definitions. The foregoing calculation uses the old definitions, which put the farm population in the labor force at 6,371,000. On the new definitions, the numbers are only 5,196,000. Most of the change (all but 225,000) is in women.

foods — dairy products, eggs, and meat? Why, in short, did not British agriculture transform more thoroughly from wheat to livestock after the fall of the price of wheat relative to that of foodstuffs?

The period of High Farming,[115] begun in the 1830s, brought British efficiency in arable cultivation up to new peaks after the agricultural revolution of the eighteenth century. Deep plowing, better drainage, chemical fertilizer, and machinery constituted the technical side of the change,[116] along with stall feeding and selective breeding in livestock; there were, in addition, continued investment of urban accumulated wealth in the purchase of country property and government loans for drainage in the 1840s and 1850s. More scientific farming was advocated as a means for the farmer to adapt to the repeal of the Corn Laws.[117]

The fears of agriculture over the Corn Laws repeal proved groundless, whether because of increased efficiency in supply or expanding demand. Wheat prices held steady during the 1850s, despite rising imports.[118] But dairy and meat prices rose 40 percent between 1850 and 1860 under the pressure of rising demand.[119] Big reductions in customs duties occurred in butter and cheese in 1846, 1853, and 1860, and on eggs in 1853 and 1860. Duties on livestock were removed in 1846, along with those on ham and salted meat. The tariff on bacon was taken off in 1853.[120]

Here was the growing market for foodstuffs in Britain. Income elasticity was high, and urban incomes were rising. While British production of animal foodstuffs increased, imports rose even faster than

[115] It is not altogether clear in the literature whether High Farming derived its name from its high content of scientific and experimental practice, as opposed to traditional practice, or from high profits. In regarding 1853 to 1862 as the golden age of British agriculture, historians follow Lord Ernle (*English Farming, Past and Present*, 1937, p. 373) who also states (p. 346) that "so far as the standard of the highest farming is concerned, agriculture made but little advance since the fifties."

[116] Léon de Lavergne, *The Rural Economy of England* (1855), p. 1, says that the Great Exhibition of 1851 surprised the French visitor not so much by British manufactures as by its agricultural machinery. Lord Ernle notes that the Gloucester exhibition of 1853 exhibited 2,000 implements (p. 372).

[117] See Ernle, p. 374: "Mr. (later Sir) James Caird's pamphlet on *High Farming . . . the Best Substitute for Protection*, 1848, pointed out the true remedy."

[118] The volume of grain imports rose from an average of £4.3 million in 1840–1844 to £11.2 million in the five-year period after 1853 (when harvests settled down). These figures are averaged from Schlote's data (quantities multiplied by fixed prices), *British Overseas Trade* (1952), table 11, p. 140. Imports would have been higher had it not been for limitations on the supply side — the discovery of gold in Australia and the Crimean War, which closed the Baltic to Russian wheat.

[119] Saville, p. 12.

[120] Schlote, pp. 62–63.

in grain,[121] where the British farmer was to cut out a third of his acreage and where imports included some feed for British livestock. The market was there, but British producers left it to be taken over in large part by foreigners. In inexpensive meat and wool, the cheapening of transport and the settlement of new grazing lands overseas put the British producers of sheep and ordinary beef cattle at the same disadvantage as his wheat-growing colleague. But in milk, cheese, butter, eggs, bacon, not to mention fruits and vegetables, the opportunity existed.

High Farming continued through the 1870s, until the Great Depression, which in this sector began in 1879. There is doubt that the depression was general in agriculture. It hit mostly wheat farmers on heavy land, particularly in East Anglia and in the southeast. Dairy farmers near cities suffered not at all; and an observer who found no depression in agriculture in Lancashire holds that the exaggerated view of the extent of the depression comes from the fact that the Royal Commission of 1879–1882 was packed with wheat interests.[122] Third-quality beef and mutton items actually held their prices from 1876 to 1883, before starting down sharply thereafter under the impact of imports of chilled and frozen meat.[123] But dairy production

[121] The decennial import averages from Schlote, (table 11) are revealing (in millions of pounds sterling at fixed prices):

Year	Grain	Animal foodstuffs
1830s	2.1	1.7
1840s	6.2	3.4
1850s	11.1	5.6
1860s	20.1	13.3
1870s	34.1	24.6
1880s	42.1	37.1
1890s	58.0	63.3
1900s	62.0	92.8

[122] See Fletcher, "The Great Depression in English Agriculture" (1961), p. 426. Of 35 witnesses before the commission who were farmers, almost all were tenants, only 1 farmed less than 100 acres, 26 came from the wheat areas of the south and east, and only 4 from north of the Trent, of whom two raised wheat. For further evidence on the lack of agricultural depression in Cumberland, Westmoreland, Middlesex, Derby, and Cheshire, see Stearns, "Agricultural Adaptation in England" (1932), pp. 95, 97.

[123] For the best statistical series, see Besse, *L'Agriculture en Angleterre* (1910). The price data are on p. 339. First- and second-quality beef and mutton did not fall nearly so far in price and undoubtedly remained profitable after taking account of the reduction in costs. Note that meat imports had a strong geographical bias in distribution, the main consuming areas being London, the Midlands, and parts of Lancashire around Liverpool. In Yorkshire, the northern counties, the southwest, Wales, and particularly Scotland, butcher shops refused to handle or buy im-

remained profitable.[124] In the absence of adequate data on either prices or costs, it is not clear that fruits and vegetables were also a profitable occupation during the depression. Acreage figures are available for fruit during the depression only from 1888, and not for green vegetables. The trend of this acreage, and of imports, however, suggests that here was another opportunity, and one which might have retained on the farm the agricultural workers who were leaving so precipitously.[125]

British agriculture changed to some extent in the face of these incentives. Wheat acreage fell in half between 1875 and 1908, barley by a third. Olson and Harris argue that the data for wheat show a much higher elasticity of supply than is normally found in the United States, and they find it "probable that the substitution between wheat and other products was easier in Great Britain than in many other wheat growing areas, such as the American Great Plains." [126] But there is a serious question about whether supply elasticity is the appropriate concept to apply to what was taking place in Britain in this period. It is true that oats for feed rose about 450,000 acres while wheat was declining 1,600,000 and barley 650,000; and that permanent pasture expanded from 10.5 million acres to 13.9 million. But was the increase in pasture a deliberate move or a consequence of the farmer's discouragement and lack of capital? [127] They simply let it "tumble down" to grass.[128] In these circumstances, there may have been an irreversible exit from the sector over a long period, and the concept of supply elasticity, appropriate for small changes in a limited time compass, is not applicable.

Animal numbers rose, though less than the population. Between 1870 and 1908, cows increased from 3,700,000 to 4,400,000, but declined from 118 per 1,000 inhabitants to 98.[129] Other cattle increased

---

ported meat except as a very last resort (Jeffrys, *Retail Trading in Britain*, 1954, p. 129).

[124] Trow-Smith, *British Livestock Husbandry* (1959), p. 234.

[125] This was not due to the enclosures, the last wave of which was over by 1845, but to first, High Farming, which released 300,000 men from 1850 to 1870, because of increased productivity; and second, to the decline in the price of wheat after 1879. The number of agricultural workers fell 400,000 from 1871 to 1901, or from 996,000 to 597,000. (There is the view, expressed in a seminar at Nuffield College, that High Farming did not so much release agricultural workers as an independent force as it constituted a response to the loss of workers pulled by industry and not pushed by the repeal of the Corn Laws. Here again, as in so much of the analysis, it is virtually impossible to sort out cause and effect.)

[126] Olson and Harris, "Free Trade in 'Corn'" (1959), p. 165.

[127] Bear, *English Farmer and His Competitors* (1888), p. 29; and Channing, *Agricultural Depression* (1897), pp. 4–5; 324.

[128] Stearns, "Agricultural Adaptation in England," p. 90.

[129] Besse, *L'Agriculture en Angleterre*, pp. 358–359.

somewhat more proportionately, from 5,500,000 to 7,400,000 over the same period. These figures are somewhat misleading, however. If the data are put on a more solid basis to distinguish dairy herds from beef, it can be seen that between 1873–1882 and 1902–1912 the number of cows and heifers in milk or calf increased by one quarter — from 2,240,000 to 2,740,000 — while the number of other cattle over two years old declined slightly — from 1,480,000 to 1,380,000.[130]

On the whole, however, the most striking fact that emerges from the British agricultural record after 1850 is the fact that it did not respond in the pattern of output to the changed conditions of grain supply abroad and the demand for animal foods at home. In the end, it was left for Denmark, the Netherlands, and New Zealand to provide the bacon, eggs, ham, and cheese in which the British worker and middle-class member chose to take such a large proportion of their increased productivity. These countries did transform under the pressure of British demand. The question is why was it they and not the more strategically located British agriculture.

The list of reasons is a long one and tends to explain more than 100 percent of the problem. Pride of place doubtless goes to the system of land tenure, ideal for grain on large farms, but poorly suited for more labor-intensive animal husbandry. Lesser considerations include the ignorance of the average farmer, despite the interest in agronomy of the leaders of British agriculture, particularly in matters of producing and marketing animal products; the laissez-faire attitude of government and the public; and bad weather. Let us dispose of the less important causes first.

Bad weather had the effect of disguising for a time what was taking place — the troubles of agriculture were blamed on nature rather than on the flood of imports, thus inhibiting the will to seek remedies.[131] But the effects were wider. Topsoils were physically affected and became deficient in minerals. Moreover, through discouraging the farmer, the bad weather led to capital consumption, which tends to become cumulative because poorly maintained land leads to decreased yields and more pressure to take from the land without putting back.

There were other long-run effects of the natural endowment. The heavy clay lands of East Anglia and Essex were splendid for producing wheat with proper drainage, but far less satisfactory for grass. It was possible to make a living from dairying, as was demonstrated by the invasion of Scotsmen with a knowledge of milk production after

[130] Cohen, *History of Milk Prices* (1936), p. 26.
[131] Ernle, *English Farming, Past and Present,* p. 380.

rents had fallen in the nineties,[132] but this level of living was well below that which had been achieved with wheat. So too was the rent. It was too much to expect British farmers on heavy land to embrace dairying as long as there was any possibility of a restoration of wheat prices.

Second, the dispersion of rainfall in the British isles favored the west over the east. In the west the rainfall averages between 20 and 60 inches a year. East of a line from Berwick on Tweed to the Isle of Wight, however, the rainfall is less, in many areas being only 20 to 24 inches.[133] The rainfall and climate in the west (and in Denmark, the Netherlands?) give it three months of free feed as compared with the east. Wheat can grow in dry areas, but not grass.

In addition to the natural handicaps, there were the man-made ones. Many instances could be cited of the disadvantage at which British agriculture was put by laissez faire. Royal commissions investigated the agricultural depression, but were unwilling to recommend positive action to meet it.[134] The 1886 *Report* opined that the "depression in agriculture is not likely to exhibit any material improvement until the competition of soils superior to our own has worked itself out." [135] And Channing says of the 1896 *Final Report* (of the commission of which he was a member): "It is vigorous and uncompromising only in its defense of the existing land system. If it has any real policy anywhere, it is that things must be left to take care of themselves." [136]

Complaints from farmers included long tolerance of labeling margarine as butter, the absence of sanitary regulations, and the unfairness of railway discrimination against local and in favor of imported produce. Government aid to agricultural education lagged. On the other hand, there was farming opposition to technical education: "In running my eye over the account which I wrote of English agriculture in 1850, I find descriptions of good farming in nearly every part of the country which differ very little from the practice of the

[132] *Ibid.*, pp. 384–385.

[133] Russell, *World Food Supplies* (1954), p. 26.

[134] It is not entirely correct to say that no action was taken by the government. An attempt was made to hold agricultural workers on the land by furnishing them allotments (to replace their commons rights lost earlier by enclosure) — thus the Allotment Act of 1887 and in 1892 the Small-Holdings Act and the Local Government Act. These steps in favor of "peasant proprietors" whose backs the landed gentry needed (Martin, *The Secret People*, p. 181) were not altogether out of the tradition of the Poaching Prevention Act of 1862, which made it possible for a villager carrying a bundle after working hours to be searched (p. 167).

[135] Stearns, "Agricultural Adaptation in England," p. 101. See also note 147 below.

[136] Channing, *Agricultural Depression*, p. xi.

present day." [137] There were the ubiquitous complaints about middlemen and the costs of distribution; but here the remedy lay in the hands of the farmers, had they been able to organize cooperative marketing.[138]

The farmers themselves raise the same sort of questions as about those in France, but at a much higher level of technological efficiency. There were agricultural shows and prizes for livestock throughout the last three quarters of the nineteenth century. New herd books and breeding associations for new breeds came into being, especially in the last quarter. But these may have hindered, rather than helped, since the judging was on the basis of appearance rather than of performance, "a rich man's plaything [with the] practical value obscured." [139] An important reason for the loss of the butter market to foreigners was the lack of uniformity in quality and packaging. The latter was a partial cause of higher freight rates. In quality it was not the average level but the variability about the mean that counted: "Large dealers will not look at people who merely sell butter, but not of uniform quality." [140]

The major weakness of the farmers, however, was their ignorance of new methods and unwillingness to learn. Bear states that the dairy farmers had the worst possible form of ignorance — "the lack of knowing of their ignorance." [141] There was superstition: prejudice against the use of scales to weigh livestock so that farmers continued to estimate weight, despite the legislative requirement of a weigh-bridge. A Dutch attempt to introduce sugar beets onto British farms failed because of difficulty in persuading farmers to try the crop at all, and then to cultivate and weed properly.[142] The Earl of Leicester in Norfolk, son of the great Coke, grassed down his farm in Norfolk to sheep but despaired of his tenants having the sense to follow his example.[143]

---

[137] Caird, *Landed Interest* (1878), p. 28.

[138] I have discussed elsewhere ("Group Behavior and International Trade," p. 43, n. 39) the failure of the British to develop cooperatives. But note that the explanation which attaches primary importance to English character — as in H. Rider Haggard, *Rural Denmark* (1911), and Besse, *L'Agriculture en Angleterre* — contradicts the usual French view that Britain was characterized by a "spirit of association" while France, which had an effective peasant cooperative movement, was not. See above, Chapter 5.

[139] Trow-Smith, *British Livestock Husbandry*, II, 235; Ernle, *English Farming, Past and Present*, p. 387.

[140] Channing, *Agricultural Depression*, p. 45.

[141] Bear, *English Farmer and His Competitors*, p. 104.

[142] Robertson-Scott, *Sugar-Beet* (1911), *passim*. The author notes that to overcome the prejudice and arrogance of British farmers it was necessary for the Dutch company to change the expression in its booklet from "Instructions to Farmers" to "Hints on Cultivation."

[143] Fletcher, "The Great Depression of English Agriculture," p. 431.

Finally, the state of farm accounting was abysmally low, and there was little idea of the cost of raising meat.[144]

The main handicap, however, was that the system of land tenure and farm size, so admirably suited to wheat and the social requirements of a rising plutocracy, could not readily be readapted to livestock. Of the 560,000 tenant farmers in Britain, 100,000 had farms of more than 100 acres; 5,000 had between 500 and 1,000 acres; and 600 had more than 1,000. Farmers were six times more numerous than proprietor-operators.[145] A convention grew up whereby the landlord provided the whole of the permanent equipment of the land — roads, fences, drainage, buildings, water supply — and the tenant contributed the working capital — implements, livestock, and so on.[146] Until 1892 leases were rigid on what crops should be grown, when, and what could and could not be marketed. There was no incentive for tenants to improve the land.[147] Leases were annual in England, in contrast to nineteen- or twenty-one-year terms in Scotland. Rents went up easily until 1875, but came down slowly, except when a farm went vacant. From 1879 to 1894 they were often paid out of capital, except where a new tenant took over. Where the owner in the weekending class[148] obtained his major satisfaction in the possession of land from the social status it conferred, there was little incentive, after the age of Townshend, Tull, and Young, to respond to the challenge of the change in relative prices.

There was also a technical reason. Bear and Channing emphasize that the rewards of shifting from arable to grass and pasture farming come from making the change before the land has been mined to any extent. "The chances of success were increased by having the best stocks, the best seeds, the best cake and manures, the best equipment

[144] Bear, pp. 71–81.

[145] Caird, *Landed Interest*, pp. 58, 60.

[146] Orwin, "Land Tenure in England" (1929), p. 3.

[147] Bear, pp. 14–16. The Agricultural Holdings Act was passed in 1883 to enable tenants to claim compensation for improvements. It proved highly one-sided in operation, however; and Bear and Channing indicated that a tenant would be foolhardy to bring a claim under it, given the necessity for documentation, on the one hand, and his vulnerability to counterclaims for violation of restrictions and to substantial penalties, on the other.

[148] The expression is that of J. Robertson-Scott in *England's Green and Pleasant Land* (1931). The five-day week for the upper middle class came into existence in the 1850s or early 1860s. The boom in land values occurred in the expansion of 1866–1873 (see Thompson, "The Land Market in the Nineteenth Century," 1957), but more land in terms of acres may have changed hands in 1855–1864 (p. 300). In the early 1870s perhaps 500,000 to 600,000 acres, or 3 percent, of an estimated 18 million acres of marketable land changed hands annually. The owners of many of these farms had industrial incomes, were interested in well-run farms and profits, along with sport and social status, but were not dependent upon farming or farm rentals and preferred a "good" tenant to a profitable one.

and the best labor. It is the letting down of the land which is the dire
and unfailing precursor of the ruin of the farmer." [149] This of course
requires capital. Bear says that to urge the farmers to engage in what
is termed "intensive farming" without better security than the law af-
fords them at present is something like asking them to make bricks
without straw.[150]

But the major reason, in my judgment, is neither technical nor legal,
but economic. It would be useful to see whether owner-farmed holdings were shifted more fully to livestock than tenant farms were. It
seems probable that this was the case. Livestock calls for labor-intensive, capital-intensive small farms, in contrast to the land-intensive
growing of wheat. To change over a tenant-farmed holding would require dividing the farm, building new barns, if perhaps not dwellings,
and would call for investment in livestock by two farmers, one for
each half of the original tract. The market mechanism is unlikely to
produce this sort of coordination, partly for the fact that prices have
a sizable element of inertia in them and also because of the uncertainty as to how the costs and benefits of the changeover are to be ap-
portioned among the investors, workers, and income recipients. The
family-size Danish or Dutch owner-farmed holding, averaging, say,
80 acres, was admirably suited to labor-intensive dairying, to make no
mention of Danish agricultural education and the cooperative movement. These holdings were vertically integrated, in contrast to the
disarticulated British mechanism. In Britain it is appropriate to regard
owner, wheat-producing tenant, and other potential tenant or tenants
as separate firms, and to observe that the gains from the change may
involve economies that are external to a particular firm from which
investment is required. The analogy with the 10.5-ton freight car discussed in Chapter 7 seems to me to be close. It evidently would have
been profitable to transform British agriculture much more thoroughly to dairying. But the economies of such a transformation appeared uncertainly related to the investment and other efforts called
for by various parties to the change. On this account it was not undertaken.

[149] Channing, *Agricultural Depression*, p. 73.
[150] Bear, p. 162.

CHAPTER 11

URBANIZATION AND
REGIONAL BALANCE

Centralization has been touched upon in earlier chapters, especially for France, in connection with resources, capital markets, population, and government. Regional questions, moreover, figured prominently in matters of agriculture and migration in the last chapter. It is perhaps useful, nevertheless, to address the questions of centralization and spatial balance explicitly and in particular to discuss three hypotheses: first, that French economic growth has been held back by lack of urbanization; second, that the domination of Paris over the rest of France has acted as a brake on French development; third, that beyond the hydrocephalic growth of Paris there has been a deep-seated regional imbalance in France between the north and east, on the one hand, and the south and west, on the other.[1] It will thus be seen that the chapter is again primarily devoted to France. Brief attention is paid to the British urbanization process as a control. British regional problems discussed in the literature have consisted largely in the social problem of structural unemployment in distressed areas, though this has prominent economic aspects as well.

Urbanization is relevant because cities provide a training ground for the development process. Urban life involves a break with rural tradition, modifying the vertical family, liberating women, providing the necessary preconditions of mobility and transformation. Cities furnish markets of scale, particularly in communication and distribution. There is no need to recur to the mere provision of hands for the factory, discussed in the last chapter. The city demands and provides literacy, education, face-to-face contact — the prerequisites of technical change.

Economists lack elaborated models of the interregional communication of economic growth. Rostow's *Stages of Economic Growth*, for example, contains almost no discussion of the relation of leading to

[1] See, e.g., United Nations, *Economic Survey of Europe in 1954*, pp. 172–195, which lists regional imbalance as one of the four main deficiencies of the French economic structure, along with agricultural backwardness, insufficient industrialization, and a weak export structure.

lagging regions, comparable to that of leading to lagging sectors. Something depends on whether migration is possible or not.[2] But it is probably more significant whether or not the lagging region has the necessary capacity to reallocate resources and to adopt new techniques. Lacking such capacity in region B, growth in region A will fail to be communicated to B, whether or not the resources in "import-competing industries" in B emigrate or merely languish.[3]

It also seems likely — although the point is speculative and impossible to test — that there is this much to the theorem of regional imbalance: if all regions have some capacity to grow — to reallocate and to adopt more progressive technology — but one or more regions are very much ahead of the others, growth in the leading regions will not be disseminated in space. The leading regions can more effectively take advantage of the opportunities for the growth they create, except in strongly supply-oriented activities. In all other lines, in those with market pull or those requiring technical skill, sizable investments, and even only the entrepreneurship to organize manpower for labor-intensive activities, the region with the substantial lead may stay ahead. It may or may not attract migrants from the retarded regions. On the other hand, when the various regions are more or less on a par, and all possess capacity for growth, the stimulus to growth felt in one region will be communicated to others.

In the first set of circumstances, there is real point to government intervention to make good the lack of investment, entrepreneurship, and training in the retarded regions. In the second, the path to optimum growth in space lies in pushing forward wherever growth will take place most rapidly and letting it spill over from one region to the others.

RATES AND PATTERNS OF URBANIZATION

Britain was urban far earlier than France. In 1801, 9.5 percent of the French lived in cities of more than 10,000 inhabitants, and 23.3 percent of the British. By 1851 the percentages were 10.6 and 39.5, respectively.[4] In 1946, one third of the French population lived in cities of more than 10,000, compared with 70 percent in the United Kingdom and the Netherlands, 53 percent in Italy, 47 percent in Ger-

[2] See the independent statement of Maurice Byé in ILO, *Social Aspects of Economic Cooperation* (1956), discussing the Common Market. He holds that growth in one country can be communicated to another so long as there is no possibility of factor movements, but that when outward migration can take place, growth in one country may merely attract resources from another.

[3] See Burenstam Linder, *Trade and Transformation* (1961), chap. ii, part A.

[4] Weber, *Growth of Cities* (1899), pp. 43, 47, 71.

many, and 45 percent in Belgium. London is a large city, with important administrative and financial functions. Paris is a manufacturing and educational center as well. The important relation is not that Paris is so big as that the potential competition is so small. In 1946, again, London had 22 percent of the British urban population and 17.4 percent of the total population, compared with 23 percent and 13.5 percent, respectively, for Paris.[5] In 1931, all towns over 100,000 in number, however, contained 16 percent of the population in France and 40 percent in Britain; and in the below-20,000 category, the figures are 69 percent and 35 percent.[6]

Moreover, the British urban pattern differs sharply from the French. B. J. L. Berry says that cities by size fall into two distinct patterns: the "truncated log-normal" distribution, in which the number of cities decreases with the increase in size in a smoothly geometric relationship, and the "primate" distribution, in which one or more large cities dominate a stratum of very small towns and cities.[7] Berry's graphs that illustrate the differences unfortunately omit France, where data for the 20,000 to 50,000 class are missing. But the difference in the patterns can be illustrated and is set out in Table 20. The British pattern ap-

Table 20. Distribution of Cities in Britain and France, by Size, 1950

	Over 1 million (A)	500,000– 1 million (B)	250,000– 500,000 (C)	100,000– 250,000 (D)	50,000– 100,000 (E)	20,000– 50,000 (F)
England, Wales	2	4	9	55	87	220
France	1	1	3	19	39	—

Source. Berry, "City-Size Distribution" (1961), Appendix A, p. 588.

proaches the log-normal and the French the primate, though it is not so near the primate as such countries as Austria and Denmark, with one city each of more than 1 million and none in classes B and C. It will be recalled from Chapter 8 that of 38,000 towns of more than 5,000 inhabitants in France, 37,000 have 5,000 to 6,000. Paris dominates France in a way that London does not Britain.

BRITISH URBAN GROWTH

The process of English urban growth is fairly familiar. The percentage of population in cities over 20,000 advanced at every census,

[5] George, La Ville (1952), p. 71.
[6] See "Urbanization," Encyclopedia of Social Sciences, p. 190.
[7] Berry, "City-Size Distribution" (1961).

but during the nineteenth century the decades which stand out are the 1820s, 1840s, 1870s, and 1880s. The 1820s are attributed by Weber to the cotton-textile areas around Manchester. In the 1840s the growing towns were those in iron districts and the ports, where the boom in foreign trade, concentrated in rails and railway equipment, had a large impact.[8] Weber does not explain the 1870s and 1880s in detail, nor the earlier effects of the immigrants from Ireland.[9] Cairncross, however, shows sharply different results for the two decades: in the 1870s the movement out of rural areas was largely to London and to the major northern industrial towns, and only in small degree abroad. But in the 1880s, although London continued to gain — at a slower rate — the northern towns on balance lost population by migration, and the rural exodus fed overseas migration. A decade later, some recovery in the agricultural areas, the readiness of the cities to receive new immigrants, and a decline in the rate of natural increase permitted a fall in the rate of emigration.[10]

The rate of growth of British industrial cities was phenomenal. Between 1851 and 1946, Liverpool, Manchester, Cardiff, and Birmingham, already large at the start, octupled, and Oxford quadrupled.[11] These rates compare with an increase of three times for Lille-Roubaix-Tourcoing in the Nord (textiles), slightly more than this for the coal cities of the Nord and Pas de Calais, and increases of slightly less than tripling for Lyon and St. Étienne.[12]

After the First World War, the growth of British cities slowed down because of, first, the decline in the birth rate and, second, the movement to the suburbs. Overvaluation produced unemployment in coal, steel, textiles, and shipbuilding, checking the growth of the north and the ports. When recovery came in the 1930s, the rise of the engineering industry in the south and the Midlands left distressed areas in Lancashire, Wales, and Scotland. These were relieved after World War II, partly by the migration accelerated by the war, partly by governmental regulation limiting investment in areas of full employment and stimulating new construction where deep pools of unemployment remained. The British were not, therefore, without regional problems and, indeed, continue to have difficulty in areas like the Tyneside and Clyde (shipbuilding). These problems, however, have been of a different order of magnitude from the French.

[8] Weber, *Growth of Cities*, pp. 52–56.
[9] Redford, *Labour Migration* (1926), pp. 110ff, does treat the movement of the Irish to Britain. "The persistence of the Irish exodus was by far the most significant feature of the British migration." His analysis ends at 1850.
[10] See chap. iv, "Internal Migration in Victorian England," in *Home and Foreign Investment*.
[11] George, *La Ville*, p. 51.
[12] *Ibid.*, pp. 112–113.

In the first place, London has by no means dominated the rest of the British Isles. Two main centers of intellectual leadership exist outside the capital, though within commuting distance, and much of the business leadership is elsewhere. The London stock market provided capital only for a limited group of industries, but the remainder had relatively little difficulty in filling their needs on the provincial exchanges.[13] There was a tradition of self-dependence in the provincial cities,[14] as well as an attachment to the land and the local community on the part of the aristocracy.[15] The urbanization process required the use of capital, or provided outlets for it, depending upon the point of view. New construction by local authorities for the period 1870–1914 is estimated by Cairncross to run between 20 and 35 percent of total construction.[16]

FRENCH URBAN GROWTH

The urbanization process in France can best be illustrated by Table 21. It shows, first, the uneven rate of increase and how much faster it was for the major centers in the years up to 1881 than before; second, the faster rate of expansion in Paris than in the other major urban centers, up to World War I; third, with the help of quinquennial figures, the importance in accelerating the urbanization process of railroad construction, war, and business prosperity.

The effects of railroad construction on population movement have been touched upon earlier in a number of places. France had been a country of old cities, with commercial and administrative functions, running from 10 to 30,000 in population, and spread out over the major roads at average distances of 30 to 35 kilometers — "seldom 50" — representing the normal daily journey of a horseman on the roads of ancient France.[17] Paris, at the crossroads of France, linked with all the major valleys, and a royal city, was an exception, along with the lesser crossroads of Lyon and the ports of Bordeaux and Marseilles. These grew slowly up to 1841 and exploded thereafter, especially be-

---

[13] See Chapter 3.

[14] Checkland observes that at about the turn of the century there was a lull in the undertaking of new ventures of municipal improvement, owing to a loss of faith in expansion. See "English Provincial Cities" (1953). But this was shortly overcome, and in Birmingham the municipalization of gas, water, and tramways, the creation of a municipal electricity supply, and the struggle for adequate schools and social amenities from the 1870s to the 1890s were followed between the wars by themes of education, transport, municipal trading, hospitals, and city extension, not to mention municipal housing.

[15] See Chapter 5. The contrast in attitude is with the French aristocrat who, as described by Stendhal, spent six months in Paris and six months in the country, where he never traveled but played cards all the time (quoted by Lhomme, *La Grande bourgeoisie*, 1960, p. 40).

[16] Table 36, *Home and Foreign Investment*, p. 169.

[17] George, *La Ville*, p. 86.

Table 21. Urbanization in France

Year	Percent of population urban[a]	Percentage change in period (decade)	
		Paris[b]	12 cities (including Paris)[c]
1851	25.5	+20.5	+19.0
1861	28.9	+36.2	+33.0
1872	31.1	+13.6	+10.0
1881	34.8	+26.1	+18.7
1891	37.4	+12.2	+9.7
1901	40.9	+16.8	+9.6
1911	44.2	+6.4	+7.4
1921	46.3	+0.6	+2.1
1931	51.2	−0.5	+5.5
1954	56.0		

[a] The census reports as urban those communes where the total population agglomeration exceeds 2,000 inhabitants.

[b] Includes boundary change in 1858, adding about 500,000. For details see Chevalier, *La Formation de la population parisienne* (1949), pp. 39–42.

[c] Includes boundary changes for Lyon (1852), Lille (1858), and Le Havre (no date given by Weber). The 12 cities are those which were over 100,000 in 1891. See *Growth of Cities* (1899), pp. 67ff.

Source. Census reports.

tween 1851 and 1861, when the major railroad network was completed.[18] Le Havre tripled between 1851 and 1866; Lille, St. Étienne, and Paris doubled, or almost so; Marseilles, Lyon, and Bordeaux increased by roughly 50 percent — all in fifteen years.

The effect of war in uprooting population was mentioned in the last chapter. It presumably accounts for much of the increase in urbanization in the decade to 1881. The effects are delayed after 1872, when the confusion of demobilization still prevailed. But there is qualitative evidence of its importance at the time in speeding migration.[19] After World War I the major effect was felt not in Paris, but in the smaller cities.[20]

[18] In absolute numbers, the twelve cities crept up from 1.2 million in 1801 to 1.3 in 1811, 1.3 in 1821, 1.6 in 1831, and 1.8 in 1841, before jumping to 2.1 in 1851, 3.2 in 1861. But see notes b and c to Table 21, on administrative changes.

[19] Clapham, *Economic Development of France and Germany* (1936), p. 168, states that the rural population, which began to decline absolutely after 1875, learned what a town was like from the War of 1870. Augé-Laribé, *Politique agricole* (1950), p. 104, attaches importance to the conscription introduced in 1870. See also, for a later date, Mendras, *Novis et Virgin* (1953), p. 43, who says that the peasant is passive in the barracks but is changed by the experience, at least superficially, and for the better. But World War I taught the men of this village in Avéyron to drink daily, instead of only on Sundays at the cafe, and gave rise to the problem of alcoholism.

[20] Phlipponneau, *Le Problème breton* (1957), p. 28, emphasizes the effect of World War I in leading to emigration.

The third major influence is prosperity. It is associated with the railroad boom in the early period and with war and the little boom of 1879–1881, which probably contributed to the high figures for the decade ending in 1881. Insofar as a business boom is based on construction, of course, the population movement feeds on, as well as gets fed by, prosperity. Thus Gravier can claim that the public works of Haussmann attracted millions of miserable peasants to Paris, while Halbswachs had insisted thirty years earlier that Haussmann and his architects followed but did not determine the expansion of the city.[21]

Industrialization affected some of the small administrative centers — Tours, Le Mans, Limoges, Grenoble; some isolated industrial agglomerations — of various sizes, ranging from Albi with 35,000 to the mushroom cities of Lorraine, Clermont-Ferrand, Le Creusot, and so on; one or two ports, like Marseilles, which grew from 195,000 in 1851 to 914,000 by 1936, before falling back after the war; Paris, discussed below; and the large zones of industrialization, like Lille-Roubaix-Tourcoing in textiles and Béthune, Douai, Denain, and Valenciennes in coal and steel. St. Étienne in the Upper Loire, according to George, falls between the isolated industrial agglomeration and the large industrial zone.[22] Purely commercial and administrative cities grew much more slowly than the industrial; but many of these, as in the coal and steel area of the Nord–Pas de Calais, after substantial growth remained in the 35,000 inhabitant class.[23] From 1872 to 1936, the French living in cities over 100,000 rose from 9.1 percent of the population to 16.0 percent, whereas the British had reached 16.0 percent a century earlier, in 1831, and by 1936 were over 40 percent.

One can only speculate on the causes and effects of this curious penchant for the small city. It has been referred to above that the small French city is less turned inward on itself than is commonly believed, as the studies of Bettelheim and Frère at Auxerre (25,000) and Clement and Xydias at Vienne (26,500 at its peak in 1871) demonstrate. My discussion has also dealt with the "balanced regions" concept of Dunham, which may have something to do with it, the shape

[21] Gravier, *Paris et le désert français* (1958), p. 54; Halbswachs, *La Population et les tracés de voies à Paris* (1928), p. 265.

[22] George, *La Ville*, p. 95.

[23] In 1851 Valenciennes with 23,000 inhabitants and Douai with 20,500 were the only cities in the coal and steel area of the north with more than 10,000 inhabitants. Only a dozen had more than 5,000. By 1946 there were sixty cities of more than 5,000, including some like Bruay-en-Artois which had grown from 712 inhabitants in 1851 to 32,000 in 1946; but the largest were Valenciennes with 38,700, Douai 37,300, Lens 34,200. George comments that urbanization remained diffuse, showed a lack of concentration, and appeared disorganized (*ibid.*, p. 105). Pinchemel (*Les Niveaux optima des villes*, 1959) holds that cities of 50,000 to 100,000 are below the efficient level, which is above 100,000, but that there is something to be said for the city of 35,000.

of the railroad network, the family farm. It is impossible to establish how much if anything these factors had to do with the prevalence of the small city, or to what extent these cities were blighted by Paris.

The effects of the small city have not been neglected altogether, especially under scale and in retail distribution.[24] But they doubtless go beyond this. The dominance of Paris *and* the small size of most communities outside it breed defeatism at the local level. Only at the extreme periphery — in Savoy and Lorraine — did regional banks flourish, apart from the sizable agglomeration of Lille-Roubaix-Tourcoing. Moreover, with the exception of Lyon, which had both large size and an independent tradition, there was something wrong with each substantial city. In Rouen the inferiority complex vis-à-vis Britain was at its most acute; it was the home of protectionism. Marseilles, an enormous agglomeration, lacked ties to its region, though it served the hinterland of all France as a military and colonial port.[25] Bordeaux was purely commercial, hurt by the loss of colonial trade in sugar and too far from the center to attract manufacturing. Lille-Roubaix-Tourcoing had a strong commercial and financial tradition in Lille, but for the rest consisted of overgrown villages, swamped by industrial expansion, with little tradition or individuality. Paris was not only comparable to New York and Washington, as was London, but also to Chicago in transport, Detroit and Cincinnati in manufacturing, and Boston in letters and education.

PARIS AND THE FRENCH DESERT

Blame for the dominance of Paris in France has been variously ascribed to Louis XIV for assembling the court in Versailles, to the departmental system of Napoleon I, and to the beautification of the city by Louis Napoleon and Haussmann. The interesting change, however, occurred after the middle of the nineteenth century, and probably toward its end. The Paris of 1850 was one of artisans and shopkeepers.[26] Even Zola's Paris was said to be limited to these groups, after administration, finance, and culture.[27] Clothing, luxury articles, and printing are explicable in these terms. By 1959, however, the Paris district, consisting of Seine, Seine-et-Oise, Seine-et-Marne, and five communes of Oise, had 7,800,000 persons, 17 percent of the population of France in 2.3 percent of the territory; 275 persons per hectare, as contrasted with 149 in Moscow, 109 in London, and 99 in New York;

[24] See above, Chapter 8.
[25] See George, *La Ville*, p. 97; Carrère and Dugrand, *La Région méditerranéenne* (1960), pp. 7, 49.
[26] George, p. 122.
[27] Gravier, *Paris et le désert français*, p. 53.

83 percent of the newspapers and magazines; 66 percent of the men of letters; 71 percent of the salaried workers in insurance; 51 percent of the salaried personnel in banks; 42 percent of the students; 25 percent of the functionaries; not to mention 77 percent of the French production of optical goods; 67 percent of automobiles; 60 percent of aircraft (after 25 years of dispersal activities); 55 percent of the electrical-goods industry; and 44 per cent of chemicals. In 1801 Paris was six times the smallest department in France in population; in 1946, 62 times.[28]

Two points of interest arise in the centralization process. For one, Gravier asserts that the centralization of banking was less sharp than other functions and points to the growth of the Crédit Lyonnais, founded in 1863, and its centralization in 1918.[29] Morazé regards the centripetal process as having been sped by the Bank of France, which shut down regional credits in 1930, an action on which I have already commented.[30] Neither point seems justified. Centralization in banking goes back at least to the campaign of the Bank of France for monopoly of the note issue, acquired in 1848, and Bouvier dates the shift of focus of the Crédit Lyonnais from Lyon to Paris as 1869, six years after its founding and four years after the establishment of the Paris branch of the bank. Henri Germain's first wife, the daughter of a Lyonnais silk family, died in 1867. In 1869 he married a Parisian lady and took up residence in the capital. In 1871 the two branches of Lyon and Paris were of equal importance. In 1879 the Paris branch was greatly enlarged. By 1882, after the crash of the Union Générale in Lyon, the Paris manager became the director general, ranking ahead of the Lyon manager.[31] The shift was foreshadowed in 1879 by the request of the Beziers branch to deal with Paris directly, rather than through Lyon, and by the fact that Henri Germain did not visit Lyon once during 1881.[32]

A point of significance concerns the engineering industries which Gravier asserts were established in Paris in the 1890s, and developed there especially during World War I.[33] The explanation is that entrepreneurs liked living conditions in the metropolis, which also possessed a transport network, a supply of trained labor, and proximity to the market. Any pull to the steel centers of the north and east was

[28] *Le Monde*, February 15–16, 1959; Gravier, p. 125.
[29] Gravier, p. 20.
[30] Morazé, *La France bourgeoise* (1952), p. 194. See above, Chapter 3. Note that the regional banks organized to resist the centralization process in 1904. See Pose, *La Monnaie* (1942), II, 484.
[31] Bouvier, *Le Crédit Lyonnais* (1961), esp. part 2, chap. iv, "The Two-Headed Bank."
[32] Labasse, *Les Capitaux et la région* (1955), p. 443; Bouvier, p. 275.
[33] Gravier, pp. 53, 56, 169.

neutralized by the danger of war in that direction.[34] The Upper Loire exerted some attraction, to which Berliet at Lyon responded;[35] and the sober workers of the Franche-Comté helped Peugeot flourish there.[36] But Gravier believes that there was a policy of urban and industrial concentration, though he produces no evidence to support it. The armament industry was located at the center,[37] as was the "growing point" represented by the automobile industry.

Unfortunately, Gravier has his facts wrong about automobiles. There was no observable concentration before 1914, when there were 200 producers. Less than 40 were situated in Paris; the rest, except for Bollée at Le Mans, were in the north and east.[38] The war changed the situation, to be sure. The number of firms shrank to 85, but three had 48 percent of the output; and 70 percent of the total production was in Paris. Mossé attributes this to proximity to the centers of administrative decision in a period of state control. Renault and Citroën, especially, adopted mass production methods in Paris, with the benefit of large state orders and state credit.[39] But after 1919 new firms entered the industry again in the provinces. By 1926 the number of producers had risen to 150; and Paris had only 48 percent of the firms (though a higher proportion of output). It was the boom but especially the depression, with its mergers and failures, which shrank the number of firms to 100 in 1929, 27 in 1935, and 17 in the postwar period. The small firms outside Paris went under, and when a big firm like Citroën

---

[34] Nistri and Prêcheur, *La Région du Nord et Nord-Est* (1959), p. 133. They put it negatively, since they try to explain why the basic iron and steel industry of Lorraine did not push forward into vertical integration. "Lorraine did not interest the Nord and the Midi. At the end of the century . . . companies bought concessions and factories, but they did not push their investments and above all they organized no integration. It is not excluded that the frontier position of Lorraine contributed to the limiting of industries of transformation."

[35] See Labasse and Laferrère, *La Région lyonnaise* (1960), pp. 137–38, who explain that a number of early automotive manufacturers located in Lyon beginning in 1888, but that only Berliet made good. The others failed because they were artisans of talent, creators of high novelty who failed to go in for mass production. Berliet today, with 12,000 workers, deals with 369 separate suppliers comprising 18,000 workers.

[36] The mechanical industries of Belfort and Montbéliard, which embrace Peugeot at Sochaux, are regarded as an extension of those in Haute-Alsace after the Treaty of Frankfort. See Blanc, Juillard, Ray, and Rochefort, *Les Régions de l'Est* (1960), p. 29. But Peugeot got its start making steel frames for the crinoline hoop skirts of the Second Empire, before it moved into umbrella frames, bicycles, and eventually automobiles, and was located at Sochaux as early as 1810 (Sédillot, *Peugeot*, p. 45). It is interesting to observe that Peugeot attempted to move to the steel and coal of Lille and to manufacture trucks there, but the branch failed to flourish.

[37] For a map of the armament industry's concentration in Paris, see Gravier, *Décentralisation* (1954), p. 131.

[38] Mossé, *Localisation dans l'industrie automobile* (1956), pp. 19, 21.

[39] *Ibid.* Peugeot also benefited from state orders and finance, but in lesser degree.

became overextended, it was rescued (by Michelin). The economic and geographic concentration was the result not of policy but of the depression.[40]

Beginning in the 1930s, a policy of decentralization was adopted. In 1935 and especially in 1938, steps were taken to spread the armament industry to the west and southwest of Paris.[41] More than one plant may also have been established or moved out of Paris, to escape the Front Populaire.[42] But the real discontinuity came during the war. The division of France into occupied and unoccupied zones required initiative outside of Paris.[43] Moreover, the geographers became acutely conscious of the paralyzing effects of Paris on the rest of the country, and they produced a series of studies in support of a more active policy of regional economic management, especially decentralization.[44] The attraction of Paris for economic vitality and brains has by no means been destroyed. But while local talent is still being seduced to the capital,[45] and some regions remain unattractive for private investment, expansion is now most rapid in areas far from Paris — Nice, Annecy, Grenoble[46] — and the economic awakening has affected a number of cities in the Paris basin which previously had been overwhelmed by the center.[47]

[40] Ibid., p. 25.

[41] Gravier, Paris et le désert français, p. 95. Sixty-two firms and 15,000 workers were affected. One city which particularly benefited from airplanes was Toulouse (ibid., p. 163).

[42] Gouhier, Naissance d'une grande cité (1953), p. 76. Renault bought land in Le Mans in 1920–1922, but started to build there only after the sit-down strikes of 1936 at Billancourt near Paris.

[43] Gravier, Paris et le désert français, p. 96.

[44] Ministère de l'Économie Nationale, Rapports sur la décongestion (1945), vols. 1–6.

[45] Labasse, Les Capitaux et la région, p. 500, notes that the head offices of three firms moved to Paris from Lyon during the single year 1950, though the president of one continued to live in Lyon (p. 493). Some offset to this continued centralization was received through the establishment of a number of regional branch offices of national firms in Lyon.

[46] See Labasse, ibid., pp. 339, 455, 500.

[47] George and Randet, La Région parisienne (1959), p. 156, argue that while Gravier was wrong in asserting that Paris blighted all of France — for example, not Lyon or Lille — he was right for the distance of 200 kilometers around Paris. This region was strongly stimulated by the policy measures taken by the government after 1950. George and Randet observe the growth in such places as Orléans, Chartres, Reims, Châlons-sur-Marne, Amiens (p. 157). Gravier recognizes the renaissance of Châlons-sur-Marne (Décentralisation, p. 324), but asserts that Reims, where the woolen industry declined from 18,000 to 8,000 between 1896 and 1931 had been overwhelmed by Paris and repeated invasions, lacked the local initiative of Lille, Grenoble, and Strasbourg, and exhibited an atmosphere of individualism and dullness. Reims established a Committee of Studies and Improvement in 1943, but for ten years the organization for local planning grew rather chaotically. See Labasse, La Planification régionale (1956–60), p. 153. See also Carrère and Dugrand, La Région méditerranéenne, p. 143, who complain

How far centralization in Paris has been reversed, and the extent to which this is the consequence of policy or "natural forces," take us beyond the period of our interest. The hydrocephalic growth of Paris was taken seriously during the war, and legislation was enacted in 1950 to direct the location of plants outside Paris. Prohibitions on investment in Paris and incentives to investment farther afield were strengthened in 1955, when they began to take effect.[48] But greater mobility on roads contributed to the revival of the vitality of small towns,[49] and the change in attitudes toward family, consumption, and economic expansion was accompanied by, or gave rise to, a renewal of local initiative.

REGIONAL DEVELOPMENT

Outside of Paris not all regions grew at exactly the same rate, and France is said to suffer not only from the dominance of Paris but also from regional imbalance. The north and northeast have prospered relatively to the west and south. Twenty-six of ninety departments, all north and east save five, have 65 percent of the French production, whereas sixty-three departments with much more than half the area of France have less than 35 percent.[50] Average income per active member of the labor force varies from 160 percent of the French average in Paris and the Nord, to less than half that level in Brittany and the far southwest. A line from Rouen to Marseilles leaves what André Philip has called dynamic France to the north and east, static France to the west and south.[51] Lerner and Gorden say that geographic lines of this sort have no validity and that the real difference between dynamic and static France is between the urban areas and the rural.[52] The Economic Commission for Europe's study of regional imbalance, however, makes it clear that the shaded areas of Marseilles, Toulouse, Nantes, and St. Étienne to the west and south of the line have a gross industrial product per head of only 85 to 100 percent of the French average, as contrasted with more than 160 for Paris and the Nord.[53]

As indicated earlier, economists know relatively little about the interregional communication of growth. Perroux has a theory of *pôles*

---

that two thirds of the first 207 factories receiving the assistance of the Fonds National de Développement were located within 200 kilometers of Paris.

[48] See Faucheux, *La Décentralisation industrielle* (1959).

[49] Gravier, *Paris et le désert français*, p. 113. In the United States, the automobile is accused of destroying the village.

[50] INSEE, *L'Espace économique française* (1955), p. 51 and map 74.

[51] Quoted by Lerner and Gorden in "Static and Dynamic France," unpublished manuscript (1960), p. 11.

[52] *Ibid., passim.*

[53] United Nations, *Economic Survey for Europe in 1954*, map 5, p. 183.

de croissance, or motor industries, but little has been done to give it concrete form. Gravier is persuaded that large public works have no power to stimulate local growth and may succeed only in depopulating an area.[54] Extractive industry has no multiplier effect, and heavy industry in the first stage has no motive capacity and only local significance.[55] The economic geographers of the Lyon area are negative on the chemical industry. Chemical companies dominate but do not stimulate.[56] Capital-intensive and requiring little labor but cheap land, they build in the country, move their head offices and research laboratories to the city, and contribute little to economic growth.[57] And small-scale labor-intensive industry around Lyon[58] and geographically poor regions like the Massif Central [59] have both been termed zones or poles of repulsion for industry.[60]

There is less agreement on what constitutes a *pôle de croissance* or growing point. Electric power and irrigation[61] are singled out by Gravier, along with metallic mining, which is better than extractive mining but not absolutely good, and automobiles, that excellent industry. Clothing is good, but not shoes. The best industries for growth are those with large intellectual and small capital requirements. The existence of a university is an important element in the growth of an area and helps to explain the success of Grenoble and Caen.[62]

These generalizations rest on a narrow factual basis. Extractive industry did stimulate economic growth in the north in the nineteenth century, and iron and steel production has led to the development of engineering industries in Birmingham, Sheffield, the Ruhr, and Pitts-

---

[54] *Paris et le désert français,* p. 150.

[55] *Ibid.,* pp. 161, 163, 165. Coal used to have power to stimulate, but has lost it.

[56] Labasse and Laferrère, *La Région lyonnaise,* p. 137.

[57] Labasse, *Les Capitaux et la région,* p. 493. Note that the chemical industry was induced to locate in the Lyon area by the existence of the silk industry, which attracted both dyestuffs and artificial fiber (p. 473).

[58] *Ibid.,* p. 496.

[59] Gravier, *Paris et le désert français,* p. 262.

[60] Estienne and Joly, *La Région du centre* (1961), p. 8. The Center suffers from its position with the headwaters of various rivers flowing away from it in all directions and natural routes skirting around it. The economic and demographic forces there are centrifugal rather than centripetal.

[61] Gravier, p. 148. But note that it is the delivery, not the production of cheap electricity, which is attractive. C. A. Colliard notes in his introduction to Lefèbvre, *Localisations industrielles* (1960), p. xv, that the French Alps lost their original advantage in cheap electricity after 1930 when techniques of distant transmission of electricity improved. Lefèbvre cites (p. 120) a report that the distant transport of electricity at 225,000 volts is still more expensive than the transport of an equivalent amount of coal of good quality, though cheaper than coal of poor quality. Note that the southwest has not benefited from the late development of hydroelectric power in the Pyrenees.

[62] Gravier, pp. 162, 165, 167, 169, 173.

burgh, if not in Lorraine. The notion that clothing is a growth leader evidently has the matter backwards; the industry is market-oriented and attracted to centers of population and communication. One could criticize the fine-spun argument about electricity; suggest that the remarks about automobiles fail to explain why the industry failed to spread everywhere, and particularly in Lyon, St. Étienne, Le Mans; raise the question of why Poitiers, a university town, is so underdeveloped industrially. Gravier deserves commendation for his courage in breaking away from the customary French generalization about the necessity for large firms, for supporting the establishment of small firms which contribute to regional growth both by growing separately and by peeling off cadres that form new companies.[63] But if such firms are largely intellectual-intensive and have limited capital content, there is no reason why they should fructify the local area. The cadres can remove to Paris.[64] The general-equilibrium argument that applies when factors are assumed to be immobile can be turned inside out when interregional factor mobility is permitted.

The fact is that regional analysis can shed very little light on the development problem. Development once started is likely to keep on going. The north had known intensive activity in France for several centuries and was the growth leader of the nineteenth century until the 1890s. It benefited particularly from the discovery of coal in 1847, which quintupled production in twenty-five years. At the beginning of the twentieth century, coal production amounted to 28 million tons, or two thirds of French production. The coal companies had no interest in merging with steel or in taking advantage of the growth of Lorraine steel after 1890. Where these firms wanted vertical integration in coal, they had to seek interests in Belgium, Lorraine, or, like the Lorraine steel plants, in Germany. In coal, the Nord became a center of protectionism. The urbanization process was one of finding shelter for workers — often hovels, including first caves, later company housing — rather than the gradual evolution of ancient administrative cities. Education, sanitation, and housing lagged well behind the French average, and infant mortality was higher in the city than in the country, unlike the rest of France.[65] Here was little of the civilizing urbanity which Lerner and Gorden consider fundamental to growth

[63] *Ibid.*, p. 175.

[64] See Lebréton, "Une Expérience de la dispersion industrielle dans l'électro-chimie" (1946), p. 65, who states that Ugine, the company whose experience he describes, has difficulty retaining its cadres of administrators and research staff when they become too old for mountain climbing and skiing, bored with the monotony and austerity of the mountains, and concerned with the schooling of their children.

[65] See Nistri and Prêcheur, *La Région du Nord et Nord-Est*, pp. 85ff.

or, apart from Lille, of the intellectual vigor sought by Gravier. The Pas de Calais was capable of growing in coal output up to World War I, but general economic development did not occur until the economic and social pattern had been broken up by the war.[66]

Lorraine's growth has its roots in phosphoric iron ore and the Thomas process, after allowance for the response to 1870 and local financing and capital imports. What prevented the steel industry here from going forward into engineering industries? It was some distance from markets in France. Basic Bessemer started out with a bad reputation, as in Britain. Its frontier position may have limited investment by Paris financiers. After the loss of Strasbourg, there was no real cultural center. Strasbourg was not replaced by the "mushroom towns" of Nancy and Metz, nor Mulhouse in textiles by Epinal. Nistri and Prêcheur believe that the natural steel market of the area lay to the north and east rather than to the west. In addition, and despite active recruiting of labor in the countryside and immigration, there was a shortage of labor. Refugees from the lost provinces of Alsace-Lorraine strove to get away from the border.

One may ask why Lyon, Marseilles, Toulouse, Bordeaux, or Nantes did not give rise to spreading growth in the local region, responding and contributing to the growth of Paris, the Nord, and Lorraine. Toulouse, Bordeaux, and Nantes were too far away, and were connected with the rest of France and with each other (except for the Midi Canal between Toulouse and Bordeaux) mostly through Paris. Lyon and Marseilles did respond and contribute to national impulses, and the former played an important regional role. But the impulses petered out against the Jura, the Alps, and the Massif Central.

Regional disequilibrium, of which so much is made by the Economic Commission for Europe, can be regarded as desirable when it serves as a means of communicating progress in one area to another. The rise

---

[66] Ariès sketches a population history of the Black Country of the Pas de Calais, which, for the period prior to World War I, is strikingly reminiscent of the bidonvilles of underdeveloped countries today (*Populations françaises*, 1948, pp. 202–263). The town center was not the church or the Hotel de Ville but the company office. Twenty thousand inhabitants of a single community were not organized into specialized occupations, exchanging goods and services: all were miners, with one class, one mode of life, and one language, the argot of the mine. Life was comparable to that in the army, in which the individual loses himself in the group to such an extent that emigration is impossible, for the individual would feel uprooted elsewhere. Within the family, life was bestial and resulted in a high birth rate. This existence was broken up by World War I. Thereafter the demand for labor in other lines and other areas created the opportunity; the destruction of group life let the separate miners take advantage of it. Immigration from abroad was necessary to staff the mines. The local French went into storekeeping, bakeries, hairdressing. The area lost its primitive character, and the birth rate settled down nearer the French average.

of Paris or the Nord creates opportunities for business in other areas, both in demand for their production and as sources of supply of new or cheaper inputs. But the gap must not be too wide — either in distance or in levels of production. If it is wide, it is easier to move out, to migrate to Paris; but if migration is not possible among the various regions of France, the stimulus is not fruitful. Without entrepreneurship the Midi cannot provide the products which a larger market in the Nord would accept, nor can it make use of the cheaper labor.

BRITISH DISTRESSED AREAS

I have not studied the distressed areas of Britain and can only suggest that the regional model there would be one of highly specialized resources which experience difficulty in transforming after an abrupt reduction in demand. It is likely that the transformation could be effected slowly in ordinary circumstances, as depreciation allowances were withdrawn from local investment and youth was redirected to industries elsewhere. A sizable structural change, however, would require a discontinuous change in demand to draw labor away and to induce entrepreneurs to abandon plants that made losses but could make a contribution to overhead costs. Such a change came during World War II, cleaning up the persistent unemployment in the distressed areas in coal, which had proved so unyielding during the prosperous 1930s.

The difference between the distressed areas of Britain and the backward regions of France is obvious. The former had transformed once, but found difficulty in retransformation. The latter had never really been caught up in the process of specialization, investment, and technical change. The analytical distinction may not be important for policy: the backward or depressed areas may have to be liquidated through emigration or stimulated through measures for attracting investment. But there will be differences. One will have a certain amount of labor skill and entrepreneurial experience, along with a pattern of habits that may inhibit transformation; the other will lack experience but, if it can be at all trained to the industrial pattern, may be capable of moving in the appropriate directions.

CHAPTER 12

FOREIGN TRADE

Of the many possible interrelations between foreign trade and economic development, most of which could be illustrated by the economic history of France and Britain in the last century, this chapter can deal with but a few. It is limited, first, to some simple models[1] in which expansion and contraction of exports and imports as affected by foreign demand, capital movements, tariffs, and the removal of tariffs may be said to have altered the rate of domestic development; and second, much more briefly, to some criticism of French foreign trade for its rigid structure and its concentration of exports on foodstuffs and raw materials. The theme of the first and major portion is this: if expanding exports or imports, and contracting exports or imports, can either promote or slow down economic growth, it is inappropriate for the economic historian to assert that such-and-such a change in growth was caused by such-and-such a change in foreign trade, without specifying the circumstances that limited the possible relationships to the one he picked.

EXPORTS AS A LEADING SECTOR

The first model is one in which expanding foreign trade stimulates growth. A rise in exports leads to an increase in national output. This is an example of what Rostow calls "a leading sector." [2] An economist may express some surprise that the relatively straightforward statement of this relationship, with a small amount of historical illustration, should be set forth as a discovery in a 1960 issue of the *Economic History Review*, since the idea is one of long familiarity.[3]

[1] In limiting the discussion to simple models, I exclude a complex interrelationship made familiar by the work of Cairncross, Clark, Lewis, and Rostow, among others, in which capital exports lead to expanding production overseas, improved terms of trade for the leading country, and increased real income in the latter. I have expressed some skepticism on these scores in *The Terms of Trade* (1956), esp. chap. vi.

[2] *Stages of Economic Growth* (1960), pp. 52ff. It is not necessary, of course, to adopt the "stages" schema to attach importance in growth to leading sectors.

[3] See Berrill, "International Trade and the Rate of Economic Growth" (1960). This will emerge particularly from the discussion of its inverse: that a decline in

But the connections between foreign trade and growth are not always made clear. The pure types are several. First, in a full-employment economy, a favorable change in demand abroad or an innovation reducing costs at home may expand exports, improve the terms of trade (whether net barter or single factoral), and enlarge the gains from trade. This will increase income and in turn lead to still higher incomes, through higher savings, more investment, and, with a constant capital coefficient, more output. Trade is tied in with a Harrod-Domar growth model, and more trade means more growth.

Second, unemployed or underemployed resources may exist in the economy. In Perroux's phrase, the economy is disarticulated. If exports are the modern efficient sector, expanding exports allow added resources to be drawn away from the underemployed and low-productivity sector to occupations where they are more productive. This is in addition to the gains from trade. There may or may not be an improvement in the terms of trade. But even at the old terms of trade, with increased volume the gains have enlarged. A variant of this second submodel is contained in the case where entrepreneurship is lacking, investment decisions are few, and the increase in exports calls attention to an investment opportunity. This is Hirschman's "backward" linkage, which can take place either in the export industry itself or in the industries that supply it.[4]

Third, in the industries with decreasing-cost curves, export markets may enable a reduction in real costs to take place, an increase in real income, and so on. This could be said to be a variant of the first submodel, but one in which the extent of the comparative advantage, or its existence, depends on access to the foreign market.

Last in the list, although doubtless there are further possibilities, expanding exports may put pressure on domestic resources and lead to cost-reducing innovations. This is perhaps a different type of linkage from that discussed by Hirschman—he was interested mainly in investment decisions rather than in technological change. But the difference can be narrow if the rise in exports induces an entrepreneur to expand capacity and make use of known but previously unutilized techniques. In the pure form, the pressure is to devise new cost-reducing processes. This submodel is particularly relevant to those general models of growth which emphasize the importance of technical change, as contrasted with capital expansion.

Exports have been a leading sector in British growth on at least

exports, or even in their rate of expansion, can slow down economic growth. For an explicit treatment of three models in which foreign trade is a leading, lagging, and balancing sector, see my *Economic Development* (1958), chap. xiv.

[4] See Hirschman, *Strategy of Economic Development* (1958), chap. xiv.

two occasions since the Industrial Revolution: in the last two decades of the eighteenth century and in the 1850s and 1860s. In the latter period, they performed the same role in France. Phyllis Deane and H. J. Habakkuk state that the most satisfying interpretation of British experience in the Industrial Revolution is that the sudden and important acceleration in exports was responsible for British growth.[5] They observe that, even without cotton textiles and iron goods, the volume of exports increased by half between 1779–1783 to 1789–1793, and by one third again to 1799–1803. The expansion resulted from the fortunes of war, which took the American colonies and then France out of world markets. In the important cotton-textile industry, Smelser finds that the heavy foreign demand created the "disturbance" that leads, in his system, to industrial change.[6]

But our interest really begins with the 1850s. Schlote groups the forties and fifties together in calculating his average rates of growth. For exports it was 5.3 percent per annum, for imports 4.5.[7] I the relationship between total foreign trade (exports plus imports) and national income be measured throughout the nineteenth century, and put in terms of 1913 as a standard, it can be seen that foreign trade is a steadily rising proportion of national income throughout the period. The index of relation rises very rapidly in the fifties and sixties — from 36.8 in 1840–1849 to 55.9 in 1850–1859 and 78.6 in 1860–1869. A similar index of relationship between total overseas trade and industrial production did not rise so consistently throughout the century, but shows big increases, from 55.4 to 67.1 and 75.6, over the same decades.[8] The period is well summed up by Leone Levi, who said in

---

[5] "The Take-Off in Britain" (1960), paper submitted to the September 1960 meetings of the International Economic Association at Konstanz. Professor Habakkuk has kindly shown me the paper in typescript.

[6] *Social Change in the Industrial Revolution* (1959), p. 62.

[7] *British Overseas Trade* (1952), p. 42. It is worth setting down the series, beginning with 1840–1860:

Period	Imports	Exports
1840–1860	4.5%	5.3%
1860–1870	4.4	4.4
1870–1890	2.9	2.1
1890–1900	2.6	0.7
1900–1913	1.5	3.3

An indication of the greater importance of the fifties over the forties is given by the figures (from Habakkuk, "Free Trade and Commercial Expansion," 1940, p. 803) that export values increased 40 percent in the 1840s, 90 percent in the 1850s, 47 percent in the 1860s, and 12 percent in the 1870s.

[8] Schlote, *ibid.*, pp. 49, 51. These are current values, but the index of relationship on a deflated basis gives 43.2, 60.0, and 71.9 for the forties, fifties, and sixties, respectively.

1880: "The increase of commerce of the United Kingdom during the last one hundred years is something wonderful." [9]

The parallel development in France can be adequately demonstrated with value figures differently centered, and for exports and imports combined. These show the same pattern. Foreign trade grew at 45 percent in the decade 1836–1845, 46 percent in 1846–1855, 111 percent in 1856–1865, and 48 percent in 1866–1875.[10]

The factors responsible for this expansion in foreign trade are well known. Factory legislation and railway investment in Britain led to productivity changes, increased specialization, and lower costs. Gold discoveries in California and Australia, falling ocean-transport costs, and rapidly expanding British overseas investment spurred the expansion of exports. Loans were made for railroads in India, to Turkey and Egypt in connection with the Crimean War, to Egypt again during the cotton famine, and to the United States for railroads. Total British loans during the period were roughly £1,000 million, of which two fifths were directed to the empire.[11] French foreign investments went from something like 2,000 million francs in 1850 to 16,000 (nominally 22,000) in 1880.[12] Since a major portion of the difference between the actual and nominal figures for 1880 was write-offs for losses, gross lending over the period approached 20 billion francs or £800 million. French loans in this period went largely to Germany, Austria, Spain, and Switzerland and into railroads and banking. But French firms invested substantially in Egypt and Turkey during the cotton famine.[13]

There is a temptation to exaggerate the importance of gold and to ascribe some of the growth to internal monetary expansion based on increases in reserves.[14] The direct effects are more obvious and were short-lived. Australia leapt from seventh place among Britain's customers in 1850 to second in 1853, before the slump of the following year. But these effects were offset in considerable part by the Indian absorption of silver. British gold reserves did not rise until 1866, when, after Indian cotton growing had waxed and waned, India

[9] *History of British Commerce*, p. 540.

[10] Marczewski, "La Croissance de l'économie française, 1700–1957" (1959), table 10.

[11] Habakkuk, "Free Trade and Commercial Expansion," p. 788.

[12] Cameron, *France and the Economic Development of Europe, 1800–1914* (1961), pp. 78ff.

[13] See Landes, *Bankers and Pashas* (1958). Landes remarks on the differences between French and British lending, the former only to a small extent, the latter largely an outgrowth of trade relations (p. 56, n. 2).

[14] See Marjolin, *Prix, monnaie et production* (1941). The rate of production to stocks reached 4 percent in 1852 and then declined steadily to between 1 and 2 percent in 1890. It was still over 2 percent in 1870 (p. 185).

learned to import goods as well as specie.[15] The French role was to convert the overvalued gold exported by the producers and received for the British net balance into undervalued silver shipped to the East.[16] But Indian hoarding must be scored against new production.

Which of the various versions of the model applies? In Britain the fourth, in France, the first. This answer is a loose one. Reallocation from agriculture to industry was prominent in Britain, and technological progress stood out in France. But the change from wrought iron to steel, and the Bessemer and Siemens-Martin processes, were stimulated by the surging demand for railroad equipment and the bottlenecks it produced in Britain,[17] and France experienced the most substantial reallocation of underemployed agricultural labor to urban construction, railroad construction, retail distribution, and manufacturing of the entire nineteenth century.[18]

There were two further periods for France when exports may be said to have been a leading sector: 1896–1913 and 1921–1929. The stimuli were very different. Immediately before World War I, and despite the tariffs of 1892, 1902, and 1910, exports rose for three reasons: new industries, especially iron ore, but to a lesser extent automobiles and chemicals; colonial preferences, especially for textiles; and the widely dispersed influence of heavy capital exports. The first decade of the interwar period, on the other hand, is divided into two parts: up to 1926, exports were stimulated by capital flight; after the *de facto* stabilization of the franc, when the private movement of capital reversed itself, exports continued to grow in real terms because of the undervaluation of the currency. But in both instances, the rate of expansion of the volume of exports exceeded that of industrial production.

It is a substantial step from the high British rates of growth in exports and in the total economy between 1850 and 1875 to the claim that the slowing down of the growth rate in exports slowed down the growth rate in the economy. Two variants of such a thesis have been put forward, one by J. R. Meyer, another by W. A. Lewis.[19]

Meyer uses an input-output model because he wants to explain why the rate of growth of national income fell more than the rate of growth

[15] Habakkuk, pp. 769, 775.

[16] See Hughes, *Fluctuations in Trade, Industry and Finance* (1960), pp. 247ff.

[17] See Habakkuk, p. 802, and, by the same author, "Basic Conditions of Economic Progress" (1955), esp. p. 154.

[18] The percentages of the active labor force engaged in agriculture, fishing, and forestry fell from 63 percent in 1845 to 52 percent in 1856 and 50 percent in 1866.

[19] Meyer, "Input-Output Approach to the Influence of Exports" (1955). Lewis foreshadows his theory in *The Theory of Economic Growth* (1955), pp. 279, 345, and develops it systematically in "International Competition in Manufactures" (1957).

of exports. With it he is able to take into account indirect effects, as well as direct. He shows that if exports had continued to grow to 1907 at the same rate that they had from 1854 to 1872, the rate of growth would have been 4.1 percent a year instead of the 1.75 percent actually attained and the 3.05 percent rate for 1854–1872. This result, it is claimed, tends to confirm the hypothesis that if the growth rate of exports had been maintained, the United Kingdom could have maintained its rate of growth in industrial production.[20] The technique assumes that the pattern of exports would remain unchanged and that textile exports would have grown to £493 million in 1907 instead of the actual figure of £129 million; iron, steel, engineering, and ships to £205 million instead of £95 million; and total exports to £1,403 million instead of the actual £477 million.

As Meyer recognizes, there are conceptual difficulties with the analysis. It is arbitrary to regard exports as the only independent variable, with consumption, capital formation, and government expenditure dependent upon it. Second, the use of fixed coefficients of input-output analysis, while appropriate perhaps for short-run changes, excludes the possibility of expansion through increases in technical efficiency and assumes unlimited expansive capacity as the only source of growth. Meyer attempts to extricate himself from this dilemma by asserting that natural resources cannot have held down growth because of the possibility of imports; but this result is a distortion of input-output relationships and undermines the validity of the technique.

Most significant of all, however, is the assumption that growth is possible with a fixed pattern of demand as well as of inputs. The law of diminishing returns in consumption ensures that a given bill of goods cannot expand at a constant rate either indefinitely or over decades. The "law" of diminishing foreign trade asserts that as a country's income rises beyond a certain point, foreign trade will form a smaller and smaller proportion of national income because of the high income elasticity of demand for services which are less traded than movable commodities.[21] This law is by no means fully established, and, in any event, the proportion of foreign trade to national income in Britain and France rose after 1872, or at least from the low of the Great Depression.[22] But in no case must a given component of income

[20] Meyer, p. 17.

[21] See Deutsch and Eckstein, "National Industrialization and the Declining Share of the International Economic Sector" (1961).

[22] One can choose among a variety of estimates with somewhat different results. See two series in Deutsch and Eckstein, *ibid.*, Schlote/Quittner–Bertolasi which shows a peak at 1910–13, and the Schlote/Prest figure which gives 1870–79 as slightly higher, 59.9 as against 58.8. Kuznets in *Six Lectures on Economic*

follow an exponential growth pattern to make exponential growth of income possible: it is enough that sufficient numbers of new industries enter into production, whether for home demand or foreign, and follow the normal Gompertz growth curve, first rising rapidly at ever increasing growth rates and then at decreasing rates until the series levels off at an asymptote. The world demand for exports is not infinitely elastic at existing prices, any more than the supply of British exports may be. The input-output technique may provide a useful *reductio ad absurdum:* British growth could not have been achieved through expanding exports and an unchanged pattern. It would have produced a ridiculously large amount of textile exports, in terms both of production and of consumption abroad. Therefore, more demand would have to spring up somewhere else, for example, in the home market, and resources would have had to be transferred to it. But this cannot be used to prove, or even lend support to, a hypothesis that the falling rate of growth of exports was responsible for the falling rate of economic growth.[23]

Lewis' model relies on a less direct mechanism. Exports are needed not for their direct stimulation of investment and other spending, but to prevent the deflation that might otherwise occur because of an adverse balance of payments. In a country with a narrow resource base, buoyant domestic investment must be accompanied by expansion of exports in order to finance the imports of raw materials and foodstuffs generated by that home investment. If such exports are not forthcoming, deflation is required to balance the international accounts, and investment and growth get cut back.[24]

Such a model is a perfectly logical one and applies very well to, say, India, or even Britain today. How relevant is it, however, to 1850–1913? Lewis anticipates a counterargument on this score when he brushes aside a number of excuses, including one which points to the balance-of-payments surplus of the period, the slow rate of

---

Growth (1959), p. 101, has a substantial decline from 1880–89 to 1900–09, but uses a somewhat different definition. His French figures, however, show a very slight rise. In *The Terms of Trade,* p. 301, I calculated a ratio for France of exports to national income: 1872, 16 percent; 1900, 15 percent, 1913, 20 percent. For the United Kingdom for the same dates, the percentages were 27, 16, and 22.

[23] Coppock, "The Climacteric of the 1890s" (1956), blames the decline in the rate of growth directly on the fall in the rate of growth of exports, but the connection is capital accumulation (p. 27). He ascribes the decline in the rate of growth of exports to the adverse terms of trade of primary producers, along with the industrialization of Western Europe, the United States tariffs in importing countries, and price discrimination. In his "Causes of the Great Depression" (1916) Coppock lays less stress on exports, which cannot explain the depression in the United States and Germany (p. 221), and more on the decline in housing in the 1880s (p. 228).

[24] "International Competition in Manufactures," p. 585.

growth, and the limited need for imports up to 1913. But he never really does dispose of this counterargument. He suggests that the direct model may possibly apply instead — that the slow growth rate of exports was responsible for the slow growth rate of income.[25] This is not rebuttal but abandonment of the initial position. And it is hard to see how he can stand by the indirect model: interest rates were low, capital was exported, raw materials and foodstuffs were available on favorable terms of trade. Lewis even points out that the volume of manufactured imports grew faster between 1883 and 1913, at 3.4 percent, than those of raw materials (1.8 percent) or foodstuffs (2.0 percent).[26] Such deflationary pressure as existed in the late 1870s and early 1890s came largely from the decline of world prices, rather than from monetary restraint at home.

Although Lewis' indirect model is not applicable to the British experience from 1875 to 1913, it has the advantage over the direct one of assuming that impulses for growth come from more than one direction. It is in fact the model in which exports play a balancing role to enable home investment to take the lead. If home investment results in a spillover of demand into imports, exports (or foreign borrowing) must grow at some appropriate rate. But it can hardly apply in a capital-lending country where the rate of lending is rising.

DECLINE FROM OVEREXPANDED EXPORTS

The rate of growth of British exports in the last quarter of the nineteenth century was bound to decline. An exporter with 75 percent of the world market in a commodity, as the British had at various times in cotton textiles, iron rails, galvanized iron, tinplate, locomotives, ships, and coal, could not expect to maintain it. New entry will take place into such markets in some of the importing countries themselves, as they industrialize and, as they begin to export, into third markets.

To sustain domestic growth and pay for necessary imports, the country faced with rising industrial competition can follow one of several courses. It can withdraw from the market for standardized commodities, in which foreign competition is likely to emerge first, and upgrade its industry to higher-quality products.[27] Some of this process is automatic, as the domestic consumer with increased income demands an improved product, and as manufacturing inexorably

[25] *Ibid.*, p. 580.
[26] *Ibid.*, p. 585.
[27] For an interesting discussion in detail of the greater competition in the cheaper products, and the necessity to improve quality, see Allen, *Birmingham and the Black Country* (1929), pp. 409, 443.

alters the composition of output to accommodate this change.[28] A second alternative is to pare costs and attempt to hold on to existing markets. A third is to redirect the identical goods at roughly the same costs to new markets, often with the aid of capital exports. To the extent that the third alternative is adopted, it sustains income in the short run. By relieving the pressure for technological change, however, and by building up export markets which in turn must crumble before domestic industrialization and third-country competition, it can be said that the important problem was evaded. It is on this analysis that capital lending and growing commodity exports after 1885 can be regarded as having slowed down the British growth rate. There can be no guarantee, of course, that the growth problem would have been solved if it had been faced. It is argued that expansion of exports in cotton textiles, railway materials, galvanized iron sheets, and tinplate after 1880 postponed the necessity to improve productivity in these areas and slowed down the long-run rate of growth. This assumes that if these exports, and the capital lending which financed them, had not been forthcoming, Britain would have been aware sooner of its technological faltering and taken steps to meet it.

The share of British exports going to the empire declined from roughly 35 percent in the late 1850s to 25 percent in the early 1870s, and then rose to more than 35 percent in the period 1911–1913 (after reaching a peak of 38.5 percent in 1902).[29] The proportion of exports going to agricultural countries, as opposed to industrial, increased gradually from 56.3 in 1854–1857 to 69.6 in 1909–1913.[30] If the rising coal exports to Europe are excluded, to restrict the analysis to finished manufactures, the percentage climbs from 59 to 76.[31]

It may be worthwhile to furnish concrete examples. A revolution in the consumption of canned goods in the United States and the spread of tinned gasoline and kerosene throughout the world led to an increase in the number of canners in the United States — from 97 in 1871 to 411 in 1880 and 886 in 1890 — and produced a boom in tinplate, especially in the period 1875–1880. One hundred new mills were constructed in Britain in 1879 alone. But there was little technological change. Exports from the United Kingdom to the United States rose from 86,000 tons in 1871 to 215,000 tons in 1882 and more than 300,000 in 1890. Then came the McKinley tariff and a collapse of

---

[28] An interesting example is the American automobile, which had more than 75 percent of world markets in the 1920s but in which design "improvements" proceeded at a rate that priced the product out of world markets (to the extent that rising costs did not do so).

[29] Schlote, *British Overseas Trade*, appendix table 20b, pp. 161–162.

[30] *Ibid.*, table 31, p. 82. The figure 38.5 for 1867–1869 is evidently a misprint.

[31] Calculated from table 34, *ibid.*, p. 86.

the American market for British sales. After a difficult period in the
1890s, new markets were found in the Far East, Southeast Asia, India,
and South America. But while the United States made rapid technological progress behind its tariff wall, and ultimately developed an
export capacity, British technology remained stagnant until forced to
convert to hotstrip and cold rolling methods by American export competition after World War I.[32]

The picture is reproduced on a broader canvas in cotton textiles.
The general outline is familiar and need not be sketched, although
Table 22 helps to make it dramatic. Of the expansion from five to

Table 22. Percentage Distribution of Cotton Piece-Good
Exports by Great Britain, 1820–1913

Year	Europe	Turkey, Egypt, Africa	America (excl. U.S.)	U.S.	India	China, Java, etc.	Other
1820	51	4	22	10	6[a]		8
1850	16	14	27	8	23	8	4
1880	8	13	15	2	40	14	8
1900	6	14	14	1	40	18	7
1913	6	14	10	1	42	16	11

[a] Figure for both areas.

Source. For 1820 to 1900, Cd 1761, *British and Foreign Trade and Industry,
1854–1903*, p. 444; for 1913, *Annual Statement of the Trade of the United Kingdom* (1913).

seven billion yards between 1900 and 1913, when Manchester had
its last boom, fully half went to India. The rate of technological advance had slowed down after 1870, and the ring spindle and automatic loom were virtually neglected.[33] But the industry succeeded in
achieving the removal of the Indian 5 percent revenue import in 1882
and the equalization of the excise tax on British and Indian output in
1896.[34] High proportions of a similarly standardized product went to
India in galvanized iron sheets, used in roofing. India took 31 percent
of British exports of galvanized iron sheet, which formed a rising
proportion of total iron and steel exports, and all but 1 percent of such
imports by value came from the United Kingdom.[35] The loss of the

[32] The facts in this paragraph are taken from Minchenton, *British Tinplate Industry* (1957), esp. pp. 51, 55, 63, 80.

[33] Jones, *Increasing Return*, parts 2 and 3; Allen, *British Industries* (1939),
p. 247.

[34] Redford, *Manchester Merchants and Foreign Trade* (1934), chaps. iii and iv.
See also Pares, "The Economic Factors in Empire" (1937), pp. 430–431.

[35] *Annual Statement of the Trade of the United Kingdom*, 1913; Saul, *Studies
in British Overseas Trade* (1960), p. 202.

European and United States rail market in the 1850s and 1860s was also offset by expanding sales in less developed countries. But it is interesting that when British railroads were turning to foreign locomotives, at least for prototypes,[36] heavy exports to Argentina and India took place, assisted by British finance. In Canada, where the borrowers exercised a choice, purchases were financed in London but orders placed in the United States.[37]

The Canadian illustration shows that British capital exports were not tied to merchandise sales. Saul emphasizes that British capital lending assisted exports not so much directly as through stimulating growth and increases in income abroad and through financing multilateral payments. But the bilateral component was high, particularly in India and Latin America. Investment may have played only a small part in financing the sale of cotton textiles to India, but it did contribute crucially to railroad goods.[38] And the spurt of lending to Argentina after 1885 led to an enormous expansion in Argentine imports from Britain.[39] British lending to the faster-growing dominions frequently financed imports of complex capital equipment from the United States and Germany, but this aid to multilateral trading was offset by the impressive French contribution of a similar sort, which doubtless benefited British exports of simple manufactures to borrowers from France.[40]

If capital exports were not consciously adopted to push exports of relatively primitive manufactures, neither was colonial expansion. Exporters strove to keep free trade, and ultimately preferences, in colonial areas, both in France and Britain, but the evidence is strongly against the view that the acquisition of colonies was dictated by the desire to offset constricted markets.[41] In France, moreover, produc-

[36] Saul, *ibid.*, p. 36, reports imports of locomotives after 1898 by the Midland, Great Northern, and Great Central railroads.

[37] Saul, p. 182, notes purchases between 1909 and 1914 of 719 locomotives from the United States and 11 from Britain.

[38] *Ibid.*, pp. 87, 208. Habakkuk claims that in the 1850s the Indian Railway loans went one third for Home charges, one third for wages and administrative expenses, one third for the payment of rails, engines, and ship freight ("Free Trade and Commercial Expansion," p. 799).

[39] See Ferns, "Investment and Trade between Britain and Argentina" (1950).

[40] French loans to tsarist Russia from 1880 to 1913 amounted to 10 billion francs, while total exports amounted only to one tenth of that amount. See White, *French International Accounts* (1933), p. 145. A considerable part of this effect was owing to the fact that Russian loans floated in Paris were used to pay off old debts due in London and Berlin which those markets were unwilling to refund. See Cameron, *ibid.*, pp. 422–424.

[41] Gallagher and Robinson, "The Imperialism of Free Trade" (1953). Young points out (*Portrait of an Age*, 1936, p. 180) that imperialism was a fact of the 1890s, which of course were prosperous. For a contrary Marxist view attributing it to the search for markets to offset domestic underconsumption, see Dobb, *Political Economy and Capitalism* (1937), pp. 227ff.

tion of quality manufactures was not suited for colonial consumption. Apart from cotton textiles, the colonies were more important economically as a source for raw materials than as an outlet for manufactures.[42]

Thus the response to the narrowing of European and American markets[43] was to find new outlets for the same goods and to assist in financing continuously rising exports, both directly and indirectly. There was little attention given to stepping up the rate of innovation, producing new goods, or discovering new and cheaper ways of making old. The Nottingham and Leicester hosiery trades were more lastingly affected by the McKinley tariff than the German, and the same is true of British lace exports as contrasted with those of France, Germany, and Switzerland.[44] The rate of productivity increase declined throughout the economy, whatever the connection to technical change.

If it is assumed that the causation ran from the economy to exports, what factors contributed to the failure to adapt to changing world markets and the attempt to prolong the existing pattern of exports? A wide variety of points has been made. Lewis suggests that British business lost "the irresistible urge to invest"; Williams that the British exporter failed to adapt his product to the foreign market. Some observers blame the merchant system, under which intermediaries prevent the manufacturer from learning exactly what the needs of the customer are, although Marshall defends it. In some markets British standards for domestic sale were of too high a quality for wide foreign appeal.[45]

This is a complex matter, requiring deep analysis of the process of British growth in the late nineteenth century. The quick answer, however, is that great specialization can be achieved only at the cost of flexibility, unless far-reaching and expensive steps are taken to guard against ossification. The British textile industry, and to a lesser degree the rail, galvanized iron sheet, apparel, footwear, and similar export

---

[42] Brunschwig, *L'Impérialisme colonial français* (1960), p. 94.

[43] This must not be regarded as simple protectionism since, behind the German and United States tariff walls, techniques were changing and costs falling. And in such markets as the French from 1860 to 1881, where tariffs were low, the position was not vastly different.

[44] See Saul, *Studies in British Overseas Trade*, pp. 160–161.

[45] Lewis, "International Competition in Manufactures," p. 585. He believes that the British had an "irresistible urge to invest" in cotton textiles and iron, but that it failed to spread to the newer industries. Along with this, the will toward and techniques of exporting are needed. Williams, *Made in Germany* (1896), p. 172. Compare this view of the British exporter in the 1890s with the French banker's letter of 1865, which said that the British dominated the Egyptian market to the extent of 75 percent because they were ready to adapt their products to the tastes of the local population, and lent money generously (Landes, *Bankers and Pashas*, p. 271). On the merchant system, see above, chapter 7.

industries, were highly specialized in production and marketing. They achieved great efficiency for a given set of tastes, income, and technology. It is not clear, however, that the system was readily adaptable to changes in these areas. When a market is lost, it is easier to find new markets for the same goods, made in the same way, than to adapt selling and production techniques, to pare costs, or to modify the product. The manufacturer lacks firsthand knowledge of changes desired by the customer; or the merchant may not know how a new article will suit old users. Perhaps the most striking example of this is found in the widespread hostility of users to basic Bessemer steel as opposed to Siemens-Martin acid. The former, based on British inventions, suited British resources; acid required imported iron ore. Initially hostile to Bessemer, some fabricators turned to cheaper imported supplies at the end of the century, when the domestic industry was slow in producing it. It is entirely possible that, even with direct selling, the manufacturer would have shifted markets rather than altered his product or production techniques. But with the merchant system and its lack of contact between producer and customer, this response seems inevitable.

This is presumably what Robinson meant when he suggested that Britain had been too specialized in the late nineteenth century and that a more balanced allocation of resources between manufacturing and agriculture, with less emphasis on exporting, as in Germany, might have run less risk.[46] Liesner's reply that Britain benefited substantially from cheap food, while Germany devoted an undue proportion of its manpower to agriculture, does not meet the point, insofar as specialization may be deemed highly efficient in the short run but likely to inhibit the power to produce changes or to adapt to change.[47]

Lewis is disposed not to believe that the old country loses by too complete specialization, even though the British case "fits this formula

[46] Robinson, "The Changing Structure of the British Economy" (1954); Saville ("Some Retarding Factors in the British Economy before 1914," 1961, p. 58) is after the same idea when he says that Britain was unable to overcome the handicaps of the early start, obsolescent industries and institutions capable of providing capital to domestic entrepreneurs, because the country was "too prosperous" following the expansion of exports between 1870 and 1914. This expansion, however, coincided with the failure to develop new exports in automobiles, electrical equipment, and dyestuffs.

[47] Liesner, *The Import Dependence of Britain and Western Germany* (1957). At the peak of its world supremacy in shipbuilding, around 1905, Britain was much more efficient than other nations, despite the use of relatively large amounts of backward equipment, owing to the craftsmanship of the British worker and intensive specialization, both in the yards and especially in component manufacturing. But by this time technological leadership was passing to the Scandinavian countries. See Svennilson, *Growth and Stagnation in the European Economy* (1954), p. 155. Innovation in this industry required cooperation between shipowner and builder, as well as between assembler and component manufacturer.

suspiciously well." But his reasons — the balance-of-payments surplus and the assertion that Britain could be as effective as any other country at organizing exports, if it had wanted to[48] — are not convincing. There is no attention paid to the problem of effecting change with highly specialized discrete units that have grown efficient in a given procedure. Saul approaches the end of his studies wondering whether ease of entry in empire markets for textiles and railway materials may not have dulled the senses of many exporters and encouraged concentration in the wrong products. He concludes by listing the benefits derived from the empire's role in multilateral settlements; these still his doubts.[49] However, if the growth process requires continued technological progress and a reallocation of resources to new products, expanding exports in traditional lines may, over time, slow down the rate of growth.

The thesis that the moderate expansion of British exports from 1890 to 1914 slowed down British growth in the long run, and that a further expansion of the same character would have been even worse for British growth, can be tested against the interwar period. In the 1920s the overvaluation of the pound sterling from 1924 to 1931 inhibited exports of coal, textiles, and ships, after the brief postwar boom. The decline of income in the export sector led to massive unemployment and, through the multiplier, to a stagnant economy. But the way was cleared for the renewal of economic expansion in the necessary direction. Housing picked up from 1924, as well as the new light industries on the Great West Road near London in the south, the automobiles, chemicals, and so on, which were to flourish in the 1930s. The process of conversion was painful and necessary. It is impossible to judge whether an exchange rate nearer equilibrium would have encouraged exports from the declining industries and held up their decline more than it would have stimulated demand for the products of the rising industries. The improvement of the terms of trade which came with devaluation in 1931, and the intensification of the depression abroad, made possible the diversion of purchasing power from imports to housing and the newer industries, thereby stimulating growth. But in the 1920s, conditions probably had to get worse before they could get better. To change out of textiles, coal, and shipbuilding would have been impossible as long as these were marginally profitable, no matter how low the average profits compared with returns in other industries. The dogs were too old to learn new tricks except under stern necessity. If this judgment is

[48] Lewis, *The Theory of Economic Growth*, pp. 346–347.
[49] Saul, *Studies in British Overseas Trade*, pp. 220, 229.

correct, the overvaluation of the pound sterling in 1924 may have sped British growth in the long run while it was hurting it at the time.

CHANGES IN IMPORTS AND GROWTH

By analogy with exports, increased imports through reduced tariffs can help or hinder growth, and reduced trade from raised trade barriers is also capable of acting in either direction. Here again there are several models, to limit it only to simple varieties. Among them are the gains-from-trade, in which increased income from increased trade raises the level of income and savings from which the Harrod-Domar compound-interest formula operates; the multiplier-accelerator, which requires the existence of under- or unemployed resources; the infant-industry, where the stimulus of reduced imports and higher prices enables an industry to find a more efficient point on its long-run falling cost curve; the linkage model, where cheap imports of raw materials or equipment stimulate an industry which uses these as inputs; and the competitive model, where imports spur domestic innovation and other cost-reducing activity in the same lines.

Concern here is mostly with France. But the repeal of the Corn Laws assisted British economic growth in the 1850s and 1860s by enlarging the gains from trade. The multiplier-accelerator model does not apply, since an autonomous increase in imports leads to contraction, not expansion, except in the complex version where the increased imports stimulate output abroad and the full foreign repercussion leads to expanded exports. There is, of course, a serious identification problem. Most of the expansion in imports in this period came from rising incomes generated by expanding exports and investment, rather than from the decline in tariffs. But some of the increase in exports may have been induced by the autonomous expansion in imports and the foreign repercussion. It is worth recalling that the induced response does not altogether offset the change in income under the multiplier-accelerator model, although it moderates the income change and ultimately brings it to a halt. It is not the export or import surplus which produces the income change, but the shift in the parameter and the multiplier. It is suggestive of the irrelevance of this model that the import surplus rose in 1847 and 1848 above previous levels but subsided again for the next five years.

Germany and the United States used protection to assist their industries. Protection, Habakkuk says, can either spur an industry to win the home market or dampen the stimulus to change provided by the competition of initiating industries. The former is true of Germany, the latter of France.[50] Import substitution has been characterized as a normal part of the process of growth.[51] But in the French experience tariffs have hurt: "Tariff policy isolated France and accounted more than anything else for the economic stagnation in France in the first half of the nineteenth century." [52] Lhomme attaches particular significance to the three metallurgical groups in Lorraine, Paris, and the Center which resisted the rail imports and, together with the government's hesitations, slowed down French railway building.[53] Habakkuk suggests that Germany's completion of its railway network ten years before France may have been an important factor in accelerating German growth over French.[54]

Nor is it only for the early part of the century that the tariff is blamed for slowing down French growth. There are timing difficulties for the later period. The denunciation of the treaties of the 1870s, the 1881 tariff on grain, and the 1882 one on woolens were on the whole mild preludes to the Méline tariff of 1892 and the subsequent increase of 1910. But economic growth was rapid from 1896 to 1913. Trade more than doubled in this period, with the help of capital exports and despite the tariff, and the model applies in which exports are a leading sector, drawing resources into high-return occupations from underemployment. Clapham in fact argues that the tariff on industrial goods acted as a stimulus of the infant-industry variety.[55] But most observers argue, with Bettelheim and Luethy,[56] that tariffs caused France to isolate itself from progressive and competitive tendencies abroad, to turn inward, to allow its markets to be dominated by "Malthusianism," under which coalitions of interests maintain production at relatively low levels and high prices.

[50] "Basic Conditions of Economic Progress," p. 168.
[51] See Chenery, "Patterns of Industrial Growth" (1960).
[53] Gerschenkron, "Comment" (1956), p. 376. See also Cameron, *France and the Economic Development of Europe,* p. 36. But note (*ibid.*) that French foreign trade rose fourfold between 1816 and 1850 (1860?). Dunham believes that economic historians overemphasize the role of the tariff because they have more information on these schedules than on other aspects of the economy (*The Industrial Revolution in France,* 1951, pp. 212, 298). Lévy regards it as a mistake to date the movement for lower tariffs only from 1860. In his view the revolution for freer trade really started in 1832 under the pressure of industrialists who wanted lower metal prices (*Histoire économique de la France,* 1951–52, p. 107). Three movements for tariff reduction occurred in the prosperous phases of cycles in the 1830s, 1840s and 1850s (p. 96).
[53] Lhomme, *La Grande bourgeoisie au pouvoir* (1960), pp. 100–101.
[54] "Basic Conditions of Economic Progress," p. 165.
[55] Clapham, *The Economic Development of France and Germany* (1936), p. 264. Clapham calls the Méline tariff great (p. 263).
[56] Bettelheim, *Bilan de l'économie française* (1947), pp. 53, 171ff; Luethy, *France against Herself* (1955).

Some writers attach primary importance to French agricultural tariffs, which may have prevented a rationalization of agriculture and the transfer of labor to the industrial sector. On the other hand, France's leading agricultural economist, Augé-Laribé, is persuaded that French agriculture suffered more from the tariff on industrial products than the rest of the economy did from the protection accorded to farmers.[57] The most careful investigation concludes that it is virtually impossible to decide which sector of the economy was favored over others in tariff policy.[58]

There was little support in France for the liberal trade policies of Michel Chevalier and Napoleon III, for various reasons (largely accidental). The silk interests of Lyon had been hit in the fifties with pébrine, which raised their costs relative to those of Italy and Japan, and put the industry on an import-competing basis. More far-reaching was the phylloxera after 1875, which produced an identical result in wine, the main beneficiary of the British concessions in 1860. In the cotton-textile trade, the one free-trade area, Alsace, had been lost in the Treaty of Frankfort.[59] With virtually no support for freer trade from export interests, the French policy was tariffs for all, including, absurdly, tariffs on raw materials. The colonial party fought to obtain exemptions for the newly acquired colonies in the Méline tariff, but on political rather than economic grounds.[60] They failed to secure their point in 1892, but in 1902 colonial preferences were enacted.

The French policy of tariffs for all interests can hardly be said to have been a stimulus to growth. Jean Weiller even wonders whether the tariffs hindered the growth of foreign trade; it would seem that it must. But how, then, does one explain the equally slow or rapid development of British foreign trade?[61] The "generalized protection" of France did not represent positive steps toward change — it was negative action to preserve the structure of French foreign trade and, behind that, of French output.[62] The sectors which are said to have led French growth from 1896 to 1913 were not import-competing or import-substituting, except to a slight degree in chemicals; the leaders were iron ore, steel, and automobiles, which were exported, and electricity, a purely domestic industry.[63]

[57] See the references in Chapter 9, note 45.
[58] Latil, *Revenu agricole* (1956), pp. 287ff.
[59] Fohlen, *L'Industrie textile* (1956), p. 70. Alfred Motte, the cotton manufacturer at Roubaix, was also a free-trader, but he was exceptional.
[60] Brunschwig, *L'Impérialisme colonial français*, p. 94.
[61] In Duvaux and Weiller, "Économie française, échanges extérieurs, et structures internationales" (1957), p. 50.
[62] Weiller, "Long-run tendencies in foreign trade" (1943).
[63] The French chemical industry was also hurt by duties on sulphur and saltpeter. See Haber, *Chemical Industry in the Nineteenth Century* (1958), p. 42. See also Chapter 13 below.

So the infant-industry argument does not apply. Nor can it be said that protectionism slowed down growth, which was rapid from 1896 to 1913, except perhaps in the long run by solidifying the backward position of agriculture. The tariffs on timber, coal, and ferro-manganese cannot have helped, but tariffs on steel were raised only in 1910 after the rapid expansion had run most of its course up to World War I. The tariff enactments of 1892 and 1910 slowed down growth, but only in the long run and indirectly, by weakening the pressures on French resources to adapt to market forces.

There is still another possible relation between growth and trade, one raised by the French tariff on wheat and possibly that on cotton textiles: strong deflationary pressure on the economy from abroad is hardly conducive to growth. It may be necessary to remove it before growth can proceed (as discussed at some length in Chapter 10). The existence of such pressure cannot be judged from the multiplier model, in which export surpluses show an excess of expansionary pressure from abroad and an import deficit shows net deflation. There may also be price pressure. Economists and historians in the post-Keynesian era sometimes reason as if only the multiplier pressure counted — for example, when it is argued that the United States sinned against the canons of international cooperation in devaluing its currency in 1933 when it had an export surplus. But price pressure may not be revealed in the balance of payments, if it reduces income and imports as fast as or faster than exports fall. The appreciation of the dollar in 1932 drove down the prices of wheat and cotton to fifty cents a bushel and seven cents a pound. The pressure on export sales was significant. But far worse was the internal deflation. It can be argued that the loss to farmers on internal sales was balanced by the rise in consumers' real income, with no net deflationary impact. But the decline in farm spending may not be matched by increased urban outlays. Money illusion may deter the consumer from enlarging his spending. And the decline in farm spending may become dynamic and cumulative. In these circumstances, which I believe apply to the fall in France's wheat price in the 1880s, steps must be taken to stem the deflationary tide. In a world of stable exchange rates, where devaluation cannot be used, the only available measure is a tariff increase. The side effects, limiting transformation, were harmful to French growth. But some such action was inescapable if growth was to be at all resumed. The mistake was to continue and extend the range of protection.

THE ANGLO-FRENCH TREATY OF COMMERCE

What of tariff reduction in France? Dunham, who is a strong protagonist of both Chevalier and the Anglo-French Treaty, argues that it helped to "bring about the full development of the industrial revolution in France." [64] The difficulties of various industries are explained in terms of other forces: cotton textiles suffered from the cotton famine and from internal competition, resulting from the completion of the railroad network; silk from changes in fashion; linen from cheap cottons and woolens and Russian flax; iron from depletion of the beds in the Nord.[65] But the stimulating force of import competition had broad beneficial effects in completing the conversion of the steel industry from charcoal to coal, accelerating the equipment of industry with machinery, expanding the foreign market for wines, until the advent of phylloxera in 1875.[66] The 40 million franc fund for re-equipment of business hurt by the treaty was fully used.

The stimulation of economic growth through imports had been tried before, in the 1786 Treaty of Vergennes; this was an attempt to shock French industry into adopting machinery, but it was soon interrupted by the revolution.[67] (A more recent and geographically limited example is the European Common Market.) On the 1860 occasion, an interruption came from victory of the Third Republic and the strength of its protectionist sentiment, maintained by Thiers, who wanted tariffs on raw materials as early as 1872, and by Pouyer-Quartier, the Rouen cotton manufacturer. The abandonment of freer trade may have contributed to the stagnation of growth from 1882 to 1896, though this had its roots in the banking decision to withhold credit from long-term investment in industry, the defeat of the government over the Freycinet Plan for investment in railroads, roads, and canals, and the troubles of agriculture.

But there is good reason to think that Dunham's remark in 1955 about exaggerating the effect of tariffs applies equally to the second, as well as to the first, half of the century, despite what Dunham

[64] Dunham, *The Anglo-French Treaty of Commerce* (1930), p. 179.
[65] *Ibid.*, pp. 196, 165ff, 363.
[66] Marcel Rist is interested in the effects of the treaty on the French balance of trade, as well as on French industry ("Une Expérience française de liberation des échanges," 1956), and gives it high marks on both scores. After two years French industry checked the increase in the volume of imports (p. 937). But the change from an import surplus of 520 million francs in 1861 to an export surplus of 498 million francs in 1863 was almost one third due to the decline in cereal imports, unaffected by the treaty, from 390 million francs to 53 millions in the same years.
[67] Ballot, *Introduction du machinisme dans l'industrie française* (1923), pp. 11–12.

thought in 1930. It is a mistake to think of the Anglo-French Treaty of 1860 as enacted through Louis Napoleon's decree powers in the face of unanimous opposition and as a sharp discontinuity. Nor is it necessarily the autonomous factor, with economic growth the dependent one. Tariff reductions had gone forward in 1853 and 1855, on coal, iron, machinery, and raw materials.[68] The failure of the British to sell 20 million francs' worth of goods left over from the 1855 exposition in Paris, at a reduced duty of 22 percent, greatly encouraged the forces supporting free trade in France.[69] Economic growth supported by investment in railroads, Paris buildings, ports, and public works, along with increasing exports, helped tariff reductions as much as the tariff reductions completed the transition from handicrafts to the machine and the factory, or from charcoal in steel making to coal.

The courage and leadership of Chevalier and Louis Napoleon were impressive, but they must not be exaggerated. There were forces already working for freer trade. Lhomme gets himself into contradictions when he says that the grande bourgeoisie supported the Second Empire and protectionism and that Louis Napoleon looked after its interests, despite the treaty. His escape, that Napoleon knew the interests of the upper middle classes better than they did themselves, is hardly persuasive.[70] More typical, perhaps, is the attitude of Charles de Wendel, who said to the emperor that his only regret about the treaty was that his competitor, Schneider, had been consulted beforehand and he only afterwards.[71] The treaty may have meant a great deal to the cotton manufacturers of Rouen, but it scarcely figures in the history of the Méquillet-Noblot concern at Héricourt near Belfort, for which technological change, the spread of the market through the railroad, the cotton famine, and the state of the wine and grain harvests were the major external influences.[72]

STRUCTURAL RIGIDITY

Related to the question of whether the Anglo-French Treaty of 1860 spurred French economic growth, and subsequent tariff increases slowed it down again, is the French thesis that the country has had a rigid trade structure, working against growth. Some claim that the rigidity of French domestic production has operated to keep

---

[68] Dunham, *Anglo-French Treaty of Commerce*, p. 190.
[69] Lévy, *Histoire économique de la France*, p. 98.
[70] Lhomme, *La Grande bourgeoisie au pouvoir*, pp. 237ff.
[71] Sédillot, *La Maison de Wendel* (1958), p. 193.
[72] See Fohlen, *Une Affaire de famille* (1955). The one mention of the treaty is on pp. 76–77.

the foreign-trade structure unchanged; others that threats of change from abroad have been held off by commercial policy. In the view of one French economist, French foreign trade has a "preference de structure," [73] or a tendency to settle in a given mold. And while all these strictures have been leveled against the rigid French trade structure, the Economic Commission for Europe has attacked it for its high proportion of raw materials, calling the unfavorable composition of French exports one of the weakest parts of the economy.[74]

It is generally agreed that the French economy resisted change after 1875, especially in the wheat tariff of 1881 and the Méline tariff of 1892. A student of Weiller's has tried to show that the Anglo-French Treaty did not involve a break with the French preference for a set trade structure, but the case is not persuasive.[75] From 1872 to 1952, however, the French export structure changed less than those of five other countries in Europe, although the measurements are not refined.[76] The casual comparison of the export breakdown is hindered by the differing practices among statistical bodies, and using the historical time series ignores the impact of the inclusion of Alsace-Lorraine in 1919 and, in 1948, of the Saar in the French customs union. In addition, there was a small reclassification of semifinished steels from manufactured goods to raw materials in 1948. Ignoring this, however, the French breakdown since the figures have separated foodstuffs and raw materials show the trends set forth in Table 23.

If these criticisms are correct, the French export structure is not only rigid; to the extent that it has been moving at all, it is going in the wrong direction. But this is not convincing either. For a country to be stuck in the production of raw materials, and to be able to move away from it only slowly because of its lack of an industrial base, may be a weakness. But it is a sign of strength, not of weakness, to alter a trade structure in the direction of primary products when

[73] See Weiller, *Problèmes d'économie internationale* (1950), II, 282ff.

[74] United Nations, *Economic Survey of Europe in 1954*, pp. 187–188. This judgment is concurred in by various observers, among them Duvaux and Weiller, "Économie française, échanges extérieurs, et structures internationales," p. 15; and Peterson, "Planning and Economic Progress in France" (1957), pp. 365, 373.

[75] See Coussy, "La Politique commerciale du Second Empire et la continuité de l'évolution structurelle" (1961). Among other weaknesses, the article seems to me to confuse a rigid structure with a rigidly evolving structure, which are by no means identical.

[76] Cumulating the absolute percentage changes in each of eight categories of trade for the periods 1872–1900, 1900–1913, 1913–1928, 1928–1938, and 1938–1952, Gérard Salette (in an unpublished paper for a seminar at Massachusetts Institute of Technology) found that France has an index of 118, compared with Sweden, 130; United Kingdom, 135; Germany, 158; Italy, 171; Belgium, 200. If only beginning and end years are compared, France suffers more in the comparison because more of its changes in a given category were in opposite directions, and canceled out as between periods, than was true of other countries.

Table 23. Distribution of French Exports among Broad Classes (in percent)

Period	Foodstuffs	Raw materials for industry	Manufactured goods
1878–1882	24	23	53
1908–1913	13	29	58
1920–1924	10	25	65
1950–1954	13	47	38

Source. INSEE, *Annuaire statistique, 1957*, p. 6.

the demand for iron ore, pig iron, crude and semifinished steel, baux-
ite, aluminum, chemical raw materials, and so on, is booming, and
when the demand for manufactured silk, cotton textiles, leather goods,
lingerie, and high-style goods is falling. The terms of trade may not
have favored France because it moved too slowly out of weak manufacturing lines (and such weak raw-material lines as silk, linen, and
leather).[77] And it is possible, though not self-evident, that there were
exports among manufacturers which were more favorable than the
steel, petroleum products, wood, chemical raw materials, coal, and
pig iron for which volume held "steady, and value was up because
of good prices."[78] The Economic Commission's conclusion that an
export structure is weak if it favors raw materials may apply to an
underdeveloped country with no power to transform, but not to a
country whose manufacturing capacity, to the extent that it reallo-
cates in response to price stimuli, is pulled in the direction of raw
materials.

Structural rigidity in imports is less obvious in analytical terms.
The Salette indexes for 1872 to 1952 are: France, 119; United Kingdom, 101; Germany, 96. German tariffs were applied as vigorously
as the French, and for more than half of the period Britain was
wedded to free trade. It is evident that France resisted the prospect
of wheat imports in 1881, and in 1892 and 1910 that of increased imports of a variety of raw materials and manufactures. The French
innovation of quota restrictions in the 1930s was motivated in the
same fashion by the desire to protect the peasant and was followed by
their rapid extension to manufacturing.[79] How does it happen that its
index is higher?

[77] See my *The Terms of Trade*, p. 238. Duvaux also concludes that the terms of
trade have been adverse because the French economy was unable to adapt sufficiently (p. 28).
[78] *Ibid.*, p. 25.
[79] See Haight, *French Commercial Policy* (1941) and *French Import Quotas*
(1935).

Salette offers a partial explanation: the rigidity of the domestic industrial structure is so great that small changes in demand have to be balanced by changes in imports. (This reasoning could also, of course, have been applied to exports: with constant production of an export product, a change in domestic demand could reduce or increase the amount available for sale abroad.) There is some support for the theory. French wheat consumption in the nineteenth century ran to about 90 million quintals a year. When the crop fell below 80 millions, imports were necessary. But in the present century, wheat consumption in France has fallen to 60 million quintals.[80] An unchanged domestic production can therefore lead to a substantial decline in imports as a result of a decline in domestic demand.

But if France's import structure has been changed more than those of Britain and Germany, which have imported mainly foodstuffs and raw materials for which the demand is relatively income-inelastic, it is nonetheless rigid. In 1928–1930, after the trade turmoil up to 1926 had settled down, the import structure closely resembled that of 1913 despite the territorial changes, exchange depreciation, and the changes in factors, technology, and the level and distribution of income.[81] Weiller states that the conservative character of the prewar reconstruction stemmed from the great prestige of the prewar structure — Europe hoped for 1913 prices, exchange parities, production, and trade.[82] Duvaux comments that this is not surprising, for it reflects the rigidity of the structure of production.[83]

There is much to this view. The French economy did resist change. It was capable of changing under pressure, but reluctant to do so. When change was forced on industry by an imposed reduction of tariffs, it affected agriculture adversely through increased wages. But an attempt to force change directly on agriculture by pushing down prices through imports was resisted effectively. And the example of protection for agriculture quickly led to protection for industry, for mining, for everyone.

The problem of the 1960s is an ironic variant on the problems of 1875 and 1930. Instead of resisting imports so that agriculture will not have to improve its efficiency faster, France is now stressing exports because agricultural efficiency is increasing faster than resources can be reallocated to industry and services. This is an incapacity to transform which has the stimulus to change coming from inside. And German resistance to France's overtures for a larger share of its market for foodstuffs parrot the arguments of Méline and Daladier.

[80] Duvaux, p. 22.
[81] Weiller, "Long-run tendencies in foreign trade," p. 19.
[82] *Ibid.*, p. 33.
[83] Duvaux, p. 24.

The relations between trade and growth cannot be discussed without specifying the extent to which the economy at home is growing and changing. Foreign demand and internal capacity to transform work effectively together. It makes very little difference whether demand leads and the capacity to transform follows, in which case exports stimulate growth; or whether the domestic economy leads, with an innovation, and foreign demand responds, in which case growth results in exports.

But exports can expand when the economy has lost its capacity to grow in new directions. If these exports lead the economy to devote its energy to old played-out lines, with little entrepreneurial or technological energy, they may delay economic growth in the long run, while assisting it by sustaining incomes in the present. In the same way, reduced imports lead to growth when the capacity to expand into new lines is present (the infant-industry case); but reduced imports are damaging when they sustain an economy in its refusal to submit to the strains of transformation. And increased imports can hurt when the economy is incapable of growing; or they can help when they stimulate latent capacity to transform, through the competitive effect.

In other words, one cannot really discuss the role of foreign trade in growth without indicating the underlying capacity of the economy to undertake new tasks in depth or to transform. And this economic historians have seldom done. It is not the foreign trade that leads to growth — any stimulus can do it if the capacity to transform is present or can be drawn out of dormancy. Without that capacity, a benign stimulus may lull the economy into senescence and a rude one may set it back. With it, both can lead to growth.

CHAPTER 13

LEADING AND LAGGING
SECTORS AND INDUSTRIES

After discussing the ingredients of growth and the relations in transformation between agriculture and industry, between exports and home industry, and among regions, it is time to look more closely at the relations among domestic sectors and industries. My purpose is to test British and French experience against the stage models of growth, particularly those of Hoffmann and Rostow. In the course of this analysis, I take occasion to compare the woolen and the cotton-textile industries in the United Kingdom and to sketch the growth and organization of the chemical and building industries in France.

THE HOFFMANN MODEL

Hoffmann's attention is focused on industry. In this sector he postulates a continuous shift of structure which "has always followed a uniform pattern," starting with consumer-goods industries and gradually developing capital-goods industries at a faster rate. Cross-sectional analysis of the process will produce stages, of which Hoffmann designates four: Stage I, where the ratio of net value added by consumer-goods industries is five times that of the capital-goods industries; Stage II, where the ratio is two and a half to one; Stage III, where it is one to one; and Stage IV, where it falls below unity. There is some room for variation around these averages, and the structure of foreign trade also makes a difference.[1]

Hoffmann's data are in terms of both employment by industry and an approximation of net output, derived from employment data for a selected group of industries.[2] The technique for estimating net out-

[1] Hoffmann, *Growth of Industrial Economies* (1958), pp. 2–3.
[2] Excluded from consideration are rubber; building; timber and woodworking; paper, paper goods, printing, and publishing; water, gas, and electricity; quarrying, cement, glass making, and pottery; and all other. The basis for such exclusion is largely difficulty of classification between consumer and capital goods. The industries included cover broadly two thirds of the output. Hoffmann asserts that the relation between stages would not be greatly affected by developments in the excluded industries (*ibid.*, pp. 74ff, 85ff, 94ff).

put is suspect, as Hoffmann recognizes. It consists in applying the relationships between employment and output in one country to others where output data are missing but employment estimates exist. The reasons why net productivities per worker in one country at a given time might not apply in another are set forth, but the technique is said to be justified empirically: where data can be found, net outputs per worker in various industries are fairly uniform. For the United Kingdom in 1907, 1924, 1935, and 1947, and for France in 1861–1865, net output figures are available directly from Census of Manufactures figures.[3] While four stages are recognized, data are given for only three, as shown in Table 24.

Several anomalies appear when the data are reassembled by countries: the increase in food and drink in Great Britain between 1871 and 1901 appears sharper than can be accounted for by the rise in whiskey production, and there may be an element of statistical incomparability in it. This is also likely to be true of the reduction between 1901 and 1907 from 22.8 to 18.6 percent in combined iron and metal goods, machine building, and vehicles.

The greatest anomaly in Hoffmann's theory, however, is that while Britain and France go through the industrialization revolution at different times — Britain in 1780 to 1820 and France in 1820 to 1860 [4] — they arrive at various stages of industrialization simultaneously. This is baffling. Hoffmann states in several places that historical phases of industrialization are different from stages of industrialization, the latter being defined in terms of net output ratios of consumer goods to capital goods.[5] The exercise loses point, however, if the "striking similarity" of countries at the same stage of industrialization is the result of stages of industrialization chosen on the basis of a similarity of pattern.

In Hoffmann's view, consumer-goods industries develop first because capital-goods industries require a large amount of capital, advanced techniques, and a skilled labor force, whereas consumer-goods industries can utilize the technical knowledge already possessed by craftsmen and require less capital.[6] In any particular stage, one industry will be dominant; in successive stages, new industries will come to the fore and take the place of the original dominant industry.[7] Dominant industries in general have been the food and textile

[3] *Ibid.*, p. 22.
[4] *Ibid.*, p. 111.
[5] E.g., *ibid.*, p. 3, and footnote a to table 36, p. 143.
[6] *Ibid.*, pp. 3–4.
[7] *Ibid.*, p. 4. Dominance is defined in terms of the "lead, in terms of net output, over all other industries," and the dominant industry is said to influence greatly the course of economic growth.

Table 24. Relative Net Output of Main Industries during Various Phases of Industrialization
(total industrial net output per employee = 100 for each country)

Stage	Year	Food and drink (1)	Textiles and clothing (2)	Leather goods (3)	Furniture (4)	Iron and metal goods (5)	Machine building (6)	Vehicles (7)	Chemicals (8)	Consumer-goods industries (1)–(4) (9)	Capital-goods industries (5)–(8) (10)	Ratio (9)/(10) (11)
						Great Britain						
I	1851	6.3	43.2	1.5	—	—	10.1ᵃ	—	1.3	51.0	11.4	4.7
	1871	6.4	43.5	1.8	—	—	12.1ᵃ	—	1.9	51.7	14.0	3.9
II	1901	13.9	25.7	1.4	—	—	22.8ᵃ	—	2.1	41.0	24.9	1.7
III	1907	13.4	24.5	1.6	1.7	4.4	9.1	5.1	4.4	41.2	23.0	1.8
	1924	17.7	19.8	1.7	1.0	7.9	11.6	4.7	4.4	40.2	27.6	1.5
	1935	16.6	19.0	1.1	1.3	7.2	15.7	7.9	5.0	38.0	35.8	1.1
	1948	11.6	17.3	0.9	1.1	8.7	21.9	9.6	4.8	30.9	45.0	0.7
						France						
I	1861–65	28.1	34.1	2.0	0.4	5.8	4.1	0.9	3.7	64.6	14.5	4.5
II	1896	12.7	28.8	2.3	—	—	14.9	—	4.8	43.8	19.7	2.3
III	1921	12.8	19.5	1.8	1.0	7.2	6.6	4.7	4.7	35.1	23.2	1.5

ᵃ Figure for columns 5, 6, and 7.
Source. Hoffmann, *Growth of Industrial Economies* (1958), appendix tables 40, 41, and 42.

industries in the first two stages of development and the iron, steel, and engineering industries during the third stage; but Hoffmann notes that the textile industries can continue to occupy the dominant place during the third stage. In Britain and France the textile industries were dominant in all three stages until the expansion of iron, steel, and engineering after World War I in Britain.[8]

A theory of stages of growth in which changes take place within but not between stages, and in which dominance is measured in static comparisons rather than by dynamic effects, is not very persuasive. Moreover, the behavior of one textile industry in the real world can differ from that of another, as will be demonstrated below. The Hoffmann thesis about the growth of industrial economies leaves out too much and uncovers too little to be of any great help.

ROSTOW'S STAGES

Rostow's early work on the British economy divided the nineteenth century into five trend periods in which the major difference was made by the alternating rhythm of home and foreign investment. From 1790 to 1815 there was a rapid rise in production, both in industry and in agriculture, with a big increase in exports and a more rapid expansion of producer goods than of consumer goods; 1815–1847 was a trend period with intensive domestic investment, especially in quick-yielding innovations, textile machinery, steel, and railroads. The increase in industrial production was at a maximum, amounting to 3.5 percent overall, 3.2 percent in consumer goods, but 4.2 percent in producer goods. The great mid-Victorian boom from 1850 to 1873 turned attention outward to wars, gold mining, and railroads abroad, plus domestic shipbuilding. Total industrial production grew at 3.2 percent a year, with consumer goods expanding at 2.6 percent and producer goods at 4.1. After 1873 the pendulum swung to domestic investment — in iron and steel, freighters, machine tools, telephone, electricity, and, in the 1890s, bicycles. This trend lasted to 1896 and saw industrial production up by 1.7 percent a year, consumer goods at the lower rate of 1.3 percent, and producer goods at 2.2. From 1898 to 1913, investment again turned outward, leaving unemployment at home. Total industrial production rose only 1.5 percent, with consumer goods at 1.0 and producer goods at 1.9.[9]

The main theme of Rostow's study is that changes in British investment between Britain and the outside world produced changes in terms of trade, real wages, and the course of business activity. The shift of

[8] Table 34, p. 128, and p. 131.
[9] Rostow, *British Economy of the Nineteenth Century* (1948), chap. i.

investment abroad worsened the terms of trade and reduced real
wages; its return to domestic industries improved the two. The thesis
has been attacked on grounds of timing, its use of unemployment
figures, and the focus on the division of investment rather than on the
total.[10] The theory supports Hoffmann to the extent that producer
goods rise continuously at faster rates than consumer goods.[11] Rostow's
concern with the division of investment between home and abroad,
and the role of the terms of trade, gave way subsequently to an
equally mechanical, but different, theory of stages.

The stages of growth form a more fully elaborated theory. The
first two stages — the traditional society and the preconditions for
"take-off" — do not concern us, since they are antecedent to our time
period for both France and Britain. Thereafter comes the take-off,
when resistance to growth is overcome and growth becomes a self-
sustaining and normal condition. Growth does not begin everywhere
at once, but centers first in primary-growth sectors, from which it
spills over into supplementary-growth sectors that respond directly
to the leading sector and into derived-growth sectors that react to
increases in income, population, or production.[12]

The fourth stage is called the drive to maturity and consists of the
spread of the efficient techniques developed in the leading sector
during take-off. Maturity is reached when a society has effectively
applied the range of its modern technology throughout the economy.
The stage after maturity is called the age of high mass consumption.
It may not be reached immediately because of the pursuit of national
power, the institution of the welfare state, or relative stagnation.
Rostow states that "it cannot be emphasized too strongly that the
stages of growth are an arbitrary and limited way of looking at the
sequence of modern history: and they are, in no absolute sense, a
correct way." [13]

The stages for Britain and France are said to fall as follows.[14]

	Britain	France
Take-off	1783–1802	1830–1860
Maturity	1850	1910
High mass consumption	1935–	1950–

The drive to maturity can be defined less precisely than take-off or
the age of high mass consumption and must be given in round num-

[10] Saville, "Comment on Rostow's *British Economy of the Nineteenth Century*"
(1954).
[11] The indexes used are those constructed by Hoffmann.
[12] Rostow, *Stages of Growth* (1960), p. 52.
[13] *Ibid.*, p. 1.
[14] *Ibid.*, pp. 38, 59, xii (chart).

bers. This is because of the possible interval between maturity and the following stage, and the definite character of take-off and mass consumption, each with prominent leading sectors, in contrast with maturity when leading sectors may fall away.[15]

Unlike that in the *British Economy in the Nineteenth Century*, this schema originally made no provision for the Great Depression of 1873. The length of the depression in the 1930s resulted from the need of the leading sectors of the age of mass consumption — automobiles, suburban home building, and so on — for full employment and an atmosphere of confidence.[16] In a subsequent paper, however, Rostow said:

> I am inclined to think that when we have fully examined the 1880s we shall find the widespread deceleration in that era related in part to the process of disengagement from the railroad era and to the process of catching hold fully of the potentialities implicit in the new leading sectors: steel, electricity, and chemicals. I am reasonably certain that, as time passes, we shall interpret a significant element in the interwar sluggishness of Western Europe as due to the process of disengagement from the old leading sectors of pre-1914 [a] and wartime years and to the rather slow preparation for the age of high mass consumption which in the 1930s at last fully seized Western Europe as the old men of steel and electricity and heavy chemicals have been superseded by the bright young men of automobiles and plastics, electronics and aeronautics.
>
> [a] The statistical evidence on rates and patterns of growth for Germany, Great Britain, and the United States suggests that the pre-1914 leading sectors may have begun to lose their capacity to sustain the rate of growth toward the close of the pre-1914 decade.[17]

This characterization of the Great Depression as a pause between stages finds an echo in a parenthetical remark by G. C. Allen on Birmingham. This writer regarded the period from 1876 to 1886 as a watershed between the period of British unchallenged predominance and the era of international competition, and he attributed the prolonged nature of the depression to the necessity of redistributing productive forces and eliminating marginal firms because of technical change abroad.[18] I am not aware, however, of a comparable interpre-

[15] *Ibid.*, p. 59n.
[16] *Ibid.*, pp. 77–78.
[17] Rostow, "Leading Sectors and the Take-Off" (1960), p. 14.
[18] Allen, *Birmingham and the Black Country* (1929), p. 211. This view seems to suggest improvements in efficiency in the same industries and changes mostly by firms, rather than the development of new industries and the entry of new firms (and the exit of old). Later, at p. 438, Allen characterizes 1785–1860 as the malleable iron age for Birmingham; 1860–1886 as the end of the iron age, the start of foreign competition, and readjustment and slow growth; 1886–1927 as the changeover from hardware to engineering.

tation of the interwar slumps with their very different patterns in Britain, France, and the United States.

Rostow gives the leading sectors in the take-off as textiles in Britain and railroads in France.[19] On the path to maturity, Britain experienced further innovations in textiles, along with railroad booms in the 1830s and 1840s, which brought the coal, iron, and heavy engineering industries to maturity.[20] In France (and the United States and Germany) the rise of the steel and the development of its engineering uses are regarded as the central symbols of the move to maturity.[21]

Perroux has given a list of leading sectors for France (*industries motrices*) which differs from that of Rostow. First were the large credit institutions and the railroads. These were followed until 1880 by textiles and steel. Later at the turn of the century there were new industries in the lead: automobiles, electricity, chemicals, and new goods — bicycles, electrical equipment, cement, and so on.[22] Implicitly the differences are not so great. Chemicals and cement may be regarded as an engineering industry made possible by steel vessels. And the banks, which Perroux picks as a motor industry, have been left out of account in Rostow's list as partaking of a different character, along with government. But the difference in the timing of steel is important.

COTTON TEXTILES, WOOLENS, AND INDUSTRIAL ACTIVITY IN BRITAIN

It may throw light on stage theories to examine, in greatly condensed form, the behavior of two leading industries in Britain and a leading and lagging industry in France. Changes in perspective alter the general picture, and a close look will detect differences which may legitimately be ignored from a distance. But if industries which should behave differently behave in the same fashion, and those which should be alike operate differently, at the same or different stages, the usefulness of the stages analysis must come into question.

The Industrial Revolution began in cotton textiles, not in textiles generally, and in spinning rather than in weaving. Cotton spinning was already in the factory by 1800, when the take-off had been completed. Worsted spinning shifted to the factory next, by 1815; cotton weaving, by 1830. By 1850, the date Rostow gives for maturity, there

[19] *Stages of Growth*, pp. 54–55.
[20] *Ibid.*, p. 60.
[21] *Ibid.*, p. 62. Rostow adds: "And Britain, of course, joined fully in the elaboration and application of the post-railway technology." But see British technological immaturity in railroads, Chapter 7 above.
[22] Perroux, "Croissance de l'économie française" (1955), pp. 55ff.

were still 250,000 handloom weavers in cotton. These were reduced
to 40,000 by 1881. In woolens, however, the handloom weaver still
dominated in 1870.[23] The move into factories started in 1850. It was
completed for worsteds about 1880 and in woolens shortly thereafter.[24]

The expansion of cotton from 1780 to 1802 was phenomenal in Hoffmann's indexes; worsteds and woolens hardly grew at all. During the
drive to maturity, when the stimulus from the leading sector was
spreading throughout the economy, cotton expanded tenfold, woolens
doubled. Thereafter, from 1851 to 1913, when other leading sectors
had taken over, according to Hoffmann — though he recognizes the
dominance of textiles in Britain and France in all three stages — cotton
and wool grew at the same rate, roughly speaking, and this was also
the pace of industrial production generally, including building.[25] The
old leading sector of take-off continued to lead, or at least to keep up.

More interesting are the qualitative comparisons. The worsted industry was organized much like cotton textiles, with regional and
product specialization and horizontal integration, but not much in
the way of vertical integration between stages. Vertical integration in
worsted was perhaps a little ahead of that in cotton, but the latter
was only beginning in 1913. Weavers using a cotton warp had little
interest in controlling the quality of worsted yarn. Vertical integration
was the rule, however, in woolens. Here the machinery was less complex and the weaver was obliged to control yarn quality at the spinning stage.

Worsteds and woolens were both slow in putting cotton-textile
innovations into effect. This was due partly to the conservatism of an
established industry, partly to the technical difficulties of applying
cotton techniques to a different fiber, especially in combing where
effective machinery was not devised until the 1840s; innovation also
waited upon substantial supplies of imports of Australian wool, after
1830, to supplement domestic production. But once the process of

[23] Dobb, *Development of Capitalism* (1947), p. 265, discusses the survival of
domestic industry in the third quarter of the nineteenth century and observes that
the technique of the hand nailer was unaltered between 1830 and the 1870s —
well past "maturity."

[24] Similar wide disparities in the timing of mechanization of cotton, wool, and
linen spinning and weaving have been noted for France in a chart by Lhomme,
Grande bourgeoisie au pouvoir (1960), p. 176, based on data from Lambert
Dansette, *Quelques familles du patronat textile* (1954), p. 100. E.g., for France
on the average, cotton spinning had been mechanized by 1830, whereas power
looms were introduced over the period 1830–1870. In woolens, spinning was
mechanized between 1830 and 1870, weaving between 1850 and 1870, especially
during 1857–1866, which included the cotton famine.

[25] See Hoffmann, *British Industry* (1955), table 54, which gives for 1851, on
the basis of 1913 as 100, cotton yarn, 30.3; cotton piece goods, 25.8; woolen and
worsted yarns, 29.8; woolen and worsted cloth, 28.6; total industrial production
excluding building, 24.3; total industrial production including building, 28.8.

technical change started, it did not slow down after 1875, unlike cotton. Worsted suffered a blow in the shift of French taste (later followed by English) against hard finishes and in favor of the softer all-wool cloths. The shortening of skirts for riding bicycles also hurt, as did the McKinley tariff. The industry was unable to divert exports to newer markets since tropical areas did not use wool for clothing. At the same time, it was already exporting to wool-supplying markets with close ties to England — Australia, South Africa, and Argentina; and it benefited from the lack of a competitor like Japan. But instead of diverting exports from competitive to noncompetitive markets, it maintained pressure for innovation, permitted imports, shifted to exports of worsted coated yarns and tops, switched from luster (English) wool to soft (Merino-crossbred) wool.

Cotton textiles made a moderate adjustment to foreign competition by upgrading the quality of output and selling fine yarns to Europe, which absorbed 60 percent of yarn exports in 1913. The main response, however, was to build bigger spinning mills for the same product, still woven by a separate manufacturer and sold by a separate merchant in colonial and agricultural countries. The two industries grew in the same proportion from 1851 to 1913. But the cotton-textile industry was highly developed, technologically stagnant, competitively fragile, whereas woolens depended less on exports and continued to make technical progress. The United Kingdom remained ahead of the world in woolens during the interwar period and maintained a place in world markets. The obsolete cotton-textile industry was unable to compete in world markets. By 1935, in moderate depression, woolens were at 90 percent of 1913 figures, cottons at 60 percent.

The different behavior of cottons and woolens after 1875 may be owing partly to absolute size, rather than to the character of growth before 1913. Employment in cotton was 570,000 in 1851, or more than double wool's 254,000.[26] Cotton had more effective access to the London capital market. An additional factor is that woolens did not use the merchant system to the extent that cotton did, but moved closer to direct trading. Allen comments that, exporting only to temperate-zone countries, the industry was dealing with areas whose civilization and legal system were akin to that of the British.[27] This is a doubtful explanation.

The bearing of the comparison on stage theories of development

[26] By 1911 cotton had risen to 620,000; wool had fallen slightly to 248,000. A rough indication of productivity changes may be obtained by recalling that output had gone up about the same in woolens as in cotton textiles, or that inputs had gone up slightly more — from 240 million pounds to 840 million pounds in wool, compared with 700 million pounds to 2 billion pounds in cotton.

[27] Allen, *British Industries* (1939), p. 262.

should be clear. Both Hoffmann and Rostow have difficulty with the fact that both cotton and woolen textiles grew at approximately the same rates as the rest of industrial production,[28] for the stimulus to growth is supposed to change from stage to stage. Hoffmann, moreover, is explicitly troubled that his theory calls for a shift in dominance from consumer-goods industries to capital-goods industries, whereas textiles remain dominant for Britain and France through all three periods. His stages of industrialization at which consumer-goods industries progressively decline in proportion rest heavily on the apparent relative decline in textiles, along with the real growth in iron and steel and engineering.[29]

For Rostow the problem is rather that his stages call for an application and relaxation of growth forces that are greater than what seem to exist. The forward, lateral, and backward effects of the take-off in cotton textiles took twenty years or so to be realized in worsteds, but eighty years in woolens, long after the economy as a whole should have been galvanized into self-sustaining growth, with compound interest built into its habits and structure. After 1870, moreover, cotton textiles slowed down on technological improvements, and expanded sales abroad to underdeveloped countries, while worsteds and woolens settled back to a very different life of steady technological progress. And they responded to stimuli from foreign competition more than from increased demands, cheaper inputs, and concurrent urbanization.

It is hardly helpful to measure dominance as Hoffmann does, by whether one industry has one tenth of 1 percent more of the labor force or of value added than another. Similarly, it is necessary to decide whether a leading sector leads by virtue of its faster rate of growth or by virtue of dynamic performance or dynamic effects. On the first score, cotton textiles and woolens qualify as leading industries almost up to 1913. Like cotton textiles, iron and steel expanded sub-

[28] As shown by Hoffmann in *British Industry*. In his *Growth of Industrial Economies* textiles alone and textiles and clothing fell sharply as a percentage of net industrial output, especially between 1871 and 1901 (see Table 23 above). It is hard to see how the two positions can be reconciled. The former, for all its weaknesses, is likely to be a more accurate representation of output over time. When productivity in different industries is changing at different rates, inputs of raw materials are likely to be a better, though unsatisfactory, measure of output than employment, even after adjustment for differences in output per worker in different industries (which change over time).

[29] It is difficult to explain how iron and steel and engineering grew little more than textiles from 1881 to 1913 (on the basis of 1913 as 100, for 1881 the percent of iron and steel was 55.4; iron and steel products, including machine tools, 46.8; cotton yarns, 65.7; cotton piece goods, 59.7; woolen and worsted yarns, 56.4; woolen and worsted cloth, 55.2) when employment in the former rose as a percentage of all industrial employment from 12.6 to 18.3, and textiles fell from 28.2 to 21.0. The increase in productivity and in capital-intensity in textiles as compared with metals and engineering was not that great.

stantially in output from 1870 to 1913, but the rate of productivity increase was low — lower, in fact, than that of woolens, which expanded by approximately the same amount. The dynamic effects of all three industries, moreover, were probably less in this period than those of foreign competition[30] and the beginnings of American direct investment.[31]

CHEMICALS AS A LEADING SECTOR IN FRANCE

We have already seen that Rostow and Perroux differ on what are the leading sectors in France between 1850 and 1875 — whether railroads or banking and textiles, then steel. For the period of rapid French growth from 1896 to 1913, there is some dispute about steel. Rostow believes that steel is a leading sector in Western Europe in this period, along with electricity and chemicals. Perroux puts it earlier. There should be little doubt on this score. Without Alsace-Lorraine, crude-steel production in France rose from 400,000 metric tons in 1880 to 700,000 in 1890; 1,600,000 in 1900; and 3,400,000 in 1910. Steel clearly belongs to the 1896–1913 period.[32] But Perroux's list for 1896–1913 consists of automobiles, electricity, chemicals, and new goods. Since he and Rostow agree on chemicals, the industry is worth examining as a growth leader.

Note first that Hoffmann's figures in Table 24 show no dramatic change in the position of the chemical industry between 1896 and 1921, although this source is questionable. The industry did expand in output; in 1896 the industry employed 84,000 people, or 15 out of every 1,000 employed in industry, compared with 110,000 in 1901 and 125,-000 in 1906 (21 per 1,000 industrial employees).[33] Production expanded, particularly in sulphuric acid, which rose from 625,000 tons in 1900 to 1,200,000 tons in 1913 (largely the output of Kuhlmann and St. Gobain), and soda from 190,000 tons in 1895 to 276,000 tons in 1905 (80 percent by the Belgian Solvay Company).[34] Fertilizers showed some growth: from 42,000 tons of nitrates in 1898–1902 to

[30] Burn, "American Engineering Competition" (1931).

[31] Dunning, "Growth of United States Investment in United Kingdom Manufacturing, 1856–1940" (1956), pp. 240ff.

[32] Figures from OEEC, *Industrial Statistics, 1900–1955*, p. 93. Iron-ore production was also a leading industry, working in large part for export. In Britain, which was shifting to an import basis and had thinner ore, production rose from 14,000,000 tons in 1890 to 16,250,000 in 1913. Over the same period French output rose from 3,500,000 to 21,900,000. See Ministère du Commerce, *Rapport général* (1919), I, 58.

[33] Figures from the 1906 census report. Hoffmann gives 2.6 percent of all industrial employees in 1896 and 2.9 percent in 1921.

[34] Haber, *Chemical Industry during the Nineteenth Century* (1958), p. 110.

73,000 tons in 1913 and 9,500 tons of potash to 42,000 over the same period. These figures, however, were small. It was in superphosphates that the French expanded significant production, from 186,000 tons of phosphoric oxide in 1898–1902 to 352,000 tons in 1913.[35] This expansion was based on the discovery of rich Tunisian deposits in 1894, which were rapidly exploited after 1900, while the lean French deposits were allowed to fade. French peasants could be induced to use phosphatic fertilizer rather more readily than nitrogen, which was not always stable in the form used. Nor did the French apply potash in any substantial amount to the land, consumption averaging 90 kilograms on each hectare compared to the German 1,500.[36] Production of superphosphates stimulated the demand for sulphuric acid. Apart from fertilizers, the demand for heavy inorganic chemicals came, as always, from other branches of the chemical industry, including soap, and from textiles and paper. Materials for the industry were provided by imports of sulphur from America, phosphatic rock from Tunis, along with the traditional French production of salt. Potash could be obtained from Germany; and ammonium sulphate could be recovered from coke and gas operations, if the industry was unable or unwilling to produce *goudron* (coal tar) itself.[37]

This record in heavy chemicals is not impressive. The French had successes to their credit in rayon[38] and electrochemistry, based on hydropower.[39] But these industries were still tiny in 1913. On the other side of the ledger was the French failure in soda, when the Le Blanc process of 1825 was outstripped by the Solvay method, invented in 1863. The industry fought on with ingenuity to make the Le Blanc process economical, but without success. The other major failure was the famous case of La Fuchsine, a company formed in 1863 to exploit the 1859 aniline-dye invention of Verguin, trying to patent the product

---

[35] *Annuaire statistique, 1936,* pp. 374* – 375*.

[36] Baud, *Les Industries chimiques régionales de la France* (1922), p. 88.

[37] See above, Chapter 2, for a discussion of how much this was because of a lack of coal.

[38] Robson, *Man-Made Fibers Industry* (1958), p. 17. Count de Chardonnet patented the nitro-cellulose process in 1885, and commercial production began four or five years later. Production reached 40,000 pounds in 1891 and 2,900 tons in 1913. Calder states that France discouraged the viscose artificial-silk industry in an effort to protect natural silk. "Failing to get adequate support, French industrial chemists took their artificial silk processes elsewhere [abroad]." See "Technology," in Dewhurst et al., *Europe's Needs and Resources* (1961), p. 795.

[39] See Gignoux, *Enterprise française* (1955), on Pechiney, and Lebréton, "Une Expérience de la dispersion industrielle dans l'électrochimie" (1946). La Société Électro-Chimie was founded in 1889 to produce chlorine and sodium electrolytically. The first 500 kilograms of aluminum had been produced by Allais-Camargues at Salindres in 1860. By 1900 production was 1,000 tons; by 1910, 10,000 (Jeanneney, *Les Transformations économiques,* 1954–55, p. 97).

rather than the process.[40] When this failed and the Swiss and German production of fuchsine (a red synthetic dye) by different methods could not be legally stopped, the financier-administrators of La Fuchsine, against the wishes and warnings of the original engineers and producers, decided to try to wipe out their competitors by driving down the price. This maneuver was unavailing and, with local sales in Lyon suffering from the depression in silk in 1864–1866, the administrators sold the patents to Paris industrialists and liquidated the company, to the bitter resentment of Lyon as a whole and especially the original manufacturers and engineers. The latter emigrated and aided in the establishment of the Swiss organic-chemical industry. The St. Denis dye company in Paris never amounted to anything, having only 200 men in 1870 and growing but little thereafter. When a general chemical company of less than 300 employees — Kestner in Thann (Alsace), which made some dyes — was lost to France in 1870 through the Treaty of Frankfort,[41] the setback in dyestuffs was complete. By 1913 Germany was producing 90 percent of the world's production of synthetic dyes.[42]

The chemical industry, then, hardly qualifies as a growth leader during this period, either in heavy inorganic chemicals or in the entire industry.

The automobile industry is more interesting in a number of respects. French production in 1913 was double that of Britain, and French exports in 1911 and 1912 were larger by value than those of the United States. Half of the French automobile output, in fact, was exported, and half of this to Britain.[43] Growth was very rapid, but numbers were small. Production grew from 2,000 in 1900 to 45,000 in 1912. The United States was producing 360,000 cars in 1912, when its exports were 154 million francs to the French 212 million. Firms in the industry were larger, on the average, than most metalworking branches: 33,000 workers (or one fourth of the working force in chemicals) in 48 factories, for an average of 666 workers per factory. If components are included, the labor force rises to 100,000, but the average size of

[40] For a detailed account of the La Fuchsine fiasco, in which Henri Germain of the Crédit Lyonnais had a major role, see Bouvier, *Le Crédit Lyonnais* (1961), esp. pp. 374–381, where he states that the Fuchsine experience was decisive in turning the Crédit Lyonnais away from enterprise to security flotation. Another full account of the episode is given by Laferrère, *Lyon, ville industrielle* (1960), pp. 153ff.

[41] Haber, *Chemical Industry during the Nineteenth Century*, p. 113.

[42] The French government protected the natural-dye industry by requiring the use of garance for uniforms, though the synthetic alizatin dye was better. Note how long the ochre industry hung on in Péyrane in Wylie's *Village in the Vaucluse* (1957), p. 21.

[43] Ministère du Commerce, *Rapport générale*, I, 369.

plant would drop precipitously.[44] These were luxury cars, however, not produced in series, and the industry was mainly interested in mechanical perfection and prizes.[45] Not until after the spurt of World War I could the industry properly be said to have been an engine of growth.[46] And even here there is a question of whether the growth effects were localized or dispersed. The Peugeot firm at Sochaux was successful and, along with Alsthom in electric locomotives at Belfort and Japy in typewriters at Montbéliard, produced a concentration of some 47,000 workers in the mechanical industries. Although this has been called a regional growing point,[47] the region as a whole did not respond to it. Outside of 4 establishments of more than 1,000 workers, there were but 20 of 200–1,000 and 36 of 50–200 before reaching real diffusion.[48] The mechanical industry, led by automobiles, constituted less of a growing point than an island of growth in an underdeveloped sea.

What is then meant by a leading sector — industries with the fastest relative growth? the largest absolute growth? the largest degree of technical change? the greatest effects on technical change in other industries, by force of example or analogy? producing the largest increases, actual or potential, in the demand for outputs (or the supply of inputs) of other industries? or some weighted or unweighted combination of all of these? In any case, the leading sector must be one where change is independent. If so, it is hard to rate chemicals as a leading sector in French growth in the period 1896–1913. Its changes were induced rather than autonomous. Its growth was large neither absolutely nor relatively; its technical change was small; its effects in inducing technical change in other industries are debatable.

Electricity qualifies in terms of the degree of technical change and the rate of growth. But the absolute growth and the dispersion effects

[44] The number of suppliers was still 1,000 in 1919, when the producers were 200, and went down only to 467 in 1954, when the producers had shrunk to 17. While there are a few large suppliers, especially in tires where three firms have 88 percent of the business, the average number of employees per firm was 79 among the suppliers as compared with 6,800 in automobile construction. See Mossé, *Localisation dans l'industrie automobile* (1956), p. 32. See also, Chapter 11, note 35.

[45] See Ministère du Commerce, pp. 308–309, where the history of the French automobile industry is set forth almost entirely in terms of prizes won at exhibitions.

[46] Note that production in 1929 was 6.5 times that in 1913 (Jeanneney, p. 97). Rostow reserves the automobile as a leading sector for the period of high-level mass consumption and is interested in its effects on the petroleum industry, road building, the building of suburbs, changing retail distribution, and so on — a much wider effect than those on the supplying industries. See *Stages of Growth*, p. 77.

[47] See Blanc, Juillard, Ray, and Rochefort, *Les Régions de l'Est* (1960), p. 109.

[48] *Ibid.*, p. 96.

were both limited because of its small size. Output rose from 20 in 1900 to 100 in 1913, but the small size of this base is seen by the further rise to 1,000 in 1937 and 2,300 in 1953.[49]

The rapid growth of the French economy in the period from 1896 to 1913 rested in absolute terms on iron ore, steel, and textiles. These industries were absolutely large to begin with and grew at rates faster than total industrial production.[50] Technological change occurred in steel making, through the enlargement of plant, and in iron ore, with the solution of mining problems. It was not substantial in textiles. But the figures raise the important theoretical problem of whether the notion of a leading sector has any meaning when the qualitatively significant industries are quantitatively insignificant, and when the industries with big weight in the indexes undergo little technical change.

THE LAGGING SECTOR — BUILDING

The French economy is said to have reached maturity about 1910, and maturity is defined as "the period when a society has effectively applied the range of [the then] modern technology to the bulk of its resources." [51] There is "need to allow for regions or sectors of the economy to resist the full application of the range of modern technology," Rostow points out, citing the French technologically backward peasantry and France's tendency to export capital, despite technologically lagging industrial sectors.[52] The technological definition of maturity, then, must be an approximation.

In an interesting *tu quoque* defense of agriculture, Latil says that, for everything one can say about agriculture, one can find another sector of the French economy in the same quandary. Agriculture is a primary industry; so is mining. Its adherents earn low incomes; this is equally true of common labor. It is a declining industry; but so are textiles, small-scale business, commerce. It lives by protection; so do many other French industries. It has a low rate of technological progress; so does building.[53] He might have gone further and said

[49] Jeanneney, p. 97. In absolute terms the industry grew from 300 million kilowatt-hours in 1900 to 1,800 million in 1913; to 16,000 million in 1929; and to 64,500 million in 1959 (*Annuaire statistique, 1961*, p. 130).
[50] The index of industrial production rose from 100 in 1900 to 156 in 1913. Steel production outside of Alsace-Lorraine rose from 1.6 million tons to 7.0 million; iron-ore production, from 6,100,000 tons to 21,900,000. The increase in textile production is reflected in the fact that imports of cotton went from 146,000 tons in 1890 to 346,000 in 1912. Capronnier, *La Crise de l'industrie cotonnière* (1959), p. 37.
[51] Rostow, *Stages of Growth*, p. 59.
[52] *Ibid.*, p. 67.
[53] Latil, *Revenu agricole* (1956), p. 313.

that anything bad one can say about agriculture also applies to building, assuming that calling agriculture a primary industry is not an aspersion.

Rostow is right in raising the question of technologically backward areas for France. There are not only agriculture and the artisanal elements in industry.[54] There is building, which accounts for 20 percent of industry and 7 percent of the total labor force. Building has been called a "large, backward, leading industry." [55] It and agriculture together account for a large part of the difference in absolute levels of income between Britain and France.[56]

Building is regarded by Chatelain as a motor industry. "When building goes, everything goes." [57] "Much building means prosperity." These bits of folk wisdom suggest the critical nature of the industry. Its backwardness is revealed not only by comparison with Britain, but by the Economic Commission for Europe's calculation that it, and agriculture, alone of all sectors in 1954, were below the national average in terms of output per worker, calculated, as in Table 25, by dividing the percentage of output per sector by its percentage of employment, including unpaid female workers. The figures reflect, of course, more than the economic efficiency of the separate industries, showing in particular their capital intensities. But it is striking that services as a whole, particularly trade and other services which are labor-intensive, should have so much higher output per man than building, where the opportunity exists to employ capital.

The troubles of the building industry, which persist today, have

[54] See Chapter 8. Note that Table 9, which shows that 87 percent of industrial establishments had 1 to 5 workers in 1906, omitted self-employed workers with no helpers (isolés), amounting to 1,400,000 with the isolés not in establishments numbering 4,200,000.

[55] Chatelain, "Une Grande industrie motrice française attardée: Le Bâtiment" (1958).

[56] For the difference in the structure and output of the building industry in France and Britain in 1955, see the following table from Passe, *Économies comparées* (1957), p. 29 (figures in thousands):

	Total active population	Independent workers, employers	Wage earners	Number of dwellings constructed	Area of industrial building (sq. meters)
France	1,392	253	1,139	210	1,587
Great Britain	1,526	142	1,384	324	3,570

This table, from official sources, illustrates not only the greater productivity but also the different organization of the British industry.

[57] See also Labrousse, *L'Évolution économique de la France et du Royaume Uni* (1954), p. 75: "In that transformed France [referring to the Second Empire], building went" (*le bâtiment va*).

Table 25. Output, Employment, and Output per Man
by Sectors, France, 1954

Sector	Output (percent of total)		Employment (percent of total)	Output per man (percent of national average)
Agriculture	18		32	57
Industry	40		35	116
Mining and quarrying		2.6	2.0	130
Manufacturing		30.6	25.2	121
Electricity, gas, water		1.6	0.7	229
Construction		5.5	6.9	80
Services	42		33	123
Transport and communication		7.2	5.1	141
Trade		11.9	9.7	122
Other services		22.5	18.5	121
	100		100	(Average) 100

Source. United Nations, *Economic Survey of Europe in 1956*, chap. vii, p. 20.

an ancient origin, but the subject remains shrouded in mystery because of the paucity of data. Early information is derived from the
tax on doors and windows, with figures after 1870 divided into those
buildings with more than and those with less than six openings.[58]
Later in the century there are more data, fairly full for Paris though
fragmentary for the rest of the country.[59] Even the complete data are
not always comparable. The number of entire houses constructed in

[58] In 1822 there were 6,400,000 buildings subject to tax; in 1841, 7,500,000; in
1870, 8,500,000, of which 5,700,000 had less than six openings and 2,800,000
had six or more openings. See *Annuaire statistique, 1878*, p. 506. Employment
data from the quinquennial censuses cannot be used, even if one had some idea
of the course of output per man, because of the shift of the census definition of
employment, between 1861 and 1866, from persons attached to the industry to
persons active in it. For a highly seasonal industry like building, where attachment
can vary in degree, it is impossible to interpret the change in number of people
employed in building from 2,120,000 in 1861 to 833,000 in 1866. Even the
doubling of employment between 1851 and 1856 — from 940,000 to 1,943,000 —
is no very accurate measure of the change in the labor input. After 1866 there are
no more data until 1886, when the active labor force was 640,000. Subsequent
numbers are 1891, 620,000; 1896, 553,000; 1901, 572,000; 1906, 550,000. To
move from employment to output, however, is peculiarly difficult in French
building.
[59] See Chapter 1.

Paris is unhelpful for revealing housing changes because it ignores demolitions and additions to structure. It has the further disadvantage, both for lodging and for construction, that it makes no distinction among houses by number of stories or cubic footage.[60] Data on these measures are available for Paris from 1920 and from 1938, but on an authorization, not a completion, basis. For France as a whole an index from 1900 exists, but it links different series based on authorizations, quantity of manpower employed, or materials utilized and is not very good.[61]

Demand for housing was held back by slow rates of population growth. But housing demand varies with migration, rather than with total population. This is true for Paris,[62] and probably for the rest of

[60] Direction de la Statistique, *Le Logement à Paris* (1946), table 82, pp. 105–106. The series is worth setting out from 1872 to 1913 to show the shape of the 1880 boom and the absence of any big response during the 1896–1914 growth period. A shift to apartment houses during this period, if one took place, would make the figures worthless.

1872	877	1883	2,400	1894	1,415	1905	1,078
1873	1,392	1884	2,501	1895	1,361	1906	1,051
1874	1,258	1885	1,806	1896	1,415	1907	985
1875	1,160	1886	1,593	1897	1,389	1908	986
1876	1,034	1887	1,220	1898	1,168	1909	841
1877	1,078	1888	1,178	1899	1,091	1910	873
1878	1,800	1889	1,043	1900	653	1911	1,186
1879	1,383	1890	1,408	1901	935	1912	1,136
1880	1,444	1891	1,409	1902	1,227	1913	1,322
1881	1,772	1892	1,276	1903	1,215		
1882	1,992	1893	1,430	1904	1,064		

[61] Jeanneney, *Les Transformations économiques*, p. 96, notes that, on this basis, building rose from 75 in 1900 to 100 in 1913, fell to practically zero in 1919, hit 137 in 1930, 51 in 1938, and had climbed back to only 71 in 1952. I do not know whether the rise from 1900 to 1913 is affected by the purely sporadic drop in 1900 shown in new construction of houses in Paris, or whether a series which compared 1913, say, with the average of 1894–1896 would show only a sideways movement.

[62] The annual average increase in number of new houses and in population per decade in Paris from Direction de la Statistique, *Le Logement à Paris* (p. 107), is revealing in this connection. The 1851–1860 figures include gains from an enlargement of administrative area.

Years	Houses	Population	Years	Houses	Population
1833–1840	260	13,350	1890–1900	1,261	23,875
1841–1850	260	12,550	1901–1910	1,025	19,150
1851–1860	3,240	51,850	1911–1920	650	8,225
1861–1870	510	27,103	1921–1930	650	3,325
1871–1880	1,269	34,675	1931–1937	625	4,175
1881–1890	1,742	20,225			

See also INSEE, "Logement en France depuis cent ans" (1957), p. 1007, which gives rough orders of magnitude in building for France as a whole by five-year

France before World War I. During the 1920s there were two main effects on demand: rent control and inflation, which killed output of rental housing, and government finance of the reconstruction of devastated areas, which limited building to those areas.[63] When this stopped, building died away almost entirely during the 1930s. Since World War II, the gradual erosion of rent controls, and the rise in the rates of population growth and urbanization, have raised demand to new heights, where supply has had trouble following.

The importance for migration of government expenditure for social-overhead capital, including railroads, the boulevards of Paris, and the reconstruction of ports, has been referred to earlier.[64] An important element in the demand for housing was the distribution of income. At the end of the nineteenth century, new building was largely for the rich.[65] Houses for the masses were inadequate in size, sanitation, amenities, and amount, in both city and country. Urban rents for the working man rose, and vacancies fell.[66] A series of laws enacted in 1894, 1906, 1908, and 1912 to stimulate investment in "cheap" housing was not effective.

On the supply side, there were two problems: finance and technical organization. Finance was stimulated, especially for Paris, by the establishment of the Crédit Foncier which, according to the Inspection Générale des Finances, financed a large proportion of the new construction by issuance of securities. It also bought and sold properties. When the rate of interest was too high to assure the profitability of construction, subsidies on interest and fiscal exemptions were agreed upon. This mechanism was ended by rent control and successive devaluations.[67] Capital turned away from what used to be considered a sure investment, one for the "father of a family." [68] Or, as another writer put it, the peasant attitude toward buying land which used to

---

periods, and shows the highest periods for 1856–1861, 1861–1866 (200,000 each), 1921–1926 (400,000), and 1946–1954 (600,000). The 1960 goal was 240,000 dwellings a year. Unfortunately, the increases in housing of 200,000 for the years 1896–1911 cannot be compared effectively with earlier and later periods because the system of estimation changed.

[63] Notice the failure of Paris building to rise in the 1920s above the wartime level. Not all the building in the north and east was governmental; much was financed by companies for their workers, especially the SNCF and the coal companies. See George, La Ville (1952), p. 105.

[64] See esp. Chapters 9 and 10.

[65] George, La Ville, p. 113.

[66] D'Avout, Le Crédit immobilier en France (1914), p. 5.

[67] Inspection Générale des Finances, Les Interventions dans le logement (1952), pp. 71–72. This report states that devaluation was more important than rent control for finance because the borrower enjoyed the speculation, being interested in capital gains rather than rental income. For the contrary view, see Institut de Conjoncture, Étude économique sur le problème du logement (1944).

[68] Gigou, Le Problème du logement en France (1945), p. 3.

motivate the building entrepreneur has changed. Tastes turned from housing to food and, more recently, to automobiles.[69]

The main problem, however, was the organization of the industry — in 1850, 1913, 1929, and today. Chatelain has said that in fact two industries exist — one which handles large public works and is made up of big firms; another narrowly characterized as building, which is carried on largely by artisans.[70] It is not clear where the support for this distinction comes. The Inspection des Finances, which investigated building for the government, focused its attention on the Habitation à Loyer Modéré (HLM) low-income housing and found that 80 percent of the enterprises had less than five workers.[71] A thorough study was made of the finances of these enterprises, which were said mostly to be permanently in a crisis for cash. Delays were appalling: France, the country of expensive construction, was the country of slow construction. In one case it took eighteen months of formalities before putting down the first stone of an HLM building, then two years to finish it.[72] The Inspection and the industry were agreed that the big task was to achieve a more effective distribution of responsibility for design, construction, and costs between the architect and the entrepreneur. The Inspection thought that the architect should be made responsible to the contractor; the industry, for which an architect was the rapporteur, thought that the task should be assigned to the architects.[73]

Technically, French building has had some significant achievements. Chatelain states that the public-works industry was already capital-intensive in 1860, making use of electric lights, elevators, compressed air.[74] The tower crane was a French first. The industry changed from stone to brick and then to reinforced concrete. But it remained inefficient. In company housing, Michelin tried to get the Limousin mason to streamline his methods, but met the proud resistance of a thousand-year tradition. In the postwar period, the industry has close to 10 percent of foreigners and an additional 3.5 percent of Africans. It needs to develop immigration, apprenticeship and professional edu-

[69] Chatelain, "Une grande industrie motrice attardée," pp. 581–582.
[70] Ibid., p. 573.
[71] Inspection des Finances, p. 44.
[72] Ibid., p. 13.
[73] Gigou, p. 8; Inspection des Finances, p. 119. The Inspection thought that architects had too difficult a time in shifting from the long period of inactivity in the 1930s to full swing after World War II, noting that much of their work had to be done over again on the job, that site work was badly organized, and so on (p. 47). It was noted also that Le Corbusier's brilliant apartments in Marseilles took four and one-half years to complete, instead of the scheduled one, and cost 28 percent above the estimates (p. 60).
[74] Chatelain, p. 578. Any visitor has it borne in on him forcefully that Paris was one of the earliest cities to acquire elevators.

cation, new materials, new techniques, organize work better on the site, and so on. All agree that building is expensive and unprofitable.[75]

Like agriculture, building is relatively backward in all countries, and there are evident reasons which explain the fact. But the position has been worse in France. Partly this may originate in the industry's early connection with agriculture — its strong seasonal character,[76] with employment of migratory and casual labor.[77] It is like stevedoring, which until recently resisted the application of capital and relied on the brute strength of the dregs of the labor supply.

The question remains, however, whether there was not a special French handicap in organization, with the peculiar division of responsibility for building among client, contractor, and architect that inhibited technological advance. The position is similar to that of tenant and owner in British agriculture which, it was suggested in Chapter 11, slowed down transformation there. When it is unclear how the costs and benefits of technical change are to be borne and distributed, the market mechanism may not work effectively in achieving technical advance.

My interest is not in industrial organization, however, or in the level of efficiency, but in growth. This may be as much a matter of technical change as of capital/output ratios, shifts of demand through the operation of Engel's law, and so on. To the extent that the theories of stages of growth ignore differences in the capacity of different societies to initiate and apply technical change, not only generally but sector by sector, such theories have little explanatory or predictive value. It is all very well to set out the caveats and to state that one cannot emphasize too much that the stages are arbitrary, or that the sec-

[75] It goes without saying that this point is made by the industry. See Federation National du Bâtiment, *Sortir la construction de l'impasse* (1956), p. 51, which gives profits at only 3 percent and asks whether this is equitable. The Inspection des Finances mentions that at Rennes 31 percent of entrepreneurs (including those with deficits) had profits of less than 1.5 percent of turnover. In a second report, *Organismes d'habitations à loyer modéré* (1952), the Inspection notes that real costs of building in constant francs increased 50 percent above prewar levels. See also George, *La Ville*, p. 113, who observes that in the realm of financial speculations of the last hundred years, house construction has been one of the least profitable.

[76] The industry takes August off for vacations, just like other industries, despite the fact that it is the best month in the year for construction (see Leavasseur, "La Construction de logement en France et en Allemagne," p. 33). Leavasseur observes that France has the benefit over Germany of a milder winter, though it has not made such great efforts for winter building (*ibid.*, p. 34). This is another example of the truth that objective conditions count less for economic development than the nature and extent of the response to them.

[77] See above, Chapter 4. Néré notes that the building industry and public works in France often played the role of regulator, absorbing workers temporarily unemployed in other industries ("Une Statistique du salaire et de l'emploi en France," 1955, p. 227).

ondary effects of rapid growth in a sector suffused with new technology are not automatic.[78] But, in the last analysis, the proponents of stages come to believe that the procrustean bed fits everyone.

THE STAGE OF MASS CONSUMPTION

One final question on stage theories is relevant to our period, and in fact covers most of it: the eighty-five-year delay in Britain in moving from "technical maturity" (in 1851) to the age of mass consumption (after 1935). This seems to bother Rostow, who devotes two passages to it which are not identical. In the *Economist* article the explanation is, first, that durable consumer goods did not exist[79] — apart from housing and, beginning in the 1890s, the bicycle — and that rising British real income was spent on more and better food, clothing, housing, public utilities, and transport; second, that the rise in real income and population was in fact slowed down by a "policy" of capital exports.[80] In *Stages of Economic Growth,* on the other hand, it is agreed that the explanation that the British could not consume durable goods because the automobile had not been invented is satisfactory for many purposes. But a case is made that British experience involved a gap and for three reasons: (1) if incomes and consumption had been high enough, technology might have evolved more toward durable consumer goods; (2) gaps occur in other societies; (3) British interest turned from increasing real output to social reform.[81]

It is unnecessary to summarize the changes in the British economy between 1850 and 1935 — in domestic and foreign investment, the rate of technological change, the problems of a disintegrated economy in responding to foreign competition in cheaper food and textiles or to new products and processes, especially when technical progress shifted from an empirical to a scientific phase. Moreover, there is no basis for denying the importance of the change in attitude toward real income which Rostow mentions. Like the slowdown of technological progress, however, it occurred in the 1870s rather than at maturity in

[78] *Stages of Growth,* p. 1; "Leading Sectors and the Take-Off," p. 11.

[79] This is how I interpret the sentence, "Maturity is a matter of virtuosity and the spread of technique on the supply side."

[80] "Rostow on Growth," *Economist,* August 15, 1959, p. 415. For comment on whether capital exports slowed down growth in Britain, see above, Chapter 3.

[81] *Stages of Growth,* p. 69n. The footnote concludes: "In short, even narrowly examined, much in British history in the period 1850–1900 is illuminated by the notion that this was a society which took its technological virtuosity as given and, at a decorous rate, proceeded to explore, at the margin, objectives beyond." In the following chapter Rostow notes that the national pursuit of external power and depression can also serve, along with the welfare state, as an alternative to durable consumer goods (pp. 73–74).

1851. But the major objection is this: the age of high mass consumption is needed to explain American experience and to support an independent prediction that the Soviet Union will move from capital formation and armaments to consumption. Any system of stages that applies somewhere must apply to the country that pioneered the Industrial Revolution. The attempt to rationalize the gap between maturity and mass consumption results less in support of the existence of a gap than a *reductio ad absurdum* of the theory of stages, beyond the initial discontinuity of the take-off.

CHAPTER 14

GROWTH:
SYSTEMATIC OR RANDOM?

I have examined the most widely held theories about the course of economic growth in Britain and France. Before concluding, it may be in order to attempt a rapid review of a few quite different explanations, ones that do not share the same degree of popular support. Most of these look to what are in most systems exogenous phenomena — the harvest, the gold supply, war — although the independent variables in one system may be dependent from a wider perspective. A paragraph or two is also due the systematic Marxian theory of economic crisis under capitalism, despite my ignorance of the subtleties of the theory.

More fundamentally, the question must be raised about whether the course of economic growth in Britain and France has been the result of an unfolding series of accidents or random events in which the contingencies have overwhelmed the constants. This question is not new in these pages. It has been raised in connection with the repeal of the Corn Laws, the Revolution of 1848, and especially the extent to which government policy is the result of a chance interaction of personality, intelligence, and circumstances, or whether countries achieve in some sense the leadership they deserve.[1]

This is, of course, the core of the theory of social causation. Do accidental disturbances affecting societies that respond in systematic ways produce accidental or systematic results? The question is not only an interesting philosophical riddle. It also calls for a quantitative answer in which the relative strengths of the stimulus and the response are judged. It is possible to go only a short distance toward this quantitative answer, but the journey is necessary.

THE HARVEST

Under this heading we may group all kinds of natural phenomena — good and bad harvests; plant, animal, and, if it had been of economic

---

[1] See above, Chapters 10, 1, and 9.

significance in 1851–1950, human disease; bad weather in its industrial effects. Bad weather had profound effects at the beginning and at the end of the period: the disastrous crop year of 1846 accelerated the repeal of the Corn Laws, the Irish emigration, the political revolution of 1848 in France, and the ensuing demographic revolution; the winter, spring, and summer of 1947 led to the intensification of the cold war and would have brought disaster had it not been for the Marshall Plan.[2] Bad weather at the end of the 1870s also contributed, along with the animal diseases of rinderpest and liverrot, to the view that British agricultural troubles were the result of natural causes rather than of the iron steamship, the transcontinental American railroad, and the settling of Civil War veterans on Minnesota and Dakota homesteads. The Great Depression in British agriculture was a calamity which stretched from 1879, the wettest, to 1894, the driest, year in memory.[3] Plant disease in its turn has had important effects on the course of French economic growth and policy: phylloxera in wine combined with the fall in world wheat prices to apply strong deflationary pressure to France in the 1880s. Together with pébrine in silk and the loss of Alsace-Lorraine after the Franco-Prussian War, it scattered the handful of supporters of Louis Napoleon's policy of freer trade by undermining the main export groups.

Agricultural difficulties were not significant for the course of British growth at any time during our period, because of the small size of the sector — 20 percent of the national income in 1850 and 26 percent of the male labor force.[4] In France, the Revolution of 1848 produced few long-run political changes, and the demographic discontinuity was superimposed on a general declining trend. The phylloxera, moreover, operated in strong conjunction with social forces. Augé-Laribé notes that the prosperity of the Midi before phylloxera had been demoralizing. The area never had much discipline or respect for law. It was a country of contraband, of extremes, without resignation, patience, or stability. It is this character, he states, which determined the sector's history. Ultimate recovery after 1900 was achieved through study and education. In the meantime, there were adulteration, fraud, a shift from quality to quantity, riots, strikes, more laws and more violation of them.[5]

After 1892 the slow pace of agricultural improvement lowered the overall rate of growth on the average, but probably without significant causal effects. A short crop might produce significant balance-of-

[2] Smith, *The State of Europe* (1949), pp. 23ff.
[3] Young, *Portrait of an Age* (1936), p. 145.
[4] Clapham, *Economic History of Modern Britain* (1952), II, 22.
[5] *Politique agricole*, pp. 84, 175, 178ff.

payments fluctuations,[6] or contribute to inflation by giving the peasants a weapon with which to ensure that the burdens of the economy do not fall on them. The impact on overall growth, however, was not important.[7]

Finally, Britain and France experienced many of the same natural phenomena with substantially different reactions: the crops of 1846 and 1847; the bad summers of the late 1870s; the cheap wheat of the 1880s; the frost, floods, and drought of 1947. The operation of any system is subject to random external perturbations. If two systems respond differently to the same disturbance, the system is more significant than the stimulus. British farmers in the 1850s went on improving techniques; the French peasant reduced the size of his family. In 1947 the British applied more austerity; the French, greater inflation. In the 1870s and 1880s one could say that the response was different: the liquidation of agriculture in Britain and the tariffs of 1881 and 1892 in France. But one could also claim that both suffered a depression in consequence of the price decline. The case is strong for France, but weak for Britain. In the 1880s as much as 64 percent of Britain's wheat was met by imports.[8] In this circumstance, cheaper wheat might be regarded as an expansionary rather than a deflationary influence. If we conclude that France and Britain responded differently to natural disaster, we can hardly regard Nature as the determinant of the path of growth.

GOLD PRODUCTION

The case is often made, and as frequently criticized, that the course of economic growth has been determined by changes in demand and supply for gold. On this showing, gold discoveries in California and Australia in 1849 and 1851 explain the boom in the third quarter of the nineteenth century. The Great Depression resulted from the shift of Germany from the bimetallic standard to gold, after 1871, and the resumption of specie payments in the United States in 1879. The subsequent recovery in the 1890s can be attributed to the Rand strike in 1890. The theory encounters greater difficulty after World War I than before. Monetary experience in Britain could be attributed to the lack

[6] See White, *French International Accounts* (1933), p. 139.

[7] The disastrous winter, spring, and summer of 1947 were highly inflationary in France, and of great political importance in encouraging the Soviet Union to adopt a more aggressive posture in the cold war. But major importance attaches to the impact of the winter frost in revealing the fragility of British industrial recovery, rather than on French agricultural production, even in its weakened postwar state.

[8] Olson and Harris, "Free Trade in Corn" (1959), p. 147.

of gold support for the currency, after the wartime expansion of the fiduciary issue of the Bank of England to absorb the Bradburys; and the recovery of the 1930s could be ascribed to the new high price of gold. Even the slowness of British growth after World War II might be laid at the door of a fixed gold price. But the radically different French experience after World War I requires a different theory. If it remains monetary, it has to be put in terms of under- and overvaluation of the franc and the pound, respectively, in the 1920s and of the pound and the franc, respectively, in the 1930s. This is a monetary explanation which goes beyond gold. Overvaluation of the pound was treated, along with reparations and the forty-hour week, in the discussion in Chapter 9 of whether governmental policy was a random phenomenon or emerged from the sociopolitical forces that shaped the economy.

The role of gold production raises questions of all sorts which true believers have no difficulty in disposing of while heretics remain unconvinced. How did the discovery of gold in California in 1849 produce a big rise in French exports in 1849, as Sée claims,[9] for example? And if the mechanism worked so rapidly then, why did it function so slowly in the 1890s, the depression continuing to deepen after the Witwatersrand strike of 1891 until 1895 or 1896? Marjolin says that there is no necessary constant lag and that the rise of prices can even anticipate the discovery of gold through speculation.[10] What is the mechanism — a monetary one or one that operates through income? If the former, how do we account for the fact that the gold reserves of the Bank of England did not expand until 1866, when India stopped absorbing the silver replaced by gold? [11]

In the Great Depression the major question is how the shortage of gold produced depression while interest rates were low and demand for money slack. The discussion has been ably summed up by Rostow, complete even to the two views normally produced by Keynes on a

[9] *Histoire économique de la France* (1942), II, 236.

[10] *Prix, monnaie et production* (1941), p. 168n. There is the possible explanation that the Californian and Australian discoveries were of alluvial deposits, which quickly resulted in output, while the South African discoveries required investment in deep mines that began to produce in quantity only in 1896.

[11] See above, Chapter 12. Habakkuk, "Free Trade and Commercial Expansion" (1940), p. 775. Hughes says that gold was pouring into Britain in embarrassing quantities in 1851, and that gold was retained in England in circulation, if not in the central reserve (the coin circulation was perhaps twice the note circulation), *Fluctuations in Trade* (1960), pp. 243, 247. But note that at the time of the Civil War gold was in short supply because of the offset of Indian hoarding, and that Australian and Californian consignments came to hand at the most critical junctures (Habakkuk). The expansion went on in Britain for almost a decade more, through 1873, and, after the disruption of the 1870s, through 1882 in France.

single subject.[12] And Rostow votes against any explanation that discusses prices and gold, or prices and interest rates, but omits the vital question of investment and omits any mechanism by which the lack of gold could produce depression simultaneous with low interest rates.[13]

For the final period, there is the timing already referred to, the question of absolute versus percentage gains in the world gold supply, and the role of technological change in France. Marjolin's explanation of the Great Depression relies on percentage changes, since the absolute level of production held up well. His charts show a rise of gold output in absolute terms about 1847, reaching a peak about 1851, and holding that level until 1870. Thereafter the rate of output fell only very slightly all the way to 1891. In percentage terms, however, the rate of increase in the cumulated world gold stock reached more than 4 percent in 1852, slid down steadily to above 2 percent in 1870, and close to 1.5 percent in 1890.[14]

It is possible, of course, to think in terms of a relative shortage of gold during the Great Depression and to deal in the absolute amount of gold produced. Thus the fall in prices would result from the encounter between a big increase in goods production and roughly the same amount of gold production. But this ascribes causal significance to the output and only secondary importance to the gold which failed to balance. Marjolin's analysis starts out with the absolute amounts of new gold produced in the 1850s and then shifts to relative changes.

For Rist, the role of gold is incontestable and decisive — not perhaps sufficient, but necessary. The mechanism was the gap between the rate of interest on the financial market and the yields of enterprises, the former being in excess of the latter, even though very low. Its effects were also felt through influence on technical progress and on the psychology of producers.[15] Marjolin does not attempt to combine the monetary and the productivity explanations of price changes, but after contrasting them he votes for the monetary.[16]

The weight of historical opinion, however, comes out on the other side. The gold discoveries were real causes of economic expansion in the 1850s and the 1890s. But they were not the only or the most important causes.[17] In Britain the rapid expansion of the 1850s was

[12] Rostow, *British Economy in the Nineteenth Century* (1948), chap. vii. Both of Keynes's theories are from his *Treatise on Money* (1950); see p. 156.

[13] *Ibid.*, pp. 159–160. See also Coppock, "Causes of the Great Depression" (1961), p. 219.

[14] *Prix, monnaie et production*, chart, p. 185.

[15] Rist, introduction to Marjolin, *ibid.*, pp. viii, ix.

[16] Marjolin, *ibid.*, p. ix.

[17] Court, *Concise Economic History* (1958), p. 197.

due to factory legislation, trade unions, new railways, new gold, but
also to the character and extent of British overseas investment, which
stimulated technical change.[18] In the 1890s the main causes of the rise
in prices and the active employment of resources in Britain were found
in the export of capital from Great Britain; the economic expansion
of the United States and of the areas of recent settlement; and the
rise of new techniques in Western countries that demanded industrial
investments on a great scale. Developments among the new primary-
producing countries of the world, according to Court, were sufficient
to account for the 1900–1914 expansion, without gold.

In the Great Depression, in turn, although the gold discoveries of
a quarter-century earlier had spent their expansionary force, the real
pressure came not from the decline in monetary demand so much as
from the rise in physical supply — the consequence of the expansion
of the previous boom and, in particular, of the cheapening in transport
that linked world production in a single market. These developments
were more important than the declining rate of increase in world gold
stocks.[19]

Historians, as apart from economists, have emphasized the institutional rather than the quantitative aspects of the monetary phenomena,
and especially of the French indemnity. Young refers to "the disturbance of the French indemnity and the wild speculation which followed it in Germany." [20] Newbold sets out a more elaborate chain of
explanation for the Great Depression, starting with the American
expansion of silver production that led to the demonetization of that
metal, the German building of a gold stock, the shift of the Latin
Monetary Union from bimetallism to gold, and the French indemnity.[21]
To explain the slowing down of French and British growth after 1870
and 1873 by the random coincidence of silver discoveries in Nevada,
and the combination of the German levying of a large indemnity
and the French insistence on paying it, is to rob economic history,
perhaps rightly, of broad systematic forces.

WAR

The two world wars clearly had a massive impact on the British and
French economies of the twentieth century. If we assume that these
wars originated outside of the economic system — a position which

[18] Habakkuk, "Free Trade and Commercial Expansion," p. 804.
[19] Court, p. 198. Coppock, "Causes of the Great Depression," emphasizes
demand, but its real rather than monetary aspects.
[20] *Portrait of an Age,* p. 125.
[21] "Beginnings of the World Crisis" (1932), p. 435.

Marxists would not accept — did they determine the course of growth? The issue barely arises for the nineteenth century. The Crimean War in 1856 [22] and the Boer War in 1899 had economic repercussions. The Revolution of 1848 and the Franco-Prussian War were more deeply felt in France, but were still far from determining the course of economic growth. We have seen the effects of the Revolution of 1848 on population growth and of the Franco-Prussian War on peasant mobility, exploration for mineral resources, investment in French Lorraine, and technical change in French woolens. The loss of Alsace-Lorraine had no substantial effect in holding back the development of iron and steel or chemicals, as is occasionally alleged, though the loss in cotton textiles, including the printing and dyeing branches, was more serious, resulting in the withdrawal of support for freer trade.

A powerful nineteenth-century influence, especially on textiles, was exerted by the Civil War in the United States, with its contribution to sharp shifts in investment in textiles, on the one hand, and to foreign lending in India and Egypt, on the other. But none of these can be said to have provoked any decisive turning point for economic growth between 1850 and 1914.

The massive conflicts of the twentieth century evidently have had more important consequences. But it is difficult to be certain what they are. Paretti and Bloch observe that the wars at a minimum constituted an interruption to normal economic expansion. Writing of Western Europe as a whole, they note that if the periods of both wars are eliminated, Western Europe has grown at virtually the same rate as the United States — by 3.4 percent a year, compared to 3.7 percent. Industrial production in 1929 and 1937 was 68 and 69 percent of the prewar trend, or roughly the same in relation to trend as in 1920.[23] World War II, on the other hand, was different: by 1955 the loss occasioned by the war had been entirely made up. World War I left a gap that represented virtually a permanent setback; World War II caused an interruption, rapidly overcome,[24] or possibly a stimulus. There are thus at least two kinds of world wars in their effects on growth, if these conflicts did shape subsequent economic events.

But there is a further reason not to regard economic growth as having been determined entirely by war: the wide difference in British and French experience in the 1920s and the 1930s. Industrial production was roughly twice as large in Britain as in France in 1901 (8.5

[22] Coppock, "Causes of the Great Depression," pp. 222–223, ascribes the depression to the decline in demand owing to the change in trend in railroad investment, the capital-saving character of innovations in shipbuilding, and the falling off of the wars which had characterized 1850–1875.

[23] Paretti and Bloch, "Industrial Production in Western Europe" (1956), p. 202.

[24] Ibid., p. 203.

and 4.7 percent of the Western European 1955 total), and again
roughly twice as large in 1937 and 1955 (18 and 9.3 percent in 1937;
30 and 14 percent in 1955). In the 1920s, however, Britain in 1929
was 13.5 percent of the 1955 Western European total and France 10.5
percent, or somewhat more than three-quarters of the British amount.[25]
In general, Britain and France had grown by roughly the same order
of magnitude between 1901 and 1955; but at the halfway point in
1929, France had expanded twice as rapidly as Britain; and during
the last half of the period, Britain grew twice as rapidly as France.[26]
There were differences in the war experience of each country, to be
sure — deaths and wounded, physical destruction, and the intensity of
diversion from the tenor of peacetime existence were more far-reaching for France than for Britain in World War I. For World War II it
is perhaps impossible to compare the intensity of effects, but suffice it
to say that between uninvaded Britain, with six years of hard fighting,
and occupied France, with only a limited amount of formal war but
with prison camps and resistance, the character of the experiences was
different. But it is hardly these differences, in themselves, which account for the disjointed pace of French and British growth.

There is a theorem that war hastens the rate of change in the established direction. Allen remarks that the war sped the transformation
in Birmingham from hardware to engineering, that it strengthened
growing industries, and, after a temporary stimulus, weakened declining industries.[27] The rise of the metal-transforming industries in
France during World War I, especially automobiles, and the spur to
electricity expansion have also been noted.[28]

But war has had two important effects for France which passed
Britain by. In the First World War there was wholesale destruction,
which led the state into a substantial program of investment, on the
one hand, and cleared the decks for a certain amount of modernization,
on the other. The big expansion of French industry to 1929 was in
steel; and it was here, and in the associated state canal system, railways, and private coal mines (which were electrified), that the increase in output and productivity was great.[29]

The more far-reaching and elusive change occurred in World War
II. Accompanying a change in the French attitude toward the family,
there was a deep-rooted alteration in the importance attached by

[25] *Ibid.*, table, p. 191.
[26] *Ibid.*, table, p. 203. On the basis of 1901 = 1, Britain was 1.6 in 1929; France,
2.2. If 1929 = 1, however, Britain in 1929 had reached 2.2; France, 1.3. For the
whole period, 1901 = 1, 1955 brought Britain to 3.5; France to 3.0.
[27] *Birmingham and the Black Country* (1929), p. 373.
[28] See Chapter 13.
[29] Burn, *Economic History of Steelmaking* (1940), pp. 408ff.

society to economic expansion and advance, to effective economic performance. Whether the change was sparked by the Inspection des Finances or was widespread in every echelon of French culture; whether it relied on a small group of planners or was carried out empirically by technocrats at all levels of industry; whether it relied exclusively on increased investment or mainly on changing technology — these are subjects that lie beyond the scope of the present discussion.[30] But war had a great deal to do with the change in attitude. And this was a significant difference between the British and the French experiences: the British had won the war; the French, though they belonged to the winning side, had lost it.

The temptation to conclude that winning wars is hard on economic developments, losing them helpful, is fairly easily resisted. Defeat can exercise a unifying pressure or lead to the sublimation of patriotic urges in economic forms. Jena brought intelligent and patriotic officials to the front in Germany, and this was a forerunner to unification.[31] The loss of Schleswig-Holstein spurred Danish transformation from grain to butter. The uprooted Lorrainers, after some delay, led the fastest-growing iron and steel industry in France between 1896 and 1913; and Herzog at Elbeuf was the innovator in French woolens after his removal from the ceded territory. German post–World War II economic revival owes much to the sublimation of defeat and expulsion in grinding work. But the United States and Belgium found independence stimulating in 1781 and 1830,[32] as Germany found its victory in 1870 and the United States in 1919, if not to the same extent in 1946. And Italy has scored economic achievements from 1946 to 1960, despite the ambiguous outcome of its war for the country.

The most that can be said of war is that it is a stimulant, that its destruction may remove blocks to change, and that on rare occasions it gives rise to a discontinuity which may favor growth. In World War I France experienced the purging destruction; in World War II, the discontinuity. On both occasions Britain emerged with some new capital, but with much of the old still intact — and with an enervating sense of having achieved a goal with little need to struggle on. There is the further point that the British civil service and political leadership moved into peace exhausted by the battles behind them, while the French, refreshed through the maquis or grown impatient under occupation, were virtually "new men." After World War I Britain

[30] See my "Postwar Resurgence of the French Economy" (1963).

[31] See Cameron, *France and the Economic Development of Europe* (1961), p. 26.

[32] "The conservatism and apparent lack of enterprise that seemed to characterize the Belgians soon disappeared after they won national independence." *Ibid.*, p. 335.

thought that defeat of Germany and Japan had removed its major international competition. A quarter-century later, the belief was widespread that the brilliant success of financial policy and fair shares in wartime could be repeated for postwar recovery, independent of hard work and technical ingenuity.[33] One weapon of wartime finance, deferred pay, constituted a commitment to postwar consumption. Hancock and Gowing put it mildly when they say: "There existed an implied contract between Government and people; the people refused none of the sacrifices that the Government demanded for the winning of the war; they in turn expected that the Government would show imagination and seriousness in preparing for the restoration.[34]

Unlike the French, who greeted peace with the resolve to restore the national honor and to achieve economic expansion — two complementary tasks — the British emerged from six years of war prepared not to earn, but to enjoy, the fruits of victory. War has far-reaching economic effects, but they are unsystematic, unpredictable, and may work through noneconomic mechanisms.

THE MARXIST INTERPRETATION

Like those discussed in the previous chapter, the Marxist theory of economic development is one of stages. There is the original or primitive accumulation of capital, the rise of industrial capitalism with the reproduction of individual and social capital, and then the final stage of capitalism with overproduction, underconsumption, economic crisis, the pauperization of the proletariat, revolution, and the establishment of socialism. According to this theory, the primitive accumulation of capital took the form of enclosures in Britain and in France of the theft of peasant rights in common land and long leases. During the rise of industrial capitalism, mechanization helped to depress the condition of the proletariat, denigrating the importance of muscle and making it possible to hire women and children. The pauperization of the proletariat can be absolute or relative, but it means that the masses lack the purchasing power to take off the market the goods produced. Underconsumption leads to bigger and bigger surpluses and declining profits. Exporting this surplus fails to help because exports lead to imports (no export of capital?). With the ultimate establishment of socialism, the unstable system of capitalism can be replaced by a planned economy in which economic growth is harmonized.

[33] See Hancock and Gowing, *British War Economy* (1949). The theme of fair shares runs through the entire book — see pp. 50, 51, 211, 305, 338, 501, 511, 536. For the successes of financial policy, see esp. pp. 165ff, 220ff, 324ff, 501ff.
[34] *Ibid.*, p. 541.

This stage theory suffers the disability that, while Marx and his intellectual followers can identify the period of primitive accumulation and the rise of industrial capitalism, the next two stages — when capitalism founders and when revolution leads to socialism — have had, like the Second Coming, to be postponed from time to time. Marx and Engels thought they were close in 1848, and at frequent intervals subsequently. Hyndman fixed 1889 as the date for the revolution, a full century after 1789.[35] Eliane Mossé attempts to demonstrate relative pauperization with budget studies and concludes that the condition of the workers deteriorated sharply from 1800 to 1840, when big industry was getting started, to reach a low in 1840–1850. The situation was then stagnant to 1880–1890, with several partial ameliorations, before deteriorating again to 1913, when the system was saved by war. At this stage, the workers were worse off than in 1880–1890, though better off than in 1850.[36]

Although Mossé's deflators are suspect,[37] there can be no doubt that the working classes were in desperate condition in the 1840s, and not only because of the rise in the price of bread in 1846–1848 at a time when the substitute potatoes were also in short supply. Lasserre's picture of working conditions in Lille between 1830 and 1848 makes it clear that there was little margin above subsistence.[38] But from 1850 on there was substantial improvement. The editor of one English translation of Zola's *Germinal* is obliged to explain that, writing of what is estimated to be 1867, Zola presents the unwary reader with a description of the standard of living of a mining community that includes "conditions which applied twenty years previously but are no longer true." [39] The peasants' existence also improved up to 1870 but was set back sharply by the depression. Before this pauperization had time to bring socialism, however, the recovery of the 1890s and the renewed flow of labor off the farm turned the tide.

It was easy to forecast collapse of the capitalistic system again in the 1930s, during the period of the right-wing rioting, when the Third Republic was rescued by the sit-down strikes and the Front Populaire. Or the converse: the ruin of the Third Republic by the Front Populaire and its salvation, after Munich, by the Reynaud government, which killed the five-day week, levied new taxes, adopted budgetary econ-

[35] Cole and Postgate, *The British People* (1961), p. 416.
[36] Mossé, *Marx et la croissance dans une économie capitaliste* (1956).
[37] See the appendix at the end of this book.
[38] *La Situation des ouvriers de l'industrie textile* (1952), chap. vi.
[39] See Tancock, introduction to the Penguin edition of *Germinal* (1954), p. 9. The theme of the miners' hunger pervades the book, and even Étienne Lantier, the mechanic who has been discharged from a railway shop in Lille, is bemused by getting enough to eat (see pp. 24, 25).

omies, and instituted a more liberal regime for prices, credit, and work.[40] Whatever the stage, the collapse of capitalism or its recovery, it was again interrupted by war. After the war Charles Bettelheim discussed the weaknesses of the French economy in these unideological terms — albeit with the main thesis that France is monopoly-ridden and that a social revolution and nationalization of sectors are needed to correct its decadence and stagnation — so that one is surprised to hear him called a Marxist.[41] But by 1955 Bouvier-Ajam was publishing a study of economic conditions in France which concluded that industry, agriculture, and trade had seriously deteriorated, that the workers were in a precarious position, and that consumption by the masses was near the subsistence level.[42]

Similar analyses exist for Britain. There is, for example, the wide-ranging controversy along Marxist–anti-Marxist lines over whether the standard of living in England declined or improved during the rise of industrial capitalism.[43] But the questions can be posed more widely than simply in terms of the immiserization of the proletariat, and attention should be directed to our later period. Maurice Dobb claims no infallibility for Marx, but merely that he was right more often than any other nineteenth-century economist on the main tendencies: economic concentration, the class struggle, the growth of organized labor, and the arrival of socialism.[44] He goes on, however, in his three books to deal with the more familiar Marxian predictions and to explain them away with frequent frank and damaging admissions. In *Capitalism Yesterday and Today* (1958):

> [Marx] only called the "falling rate of profit" a tendency [p. 38]. There is some indication in . . . profit trends that the period around World War I may have represented something of a climacteric. But the indications are far from clear; nor if so, is it clear exactly why [p. 43]. It is commonly supposed that Marx forecast a steady decline of real wages as capitalism developed and that he has been proved wrong. This I believe is a misunderstanding. . . . What mattered for Marx was less the precise way in which such tendencies worked out than the *contradictions* [italics in original] and hence the social conflicts which they cradled [pp. 38–39].

In *Studies in the Development of Capitalism* (1947), where Dobb's statement that fortuitous factors may overwhelm the scientific laws of history is significant:

[40] See Reynaud, *Thick of the Fight* (1955), pp. 199–203.
[41] *Bilan de l'économie française.*
[42] *L'Économie française au milieu du xx° siècle* (1955).
[43] See Hobsbawm, "The British Standard of Living, 1790–1850" (1957), and Hartwell, "The Rising Standard of Living in England" (1961).
[44] *Capitalism Yesterday and Today* (1958), pp. 37–38.

The tendency of wages to decline due to monopoly [is] obscured by largely fortuitous factors . . . including a number of special features [which] do not fit the simplified model: real wages rose [because of] the strength of organized labor and [the improvement in] the terms of trade . . . the increase in real productivity . . . and the persistence of small firms [pp. 330–334].

[The tendency of capitalism toward crisis is a result of underconsumption, although this was] not true in the 19th century except in the Great Depression [p. 357].

The classical picture is that change in investment leads to a crisis because of a rise in wages. There are signs that something like this characterized the investment situation in the 1870s — the Great Depression [p. 286].

There may be some obscurity about the causation of the Great Depression [p. 309].

[Underconsumption was staved off] by cartels . . . imperialism with its protected markets and capital exports of the Indian summer of 1896–1914 [pp. 310–311].

Underconsumption is now chronic [p. 292].

Interwar problems were deep-seated, and the difficulties were not due merely to wartime dislocation . . . [but to] underconsumption due to monopoly with many unemployed [p. 319].

There is a growing obsession of capitalism with limitation of markets [p. 357].

And in *Political Economy and Capitalism* (1937):

It was far from the intention of Marx that his analysis of capitalist society should provide a few simple principles from which the whole future of that society could be mechanically deduced. . . . The laws of the higher stages of organic development could not necessarily be deduced, at least in toto, from those of the lower stage. . . . Lenin's analysis of the new stage appears to contradict Marx but relates to a different stage — Imperialism. These features reinforce rather than nullify Marx [pp. 248–249].

Judging from these various statements of the leading academic exponent of Marxism, there is little reason to expect an explanation of the course of British economic history since 1850 in terms of Marxist analytics that rely on the falling rate of profit, the immiserization of the working class, monopoly, and capitalistic crisis.

CHAPTER 15

HISTORY AND ECONOMIC GROWTH:
A SEARCH FOR A METHOD

These pages have provided a number of conclusions of a negative character. For example: it makes just as much sense to say that faster French economic development would have produced more coal as that more coal would have produced faster French development; or that the expansion of British exports after 1875 rather than the failure of exports to expand faster held back economic growth. Some positive conclusions at this level have been offered: the British amateur tradition is excellent for getting an Industrial Revolution started, but not well suited for taking it into the age of electricity, chemistry, and metallurgy. On the other hand, French professionalism in education and science is necessary but not sufficient for growth: the technocrats must somehow obtain an outlet for their energies.

This work has not, however, produced any substantial generalizations that would explain why Britain has maintained a higher level of output per capita than France and has grown now faster, now slower. What has been revealed is the virtual impossibility of proving anything positive about theories of growth through the use of history, and the propensity of economic historians, with rare exceptions, to overgeneralize. It is obvious that these are highly discouraging as general conclusions.

The difficulty is that there is no single theory of economic growth, nor — leaving aside Rostow's stages of economic growth discussed in Chapter 13 — any unified explanation of the course of economic history. Most theories are at best partial. With more capital formation there is likely to be faster growth, or perhaps growth at the same rate from a higher level; and the same is true of more natural resources, more social cohesion, technological education, agricultural mobility, wider markets, and so on. The partial character of our theories and their qualitative nature prevent us from saying how much wider markets should be to compensate for a loss in social cohesion, or how far the existence of the École Polytechnique compensates for the thinness of French coal seams. In analyzing changing rates and levels of growth over long periods, we need to know not only the necessary ingredients of the development process, but also which ingredients, necessary or not, are by themselves and in various combinations sufficient for growth at slow, moderate, and rapid rates. A general theory of growth must be a theory of coefficients of substitution among ingredients in the growth process.

Lack of any such general theory, however, does not inhibit economic historians from sometimes using the partial theories as if they had total validity. Single-valued explanations abound in a world of multiple causation. Hardly a book or an article is free from such expressions as "It is impossible to exaggerate the importance of," which imply a single cause. It is entirely appropriate for the economic historian to explore the effect of a single variable on the workings of an economy — appropriate and important. But the importance of any such force, whether aristocratic values, Protestantism, capital exports, or equal inheritance in farmland, can be judged in a final way only in the general setting.

General explanation of the growth process is a complicated task in many ways. We can never be sure, in an individual case, whether the economic historian needs a static or a dynamic model. He must solve the identification problem of distinguishing between the independent and the dependent variable, or he must refrain from doing so in those instances when variables interact in a positive feedback system. Finally, after parameters and dependent variables have been distinguished in the appropriate static or dynamic setting, there is the tricky business of determining when small quantitative differences in relationships affect the quality or direction of the interaction, as well as its extent.

The difference between static and dynamic models has been touched upon frequently here. Is it desirable to have the price of labor low to encourage its use and raise the rate of profit, or should it be high to stimulate labor-saving innovation? It is unusual for the same author to use both models in close juxtaposition for the same factor.[1] For different factors, or for the same factor at different times, there is no such inhibition. France suffered from cheap labor and expensive coal. Britain gained in the early Industrial Revolution from inexpensive coal,

[1] See Dobb, *Studies in the Development of Capitalism* (1947): dearness of labor in the eighteenth century led to labor-saving invention (p. 276); rising wage rates led to business depression in the nineteenth (p. 286). Dobb is conscious of the difficulty and states (p. 277) that labor must be simultaneously cheap and dear, that is, abundant but not too abundant. And of course there may be a difference in effect between rising and high wage rates, though height can only be judged in relation to past experience or to relative rates in other countries.

but suffered in the late nineteenth century by a lack of pressure to improve fuel technology. Nor do observers find it necessary to agree on the simple facts: French economic growth was held back by the cheapness of labor, which discouraged labor-saving invention; or French economic growth was held back by the refusal of the family farm to release labor to industry, which can only have had its effect through rising wages. Or, at an early stage in both France and Britain, abundant crops stimulated industrial output through raising wage rates and labor income, which spills over into demand.

Take how little we know about the effect on growth of income distribution. Skewed distribution may assist growth by building savings and reducing the cost of capital, or it may retard it by holding back the demand for consumer goods. It can also affect labor inputs. In some instances, the lure of high rewards will stimulate entrepreneurs and others to work hard and take risks. In other circumstances, the lowest-paid wage earners will work only to the extent required by necessity, and higher-income recipients, who have arrived, will also fail to exert themselves. On the other hand, fairly equal income distribution may stimulate growth through its effects on demand, or it may retard it through the operation of the doctrine of fair shares, under which it is futile to work harder than your neighbor because you earn both his disapproval and the unwanted attention of the tax collector.

Or what of aristocratic values, which are said to have slowed down economic growth in France by barring mass consumption, perpetuating the inefficient small shop, denigrating business achievement, and so on? Aristocratic values also dominated life in England. The bourgeoisie, according to Young, was "never isolated long enough to frame ideals and standards of its own." [2] Since membership in the gentry was open, however, these values served as a stimulus to economic activity until a place in the country had been acquired. After that, economic energy might flag, or be sustained in the effort to acquire a larger place. Unfortunately, we cannot state that income distribution, aristocratic values, rising imports, or anything else was responsible for a change in the rate or level of economic growth without specifying the model in detail and justifying its use.

The identification problem is closely linked to the choice of a model, since the same variable may be taken as independent for a small model but, in a larger setting, as dependent. Even in a single model, however, it is difficult in the real world to know how the models work. Does population growth promote growth by increasing demand, slow it down by diverting capital from deepening to widening, add more to

[2] *Portrait of an Age* (1936), p. 84.

consumption than to the labor force, and so on? With an agricultural
and an industrial sector, are growth rates linked through goods or
through factor markets? Where innovation occurs at home and exports
expand, did the first lead to the second, or the reverse; are they independent, or both dependent on a third outside event or condition?

Finally, there are critical distances. If import prices fall to a limited
extent, they may lead to a mild decline or, if capacity to transform
exists, to a positive dynamic increase in productivity. A wider fall, on
the other hand, may lead only to damage, in the presence of the same
capacity to transform, because the decline in price overwhelms the
positive powers. It is likely that the powers of transformation of
French agriculture and French industry differed, but the increase in
industrial imports after 1860 was stimulating, that of grain after 1875
debilitating.[3]

A similar question arises over French urbanization. Paris is said to
inhibit the growth of other cities, because it siphons off their productive resources more than its demand stimulates them. Lille, Douai,
Denain, and Valenciennes, on the one hand, and Lyon, St. Étienne,
Grenoble, and Roanne, on the other, reinforce one another's growth because of their proximity, while Toulouse, Clermont-Ferrand, and
Montbéliard, virtually isolated, fail to contribute any stimulus to
neighboring centers.

This difficulty is illustrated by a recent article[4] listing half a dozen
factors retarding the British economy in the last quarter of the nineteenth century: entrepreneurial conservatism, lack of technological
education, obsolescent industries, redundant labor, skewed income
distribution, and financial institutions favoring the export of capital.
The writer concludes that the economy could have overcome these
handicaps had it not been for too much prosperity, the consequence
of export expansion, in traditional lines. But it is not clear that less
prosperity would have evoked the positive forces needed to overcome
the blocks, or that the exports themselves were not a function of
entrepreneurial conservatism and the export of capital.

It is tempting to end this extensive exercise on a nihilistic note,
concluding that anything can and does happen in economic history
and that the historians who succeed in explaining events are myopic,
like the blind men clutching segments of the elephant.

[3] Economists are prone to draw analogies between various policy devices and
poison or alcohol, which may be useful in moderation, noxious in quantity. A
friend of mine in unpleasant situations sustains himself with the optimistic slogan,
"What does not kill, strengthens." But this of course is untrue — what does not
kill may cripple for a long life.

[4] Saville, "Retarding Factors in the British Economy" (May 1961).

Instead, however, I have prepared, in Tables 26 and 27, a tabulation of the major forces making for French and British growth and retardation by periods over the years from 1851 to 1950. A very rough attempt is made to measure their importance by grading them 1, 2, or 3 in terms of whether they exerted great, moderate, or small force in the direction indicated. Those factors that might have exerted pressure in an opposite direction in different circumstances are marked with an asterisk. A separate column is reserved for factors that are thought to have exercised no significant force in any direction in the period, though they have been important on other occasions or so regarded by others. This sort of exercise is perhaps of some help in showing how the importance of factors can change from one set of circumstances to another. The tables make no claim to fundamental truth. Others will reasonably object to the particular influences selected, finding faults of commission and omission and differing in respect to the weights.

Table 26. Forces Making for and Resisting Growth in France, 1851–1950

Period	Forces making for growth	Forces and frictions resisting growth	Potentially significant forces of negligible effect
1851–1875 Vigorous Expansion	Government spending on cities, communication (1) Railroad investment (1) Industrial banks (1) Expansion of national market (1) *Expanding exports (2) *Import competition (2)	*Resource limitations in coal, natural communications (2) Immobility of agricultural labor (3) Diversion of government attention from economy to adventure (1) Bankers' quarrels (3)	Aristocratic values Family enterprises Social division Technological aptitude Slow population growth
1875–1896 Stagnation (esp. 1882–1894)	Technological advances (3) Wheat tariff of 1881 (2)	*Fall in wheat price communicated from abroad (1) Phylloxera (3) *Social fissures (3) Overspeculation in 1881 (3) *Resource limitations (3) *Slow population growth (3)	Loss of Alsace-Lorraine Freycinet Plan

Table 26 (*continued*)

Period	Forces making for growth	Forces and frictions resisting growth	Potentially significant forces of negligible effect
1896–1913 Moderate Growth	*Loss of Alsace-Lorraine (3) Discovery of iron ore (2) New industries (2) Regional banks (3 *Booming exports due to capital exports (3) *Méline tariff of 1892 (3)	Family enterprises (3) *Resource limitations — coal (3) *Social fissures (3)	Capital exports Slow population growth Government lack of interest in economy
1919–1930 Vigorous Disorderly Expansion	Government reconstruction (1) Rising exports due to capital flight and later undervaluation (2)	Capital flight to 1926 (3) Foreign-exchange policy (3)	Social fissures Inflation War manpower losses Aristocratic values Family enterprises
1930–1939 Economic Decline	*Rising wage costs (3)	Government policies for defense of franc value and deflation (3) World depression (1) *Social fissures (1) *Monopoly (3) Family firms (2)	Technical capacity
1945–1950+ Economic Resurgence	Wartime consensus on value of economic growth (1) Government size and initiative (1) *Income redistribution (2) Technical brilliance (1) *Popu'ation expansion (2) Expanded productivity in agriculture (3) Elimination of small firms by competition (2)	Inflation (2) Social conflict, especially on Algiers (2) *Limited resources (3) *Wartime destruction (3)	Diversion of resources overseas, partly compensated by aid

Table 27. Forces Making for and Resisting Growth in Britain, 1851–1950

Period	Forces making for growth	Forces and frictions resisting growth	Potentially significant forces of negligible effect
1851–1875 Vigorous Expansion	Technological innovation (1) *Buoyant exports due to foreign demand, gold mining, capital exports (1) *War (2) High Farming (3) *Amateur spirit (2)	Government regulation (3) *Speculation in securities, cotton spinning (2)	Lack of technical training
1873–1896 Great Depression	Capital exports from 1885 to 1890 (3) Rising real wages from terms of trade (2)	Slowdown of gold output (3) Monetary disorder (3) *Expansion overseas supplies agricultural products (2) Initial excess capacity and high financial costs (2)	Family enterprises Amateur spirit
1896–1913 Moderate Expansion	*Firm export demand due to capital exports, gold output (2) *Domestic investment in traditional industries (2)	Aging entrepreneurship (3) Specialized small units joined through merchants, markets (2) Continued lack of technical capacity (2) *Amateur spirit (2)	
1919–1931 Stagnation	Accumulated depreciation (3) Wartime inventions (2)	Speculation of 1919–1920 (2) Overvaluation of sterling (1) *Decline in overseas demand for British textiles, coal, ships (2) Technological backwardness (2)	Wartime manpower losses

Table 27 (*continued*)

Period	Forces making for growth	Forces and frictions resisting growth	Potentially significant forces of negligible effect
1931–1939 Expansion Moderate	Devaluation (2) *Improved terms of trade (2) Rearmament (2) Abandonment of hope in prewar structure (1)	*Stagnant exports (3) Weak technology (2)	
1945–1950+ Slow Growth	Foreign assistance (2) Investment in new industries, engineering, electrical (1)	Leadership exhaustion by war (1) Doctrine of fair shares and continuation of class divisions (2) Loss of assets, increase of liabilities during war (3) Limited technical capacity (2)	Nationalization of coal, steel, railways, Bank of England, etc.

The main fault with this sort of summary, of course, is that it necessarily omits the subtle interconnections from one period to another: the fact that the building of Paris can stimulate economic growth under the Second Empire, but hurt it at some later period if Paris gets so big in relation to other cities that it interacts negatively with them; or the organic theory of "three generations from shirtsleeves to shirtsleeves," which Rostow calls the Buddenbrooks pattern. Success in Generation 1 (a low level but a fast rate of growth) may lead to failure in Generation 3 (a high level but a slow rate of growth). Then again, it may not. If the society is open to new elites, if the merchants give way to the industrialists, who keep evolving from textiles to steel, to chemicals, to automobiles and electronics — all may be well. But the temptation is to have enough and to turn to art, music, literature, or scholarship — a high level but with low rates of growth. And the circumstances that can indicate when British intelligence and French intellect will go now into amateur scholarship or then into economic innovation eludes tabular form.

British Victorian history is redolent of the Buddenbrooks motif, of the Indian summer that follows on the vigor of midsummer and precedes enfeebled autumn. But the France of the Second Empire went through the "growth cycle" in foreshortened form. In 1852 and 1860

Napoleon III was interested in economic advance: in social-overhead capital, the improvement of agriculture, the stimulation of industry through import competition. Not three generations but a handful of years later, his attention had turned to foreign adventure, with its negative economic payout. The earlier programs had not been fulfilled, except perhaps for the main railway lines and Paris. But this seemed enough. The pattern is based, like much else in economics, on Engel's law which says that enough is enough. But appetites differ, and economic growth proceeds best when the leaders remain hungry, or when new leaders with new appetites for economic accomplishment appear. In 1880 much still remained to be done, and (as far as agriculture was concerned) everyone knew what it was. But no one did anything, even slowly.[5]

It may be enough for the economist to handle partial-equilibrium analysis when he is asked to advise on economic growth. It appears that it had better be. Economic history, like all history, is absorbing, beguiling, great fun. But, for scientific problems, can it be taken seriously?

[5] Augé-Laribé, *Politique agricole* (1950), p. 80.

APPENDIX

THE OVERALL DATA ON GROWTH

Some readers will want statistical series on which to base their impressions of the course of economic growth, as detailed in Chapter 1. The table here brings together data on income and industrial output, overall and per capita, from the best sources. It must be mentioned, however, that the data, especially the three lonely French figures before 1900, are not very good.

Statisticians are working hard and improvement in the data is continuous. Phyllis Deane in Britain and Jan Marczewski in France, especially, are extending and improving the figures for these countries, but there is some distance to go. So poor are the French data prior to those produced by Sauvy for the Conseil Économique — about which perhaps not enough is known—that Maddison omits France from his discussion of economic growth in Western Europe, and Paige uses overall calculations but before 1913 omits France from her charts.[1]

The difficulties of course are enormous. The French censuses of occupation, agriculture, and industry in the second half of the nineteenth century suffer from marked deficiencies. The occupational census starts off with a distressingly bad definition: from 1851 to 1861, the data represent population *dependent* upon an industry for livelihood, rather than the subsequent *active* population engaged in it. There is the further knotty question addressed in Chapter 10, of how many women and children dependent on agriculture are engaged in it. Censuses of animal numbers, reasonably accurate in Britain, a land of large farms, have virtually no value in France, a land of small holdings. Nor is the coverage of slaughterings adequate for a country of village butchers.

Services are difficult to estimate, so much so that the most thorough work of Marczewski is limited to agricultural and industrial output

[1] Maddison, "Economic Growth in Western Europe" (1959), p. 59n: "It is a pity that our sample does not include France for which the lack of production censuses, an aversion to taxation, and chronic inflation seem to have so far impeded any reasonable estimates in constant prices." Paige, with Blackby and Freund, "Economic Growth: The Last Hundred Years" (1961), p. 49.

alone.[2] For the important construction industry, there are a few indexes for Paris and one or two other cities, as noted, but nothing for
the country as a whole.

Even in manufacturing, for nineteenth-century France it is difficult
to get good annual figures which are representative. The Kuczynski
series is limited to coal, pig iron, and steel.[3] An index by Dessirier includes also apparent consumption of cotton and wool, but has been
constructed only for 1870, 1880, and 1890, as the average of a three-
year period centered on the indicated year.[4] Folke Hilgerdt converted
this index to an annual one by interpolation from apparent coal consumption;[5] the results evidently have limited validity, although this
does not prevent them from being used in modern comparisons.[6]

French official statistics after World War II are of high quality, and
it may be possible ultimately to repair the major gaps prior to World
War I. Marczewski uses seven series, in contrast with the five of
Dessirier; but it is doubtful that each of these is national in scope and
covers each year. The early work of Perroux was limited to the years
of production censuses, with other years interpolated on the question-
begging assumption of regular growth. When the base years are taken
as representative of decades, some curious results are obtained.[7] Again
there is difficulty in obtaining adequate price indexes for the deflation
of value series in practice,[8] and even in theory.[9] The result is that

[2] "Some Aspects of the Economic Growth of France" (1961), pp. 369–370.
[3] *Weltproduktion und Welthandel* (1935), pp. 20–21.
[4] "La production industrielle et la production agricole" (1928).
[5] League of Nations (Hilgerdt), *Industrialization and Foreign Trade* (1945),
p. 146.
[6] Patel, "Rates of Industrial Growth in the Last Century" (1961), p. 318.
[7] Kuznets uses Perroux's figures as decade averages and calculates growth by
assuming them as centered within the decade. His results accord with the general
view for the 1850s and 1860s, when growth was faster than in the 1870s, but show
a retrogression in the 1870s, which is hardly correct for the decade as a whole, and
higher growth in the 1880s than in the 1850s. The figure for the 1870s seems to be
based on the single year 1872, which was disrupted by the Franco-Prussian War
and unrepresentative. The 1880s are overstated by Perroux's use of the boom year
1882 because of the date of the Census of Production. The series emerges curiously then as (percent per decade):

1841–50 to 1851–60	22.5
1851–60 to 1861–70	27.0
1861–70 to 1871–80	−1.4
1871–80 to 1881–90	24.3
1881–90 to 1891–1900	21.9

See Kuznets, "Rates of Growth," p. 60. Paige comments ("Economic Growth: The
Last Hundred Years," p. 39) that the Kuznets decade averages have a "rather
high margin of error."
[8] For the most part, Perroux uses undeflated figures, despite rather substantial
price changes, and draws a sharp note of criticism from Gerschenkron (*Economic*

decennial growth percentages may smooth over fast and slow periods of growth, thereby hiding significant movement from the historian,[10] and in any event are comparable from country to country only within a fairly wide range of error.

British data are better, but even they are perhaps not all that they might be, prior to the Census of Production of 1907. The widely used

---

Backwardness, 1962, pp. 438–439). When he does deflate, he uses a geometric average of the wholesale and cost-of-living index, which, however practical, is hardly defensible on theoretical grounds as a national-income deflater.

There is a further problem when working from value figures and prices-to-quantity data, of linking the right price index to the right value estimate. This is particularly acute in agriculture, where a bad crop in one year may result in a high average price this year or the next, and vice versa for a bumper harvest. See, e.g., the Sirol indexes of agricultural output and prices in the 1840s (*Le Rôle de l'agriculture*, 1942, Appendix 4.1):

Year	Quantity index (1914 = 100)	Price index (1901–10 = 100)
1843	66	114
1844	74	105
1845	62	108
1846	52	135
1847	89	159
1848	80	111
1849	72	80

Before 1846, crop and price were inversely correlated. In 1847 and 1849, however, crop and price moved the same way as a result of lags. Any mechanical multiplication of quantity by price indexes, or deflation of money income by price indexes, without knowledge of exactly how the income data have been put together, will produce anomalous results. The position would be improved by putting the data on a crop-year basis, but this raises new questions.

[9] Coppock objects to the use by Phelps-Brown and Handsfield-Jones of a composite price deflator, made up of 60 percent cost of living and therefore 36 percent food, to deflate an output series in which food is represented by less than 14 percent. The deflator for expenditure should not be used for output, and its use distorts the timing of the Climacteric. See Coppock, "The Climacteric" (1956).

[10] Marczewski's indexes of rate of growth by decades, centered on the initial year of the calendar decades, manages virtually to wipe out the boom under the Second Empire and the Great Depression. See "Aspects of the Economic Growth of France," p. 375 (percent per annum):

1835–44	3.52
1845–54	2.45
1855–64	2.76
1865–74	2.72
1875–84	2.75
1885–94	2.20

The rates differ from one tenth the per-decade rate, given in note 7, and with which they compare curiously, by the compound rate within the decade. See Gerschenkron, "On the Concept of Continuity in History" (1962), p. 206, who suggests that the historian looking for discontinuities will have no interest in decade averages which smooth them away.

Prest index of national income goes back only to 1870, and for the early period rests mainly on the early research of Bowley on wages and intermediate income, unchecked against output figures.[11] The Prest data have been extended by Jeffrys and Walters but functionally, to include expenditure, rather than in time.[12] The prodigious work of Walther Hoffmann on industrial production, reaching into the statistical mists of 1700, has been seriously criticized by Cole and Wright as overstating the growth of the early period, and understating it in the second half of the nineteenth century.[13] Cole expresses skepticism of Hoffmann's index after 1780, which, he holds, is the basis for Rostow's theory of take-off.

Some independent checks are forthcoming. But Phyllis Deane has examined the estimates of contemporary British statisticians, which were also studied for France by the Institut de Science Économique Appliquée, and produced a rather different set of estimated rates of growth for the second half of the nineteenth century, slower for the third quarter to 1870 and faster for the fourth quarter.[14]

On these scores, this volume does not rely on the presently available estimates of national income in France and Britain since 1850, nor on the rates of growth derived from them. Nor does it recommend reliance on income data found in other works, often without a statement of sources.[15] Gerschenkron has criticized Perroux for testing quantitative research by "vague and impressionistic ideas rather than the other way round." [16] But in the present state of quantitative research, happily improving at a rapid rate, the vague and impressionistic ideas are often more revealing of the truth being sought than the statistician's ingenious attempts at measurement. He should nonetheless be encouraged to press on.

[11] Prest, "National Income" (1948); Bowley, "Wages and Income in the United Kingdom" (1937)

[12] Jeffrys and Walters, "Income and Expenditure of the United Kingdom" (1955).

[13] Hoffmann, *British Industry* (1955); Cole, "Measurement of Industrial Growth" (1958); Wright, "Output of British Industry" (1956).

[14] "Contemporary Estimates of National Income" (1957), p. 461. In percent, the rates of growth per decade are: 1851–70, 11.2; 1870–95, 25.6.

[15] See, e.g., the figures for national income in money, real, and per capita terms for France and Britain in Burnham and Hoskins, *Iron and Steel in Britain* (1943), pp. 288–289, with no sources given. Or see the series by Eliane Mossé (*Marx et la croissance*, 1956, pp. 176–177), which differs significantly from those of Perroux at the ISEA, where she worked. Mossé uses these data to demonstrate the impoverishment of the proletariat, by deflating them with her own price index. The exact composition of this index is not clear, but it includes a number of commodities of rapidly rising prices like meat, butter, cheese, and milk, where rising demand led to price increases, and underweights wheat and wine, which were stable in price.

[16] *Economic Backwardness*, p. 439.

Real National Income, Population, and Real National Income per Head

United Kingdom				France			
Net national income at 1900 prices				Gross domestic product at 1905–1913 prices (tentative estimates)			
Year	Total income (£ millions)	Population (millions)	Income per head (£)	Year	Gross domestic product (millions of francs)	Population at census dates (millions)	Gross domestic product per head (francs)
1851	—	27.4	—	1852	16,787	35.8(1851)	
1852	—	27.4	—				469
1853	—	27.5	—				
1854	—	27.7	—				
1855	508	27.8	18.3				
1856	531	28.0	19.0				
1857	502	28.2	17.8				
1858	545	28.4	19.2				
1859	553	28.6	19.3				
1860	559	28.8	19.4				
1861	591	29.0	20.4				
1862	597	29.3	20.4				
1863	600	29.4	20.4				
1864	629	29.7	21.2		[comparable data unavailable]		
1865	662	29.9	22.1				
1866	675	30.1	22.4				
1867	670	30.4	22.0				
1868	673	30.7	21.9				
1869	711	30.9	23.0				
1870	774	31.2	24.8				
1871	817	31.6	25.9				
1872	813	31.9	25.5				
1873	857	32.1	26.6				
1874	891	32.5	27.4				
1875	912	32.8	27.8				
1876	909	33.3	27.4				
1877	901	33.6	26.8				
1878	927	33.9	27.3				
1879	930	34.4	27.1				
1880	932	34.6	26.9	1880[b]	21,363	37.7(1881)	617
1881	987	34.8	28.3				
1882	1,035	35.2	29.4				
1883	1,029	35.4	29.0				
1884	1,054	35.7	29.5		[comparable data unavailable]		
1885	1,115	36.0	31.0				
1886	1,162	36.3	32.0				
1887	1,225	36.6	33.5				
1888	1,302	36.8	35.3				
1889	1,380	37.2	37.1				
1890	1,416	37.5	37.8				
1891	1,404	37.8	37.1				
1892	1,350	38.1	35.4	1892	26,423	38.3(1891)	689
1893	1,369	38.5	35.6	1902/03	32,297	39.0(1901)	829
1894	1,518	38.9	39.i	1912	37,793	39.6(1911)	956
				Year	National income (in billions, 1938 francs)	Population (millions)	National income per head (in thousands, 1938 francs)
1895	1,587	39.3	40.5				
1896	1,627	39.6	41.1				
1897	1,647	40.0	41.2				
1898	1,673	40.3	41.4				
1899	1,799	40.8	44.1				
1900	1,750	41.1	42.5				
1901	1,746	41.5	42.0	1901	240	39.0	5.8
1902	1,759	41.9	42.0	1902	240		5.8
1903	1,717	42.2	40.6	1903	247		6.0
1904	1,685	42.6	39.5	1904	267		6.5

Real National Income, Population, and Real National Income per Head
(*continued*)

	United Kingdom				France		
Year	Total income (£ millions)	Population (millions)	Income per head (£)	Year	National income (in billions, 1938 francs)	Population (millions)	National income per head (in thousands, 1938 francs)
1905	1,757	43.0	40.9	1905	264		6.4
1906	1,834	43.3	42.3	1906	270	39.3	6.5
1907	1,883	43.8	43.1	1907	277		6.7
1908	1,835	44.2	41.6	1908	279		6.7
1909	1,846	44.5	41.5	1909	288		6.9
1910	1,881	44.9	41.9	1910	288		6.9
1911	1,947	45.2	43.0	1911	300	39.6	7.2
1912	1,985	45.4	43.7	1912	328		7.8
1913	2,021	45.6	44.3	1913	328		7.8
1914	2,010	46.0	43.7	1914			
1920a	2,079	43.4	47.6	1920	270		6.9
1921	1,804	44.1	41.0	1921b	250	37.5	6.3
1922	1,917	44.4	43.3	1922	304		7.7
1923	2,011	44.6	45.1	1923	329		8.2
1924	2,038	45.0	45.4	1924	381		9.4
1925	2,070	45.1	45.9	1925	384		9.5
1926	2,071	45.3	45.8	1926	401	40.7	9.8
1927	2,259	45.5	49.8	1927	387		9.4
1928	2,277	45.5	49.9	1928	410		9.9
1929	2,319	45.6	50.7	1929	453		10.9
1930	2,294	45.8	50.0	1930	447		10.7
1931	2,270	46.0	49.2	1931	428	41.8	10.2
1932	2,271	46.4	49.1	1932	398		9.5
1933	2,422	46.6	52.1	1933	400		9.5
1934	2,504	46.7	53.6	1934	392		9.3
1935	2,616	46.9	55.8	1935	375		8.9
1936	2,717	47.1	57.7	1936	371	41.9	8.8
1937	2,728	47.3	57.7	1937	384		9.1
1938	2,725	47.5	57.4	1938	380		9.0
				1939	407		9.7
				1940	336		8.2
	[*comparable data unavailable*]			1941	266		6.7
				1942	238		6.0
				1943	226		5.8
				1944	191		4.9
				1945	207		5.2
				1946	315	40.5	7.8
				1947	341		8.4
				1948	366		8.8
				1949	414		9.9
1950		50.4(1952)		1950	448	42.8(1954)	10.6

a Southern Ireland excluded, 1920–1950.

b Alsace-Lorraine excluded, 1871–1920.

Sources. United Kingdom — B. R. Mitchell (with the collaboration of Phyllis Deane), *Abstract of British Historical Statistics* (1963): income and income per head (Feinstein's and Prest's estimates), pp. 367–368; population (registrar-general's figures), pp. 9–10. France — Gross domestic product total and per head, 1852–1912: Marczewski, "Le 'Take-off' en France" (1960), table 11; population calculated from foregoing; national income, total and per head, 1901–50, INSEE, *Annuaire statistique* (1961), estimates of Sauvy, p. 300.

BIBLIOGRAPHY

INDEX

BIBLIOGRAPHY

Abramovitz, Moses. "Economics of Growth," in B. F. Haley, ed., *A Survey of Contemporary Economics*, vol. 2. Homewood, Irwin, 1952.
—— and V. F. Eliasberg. *The Growth of Public Employment in Great Britain*. New York, Princeton University Press, 1957.
Adams, Brooks. *The Law of Civilisation and Decay*. New York, Macmillan, 1896. (Reprinted, Knopf, 1951.)
Akerman, Johan H. *Economic Progress and Economic Crises*. London, Macmillan, 1932.
—— *Structures et cycles économiques*, 2 vols. Paris, Presses Universitaires de France, 1957, 1959.
Allais, Maurice. *L'Europe unie*. Paris, Calmann-Lévy, 1960.
Allen, G. C. *British Industries*. London, Longmans Green, 2nd ed., 1939.
—— *The Industrial Development of Birmingham and the Black Country, 1860–1927*. London, Allen and Unwin, 1929.
Amé, Léon. *Étude sur les tarifs de douanes et sur les traités de commerce*, 2 vols. Paris, Imprimerie Nationale, 1876.
Andrews, P. W. S., and Elizabeth Brunner. *Capital Development in Steel*. Oxford, Blackwell, 1951.
Anglo-American Council on Productivity. *Productivity Report on Management Accounting*. London, New York, November 1950.
Anon. [various writers]. *Fortunes Made in Business*, 3 vols. London, Sampson, Low, Marston, Searle and Rivington, 1884.
Anon. *An Estimate of the Manners and Principles of the Times*. London, Davis and Reymer, 1757.
Ariès, Philippe. *Histoire des populations françaises et leurs attitudes devant la vie depuis le XVIIIe siècle*. Paris, Self, 1948.
Armengaud, André. "Les Débuts de la dépopulation dans les campagnes touloussaines," *Annales: Économies, Sociétés, Civilisations*, vol. 6, no. 2 (April–June 1951), pp. 172–178.
—— "La Fin des forges catalanes dans les Pyrénées Ariégoises," *Annales: Économies, Sociétés, Civilisations*, vol. 8, no. 1 (January–March 1953), pp. 62–66.
Aron, Raymond, *Le Développement de la société industrielle et la stratification sociale*. Paris, Les Cours de Sorbonne, 1955–56.
Aron, Robert. *Une Grande banque d'affaires: La Banque de Paris et des Pays-Bas*. Paris, Les Éditions d'Espargne, 1959 (pamphlet).
Ashton, T. S. *The Industrial Revolution, 1760–1830*. London, Oxford University Press, 1947.
Aubert-Krier, Jane. "Monopolistic and Imperfect Competition in Retail Trade in France," in E. H. Chamberlin, ed., *Monopoly and Competition and Their Regulation*. London, Macmillan, 1954.
Augé-Laribé, Michel. *La Politique agricole de la France de 1880 à 1940*. Paris, Presses Universitaires de France, 1950.

Auguy, Marc. "Structure industrielle," in Rist and Pirou, eds., *De la France d'avant-guerre jusqu'à la France d'aujourd'hui.*

Aujac, Henri. "Inflation as a Monetary Consequence of the Behavior of Social Groups: A Working Hypothesis," *International Economic Papers*, no. 4 (Reprinted from *Économie appliquée*, vol. 3, no. 2 [April–June 1950]. pp. 280–300.)

Baldwin, George B. *Beyond Nationalization: The Labor Problems of British Coal.* Cambridge, Harvard University Press, 1955.

Baldy, Edmond. *Les Banques d'affaires en France depuis 1900.* Paris, Librairie Générale de Droit et de Jurisprudence, 1922.

Ballot, Charles. *Introduction du machinisme dans l'industrie française.* Paris, Rieder, 1923.

Balniel, Lord. "The Upper Class," *The Twentieth Century*, vol. 167, no. 999 (May 1960), pp. 427–432.

Banfield, E. C. *Moral Basis of a Backward Society.* Glencoe, Free Press, 1958.

Barker, Ernest. "An Attempt at Perspective," in Ernest Barker, ed., *The Character of England.* Oxford, Clarendon Press, 1947.

Barna, Tibor. *Investment and Growth Policies in British Industrial Firms.* Cambridge, Eng., Cambridge University Press, 1962 (National Institute of Economic and Social Research, Occasional Papers 20).

Bauchet, Pierre. "La Structure d'une branche d'industrie," *Économie appliquée*, vol. 5, nos. 2–3 (April–September 1952), pp. 359–399.

Baud, Paul. *Les Industries chimiques régionales de la France.* Paris, O. Doin, 1922.

Baum, Warren C. *The French Economy and the State.* Princeton, Princeton University Press, 1958.

Beacham, A. "The Coal Industry," in Burn, ed., *The Structure of British Industry*, vol. 1.

Beales, H. L. "The 'Great Depression' in Industry and Trade," *Economic History Review*, 1st ser., vol. 5, no. 1 (1934), pp. 65–75.

Bear, W. E. *The English Farmer and His Competitors.* London, Cobden Club, Caswell and Co, 1888.

Beesley, M. E., and G. W. Throup. "The Machine-Tool Industry," in Burn, ed., *The Structure of British Industry*, vol. 1.

Bellerby, J. H. *Agriculture and Industry: Relative Income.* London, Macmillan, 1956.

Bénard, Jean. *Vues sur l'économie et la population de la France jusqu'en 1970.* Paris, Presses Universitaires de France, 1953.

Bernard, Philippe. *Économie et sociologie de la Seine-et-Marne, 1850–1950.* Paris, Colin, 1953.

Berrill, K. "International Trade and the Rate of Economic Growth," *Economic History Review*, 2nd ser., vol. 12, no. 1 (July 1960), pp. 351–359.

Berry, Brian J. L. "City-Size Distribution and Economic Development," *Economic Development and Cultural Change*, vol. 9, no. 4 (July 1961), pp. 573–588.

Besse, Pierre. *La Crise et l'évolution de l'agriculture en Angleterre de 1875 à nos jours.* Paris, F. Alcan, 1910.

Bettelheim, Charles. *Bilan de l'économie française, 1919–1946.* Paris, Presses Universitaires de France, 1947

Bettelheim, Charles, and Suzanne Frère. *Une Ville française moyenne: Auxerre*. Paris, Colin, 1950.

Bigo, Robert. *Les Banques françaises au cours de XIXe siècle*. Paris, Sirey, 1947.

Birnbaum, Norman. " 'Empiricism' and British Politics," *Commentary*, vol. 31, no. 2 (February 1961), pp. 111–116.

Blanc, André, Étienne Juillard, Joanny Ray, and Michel Rochefort. *Les Régions de l'Est*. Paris, Presses Universitaires de France, 1960.

Bloch, Marc. *Les Caractères originaux de l'histoire rurale française*. Oslo, Aschehoug, 1931. (New ed., Paris, Colin, 1952.)

Block, Maurice. *Statistique de la France comparée avec les divers pays de l'Europe*. Paris, Guillaume et Cie, 1867; 2nd ed., 1875.

Bonnet, Pierre. *La Commercialisation de la vie française*. Paris, Plon, 1929.

Bouloiseau, Marc. Review of C. Rouchon, "Techniques agricoles et évolution sociales en pays cristallin: L'Évolution de Fernoël," and J. Chautard, "L'Évolution de la propriété dans une commune de la Limagne: Seychalles," pp. 13–32 and 33–56, in *Notes de geographie humaine sur l'Auvergne*, Paris, Les Belles Lettres, 1951, and *Annales: Économies, Sociétés, Civilisations*, vol. 8, no. 2 (April–June 1953), pp. 248–250.

Bouvier, Jean. *Le Crédit Lyonnais de 1863 à 1882, Les Années de formation d'une banque de dépots*. Paris, SEVPEN, 1961.

—— *Le Krach de l'Union Générale, 1878–1885*. Paris, Presses Universitaires de France, 1960.

Bouvier-Ajam, Maurice. *L'Économie française au milieu du XXe siècle*. Paris, Librairie Générale de Droit et de Jurisprudence, 1955.

Bowley, Arthur. *Wages and Income in the United Kingdom since 1860*. Cambridge, Eng., Cambridge University Press, 1937.

Brady, Robert Alexander. *Crisis in Britain*. Berkeley, University of California Press, 1950.

Brams, Lucien. "Sociologie comparée," in Colloques Internationaux du Centre National de la Recherche Scientifique, *Sociologie comparée de la famille contemporaine*. Paris, 1955.

Brand, Lord. "Recollections of a Statesman Banker," *The Observer*, January 1, 1961.

Bresard, Marcel. "Mobilité sociale et dimension de la famille," *Population*, vol. 5, no. 3 (July–September 1950), pp. 533–566.

Briffault, Robert. *The Decline and Fall of the British Empire*. New York, Simon and Schuster, 1938.

Brogan, Dennis W. *The English People: Impressions and Observations*. London, Hamish Hamilton, 1943.

—— *France under the Republic, 1870–1939*. New York, Harper, 1940.

Brooks, Alfred Hulse, and Morris F. LaCroix. *The Iron and Associated Industries of Lorraine, the Saar District, Luxemburg, and Belgium*. Washington, U.S. Government Printing Office, 1920.

Brooks, Colin. *Our Present Discontents*. New York, Holt, 1933.

Brousse, Henri, "La Productivité du travail," *Revue économique*, no. 5 (September 1953), pp. 628–642.

Brunschwig, Henri. *Mythes et réalités de l'impérialisme colonial français, 1871–1914*. Paris, Colin, 1960.

Buffet, Jean. *Du Régionalisme au nationalisme financier*. Paris, Berger-Levrault, 1917.

Burenstam Linder, Staffan. *An Essay on Trade and Transformation.* New York, John Wiley, 1961.

Burn, D. L. "British Steelmaking and Foreign Competition, 1870–1914," Appendix 1 in C. R. Fay, *English Economic History, Mainly since 1700.* Cambridge, Eng., Heffer, 1940.

—— *Economic History of Steelmaking, 1867–1939.* Cambridge, Eng., Cambridge University Press, 1940.

—— "The Genesis of American Engineering Competition, 1850–1870," *Economic History,* vol. 2, no. 6 (January 1931), pp. 292–311.

—— "Recent Trends in the History of the Steel Industry," *Economic History Review,* 1st ser., vol. 17, no. 2 (1947), pp. 95–110.

——, ed. *The Structure of British Industry,* 2 vols. Cambridge, Eng., Cambridge University Press, 1958. (Burn's essays are "Steel," I, 260–306, and "Retrospect," II, 455–457.)

Burnham, T. H., and G. O. Hoskins. *Iron and Steel in Britain, 1870–1930.* London, Allen and Unwin, 1943.

Caboue, P. "Medium-Term Lending by French Deposit Banks and Banques d'Affaires," *Banca Nazionale del Lavoro Quarterly Review,* vol. 7, no. 30 (July–September 1954), pp. 129–145.

Caillot, Robert. *L'Usine, la terre et la cité, L'Exemple de Péage-du-Rousillon.* Paris, Les Éditions Ouvrières, 1958.

Caird, James. *The Landed Interest and the Supply of Food.* London, Cassell, Potter, and Galpin, 1878.

Cairncross, A. K. "The English Capital Market before 1914," *Economica,* new ser., vol. 25, no. 98 (May 1958), pp. 142–146.

—— *Home and Foreign Investment, 1870–1913.* Cambridge, Eng., Cambridge University Press, 1953.

Calder, Ritchie. "Technology," in Dewhurst, etc., *Europe's Needs and Resources, Trends and Prospects in Eighteen Countries.*

Campbell, G. A. *The Civil Service in Britain.* Harmondsworth, Penguin Books, 1955.

Cameron, Rondo E. "The Crédit Mobilier and the Economic Development of Europe," *Journal of Political Economy,* vol. 61, no. 6 (December 1953), pp. 461–488.

—— *France and the Economic Development of Europe, 1800–1914.* Princeton, Princeton University Press, 1961.

—— "L'Exportation des capitaux français, 1850–1880," *Revue d'histoire économique et sociale,* vol. 33, no. 3 (1955), pp. 346–353.

—— "Profit, croissance et stagnation en France au XIXe siècle," *Économie appliquée,* vol. 10, no. 2–3 (April–September 1957), pp. 409–444.

Capronnier, François. *La Crise de l'industrie cotonnière française.* Paris, Génin, 1959.

Carrère, Paul, and Raymond Dugrand. *La Région méditerranéene.* Paris, Presses Universitaires de France, 1960.

Carter, C. F. "The Building Industry," in Burn, ed., *The Structure of British Industry,* vol. 1.

—— and B. R. Williams. *Industry and Technical Progress.* London, Oxford University Press, 1957.

—— —— *Investment in Innovation.* London, Oxford University Press, 1958.

Carter, C. F., and B. R. Williams. *Science in Industry*. London, Oxford University Press, 1959.

Cartter, A. N. *The Redistribution of Income in Postwar Britain*. New Haven, Yale University Press, 1955.

Central Statistical Office, *Annual Abstract of Statistics, 1956*, no. 93. London, H. M. Stationery Office.

Centre de Diffusion Française. *The Young Face of France*. Paris, 1959.

Centre Nationale de la Recherche Scientifique. *Sociologie comparée de la famille contemporaine*. Paris, Éditions du Centre Nationale, 1955.

Chambers, J. D. *The Workshop of the World, British Economic History from 1820 to 1880*. London, Oxford University Press, 1961.

Chandler, A. D., Jr. "The Beginning of 'Big Business' in American Industry," *Business History Review*, vol. 33, no. 2 (Spring 1959), pp. 1–31.

Chandler, Lester V. *Benjamin Strong, Central Banker*. Washington, Brookings, 1958.

Channing, F. A. *The Truth about Agricultural Depression*. London, Longmans Green, 1897.

Chapman, W. J., and T. S. Ashton. "The Sizes of Businesses, Mainly in the Textile Industry," *Journal of the Royal Statistical Society*, 1914.

Chardonnet, J. *L'Économie française*, 2 vols. Paris, Dalloz, 1958.

——— *Les Grandes puissances: Étude économique*, 2 vols. Paris, Dalloz, 3rd ed., 1960–61.

Charpenay, Georges. *Les Banques régionalistes*. Paris, Nouvelle Revue Critique, 1939.

Chatelain, Abel. "Une Grande industrie motrice française attardée: Le Bâtiment," *Annales: Économies, Sociétés, Civilisations*, vol. 13, no. 3 (July–September 1958), pp. 373–385.

——— "Dans les campagnes françaises du XIXe siècle: La Lente progression de la faux," *Annales: Économies, Sociétés, Civilisations*, vol. 11, no. 4 (October–December 1956), pp. 495–499.

——— "La Main-d'oeuvre et la construction des chemins de fer au XIXe siècle," *Annales: Économies, Sociétés, Civilisations*, vol. 8, no. 4 (October–December 1953), pp. 502–506.

Checkland, S. G. "English Provincial Cities," *Economic History Review*, 2nd ser., vol. 6, no. 2 (1953), pp. 195–203.

Chenery, Hollis B. "Patterns of Industrial Growth," *American Economic Review*, vol. 50, no. 4 (September 1960), pp. 624–654.

Chevalier, Louis. "Aspects principaux de l'évolution de la main-d'oeuvre industrielle dans l'Oise dans le milieu du XIXe siècle," in Ministère de l'Économie, *Rapports*, vol. 3 (1930–39).

——— *La Formation de la population parisienne au XIXe siècle*. Paris, Presses Universitaires de France, 1949.

Chevalier, Michel. *La Vie humaine dans les Pyrenées ariègoises*. Paris, Gemin, 1956.

Christopher, Jack. "The Dessication of the Bourgeois Spirit," in Earle, ed., *Modern France*.

Ciriacy-Wantrup, S. G. *Resource Conservation*. Berkeley, University of California Press, 1952.

Clapham, J. H. *The Economic Development of France and Germany, 1815–1914*. Cambridge. Eng., Cambridge University Press. 4th ed., 1936.

Clapham, John. *An Economic History of Modern Britain*, 3 vols. London, Cambridge University Press, 1926, 1932, 1938; reprinted 1959, 1952, 1951.

Clark, Colin. *The Conditions of Economic Progress*. London, Macmillan, 1st ed., 1940; 2nd ed., 1951; 3rd ed., 1957.

Clement, Pierre, and Nelly Xydias. *Vienne sur le Rhône*. Paris, Colin, 1955.

Clough, Shepherd B. "Retardative Factors in French Economic Development in the Nineteenth and Twentieth Centuries, *Journal of Economic History*, vol. 6, suppl. VI (1946), pp. 91–102.

Cohen, Ruth L. *History of Milk Prices*. Oxford, Agricultural Economics Research Institute, 1936.

Cole, G. D. H., and Raymond Postgate. *The British People, 1746–1946*. London, Methuen; reprinted as a University Paperback by Barnes and Noble, 1961.

Cole, Humphrey. "Great Western Railway Locomotive Replacement." Unpublished manuscript, Oxford Institute of Statistics, about 1957.

Cole, W. A. "The Measurement of Industrial Growth," *Economic History Review*, 2nd ser., vol. 11, no. 2 (1958), pp. 309–315.

Collas, Henry. *La Banque de Paris et des Pays-Bas*. Dijon, Barbier-Léon Marshal, 1908.

Comité des Forges. *La Sidérurgie française, 1864–1914*. Paris, Berger-Levrault, 1920.

Committee on Finance and Industry. *Macmillan Committee Report*, Cmd 3897, 1931.

Cook, P. Lesley. *Effects of Mergers*. London, Allen and Unwin, 1958.

Coppock, D. "The Causes of the Great Depression, 1873–96," *Manchester School*, vol. 29, no. 3 (September 1961), pp. 205–232.

——— "The Climacteric of the 1890s: A Critical Note," *Manchester School*, vol. 24, no. 1 (January 1956), pp. 1–31.

Cotgrove, Stephen E. *Technical Education and Social Change*. London, Allen and Unwin, 1958.

Court, W. H. B. *A Concise Economic History of Britain*, Cambridge, Eng., Cambridge University Press, 1958.

Coussy, Jean. "La Politique commerciale du Second Empire et la continuité de l'évolution structurelle française," *Cahiers de l'Institut de Science Économique Appliquée*, series P, no. 6 (December 1961), pp. 1–47.

Coutin, Pierre. "La Décongestion des centres industriels et la vie agricole," in Ministère de l'Économie, *Rapports sur la décongestion*, vol. 5, *Études diverses* (1945).

——— "Le Développement industriel à Clermont-Ferrand, et ses répercussions sur la vie rurale des régions voisines," in Ministère de l'Économie, *Rapports sur la décongestion*, vol. 6, *Études régionales* (1945).

Crédit du Nord. Centenary brochure, 1948.

Crouzet, François. *L'Économie du commonwealth*. Paris, Presses Universitaires de France, 1950.

Crozier, Michel. "Le Citoyen," *Ésprit*, vol. 29, no. 292 (February 1961), pp. 193–211.

——— "Le Corps prefectoral en action." Unpublished paper, 1961.

——— "La France, terre de commandement," *Ésprit*, vol. 25, no. 256 (December 1957), pp. 779–797.

——— "French Bureaucracy." Seminar, Center for International Affairs, Harvard University, April 15, 1960.

Danière, A. "Feudal Incomes and the Demand Elasticity for Bread in the Late Eighteenth Century," *Journal of Economic History,* vol. 18, no. 3 (September 1958), pp. 317–331.

Dauphin-Meunier, A. *La Banque de France.* Paris, Gallimard, 1936.

D'Avout, Bernard. *Le Crédit immobilier en Belgique et en France.* Dijon, Imprimerie Darantière, 1914.

Deane, Phyllis. "Contemporary Estimates of National Income in the Second Half of the Nineteenth Century," *Economic History Review,* 2nd ser., vol. 9, no. 3 (1957), pp. 451–461.

———— and H. J. Habakkuk. "The Take-off in Britain." Paper submitted to the Konstanz meeting of the International Economic Association, September 2–11, 1960.

Demoulins, Edmonds. *Anglo-Saxon Superiority: To What Is It Due?* London, 1899.

Denuc, Jules. "Structure des entreprises," in Rist and Pirou, eds., *De la France d'avant-guerre jusqu'à la France d'aujourd'hui.*

Dessirier, Jean. "Indices comparés de la production industrielle et la production agricole en divers pays de 1870 à 1928," *Bulletin de la Statistique Générale,* vol. 18, no. 17–18 (October–December 1928), pp. 65–121.

Detoeuf, Auguste. *Propos de O. L. Barenton, confiseur.* Paris, Éditions du Tambourinaire, 1958.

Deutsch, Karl W., and Alexander Eckstein. "National Industrialization and the Declining Share of the International Economic Sector, 1890–1959," *World Politics,* vol. 13. no. 2 (January 1961) pp. 267–299.

Dewhurst, J. Frederic, John O. Coppock, P. Lamartine Yates, and others. *Europe's Needs and Resources, Trends and Prospects in Eighteen Countries.* New York, Twentieth Century Fund, 1961.

Dion, Roger. *Le Val du Loire, étude de geographie régionale.* Tours, Arrault, 1933.

Direction de la Statistique Générale, Ministère de l'Économie Nationale. *Annuaire statistique,* various years. Paris, Imprimerie Nationale.

———— Études économiques, no. 1: *Documents sur le problème du logement à Paris.* Paris, Imprimerie Nationale, 1946.

Dobb, Maurice. *Capitalism Yesterday and Today.* London, Lawrence and Wishart, 1958.

———— *Political Economy and Capitalism.* London, Routledge, 1937.

———— *Studies in the Development of Capitalism.* New York, International Publishers, 1947.

Dobzhansky, Theodosius G. *Genetics and the Origin of Species.* New York, Columbia University Press, 2nd ed., 1941.

Dumont, René. *Voyages en France d'un agronome.* Paris, Librairie des Médicis, 1951.

Dunham, Arthur L. *The Anglo-French Treaty of Commerce of 1860 and the Progress of the Industrial Revolution in France.* Ann Arbor, University of Michigan Press, 1930.

———— "The Industrial Revolution in France," in *Michigan Alumnus Quarterly Review,* vol. 57, no. 14, (February 24, 1951), pp. 148–159. Reviewed by P. L. (P. Leuillot) in *Annales: Économies, Sociétés, Civilisations,* vol. 6, no. 3 (July–September 1951), p. 401.

———— *The Industrial Revolution in France, 1818–1848.* New York, Exposition Press, 1935.

Dunham, Arthur L. Review of Morazé, *La France bourgeoise*, in *Journal of Economic History*, vol. 6, no. 1 (November 1946), pp. 197–199.

Dunning, J. H. "The Growth of United States Investment in United Kingdom Manufacturing Industry, 1856–1940," *Manchester School*, vol. 24, no. 3 (September 1956), pp. 245–269.

DuPuy de Clinchamps, Philippe. *La Noblesse*. Paris, Presses Universitaires de France, 1959.

Duroselle, Jean-Baptiste. "Changes in French Foreign Policy since 1945," in Stanley Hoffmann and others, *In Search of France*. Cambridge, Harvard University Press, 1963.

———— *De Wilson à Roosevelt, Politique extérieur des États-Unis, 1913–1945*. Paris, Colin, 1960. (English ed., Harvard University Press, 1963.)

———— "French Foreign Policy." Seminar, Center for International Affairs, Harvard University, November 23, 1959.

Dutourd, Jean. *The Taxis of the Marne*. New York, Simon and Schuster, 1957.

Duvaux, Jacques. *La Théorie de la maturité économique ou de la stagnation séculaire aux Etats-Unis*. Paris, SEDES, 1958.

———— and Jean Weiller. "Économie française, échanges extérieurs et structures internationales," *Cahiers de l'Institut de Science Économique Appliquée*, series P, no. 1, 1957.

Duveau, Georges. *La Vie ouvrière en France sous le Second Empire, Paris*. Paris, Gallimard, 2nd ed., 1946.

Earle, Edward Meade, ed. *Modern France*. Princeton, Princeton University Press, 1951.

Eckstein, Harry. *A Theory of Stable Democracy*. Princeton, Woodrow Wilson School of Public and International Affairs, Research Monograph No. 10, April 10, 1961.

Economist, vol. 192, no. 6051 (August 15, 1959): "Rostow on Growth— A Non-Communist Manifesto," pp. 409–416.

Ehrmann, Henry W. *Organized Business in France*. Princeton, Princeton University Press, 1957.

Erickson, Charlotte. *British Industrialists, Steel and Hosiery, 1850–1950*. Cambridge, Eng., Cambridge University Press, 1959.

Ernle, Lord (R. E. Prothero). *English Farming, Past and Present*. London, Longmans Green, 4th ed., 1937.

Estienne, Pierre, and Robert Joly. *La Région du centre*. Paris, Presses Universitaires de France, 1961.

Evely, Richard, and I. M. D. Little. *Concentration in British Industry, An Empirical Study of the Structure of Industrial Production, 1935–61*. Cambridge, Eng., Cambridge University Press, 1960.

Eversley, D. E. C. "The Great Western Railway and the Swindon Works in the Great Depression," *University of Birmingham Historical Journal*, vol. 5, no. 2 (1957), pp. 167–190.

Faucher, Daniel. *Le Paysan et la machine*. Paris, Editions de Minuit, 1954.

Faucheux, Jean. *La Décentralisation industrielle*. Paris, Berger-Levrault, 1959.

Fauchon, Jean. *Economie de l'agriculture française*. Paris, Génin, 1954.

Fauvet, Jacques. *La France déchirée*. Paris, Arthème Fayard, 1957.

Federation Nationale du Bâtiment. *Sortir la construction de l'impasse*, 1956.

———— *240,000 logements par an*, 1953.

Fenelon, K. G. *Railway Economics*. London, Methuen, 1932.

Ferns, H. S. "Investment and Trade between Britain and Argentina in the Nineteenth Century," *Economic History Review*, vol. 3, no. 2 (1950), pp. 203–218.

Feuilhade de Chauvin, T. de. *Une Grande banque de depôts: Le Crédit Lyonnais*. Paris, Les Éditions de l'Espargne (pamphlet), 1959.

Fletcher, T. W. "The Great Depression of English Agriculture, 1873–1896," *Economic History Review*, 2nd ser., vol. 13, no. 3 (1961), pp. 417–432.

Flinn, Michael W. "Scandinavian Ore Mining and the British Steel Industry, 1870–1914," *Scandinavian Economic History Review*, vol. 2, no. 1 (1954), pp. 31–46.

——— "British Steel and Spanish Ore, 1871–1914," *Economic History Review*, 2nd ser., vol. 8, no. 1 (August 1955), pp. 84–90.

Florence, P. Sargant. *Logic of British and American Industry*. London, Routledge and Kegan Paul, 1953.

Fohlen, Claude. *Une Affaire de famille au XIXe siècle: Méquillet-Noblot*. Paris, Colin, 1955.

——— *L'Industrie textile au temps du Second Empire*. Paris, Plon, 1956.

Fouillée, Alfred. *Esquisse psychologique des peuples européens*. Paris, Alcan, 1903.

——— *Psychologie du peuple français*. Paris, Alcan, 1903.

Fourastié, J., and A. Laleuf. *Révolution à l'ouest*. Paris, Presses Universitaires de France, 1957.

Frankel, Marvin. "British and American Manufacturing Productivity: A Comparison and Interpretation," *University of Illinois Bulletin*, no. 81, 1957.

——— "Obsolescence and Technical Change in a Maturing Economy," *American Economic Review*, vol. 45, no. 3 (June 1955), pp. 298–319.

Frost, Raymond. "The Macmillan Gap, 1931–1953," *Oxford Economic Papers*, new ser., vol. 6, no. 2 (June 1954), pp. 181–201.

Gallagher, John, and Ronald Robinson. "The Imperialism of Free Trade," *Economic History Review*, vol. 6, no. 1 (1953), pp. 1–15.

Gautier, Abbé Elie. *Pourquoi les Bretons s'en vont*, 2 vols. Éditions Ouvrières, 1950.

Gendarme, René. *La Région du Nord*. Paris, Colin, 1954.

George, P. *La Ville*. Paris, Presses Universitaires de France, 1952.

——— and P. Randet. *La Région parisienne*. Paris, Presses Universitaires de France, 1959.

Gerschenkron, Alexander. "On the Concept of Continuity in History," *Proceedings of the American Philosophical Society*, vol. 106, no. 3 (June 1962), pp. 195–209.

——— "Comment" on Hoselitz, "Entrepreneurship and Capital Formation in France and Britain."

——— "Economic Backwardness in Historical Perspective," in Bert F. Hoselitz, ed., *The Progress of Underdeveloped Areas*. Chicago, University of Chicago Press, 1952, pp. 3–29.

——— *Economic Backwardness in Historical Perspective*. Cambridge, Harvard University Press, 1962.

——— *Bread and Democracy in Germany*. Berkeley, University of California Press, 1943.

——— "Problems of Measuring Long-Term Growth in Income and Wealth,"

Journal of the American Statistical Association, vol. 52 (December 1957), pp. 450–457.

———— "Social Attitudes, Entrepreneurship and Economic Development," in *Explorations in Entrepreneurial History,* vol. 6, no. 1 (October 1953), pp. 1–15.

———— "Reflections on Soviet Novels," *World Politics,* vol. 12, no. 2 (January 1960), pp. 165–185.

Gignoux, C. J. *L'Industrie française, vocation de la France.* Paris, Boivin, 1952.

———— *Histoire d'une entreprise française.* Paris, Hachette, 1955.

Gigou, M. "Les Facteurs de l'abaisement du prix de revient dans la construction," in *Documents sur le problème du logement en France.* Paris, Imprimerie Nationale, February 1946.

Gilbert, Milton, and Irving B. Kravis. *An International Comparison of National Products and the Purchasing Power of Currencies.* Paris, OEEC, 1954.

Gille, Bertrand. *Les Origines de la grande industrie métallurgique en France.* Paris, Domat Montchrestien, no date (1948?).

———— *La Banque et le crédit en France de 1815 à 1848.* Paris, Presses Universitaires de France, 1959.

———— *Recherches sur la formation de la grande entreprise capitaliste.* Paris, SEVPEN, 1959.

Girard, Alain. "Aspects statistiques du problème familial," in Colloques Internationaux du Centre National de la Recherche Scientifique, *Sociologie comparée de la famille contemporaine.* Paris, 1955.

———— "Mobilité sociale et dimension de la famille," *Population,* vol. 6, no. 1 (January–March 1951).

———— and Henri Bastide. "Orientation et selection scolaires: Une Enquête sur les enfants à la sortie de l'école primaire," *Population,* vol. 10, no. 4 (October-December 1955), pp. 605–626.

Girard, Louis. *La Politique des travaux publics du Second Empire.* Paris, Colin, 1951.

Goblot, Edmund. *La Barrière et le niveau.* Paris, Alcan, 1925.

Goldenberg, Leon. "Savings in a State with a Stationary Population," *Quarterly Journal of Economics,* vol. 61 (November 1946), pp. 40–65.

Golob, Eugene O. *The Méline Tariff, French Agriculture and Nationalist Economic Policy.* New York, Columbia University Press, 1944.

Gordon, Richard L. "Coal Pricing and the Energy Problem in the European Community." Unpublished thesis, Massachusetts Institute of Technology, 1960.

Gorer, Geoffry. *Exploring British Character.* New York, Criterion Books, 1955.

Goreux, L. M. See INSEE, "Les Migrations agricoles."

Gouhier, Jean. *Naissance d'une grande cité, Le Mans au milieu du XXe siècle.* Paris, Colin, 1953.

Grandmougin, Eugene. *L'Essor des industries chimiques en France.* Paris, Dunod, 2nd ed., 1919.

Gravier, Jean-François. *Décentralisation et progrès technique.* Paris, Flammarion, 1954.

———— *Paris et le désert français.* Paris, Flammarion, 2nd rev. ed., 1958.

Habakkuk, H. J. "Family Structure and Economic Change in Nineteenth-

Century Europe," *Journal of Economic History,* vol. 15, no. 1 (1955), pp. 1–12.

—— "Free Trade and Commercial Expansion, 1853–1870," in *The Cambridge History of the British Empire,* vol. 2. Cambridge, Eng., Cambridge University Press, 1940.

—— "The Historical Experience on the Basic Conditions of Economic Progress," in Leon H. Dupriez, ed., *Economic Progress.* Louvain, Institut de Recherches Économiques et Sociales, 1955.

Haber, L. F., *Chemical Industry during the Nineteenth Century.* Oxford, Clarendon Press, 1958.

Hagen, E. E. *On the Theory of Social Change: How Economic Growth Begins.* Homewood, Dorsey Press, 1962.

Haggard, H. Rider. *Rural Denmark and Its Lessons.* London, Longmans Green, 1911.

Haight, F. A. *French Import Quotas.* London, P. S. King, 1935.

—— *A History of French Commercial Policy.* New York, Macmillan, 1941.

Halbswachs, Maurice. *La Population et les tracés de voies à Paris depuis une siècle.* Paris, Presses Universitaires de France, 1928.

Halévy, Elie. *A History of the English People,* 3 vols. Harmondsworth, Penguin Books, 1937. (Originally published in English, 1924.)

Hall, A. R. "A Note on the English Capital Market as a Source of Funds for Home Investment before 1914," *Economica,* new ser., vol. 24, no. 93 (February 1957), pp. 56–66.

—— "The English Capital Market before 1914—A Reply," *Economica,* new ser., vol. 25, no. 100 (November 1958), pp. 339–343.

Hancock, W. K., and M. M. Gowing. *British War Economy.* London, H. M. Stationery Office, 1949.

Harrod, Roy. *Life of John Maynard Keynes.* London, Macmillan, 1951.

Hart, P. E., and S. J. Prais. "The Analysis of Business Concentrations: A Statistical Approach," *Journal of the Royal Statistical Society,* vol. 119, part 2 (1956), pp. 150–181.

Hartwell, R. M. "The Rising Standard of Living in England, 1800–1850," *Economic History Review,* 2nd ser., vol. 13, no. 3 (1961), pp. 397–416.

Henderson, W. O. *Britain and Industrial Europe, 1750–1870.* Studies in British Influence on the Industrial Revolution in Western Europe, Liverpool, University Press, 1954.

Henriques, Fernando. "The Miner and His Lass," *The Twentieth Century,* vol. 167, no. 999 (May 1960), pp. 405–412.

Henry, L. "Sociologie comparée," in Colloques Internationaux du Centre Nationale de la Recherche Scientifique, *Sociologie comparée de la famille contemporaine,* Paris, 1955.

Hérouville, H. d'. "Remarques sur le niveau de la production manufacturière de la France," *Revue d'économie politique,* May 1955, pp. 189–223.

Hersent, G. "Notre outillage maritime," in Closon, and others, *L'Outillage économique de la France.* Paris, Alcan, 1921.

Hicks, U. K. *British Public Finances: Their Structure and Development, 1880–1952.* London, Oxford University Press, 1954.

Hilgerdt, Folke (League of Nations). *Industrialization and Foreign Trade.* Geneva, 1945.

Hirschman, Albert O. *The Strategy of Economic Development.* New Haven, Yale University Press, 1958.

Hobsbawm, E. J. "The British Standard of Living, 1790–1850," *Economic History Review,* 2nd ser., vol. 10, no. 1 (August 1957), pp. 46–68.

———— Review of Earle, *Modern France,* in *Economic History Review,* 2nd ser., vol. 4, no. 2 (1951), pp. 258–260.

———— "The Tramping Artisan," *Economic History Review,* 2nd ser., vol. 3, no. 3 (1951), pp. 299–320.

Hoffmann, Stanley R. "Lasting Elements in the French Political Tradition." Seminar, Center for International Affairs, Harvard University, October 19, 1959.

Hoffmann, Walther G. *British Industry, 1700–1950.* New York, Kelley and Millman, 1955.

———— *Growth of Industrial Economies,* trans. W. O. Henderson and W. H. Chaloner. Manchester, Manchester University Press, 1958.

Holland, David. "The Replacement of Busses in Bristol," *Bulletin of the Oxford Institute of Statistics,* vol. 24, no. 4 (November 1962), pp. 413–436.

Hoselitz, Bert F. "Entrepreneurship and Capital Formation in France and Britain since 1700," in National Bureau of Economic Reserach, *Capital Formation and Economic Growth.* Princeton, Princeton University Press, 1956.

Houssiaux, Jacques. *Le Pouvoir de monopole.* Paris, Sirey, 1958.

Hughes, J. R. T. *Fluctuations in Trade, Industry and Finance, A Study in British Economic Development, 1850–1860.* Oxford, Clarendon Press, 1960.

Hunter, A. P. "Freight Rolling Stock," *British Transport Review,* vol. 3, no. 3 (December 1954), pp. 179–201.

Hunter, Neil. *Peasantry and Crisis in France.* London, Gollancz, 1948.

Hutchison, Keith. *The Decline and Fall of British Capitalism.* New York, Scribners, 1950.

Inspection Générale des Finances. *Rapport sur les travaux de l'inspection générale en 1951, II: Les Interventions des pouvoirs publics dans le domaine du logement.* Paris, Imprimerie Nationale, 1952.

———— *Rapport sur les travaux de l'inspection générale en 1955, II: Organismes d'habitations à loyer modéré.* Paris, Imprimerie Nationale, 1957.

Institut de Conjoncture, Service Nationale de Statistique. *Bilan de l'energie en France, en Grande Bretagne et aux États Unis.* Special Study No. 5, Paris, mimeographed, no date (but after 1945).

———— *Étude économique sur le problème du logement.* Special Study No. 4, Paris, 1944.

———— *Production agricole et consommation alimentaire de la France.* Special Study No. 2, Paris, 1944.

Institute National d'Études Demographiques. *Région Languedoc Roussillon, économie et population.* Paris, Presses Universitaires de France, 1957.

Institut National de la Statistique et des Études Économiques [INSEE]. *Annuaire statistique de la France,* Paris, various years.

———— "Bilan de l'industrie française du coton," *Études et conjonctures,* vol. 5, no. 2 (March–April 1950), pp. 51–89.

———— "La Concentration des établissements en France de 1896 à 1936," *Études et conjonctures,* vol. 9, no. 9 (September 1954), pp. 841–881.

Institut National de la Statistique et des Études Économiques. *L'Espace économique française*. Paris, Presses Universitaires de France, 1955.
—— *Les Établissements industriels et commerciaux en France en 1954*. Paris, Imprimerie Nationale, 1956.
—— "Évolution des conditions de logement en France depuis cent ans," *Études et conjonctures*, vol. 12, no. 10–11 (October–November 1957), pp. 985–1376.
—— *L'Industrie française*. Paris, Imprimerie Nationale, 1953.
—— "Les Migrations agricoles en France depuis un siècle et leur relation avec certains facteurs économiques, *Études et conjonctures*, April 1956, pp. 327–376. (Mostly the work of L. M. Goreux.)
—— *Tableaux de l'économie française*. Paris, 1958.
Institut de Science Économique Appliquée [ISEA]. "La Croissance du revenu national français depuis 1870," *Cahiers de l'Institut de Science Économique Appliquée*, series D, no. 7 (1952): *Le Revenu national*.
Iversen, C. "The Importance of the International Margin," in *Explorations in Economics: Notes and Essays in Honor of F. W. Taussig*. New York, McGraw-Hill, 1936.
International Labor Office. *Social Aspects of European Economic Cooperation*. Report by a Group of Experts, Geneva, 1956.
Jasay, A. E. "The Social Choice between Home and Overseas Investment," *Economic Journal*, vol. 70, no. 277 (March 1960), pp. 105–113.
Jeanneney, J. M. *Les Transformations économiques et sociales du XXe siècle*. Paris Polygraphie, Les Cours de Droit, 1954–55.
—— *Forces et faiblesses de l'économie française*. Paris, Colin, 1956.
Jeffrys, J. B. *Retail Trading in Britain, 1850–1950*. Cambridge, Eng., Cambridge University Press, 1954.
—— "Trends in Business Organization in Great Britain since 1856." Unpublished thesis, London, 1938.
—— and Dorothy Walters. "National Income and Expenditure of the United Kingdom, 1870–1952," in International Association for Research in Income and Wealth, *Income and Wealth*, series V. London, Bowes and Bowes, 1955.
Jervis, F. R. J. "The Handicap of Britain's Early Start," *Manchester School*, vol. 15, no. 1 (1947), pp. 112–122.
Jevons, W. Stanley. *The Coal Question*. London, Macmillan, 1865.
Jewkes, John, David Sawers, and Richard Stillerman. *The Sources of Invention*. London, Macmillan, 1958.
—— "Is British Industry Inefficient?" *Manchester School*, vol. 14, no. 1 (1946), pp. 1–16.
—— "The Localization of the Cotton Industry," *Economic History*, vol. 2, no. 5 (January 1930), pp. 91–106.
John, A. H. *A Liverpool Merchant House—Being the History of Alfred Booth and Company*. London, George Allen and Unwin, 1959.
—— *The Industrial Development of South Wales, 1750–1850*. Cardiff, Wales University Press, 1950.
Johnson, Harry G. *International Trade and Economic Growth*. London, Allen and Unwin, 1958.
Jones, G. T. *Increasing Return*, ed. Colin Clark. Cambridge, Eng., Cambridge University Press, 1933.
Jousseau, J. B. *Traité du Crédit Foncier*. Paris, Marchal Bullard, 3rd ed., 1884.

Juillard, Étienne. *La Vie rurale dans la plaine de Basse-Alsace.* Strasbourg-Paris, Le Roux, 1953.

—— Review of Fauchon, *Économie de l'agriculture française,* under title, "L'Agriculture française: Problème national ou problèmes régionaux," in *Annales: Économies, Sociétiés, Civilisations,* vol. 10, no. 3, (July–September 1955), pp. 437–440.

—— Review of Chevalier, *Vie dans les Pyrenées,* in *Annales: Économies, Sociétés, Civilisations,* vol. 12, no. 1 (January–March 1957), pp. 141–146.

Kahn, A. E. *Great Britain in the World Economy.* New York, Columbia University Press, 1946.

Kaldor, Nicholas. "The Economic Aspects of Advertising," *Review of Economic Studies,* vol. 28, no. 1 (1950–1951), pp. 1–27.

Keynes, J. M. *The Economic Consequences of the Peace.* New York, Harcourt, Brace, 1920.

—— *Treatise on Money,* 2 vols. New York, Harcourt, Brace. 1950.

Kindleberger, C. P. *Economic Development.* New York, McGraw-Hill, 1958.

—— "Foreign Trade and Economic Growth: Lessons from Britain and France, 1850 to 1913," *Economic History Review,* 2nd ser., vol. 14, no. 2 (December 1961), pp. 289–305.

—— "Group Behavior and International Trade," *Journal of Political Economy* vol. 59, no. 1 (February 1951), pp. 30–46.

—— "Obsolesence and Technical Change," *Bulletin of the Oxford Institute of Statistics,* vol. 23, no. 3 (August 1961), pp. 281–297.

—— "The Postwar Resurgence of the French Economy," in Stanley Hoffmann and others, *In Search of France.* Cambridge, Harvard University Press, 1963.

—— *The Terms of Trade.* New York, Technology Press and John Wiley, 1956.

Kirk, Dudley F. "Population," in Earle, ed., *Modern France.*

Klatzmann, Jean. "La Division de la France en grandes régions agricoles," *Études et conjonctures,* vol. 12, no. 5 (May 1957), pp. 566–569.

Kohr, Leopold. *The Breakdown of Nations.* London, Routledge and Kegan Paul, 1957.

Kroeber, Alfred J. *A Configuration of Culture Growth.* Berkeley, University of California Press, 1944.

Kuczynski, J. *Weltproduktion und Welthandel in den letzen 100 Jahren.* Lepaya, G. D. Meyer, 1935.

Kuznets, Simon. "Quantitative Aspects of the Economic Growth of Nations, I. Levels and Variability of Rates of Growth," *Economic Development and Cultural Change,* vol. 5, no. 1 (October 1956), pp. 1–94.

—— "Quantitative Aspects of the Economic Growth of Nations, II. Industrial Distribution of National Product and Labor Force," *Economic Development and Cultural Change,* vol. 5, no. 4, supplement (July 1957), pp. 1–111.

—— *Six Lectures on Economic Growth,* Glencoe, Free Press, 1959.

Labasse, Jean. *Les Capitaux et la région.* Paris, Colin, 1955.

—— *La Planification régionale et l'organisation de l'espace,* 2 vols. Paris, Institut des Études Politiques, 1956–60.

—— and Michel Laferrère. *La Région lyonnaise.* Paris, Presses Universitaires de France, 1960.

Labrousse, Ernest. *Aspects de la crise et de la depression de l'économie française au milieu du XIXe siècle, 1846–1851.* Bibliothèque de la Révolution de 1848, vol. 19, La Roche-sur-Yon, Imprimerie Centrale de l'Ouest, 1956.

—— *Aspects de l'évolution économique et sociale de la France et du Royaume Uni.* Paris, Les Cours de Sorbonne, 1954 (in three parts).

—— "Panorama de la crise," in Labrousse, *Aspects de la crise.*

Laferrère, Michel. *Lyon, ville industrielle.* Paris, Presses Universitaires de France, 1960.

Lalumière, Pierre. *L'Inspection des Finances.* Paris, Presses Universitaires de France, 1959.

Lambert Dansette, Jean. *Quelques familles du patronat textile de Lille-Armentières, 1789–1914.* Lille, Paoust, 1954.

Lamèyre, Gerard. *Haussmann, Préfet de Paris.* Paris, Flammarion, 1958.

Landes, David S. *Bankers and Pashas—International Finance and Economic Imperialism in Egypt.* Cambridge, Harvard University Press, 1958.

—— "French Business and the Businessmen in Social and Cultural Analysis," in Earle, ed., *Modern France.*

—— "French Entrepreneurship and Industrial Growth in the Nineteenth Century," *Journal of Economic History,* vol. 9, no. 1 (May 1949), pp. 45–61.

—— "The Statistical Study of French Crises," *Journal of Economic History,* vol. 10, no. 2 (November 1950), pp. 195–211.

—— "Social Attitudes, Entrepreneurship and Economic Development: A Comment," *Explorations in Entrepreneurial History,* vol. 6, no. 4 (May 1954), pp. 245–272.

—— "The Structure of Enterprise in the Nineteenth Century: The Cases of Britain and Germany," *Extrait des rapports du XIe Congrès International des Sciences Historiques.* Stockholm, 1960.

Landry, Adolphe. *Traité de démographie.* Paris, Payot, 1945.

La Pière, Richard T. *The Freudian Ethic.* New York, Duell, Sloan and Pearce, 1959.

Laroque, Pierre. *Les Classes sociales.* Paris, Presses Universitaires de France, 1959.

Lasserre, André. *La Situation des ouvriers de l'industrie textile dans la région lilloise sous la Monarchie de Juillet.* Lausanne, Nouvelle Bibliothèque, 1952.

Latil, Marc. *L'Evolution du revenu agricole: Les Agriculteurs devant des exigences de la croissance et les luttes sociales.* Paris, Colin, 1956.

Laufenburger, H. "Structure territoriale," in Rist and Pirou, eds., *De la France d'avant-guerre jusqu'à la France d'aujourd'hui.*

Laurent, R. "Une Source: Les Archives d'octroi," *Annales: Économies, Sociétés, Civilisations,* vol. 11, no. 2 (April–June 1957), pp. 197–204.

—— *Les Vignerons de la Côte d'Or au XIXe siecle.* Dijon, Imprimerie Bennigaud et Privat, 1958.

Lavergne, Léon de. *The Rural Economy of England, Scotland and Ireland.* London, Blackwood, 1855.

Lavington, F. *The English Capital Market.* London, Methuen, 1921.

Leak, H., and A. Maizels. "The Structure of British Industry," *Journal of the Royal Statistical Society,* vol. 108, parts I–II (1945), pp. 142–199.

Leavasseur, Bernard. "La Construction de logement en France et en Allemagne." Thesis, Paris, Fondation Nationale des Sciences Politiques, 1958.

Lebréton, M. "Une Expérience de la dispersion industrielle dans l'électrochimie et l'électro-metallurgie," in Ministère de l'Économie, *Rapports sur la décongestion*, 1946.

Lédru-Rollin, J. *De la Decadence le l'Angleterre*. Bruxelles, 1850.

Lefèbvre, Jacques. *L'Évolution des localisations industrielles, l'exemple des Alpes françaises*. Paris, Dalloz, 1960.

Lefèvre, Georges. *Politique intérieure du Second Empire*. Paris, Les Cours de Sorbonne, no date (but about 1953).

Léon, Pierre. "L'Industrialisation en France en tant que facteur de croissance économique du début du XVIIIe siècle à nos jours," in *Contribution, Communications*, First International Conference on Economic History, Stockholm. Paris, Mouton et Cie, 1960.

———— *La Naissance de la grande industrie en Dauphiné*, 2 vols. Grenoble, Presses Universitaires de France, 1954.

Lerner, Daniel, and M. Gorden. "Static and Dynamic France." Unpublished manuscript, Center for International Studies, Massachusetts Institute of Technology, 1960.

Leroy, L. *Exode, ou mise en valeur des campagnes*. Paris, Flammarion, 1958.

Leroy-Beaulieu, Paul. *L'État moderne et ses fonctions*. Paris, Guillaumin et Cie, 1890.

Leuillot, P. "Bourgeois et Bourgeoisie," *Annales: Économies, Sociétés, Civilisations*, vol. 11, no. 1 (January–March 1956), pp. 86–101.

Levasseur, E. *Questions ouvrières et industrielles en France sous la Troisième République*. Paris, Rousseau, 1907.

Levi, Leone. *The History of British Commerce*. London, Murray, 2nd ed., 1880.

Lévy, Maurice. *Histoire économique et sociale de la France depuis 1848*. Paris, Les Cours de Droit, Institut d'Études Politiques, 1951–1952.

Lévy, Robert. *Histoire économique de l'industrie cotonnière en Alsace*. Paris, Alcan, 1912.

Lewis, Ben W. *British Planning and Nationalization*. New York, Twentieth Century Fund, 1952.

Lewis, Roy, and Angus Maude. *The English Middle Classes*. London, Phoenix, 1949.

Lewis, W. Arthur. "Economic Development with Unlimited Supplies of Labour," *Manchester School*, vol. 22, no. 2 (May 1954), pp. 139–191.

———— "International Competition in Manufactures," *American Economic Review, Papers and Proceedings*, vol. 47, no. 2 (May 1957), pp. 578–587.

———— *The Theory of Economic Growth*. Homewood, Irwin, 1955.

Lhomme, Jean. *La Grande bourgeoisie au pouvoir, 1830–1880*. Paris, Presses Universitaires de France, 1960.

Liesner, H. H. *The Import Dependence of Britain and Western Germany: A Comparative Study*. International Finance Section, Department of Economics, Princeton University, 1957.

Lipset, Seymour Martin. "Democracy and the Social System." Unpublished manuscript, 1961.

Löffl, Karl. *Die Chemische Industrie Frankreichs*. Stuttgart, Enke, 1917.

Lorwin, Val R. *The French Labor Movement.* Cambridge, Harvard University Press, 1954.

Lubell, Harold. "The French Investment Program, A Defense of the Monnet Plan." Unpublished thesis, Harvard University, 1951.

Luethy, Herbert. *France against Herself.* New York, Praeger, 1955.

McCormick, B., and J. E. Williams. "The Miner and the Eight-Hour Day, 1863–1910," *Economic History Review,* 2nd ser., vol. 19, no. 4 (December 1959), pp. 222–238.

McKay, Donald C. "The Pre-War Development of Briey Iron Ores," in D. C. McKay, ed., *Essays in the History of Modern Europe.* New York, Harper, 1936.

MacKenzie, W. J. M. "Technocracy and the Role of Experts in Government: United Kingdom." Paper submitted to the Fifth World Congress, International Political Science Association, Paris, September 1961.

Macrosty, H. W. *The Trust Movement in British Industry: A Study of Business Organization.* London, Longmans Green, 1907.

Machlup, Fritz. "Three Concepts of the Balance of Payments and So-called Dollar Shortage," *Economic Journal,* vol. 60, no. 237 (March 1950), pp. 46–68.

Macmillan Report. See Committee on Finance and Industry.

Madariaga, Salvador de. *Englishmen, Frenchmen and Spaniards: An Essay in Comparative Psychology.* London, Oxford University Press, 1951.

Maddison, Angus. "Economic Growth in Western Europe, 1870–1957," *Banca Nazionale del Lavoro Quarterly Review,* no. 48 (March 1959), pp. 58–102.

Madinier, Philippe. *Les Disparités géographiques des salaires en France.* Paris, Colin, 1959.

Mantoux, Étienne. *The Carthaginian Peace or the Economic Consequences of M. Keynes.* New York, Oxford University Press, 1952.

Marcilhacy, Christiane. "Émile Zola, 'historien' des paysans beaucerons," *Annales: Économies, Sociétés, Civilisations.* vol. 12, no. 4 (October–December 1957), pp. 573–586.

Marczewski, J. "Resultats provisoires d'une étude sur la croissance de l'économie française, 1700–1957." Paper presented to the Sixth European Congress of the International Association in Income and Wealth, Portoroz, August 1959.

———— "Le 'Take-off' en France?" Paper submitted to the Konstanz meeting of the International Economic Association, September 2–11, 1960.

———— "Some Aspects of the Economic Growth of France, 1660–1958," *Economic Development and Cultural Change,* vol. 9, no. 3 (April 1961), pp. 369–386.

Marjolin, Robert. *Prix, monnaie et production: Essai sur les mouvements économiques de longue durée,* Paris, Presses Universitaires de France, Alcan, 1941.

Marshall, Alfred. *Industry and Trade.* London, Macmillan, 1920.

Marshall, T. H. "The Population of England and Wales from the Industrial Revolution to the World War," *Economic History Review,* 1st ser., vol. 5, no. 2 (1935), pp. 65–78. (Reprinted in E. M. Carus-Wilson, ed., *Essays in Economic History,* London, Arnold, 1954, vol. 1, pp. 331–343.)

Martin, E. W. *The Secret People, English Village Life after 1750.* London, Phoenix, 1954.

Martin, Germain, Henri. *Les Problèmes de crédit en France.* Paris, Payot, 1919.

Masterman, C. F. G. *The Condition of England.* London, Methuen, 1909. (Reprinted 1960.)

Maxcy, George, and A. Silberston. *The Motor Industry.* London, Allen and Unwin, 1959.

Mendras, Henri. *Novis et Virgin.* Paris, Colin, 1953.

Metraux, Rhoda, and Margaret Mead. *Themes in French Culture.* Stanford, Stanford University Press, April 1954.

Meyer, J. R. "An Input-Output Approach to Evaluating the Influence of Exports on British Industrial Production in the Late 19th Century," *Explorations in Entrepreneurial History,* vol. 8 (1955), pp. 12–34.

Miller, Francis, and Helen Hill. *The Giant of the Western World: America and Europe in a North Atlantic Civilisation.* New York, Morrow, 1930.

Minchenton, W. E. *The British Tinplate Industry.* Oxford, Clarendon Press, 1957.

Ministère du Commerce, Direction des Études Techniques. *Rapport général sur l'industrie française,* 3 vols. Paris, Imprimerie Nationale, 1919.

Ministère de l'Économie Nationale. *Rapports et travaux sur la décongestion des centres industriels,* 6 vols. Paris, Imprimerie Nationale, 1945.

Ministère des Finances. *Rapport sur les comptes de la nation,* vol. 2. Paris, Imprimerie Nationale, 1955.

Ministry of Reconstruction, Advisory Council. *Report on the Standardization of Railway Equipment,* Cd 9193. London, H. M. Stationary Office, 1918.

Morazé, Charles. *La France bourgeoise.* Paris, Colin, 3rd ed., 1952.

Moreau, Emile. *Souvenirs d'un gouveneur de la Banque de France.* Paris, Génin, 1954.

Morris, J. H., and L. J. Williams. *South Wales Coal Industry, 1841–1875.* Cardiff, University of Wales Press, 1958.

Mossé, Eliane. *Problèmes de localisation dans l'industrie automobile* (mimeographed). Paris, École Pratique des Hautes Études, Centre d'Études Économiques, July 1956.

——— *Marx et le problème de la croissance dans une économie capitaliste.* Paris, Colin, 1956.

Mourre, Charles. *D'Où vient la décadence économique de la France?* Paris, Librairie Plon, 1900.

Musson, A. E. "The Great Depression in Britain, 1873–1896: A Reappraisal," *Journal of Economic History,* vol. 19, no. 2 (June 1959), pp. 199–228.

——— and E. Robinson. "Science and Industry in the late Eighteenth Century," *Economic History Review,* 2nd ser., vol. 13, no. 2 (December 1960), pp. 223–244.

Néré, J. "Une Statistique du salaire et de l'emploi en France dans le dernier tiers du XIXème siècle," *Revue d'histoire économique et sociale,* vol. 33, no. 2 (1955), pp. 224–230.

Newbold, J. T. W. "The Beginnings of the World Crisis, 1873–1896," *Economic History,* vol. 2, no. 7 (January 1932), pp. 425–441.

Nicholls, William H. "The Place of Agriculture in Economic Development." Unpublished paper presented to the International Economic Association Round Table on Economic Development, Gamagori, Japan, April 2–9, 1960.

Nistri, Roland, and Claude Prêcheur. *La Région du Nord et Nord-Est.* Paris, Presses Universitaires de France, 1959.

Olson, Mancur, and Curtis C. Harris. "Free Trade in Corn: A Statistical Study of the Prices and Production of Wheat in Great Britain from 1873 to 1914," *Quarterly Journal of Economics,* vol. 73, no. 2 (February 1959), pp. 145–168.

Organization for European Economic Cooperation. *Industrial Statistics, 1900–1955.* Paris, 1955.

Orwin, C. S. "Land Tenure in England," *Proceedings of the International Conference of Agricultural Economists,* 1929.

Padover, Saul K. *French Institutions: Values and Politics.* Stanford, Stanford University Press, April 1954.

Paige, D. C., with F. T. Blackby and S. Freund. "Economic Growth: The Last Hundred Years," *National Institute Economic Review,* no. 16 (July 1961), pp. 24–49.

Pares, Richard. "The Economic Factors in the History of the Empire," *Economic History Review,* 1st ser., vol. 7, no. 2 (May 1937), pp. 119–144. (Reprinted in E. M. Carus-Wilson, ed., *Essays in Economic History,* London, Arnold, 1954, vol. 1, pp. 416–438.)

Paretti, V., and G. Bloch, "Industrial Production in Western Europe and the United States, 1901–1955," *Banca Nazionale del Lavoro Quarterly Review,* vol. 9, no. 39 (September–December 1956), pp. 186–234.

Parker, William N. "Coal and Steel Output Movements in Western Europe, 1880–1956," *Explorations in Entrepreneurial History,* vol. 9, no. 4 (April 1957), pp. 214–230.

——— "Comment," on Kindleberger, "Resources, International Trade and Economic Growth," in J. J. Spengler, ed., *Natural Resources and Economic Growth.* Washington, Resources for the Future, Inc., 1961.

——— "National States and National Development: French and German Ore Mining in the Late Nineteenth Century," in H. G. J. Aitken, ed., *The State and Economic Growth.* New York Social Science Research Council, 1959.

Parkhouse, S. E. Letter to *British Transport Review,* vol. 3, no. 4 (April 1955), p. 364.

——— "Railway Freight Rolling Stock," *Journal of the Institute of Transport,* vol. 24, no. 6 (September 1951), pp. 211–218, 242.

Parsons, Talcott. *The Social System.* Glencoe, Free Press, 1951.

——— and Edward A. Shils, eds. *Toward a General Theory of Action.* Cambridge, Harvard University Press, 1951.

——— and Neil J. Smelser. *Economy and Society, A Study in the Integration of Economic and Social Theory.* Glencoe, Free Press, 1956.

Pasdermadjian, H. *Le Grand magasin: Son origin, son évolution, son avenir.* Paris, Dunod, 1949.

Passe, Georges. *Économies comparées de la France et de Grande Bretagne.* Paris, Fayard, 1957.

Patel, Surenda J. "Rates of Industrial Growth in the Last Century, 1860–1958," *Essays in the Quantitative Study of Economic Growth, Economic Development and Cultural Change,* vol. 9, no. 3 (April 1961), pp. 316–330.

Pearson, A. J. "Developments and Prospects in British Transport, with

Special Reference to Railways," *Journal of the Institute of Transport,* vol. 25, no. 4 (May 1953).

Perrine, Maxime. *Saint-Etienne et sa région économique.* Tours, Arrault, 1937.

Perrot, Marguerite. *La Monnaie et l'opinion publique en France et en Angleterre, 1924–1936.* Paris, Colin, 1955.

Perroux, François. "Prises de vues sur la croissance de l'économie française, 1780–1950," in International Association for Research in Income and Wealth, *Income and Wealth,* series V. London, Bowes and Bowes, 1955.

Peterson, Wallace C. *The Welfare State in France.* Lincoln, University of Nebraska Press, 1960.

———— "Planning and Economic Progress in France, *World Politics,* vol. 10, no. 3 (April 1957), pp. 351–382.

Phelps-Brown, E. H., and S. J. Handfield Jones. "The Climacteric of the 1890s," *Oxford Economic Papers,* vol. 4, no. 3 (October 1952), pp. 266–307.

Phlipponneau, Michel. *Le Problème bréton et la programme d'action régionale.* Paris, Colin, 1957.

Pigou, A. C. *Aspects of British Economic History, 1918–1925.* London, Macmillan, 1948.

Pinchemel, Philippe. *Les Niveaux optima des villes d'après l'analyse des structures urbaines du Nord et du Pas de Calais.* Lille, CEREX, 1959.

———— *Structures sociales et dépopulation rurale dans les campagnes picardes de 1836 à 1936.* Paris, Colin, 1957.

Pitts, Jesse. "Adieu à la France de Papa." Seminar, Center for International Affairs, Harvard University, November 27, 1959.

———— "The Bourgeois Family and French Economic Retardation." Unpublished thesis, Harvard University, 1957.

———— "French Values and Their Implementation by Social Classes before World War II." Seminar, Center for International Affairs, Harvard University, October 5, 1959.

———— "The Role of the Citizen in France." Seminar, Center for International Affairs, Harvard University, May 13, 1960.

Plummer, Alfred. *New British Industries in the Twentieth Century.* London, Pitman, 1937.

Polanyi, Karl. *The Great Transformation.* New York, Farrar and Rinehart, 1944.

Pollard, Sidney. "Barrow-in-Furness and the Seventh Duke of Devonshire," *Economic History Review,* 2nd ser., vol. 8, no. 2 (December 1955), pp. 213–221.

———— "Laissez-Faire and Shipbuilding," *Economic History Review,* 2nd ser., vol. 5, no. 1 (August 1952), pp. 98–115.

Pollins, Harold. "The Marketing of Railway Shares in the First Half of the Nineteenth Century," *Economic History Review,* 2nd ser., vol. 7, no. 2 (December 1954), pp. 230–239.

Pommera, Marcelle. *Grandeur ou déclin de la France à l'époque contemporaine.* Givors, Martel, 1946.

Pose, Alfred. *La Monnaie et ses institutions,* 2 vols. Paris, Presses Universitaires de France, 1942.

Pounds, Norman J. G., and William N. Parker. *Coal and Steel in Western Europe.* London, Faber, 1957.

Pouthas, Charles. *La Population française pendant la première moitié du XIXe siècle*. Paris, Presses Universitaires de France, 1956.

Pressat, Roland. "Population," in Institut National d'Études Demographiques, *Région Languedoc Roussillon, économie et population*. Cahier No. 30, Paris, Presses Universitaires de France, 1957.

Pressnell, L. S., *Country Banking in the Industrial Revolution*. Oxford, Clarendon Press, 1956.

Prest, A. R. "National Income of the United Kingdom, 1870–1946," *Economic Journal*, vol. 57, no. 229 (March 1948), pp. 31–62.

Rabeil, Jacques. *L'Industrie cotonnière française*. Paris, Genin, 1955.

Rambert, Gaston. *Marseille*. Marseille, Société Anonyme du Semaphore de Marseille, 1934.

Ramon, Gabriel. *Histoire de la Banque de France d'après les sources originales*. Paris, Grasset, 1929.

Reddaway, W. B. *The Economics of a Declining Population*. New York, Macmillan, 1939.

Redford, Arthur. *Labour Migration in England, 1800–1850*. Manchester, University Press, 1926.

——— *Manchester Merchants and Foreign Trade, 1794–1858*. Manchester, University Press, 1934.

Reid Report, see Royal Commission in the Coal Industry.

Renier, G. J. *The English: Are They Human?* London, Benn, 4th ed., 1956.

Renouard, Dominique. *Le Transport de la marchandise par fer, route et eau depuis 1850*. Paris, Colin, 1960.

Reynaud, Paul. *In the Thick of the Fight, 1930–1945 (Le Cour de la mélée)*, trans. J. D. Lambert. New York, Simon and Schuster, 1955.

Richmond, W. Kenneth. *The English Disease*. London, Redmond, 1958.

Rideau, Père Emile. *Essor et problèmes d'une région française, houillères et sidérurgie de Moselle*. Paris, Éditions Ouvrières, 1956.

Riencourt, Amaury de. *The Coming Caesars*. New York, Coward-McCann, 1957.

Rimmer, W. G. *Marshall of Leeds, Flax-Spinners, 1788–1886*. Cambridge, Eng., Cambridge University Press, 1960.

Rist, Charles. Introduction to Robert Margolin, *Prix, monnaie et production*. Paris, Presses Universitaires de France, 1941.

——— Preface to Reynaud, *In the Thick of the Fight, 1930–1945*.

——— and Gaëtan Pirou, eds. "De la France d'avant-guerre jusqu'à la France d'aujourd'hui," *Revue d'économie politique*, vol. 53 (January–February 1939). (Publ. in book form, Paris, Sirey, 1939.)

Rist, Marcel. "Une Expérience française de liberation des échanges au dix-neuvième siècle: Le Traité de 1860," *Revue d'économie politique*, vol. 66 (November–December 1956), pp. 908–961.

Robert-Coutelle, Émile. *Le Crédit Foncier de France devant les chambres*. Paris, Amyot, no date (but after 1876).

Robertson-Scott, J. *England's Green and Pleasant Land*. London, Jonathan Cape, 1931. (Rev. ed., Harmondsworth, Penguin Books, 1949.)

——— *Sugar-Beet*. London, Cox, 1911.

Robinson, E. A. G. "The Changing Structure of the British Economy," *Economic Journal*, vol. 64, no. 255 (September 1954), pp. 443–461.

Robson, R. *The Cotton Industry in Britain*. London, Macmillan, 1957.

——— *The Man-Made Fiber Industry*. London, Macmillan, 1958.

Root, Waverly. *The Food of France*. New York, Knopf, 1958.

Rostow, W. W. *British Economy of the Nineteenth Century*. Oxford, Clarendon Press, 1948.
—— "Leading Sectors and the Take-Off." Paper submitted to the International Economic Association meeting in Konstanz, September 1960.
—— *The Stages of Economic Growth*. Cambridge, Eng., Cambridge University Press, 1960.
Rowntree, B. Seebohn. *Poverty, A Study of Town Life*. London, Longmans Green, 1901.
—— *Poverty and Progress: A Second Social Survey of York*. London, Longmans Green, 1941.
—— and R. G. Lavers. *Poverty and the Welfare State, A Third Social Survey of York Dealing only with Economic Questions*. London, Longmans Green, 1951.
Royal Commission on the Coal Industry (Reid Commission). *Report*, Cmd 2600, 1926.
Royal Commission on the Depression in Trade and Industry. *Report*, London, Eyre and Spottiswoode, 1885; indexed 1886 (C 4621).
Royal Commission on Industry and Trade (Balfour Committee). *Report*, London, HMSO (Cmd 3282), 1929.
Royal Commission on Population. *Report*, London, HMSO (Cmd 7695), June 1949.
Royal Commission on Transport. *Report*, London, HMSO (Cmd 3751), 1931.
Rueff, Jacques. Preface to Moreau, *Souvenirs*.
—— "Sur un point d'histoire: Le Niveau de la stabilization Poincaré," *Revue d'économie politique*, vol. 69 (March–April 1959), pp. 168–178.
Russell, John E. *World Population and World Food Supplies*. London, Allen and Unwin, 1954.
Salter, W. E. G. *Productivity and Technical Change*. Cambridge, Eng., Cambridge University Press, 1960.
Samuelsson, Kurt. *Religion and Economic Action*. Swedish original, 1957; English trans., London, Heinemann, 1961.
Saul, S. B. *Studies in British Overseas Trade, 1870–1914*. Liverpool, Liverpool University Press, 1960.
Sauvy, Alfred. *La Montée des jeunes*. Paris, Calmann-Lévy, 1960.
—— *Richesse et population*. Paris, Payot, 1943.
—— Conseil Économique. "Rapport sur le revenu national," *Journal officiel*, March 23, 1954.
Savage, Christopher I. *An Economic History of Transport*. London, Hutchison, 1959.
Saville, John. "A Comment on Professor Rostow's *British Economy of the 19th Century*," in *Past and Present*, November 1954, pp. 66–84.
—— *Rural Depopulation in England and Wales, 1851–1951*. London, Routledge and Kegan Paul, 1957.
—— "Sleeping Partnership and Limited Liability," *Economic History Review*, 2nd ser., vol. 8, no. 3 (April 1956), pp. 418–433.
—— "Some Retarding Factors in the British Economy before 1914," *Yorkshire Bulletin of Economic and Social Research*, vol. 13, no. 1 (May 1961), pp. 51–60.
Sawyer, John E. "The Entrepreneur and the Social Order: France and the

United States," in William Miller, ed., *Men in Business*. Cambridge, Harvard University Press, 1952.

―――― "France's New Horizons," *Yale Review*, vol. 48, no. 2 (Winter 1959), pp. 161–173.

―――― "In Defense of an Approach: A Comment on Professor Gerschenkron's 'Social Attitudes, Entrepreneurship and Economic Development,'" *Explorations in Entrepreneurial History*, vol. 6, no. 4 (May 1954), pp. 273–286.

―――― "Strains in the Structure of Modern France," in Earle, ed., *Modern France*.

Sayers, R. S. "The Springs of Technical Progress in Britain, 1919–1939," *Economic Journal*, vol. 60, no. 238 (June 1950), pp. 275–291.

Schlote, Werner. *British Overseas Trade from 1700 to the 1930s*. Oxford, Blackwell, 1952.

Schumpeter, Joseph A. *Business Cycles*. New York, McGraw-Hill, 1939.

―――― *Theory of Economic Development*. Cambridge, Harvard University Press, 1934.

Sédillot, René. *La Maison de Wendel de mille sept cent quatre à nos jours*. Paris, privately printed, 1958.

―――― *Peugeot*. Paris, Plon, 1960.

Sée, Henri. *Histoire économique de la France, II: Les Temps modernes, 1789–1914*. Paris, Colin, 1942.

Sheahan, John. "Government Competition and the Performance of the French Automobile Industry," *Journal of Industrial Economics*, vol. 8, no. 3 (June 1960), pp. 197–215.

Sherrington, C. E. R. *The Economics of Rail Transport in Great Britain, I: History and Development*. London, Arnold, 2nd ed., 1937.

Shonfield, Andrew. *British Economic Policy since the War*. Harmondsworth, Penguin Books, 1958.

Siegfried, André. *England's Crisis*. London, J. Cope, 1933.

―――― *France, A Study in Nationality*. New Haven, Yale University Press, 1930.

Simiand, François. *Le Salaire, l'évolution sociale et la monnaie*, 3 vols. Paris, Alcan, 1932.

Sinclair, W. A. "The Growth of the British Steel Industry in the Late Nineteenth Century," *Scottish Journal of Political Economy*, vol. 6, no. 1 (February 1959), pp. 33–47.

Sirol, Jean. *Le Rôle de l'agriculture dans les fluctuations économiques*. Paris, Sirey, 1942.

Smelser, Neil J. *Social Change in the Industrial Revolution: An Application of Theory to the Lancashire Cotton Industry, 1770–1840*. London, Routledge and Kegan Paul, 1959.

Smith, Howard K. *The State of Europe*. New York, Knopf, 1949.

Souchon, Auguste. "L'Agriculture anglaise et la protectionisme," *Revue d'économie politique*, vol. 13 (1904), pp. 273–308.

―――― *La Crise de main-d'oeuvre dans l'agriculture française*. Paris, Rousseau, 1914.

Spengler, J. J. "Notes on France's Response to Her Declining Rate of Demographic Growth," *Journal of Economic History*, vol. 11, no. 4 (Fall 1951), pp. 403–416.

Spring, David. "The English Landed Estate in the Age of Coal and Iron,"

Journal of Economic History, vol. 11, no. 1 (Winter 1951), pp. 3–24.

Stacey, Margaret. *Tradition and Change: A Study of Banbury.* London, Oxford University Press, 1960.

Statistical Abstract for the United Kingdom, 1913.

Stearns, R. P. "Agricultural Adaptation in England, 1875–1900," *Agricultural History*, vol. 6, nos. 2 and 3 (1932), pp. 84–154.

Streeten, Paul. "Unbalanced Growth," in *Economic Integration, Aspects and Problems.* Leyden, A. W. Sythoff, 1961.

Svennilson, I. *Growth and Stagnation in the European Economy.* Geneva, United Nations (Economic Commission for Europe), 1954.

Tapiès, Fr. de, Le Chevalier. *La France et l'Angleterre, ou statistique morale et physique de la France comparée à celle de l'Angleterre sur tous les points analogues.* Versailles, privately printed, 1845.

Taylor, Arthur J. "Labour Productivity and Technological Innovation in the British Coal Industry, 1850–1914," *Economic History Review*, 2nd ser., vol. 14, no. 1 (August 1961), pp. 48–70.

Thabault, Roger. "Les Institutions scolaires aux États-Unis," *Annales: Économies, Sociétés, Civilisations*, vol. 10, no. 1 (January–March 1955), pp. 3–26.

Thomas, Brinley, *Migration and Economic Growth.* Cambridge, Eng., Cambridge University Press, 1954.

Thompson, David. *Two Frenchmen.* London, Cresset Press, 1951.

Thompson, F. M. L. "The Land Market in the Nineteenth Century." *Oxford Economic Papers*, vol. 9, no. 3 (October 1957), pp. 285–308.

Thuillier, Guy. *Georges Dufaud et les débuts du grand capitalisme dans la métallurgie, en Nivernais, au XIXe siècle.* Paris, SEVPEN, 1959.

—— "Pour une histoire bancaire régionale: En Nivernais de 1800 à 1880," *Annales: Économies, Sociétés, Civilisations*, vol. 10, no. 4 (October–December 1955), pp. 494–512.

Tocqueville, Alexis de. *Journeys to England and Ireland.* New Haven, Yale University Press, 1958.

Toynbee, A. J. *A Study of History.* London, Oxford University Press, 1935.

Trow-Smith, Robert. *A History of British Livestock Husbandry 1700–1900.* London, Routledge, 1959.

United Nations, Economic Commission for Europe. *Economic Survey of Europe in 1954.* Geneva, 1955.

Vaizey, John. *The Brewing Industry, 1886–1951, An Economic Study.* London, Pitman, 1960.

Valarché, Jean. *L'Économie rurale.* Paris, Rivière, 1960.

—— *La Mobilité professionelle des ruraux dans une société libre.* Fribourg, Éditions Universitaires, 1953.

Veblen, Thorstein. *Imperial Germany and the Industrial Revolution.* New York, Macmillan, 1915.

Vedel, Georges. "Les Problèmes de la technocratie dans le monde moderne et le rôle des experts: Rapport sur la France." Paper submitted to the Fifth World Congress, International Political Science Association, Paris, September 1961.

Vincent, A. A. *Initiation à la conjoncture.* Paris, Presses Universitaires de France, 1947.

—— Institut de Conjoncture, Service Nationale des Statistiques, Special Study No. 3, *Le Progrès technique en France depuis 100 ans.* Paris, Imprimerie Nationale, 1944.

Viner, Jacob. *International Economics.* Glencoe, Free Press, 1951.

Warner, Charles K. *The Winegrowers of France and the Government since 1875.* New York, Columbia University Press, 1960.

Walter, François. "Recherches sur le développement économique de la France, 1900–1955," *Cahiers de l'Institut de Science Économique Appliquée,* series D, no. 9 (March 1957).

Weber, A. F. *The Growth of the Cities in the Nineteenth Century.* New York, Columbia University Press, 1899.

Weber, B. "A New Index of Residential Construction and Long Cycles in Great Britain, 1838–1950," *Scottish Journal of Political Economy,* vol. 2, no. 2 (June 1955), pp. 104–132.

Weiller, Jean. "Economie française, échanges extérieurs et structures internationales." See Duvaux and Weiller, same title.

——— "Long-Run Tendencies in Foreign Trade, with a Statistical Draft of the French Trade Structure, 1871–1939." First Preliminary Draft of a manuscript prepared for the League of Nations Economic Department in Princeton, 1943. (Kindly communicated by Professor Weiller.)

——— *Problèmes d'économie internationale,* II: *Une Nouvelle expérience: L'Organisation internationale des échanges.* Paris, Presses Universitaires de France, 1950.

Wells, F. A. *The British Hosiery Trade.* London, Allen and Unwin, 1935.

Wendell, Barrett. *The France of Today.* New York, Scribners, 1907.

Wharton, Edith. *French Ways and their Meaning.* New York, Appleton, 1919.

White, Harry D. *French International Accounts 1880–1913.* Cambridge, Harvard University Press, 1933.

Williams, Ernest E. *Made in Germany.* London, Heinemann, 2nd ed., 1896.

Williams, S. C. *The Economics of Railway Transport.* London, Macmillan, 1909.

Williams, W. M. *The Sociology of an English Village: Gosforth.* London, Routledge and Kegan Paul, 1956.

Wilson, Charles. "The Entrepreneur in the Industrial Revolution, *"Explorations in Entrepreneurial History,* vol. 7, no. 3 (February 1955).

Wilson, J. S. G. *French Banking Structure and Credit.* London, Bell, 1957.

——— "The French Deposit Banks and the Banques d'Affaires," *Banca Nazionale del Lavoro Quarterly Review,* vol. 3, no. 31 (October–December 1954), pp. 186, 199.

Wilson, Thomas. "The Electronic Industry," in Burn, ed., *The Structure of British Industry.*

Wright, J. F. "An Index of the Output of British Industry since 1700," *Journal of Economic History,* vol. 16, no. 3 (September 1956), pp. 356–364.

Wylie, Lawrence. "Criteria for Good Government as Taught in French History." Seminar, Center for International Affairs, Harvard University, March 25, 1960.

——— *Village in the Vaucluse.* Cambridge, Harvard University Press, 1957.

Young, G. M. *Victorian England, Portrait of an Age.* London, Oxford University Press, 2nd ed., 1936; reprinted 1960, paperback edition.

Youngson, A. J. *The British Economy, 1920–1957*. London, Allen and Unwin, 1960.

Zarka, Claude. "Un Exemple de pôle de croissance: L'Industrie textile du Nord de la France, 1830–1870," *Revue économique*, no. 1 (January 1958), pp. 65–106.

INDEX